Edward
Lansdale's
Cold War

A volume in the series

Culture, Politics, and the Cold War

edited by Christian G. Appy

Jonathan Nashel

Edward Lansdale's Cold War

University of Massachusetts Press
Amherst and Boston

Copyright © 2005 by Jonathan Nashel
All rights reserved
Printed in the United States of America

LC   2005010630
ISBN 1-55849-452-9 (library cloth); 464-2 (paper)

Designed by Dennis Anderson
Set in Janson Text by Binghamton Valley Composition, Inc.
Printed and bound by The Maple-Vail Book Manufacturing Group

Library of Congress Cataloging-in-Publication Data

Nashel, Jonathan, 1961–
   Edward Lansdale's cold war / Jonathan Nashel.
        p. cm.—(Culture, politics, and the cold war)
   Includes bibliographical references and index.
   ISBN 1-55849-452-9 (library cloth : alk. paper)—ISBN 1-55849-464-2 (pbk. : alk. paper)
   1. Lansdale, Edward Geary, 1908–1987.   2. Intelligence officers—United States—Biography.
3. United States. Central Intelligence Agency—Officials and employees—Biography.
4. Espionage, American.   5. Cold War.   6. Vietnamese Conflict, 1961–1975—United States.
I. Title.   II. Series.
   JK468.I6N35 2005
   327.12'092—dc22

                                                              2005010630

British Library Cataloguing in Publication data are available.

For my parents,
Richard and Susan Nashel

for one who'd lived among enemies so long:
if often he was wrong and, at times, absurd,
 to us he is no more a person
 now but a whole climate of opinion

—W. H. Auden, "In Memory of Sigmund Freud"

Contents

Acknowledgments   xi

Introduction: On the Trail of Edward Lansdale   1

1 Confidences   25

2 Selling America, Selling Vietnam   49

3 The Power of Secrets   77

4 The Perils of a Usable Past   104

5 Gazing at the Third World   127

6 Fictions of Quiet and Ugly Americans   149

7 The Half-life of Celebrity   187

   Epilogue: Southeast Asia after Edward Lansdale   208

   Notes   221

   Index   269

Illustrations follow page 126.

Acknowledgments

BOOKS TAKE TIME, and it is because of friends and family that this one was finally able to appear. First and foremost there are my parents, Richard and Susan Nashel. They believed in me and provided me with unfailing support. I am dedicating my book to them with gratitude for their love and for the love of learning they passed on to me.

Graduate school seems to have taken place in another lifetime, but some of the first people I met at Rutgers proved to be not only good friends but my best critics. George Sirgiovanni, Roy Domenico, John Rossi, Jim Fisher, Greg Stone, and Robert Johnston provided me with perspective and humor. David Engerman, William Bartlett, Brian Roberts, and Rosanne Currarrino heard more stories about Edward Lansdale than humanely should be allowed. Lloyd Gardner, Michael Adas, David Oshinksy, and Marilyn Young inspired me and supported my work: each of them offered a vision of history and a model of scholarship that I have tried to emulate.

In Indiana, I became fast friends with a wonderful group of newly minted Hoosiers. Steven Gerencser, Lyle and Erika Zynda, Lesley Walker, and Peter O'Keefe all greatly eased my adjustment to the Midwest, and I consider myself very lucky to have met them. I am professionally indebted to the tireless efforts of Maureen Kennedy in the inter-library loan office and the support and good humor of Linda Fisher and Michele Russo at the IUSB library.

At the University of Massachusetts Press I was fortunate to have Clark Dougan and Chris Appy support my work and provide a critical eye. They have both been perceptive readers and very, very patient editors.

Mrs. Pat Lansdale was gracious in allowing me to interview her and pore over photographs of her and her husband. Cecil Currey provided me with a wealth of information about Lansdale. Nick Cullather has been most helpful in broadening my understanding of the Philippines and Ramon Magsaysay. The staff at the Hoover Archives, especially Becky Mead, Sondra Bierre, and

Linda Bernard were unflaggingly patient with my demands and equally giving of their time in tracking down my many requests. Douglas Pike, then at the Indochina Archives in Berkeley, provided me with generous assistance. Archivists and librarians at Rutgers University, the Seely Mudd Library at Princeton University, the Stanford University Library, the New York Public Library, the CIA, the Columbia Oral History Research Office, the Harry S. Truman Library, the Dwight D. Eisenhower Library, the John F. Kennedy Library, the Lyndon B. Johnson Library, and the Gerald Ford Library were also friendly and informative. Of particular help were Dennis Bilger, David Haight, David Plotkin, John D. Wilson, and Michael Warner. Larry Haapanen and Chester Pach provided me with documents, and H. Bruce Franklin helped me think more about Lansdale and "The Quiet American."

For anyone who has toiled in the fields of government documents or attempted to make sense of the surreal world of FOIs, the National Security Archives in Washington is a shining star. William Burr, Wil Ferragono, and a legion of other individuals there offered me support and directed me to some of the most astonishing documents that I have incorporated into this work.

Finally, Rebecca Brittenham helped me in so many ways that I'm not quite sure where to begin. Her canny insights, love, and unending support were crucial in making this book a reality. Near the end of my writing this book, Samuel Britt Nashel was born. He has brought us a level of joy that is impossible to describe, yet is very real.

Edward
Lansdale's
Cold War

Introduction

On the Trail of Edward Lansdale

WHEN EDWARD G. LANSDALE died in 1987, his obituary made the front page of the *New York Times*. Characterizing him as a "dashing" air force officer and "counterinsurgency" expert, the *Times* retraced the trajectory of Lansdale's career and catalogued some of the reasons for his notoriety.[1] An advertising executive before World War II, he then joined the military and eventually served with the Office of Strategic Services (oss), the forerunner of the CIA. After the war he was sent as an adviser to the newly independent Philippines, where he soon established a reputation as an innovative and effective agent of American Cold War foreign policy. In fact, his actions on behalf of Philippine leader Ramon Magsaysay were credited with almost single-handedly preventing a communist takeover of that country in the early 1950s. Lansdale's success in the Philippines prompted the secretary of state, John Foster Dulles, to dispatch him to Vietnam in 1954 to perform the same miracle. "Do what you did in the Philippines," Dulles told Lansdale. CIA director Allen Dulles echoed his brother's orders, adding, "God bless you."[2]

After helping to install Ngo Dinh Diem as head of the South Vietnamese regime, Lansdale—by then an air force colonel—sought to apply some of the same techniques against communist insurgents in Vietnam that had proved so effective in the Philippines. Posted back to the Pentagon in 1956, he championed the idea of "counterinsurgency" as an alternative to the deployment of conventional armed forces—a proposal that contributed to the development of the U.S. Army's "Special Forces." As the American commitment to action in Vietnam deepened, he continued to play a role in the escalating war effort, as director of the CIA's undercover operations in Indochina and as a liaison between the U.S. embassy in Saigon and the South

1

Vietnamese leadership. So closely was Lansdale associated with the American intervention in Vietnam that many came to believe that he was the model for the protagonists in two of the most important novels of the Cold War, Graham Greene's *The Quiet American* (1955) and William Lederer and Eugene Burdick's *The Ugly American* (1958).

Nor did the legend of Edward Lansdale end there. During the Kennedy administration he was placed in charge of Operation Mongoose, the covert U.S. plan to overthrow the government of Cuba's Fidel Castro by assassination or other means, and he was suspected of masterminding other clandestine operations in the Third World. Yet even more than any actions he may have taken, it was Lansdale's personality that nurtured his celebrity. A genial charmer who moved with ease among peasants as well as presidents, journalists as well as generals, he was a CIA operative with an identifiable human face in an era of anonymous Cold War subterfuge and intrigue. His appeal was such that acquaintances as different in political outlook and temperament as William Colby, former director of the CIA, and Daniel Ellsberg, the Pentagon hawk turned antiwar activist, spoke warmly of him. If, by the time he died, Lansdale's vision of the world had fallen out of favor, an antiquated relic of waning Cold War dichotomies, the myth that surrounded the man endured, as attested by the *Times* and other major newspapers that commemorated his passing.

What the obituary writers failed to mention was that Lansdale himself had decided, in the years shortly before his death, to set the record straight by addressing—and correcting—some of the fictions that had become attached to him over the years. His 1972 memoir, *In the Midst of Wars: An American's Mission to Southeast Asia*, had only fueled some of the stories that had come to surround him; though it included some tales of high adventure, it was viewed even by friends and family as leaving far too much unsaid. A writing style that was part breathless narrative and part purple prose did not help matters: "The body politic looked as though it were about to run amok en masse" is an all too typical example of the book's literary qualities.[3] Lansdale's frantic and at times over-the-top writing style may have been a result of his preferred reading matter: spy novels, impassioned denunciations of communism, and celebratory accounts of American history.[4] As he said to a friend shortly after he finished his memoir, "I really wrote it for folks who otherwise would buy the usual run of adventure stories."[5]

A more serious problem was raised by reviewers who unmercifully challenged Lansdale's portrayal of events. First and foremost, they noted his fundamental omission of his association with the CIA. Reviewers also pointed to his failure to discuss his overseeing of—and secret payments to—

the Philippine president, Ramon Magsaysay, in the early 1950s and his having counseled Ngo Dinh Diem to wage war against his political opponents in the spring of 1955 in order to solidify, in Vietnam and in Washington, Diem's own rule. Further, Lansdale's memoir never discussed his use of CIA funds to purchase the future loyalty of Diem's political opponents, or his role in the notorious election that unseated Bao Dai and made Diem the president of South Vietnam until 1963. Not surprisingly, his shadowy efforts on behalf of Allen Dulles, for whom he pursued aims that were sometimes at odds with officially stated U.S. policy in Vietnam, also fail to appear. Finally, because Lansdale's memoir ends with his departure from Vietnam in 1956 (even though he returned in 1965 and stayed until 1968), this premature cutoff date cleanly sidesteps such activities as the notorious Operation Mongoose, in the early 1960s.

These omissions and numerous others led many reviewers to question the entire contents of the book. The historian David Chandler concluded that the memoir was nothing more than a "disingenuous" exercise. Jonathan Mirsky wrote in the popular *Saturday Review*, "There is only one difficulty with *In the Midst of Wars*: from the cover to the final page it is permeated with lies." J. L. S. Girling contrasted Lansdale's public pronouncements of American goodwill to foreigners with excerpts from *The Pentagon Papers* documenting what Lansdale had actually done. Girling concluded his review by quoting the mordant sarcasm of Antony's line from Shakespeare's *Julius Caesar*: "an honorable man, so are they all, all honorable men."[6] At first, Lansdale tried to ignore these criticisms, intimating that he was simply unable to say more, given his relationship to American intelligence agencies. By the 1980s, though, when he had long since retired from the government and the passions of the Vietnam War had subsided, his reticence seemed unwarranted, particularly since a number of exposés had already detailed his CIA connection.[7] After much soul searching and consultation with former colleagues, Lansdale agreed to an authorized biography—which meant that he had to discuss his relationship with the CIA. The result, Cecil Currey's *Edward Lansdale: The Unquiet American* (1988), thus includes Lansdale's own acknowledgment of the CIA connection.[8] Currey, an avowed admirer, shared Lansdale's conviction that the Vietnam War could have ended in an American victory if only America's leaders had listened to his ideas on how to defeat the communist revolutions then enveloping Southeast Asia. The book remains an adulatory yet thorough recounting of the man.

When I began to research the world of Edward Lansdale and Currey generously allowed me go through his papers, one photograph caught my eye—a snapshot of an elderly Lansdale in a wheelchair being pushed through

Disney World by Currey. Until then, I had thought of Lansdale in the Philippine jungles of Luzon or behind enemy lines in Vietnam, but in this photo a man who had spent a lifetime working to win the Cold War appears in his frail old age, waiting in line for a ride to the heart of an American fantasyland. Although the Lansdale of guerrilla operations and White House briefings seemed very much out of place in this American temple of leisure and fun, this photograph was a useful reminder that he spent a lifetime trying to bring the fantasy of America, including the realm of Walt Disney, to the people of the Third World. In addition to showing Mickey Mouse cartoons to Asian peasants, he became a powerful propagandist for the virtues of consumerism and the wealth generated by capitalism. Like Cecil Rhodes, the British colonizer—who, when asked the secret of imperialism, replied, "Teach the natives to want"—Lansdale understood the power and value of instilling consumerist desires in the subjects of his Cold War operations.[9] The photograph thus illuminates a key component of his character: a firm belief in the ideological assumptions driving American-style capitalism and an unabashed readiness to enjoy and spread the abundance that capitalism produced.

Another document pinpoints Lansdale in an equally curious way: a small film I came across in the National Archives that shows him giving a lecture in Vietnam in the mid-1960s. The film is silent, but the accompanying notes indicate that he was speaking about U.S. goals in Vietnam and how to foster better relations with the South Vietnamese. Look long enough at the film and spend enough time studying Lansdale's writings, and it's not difficult to imagine his words: he describes the communist-imposed "bamboo curtain" in Vietnam, claims that "Asians have this personal radar" that can tell then when Americans are being sincere or condescending, and ends his lecture-*cum*–pep talk with "the time is now for us to prevail." Even without the words, the film captures his charisma, his earnestness, his zealous belief that America could triumph against any and all adversaries. For Lansdale, the key to this success was to spread the doctrine of American democratic ideals, which in turn would inspire a powerful anticommunist movement through-out the world. He played with equal fervor, then, the roles of tourist and missionary, the carefree Disney holiday maker and the impassioned ideo-logue, but to him these two aspects of his personality were never incompat-ible, and both contributed to his successes as a CIA agent.[10]

The most cited passage in Lansdale's memoir speaks to this Americaniz-ing effort in ways that are deeply idealistic, while seemingly oblivious of the potential ill effects of such gifts upon other cultures: "When we Americans give of our substance to the people of other countries, we should give as generously of our ideology as we do of our money, our guns, our cereal grains, and our machinery. In sharing our ideology, while making others strong enough to embrace and hold it for their own, the American people strive toward a millennium when the world will be free and wars will be past."[11] Here Lansdale used the rhetoric of a secular evangelist to assure the people of the Third World and his fellow Americans that if they accepted the faith of liberalism and anticommunism, American goodwill would follow. His recourse to the language of nineteenth-century Protestant reformers, with a fervent call for America not to turn away from its special responsibility to the rest of the world, is by no means unique; there is a long history of Americans seeking to transform the world according to American principles. Secretary of State Dean Acheson proclaimed at the beginning of the Cold War, "We are willing to help people who believe the way we do, to continue to live the way they want to live."[12] Self-interest and high-mindedness have never been combined in a more concise manner, and his sentiments were shared by countless other Cold Warriors, including Lansdale. The idealism of the Lansdale passage quoted above conceals an unforgiving fact, however: when he wrote those words about building a better future for all, the United States was dropping one ton of bombs upon the people of Southeast Asia every single hour, and that rate continued for years.[13] His apparently benign injunction to "share" American ideology thus masked a military policy of vast destructiveness. This narrowness of vision characterized most of Lansdale's career. He simply saw no inherent contradiction between the fruits of capitalism and of democracy, between the rhetoric of this passage and the reality it accompanied. Assassinations, bribes, electoral fraud, and finally military force remained for him acceptable means of achieving high-minded ends.

Although he was one of the first Americans to have a Cold War mission in Vietnam, Lansdale was by no means the only Westerner who found a calling in Asia. Since Disraeli declared that the "East is a Career," countless others have had an abiding interest in this part of the world. For Americans, the East as a career-maker dates from 1784 when Boston-based clipper ships first sailed to China and brought back such exotic goods as silk and tea. Yet trade was by no means the only concern. Americans have long had a deep fascination with and delight in Asian societies and, at the same time, an intense fear and unease mixed with a racial bias toward Asian peoples. In this respect Rudyard Kipling's poem "The White Man's Burden" (1899), with its subheading, "The United States and the Philippines," becomes a touchstone for understanding someone like Lansdale. This immensely popular poem spells out both the rationale for and a critique of the missionary and imperialistic impulses that marked the American expansion into Asia throughout the twentieth century. Kipling's vision of the difficulties awaiting those who go to civilize others becomes apparent in the second stanza:

> Take up the White Man's burden—
> In patience to abide,
> To veil the threat of terror
> And check the show of pride;
> By open speech and simple,
> An hundred times made plain,
> To seek another's profit
> And work another's gain.[14]

For Kipling, the Americans had no alternative and must go abroad, as did the British, to civilize Asian "others," even those who resisted Western beneficence.

Although Lansdale would have actively denied the label of American imperialism to describe his Cold War efforts, he committed his life to reaching out with "open speech and simple" to offer Southeast Asians the benefits of American-style capitalism if they in turn would resist the lure of communism. In this respect, Kipling described him with unerring accuracy. But Lansdale's perspective was much more complexly American than the view conveyed by the poem. A series of intertwining histories can be observed as the building blocks that led him into Southeast Asia: the first American trade ships to China in 1784; the enunciation of the Open Door Policy at the end of the nineteenth century by Secretary of State John Hay and its lasting effect upon American policymakers throughout the twentieth century; Woodrow Wilson's idea that the United States had a duty to remake the world along American lines; the origins and nature of the Cold War; and the power of anticommunist thought in American domestic politics.[15] With passion and glee, Lansdale echoed the sentiments of Thomas Jefferson, embraced the Founding Fathers' vision of an "empire of liberty," and extolled Woodrow Wilson's dream of making the world "safe for democracy." He seemed convinced beyond rhetoric that his work was for the benefit of all concerned and that his actions exemplified the highest ideals embodied within American history.

The variety of American responses to Southeast Asians was brought home to me when I interviewed Lansdale's most notorious colleague, Lucien Conein. Approaching his elegant Georgian home, just outside Washington, D.C., and fittingly close to his government post at the CIA, I was greeted at the door by his part-Vietnamese and part-French wife, Elyette, and taken into a living room filled with stunning Asian artifacts. I then proceeded to interview a man who in the course of an hour used such racist epithets as "goddamn slopes" innumerable times as I asked for his thoughts and recollections about his time in Vietnam. The beauty and ugliness evident in that one encounter have remained with me throughout the research and writing of this work.[16] While it may very well be that Conein was simply testing my reactions to his performance, the complex mix of appreciation and ruthlessness that characterized his attitude, and Lansdale's, was a key component of the history of American imperialism in Asia.

Central to this history were the American missionaries and secular educators whose life ambition was to make the people of Asia more Western, more Christian, more American. This project suffered a dramatic setback in 1949 when the Chinese civil war produced Mao and not Chiang Kai-shek as the victor. American policymakers and ordinary citizens reacted to this event in ways that seem unimaginable today. From Mao's triumph until the early 1970s, Americans feared a cascade effect of countries succumbing like dominoes to communism. The color "red" became shorthand for an evil virus that threatened America and its interests. At home, American conservatives used "the Fall of China" as their rallying cry to red-bait all supposed adversaries. Their slogan became a potent political weapon because it was easily understood by the American public as a failure of American foreign policy through inaction and subterfuge, and it implied that communist infiltration of the State Department had allowed for the rise of Mao. There is much truth, then, to the argument made by Leslie Gelb and Richard Betts in their postmortem of the Vietnam War that the final domino was always the White House.[17] The "fall" of Korea, the Philippines, or Vietnam implied geopolitical and domestic costs that no Cold War American president could bear.

The origins of the Cold War and the rise of the national security state help to provide a broader explanatory context here. To be sure, this is one of the most exhaustively debated historiographical issues in American history. All the interpretations, though, emphasize the encompassing qualities of the Cold War and, in varying ways, agree with the overarching assessment of the period given by Abbot Low Moffat, a State Department official who met Ho Chi Minh in 1946: "I thought we were right back in the wars of religion" was his reflection on the origins of the Cold War.[18] Moffat would go on to decry a U.S. policy toward North Vietnam that was blind to the nationalist component embedded in Ho Chi Minh's efforts, but his advice was ignored. Instead, U.S. foreign policy embraced the policy of containment detailed by George Kennan in his celebrated 1947 article, "The Sources of Soviet Conduct." Kennan—or, as he wrote at the time, "X"—

declared that the United States must confront Soviet imperialism "by the adroit and vigilant application of counter-force at a series of constantly shifting geographical and political points."[19] Containment soon became de facto U.S. foreign policy and was applied throughout the world wherever communism seemed to be advancing.

Within a few years, however, Kennan's vision was considered an inadequate response to the multiple threats posed by the Soviet Union and China. By 1950, and on the eve of the Korean War, Moffat's fears were coming to life. The Cold War was now seen by policymakers as well as the general U.S. public as a battle against a new, modern form of evil. And "evil" is the operative word here. The standard document that incorporates the use of apocalyptic language to explain the multiple threats facing the United States after World War II is National Security Directive 68, written in 1950. The author of NSC 68, Paul Nitze (director of the State Department's Policy Planning Staff), wrote that the inherent weaknesses in the West made it easy prey "for the Kremlin to do its evil work." The word "evil" would crop up in a variety of other places in the text as well and provide a stark and totalizing vision of the world. NSC-68 argued that the entire world was confronted by this new enemy and that the United States must respond in kind because "the Soviet Union, unlike previous aspirants to hegemony, is animated by a new fanatic faith, antithetical to our own, and seeks to impose its absolute authority over the rest of the world. . . . The issues that face us are momentous, involving the fulfillment or destruction not only of this Republic but of civilization itself." What this one document reveals, other than a genuine fear of the Soviet Union, is that American anticommunist ideology during the Cold War dovetailed with the continuing devotion of American policymakers to the tenets of the Open Door, a policy enunciated at the end of the nineteenth century and designed to safeguard American interests at home and abroad. In a fascinating summation of these problems, NSC-68 argued: "The integrity and vitality of our system is in greater jeopardy than ever before in our history. Even if there were no Soviet Union we would face the great problem of the free society, accentuated many fold in this industrial age, of reconciling order, security, the need for participation, with the requirements of freedom. We would face the fact that in a shrinking world the absence of order among nations is becoming less and less tolerable."[20] These dire sentiments, reminiscent of Moffat's historical parallels, powerfully influenced Lansdale and others who made it their life mission to combat communism.

As a Cold War liberal, Edward Lansdale tapped into this anticommunist political program with the conviction of a moral reformer. His wholehearted embrace of American Cold War policies can be seen in his use of "The Good Fight" and "Yankee Do" as working titles of his memoirs.[21] He sincerely believed that because the United States was conceived in a colonial struggle, it could empathize with the colonial struggles of the newly emerging nations after World War II: "Much of Asia is emerging from colonialism, just as we did."[22] In a letter to his family from Vietnam in the mid-1950s, he wrote, "I've been living on catnaps instead of sleep and any sort of rations I could snatch up. A long hard grueling time of fighting a battle in World War III when most folks don't even understand that there is any such thing, except for a handful of Americans, a few millions in Asia, and almost any Soviet citizen."[23] Lansdale was deeply convinced that he was fighting a good and necessary battle in an ongoing if unrecognized war. "There must be a win on our side out there," he told a Senate committee in early 1965 and went on to argue that the fate of Asia and America hung in the balance. In this closed session the chairman of the committee, Senator J. William Fulbright, and Vice President Hubert Humphrey both vigorously agreed with Lansdale's assessment and spoke of how uniquely qualified he was to make that win a reality.[24]

Viewed in this context, Lansdale's principles were simply a reflection of the Cold War consensus that America must contain and confront communism everywhere. He was also influenced by the internationalist sentiment popularized by Henry Luce, the publisher of *Time*, *Life*, and *Fortune*, who wrote at the outset of World War II that the United States must realize that it was entering "the American Century" and must seize this historical moment to remake the world accordingly—a valediction that had become received truth for most liberal Cold Warriors.[25] But Lansdale's methods distinguished him from his fellow Cold Warriors, and the nature and variety of those methods reveal much about U.S. foreign policy during this period. Evolving from his complex mix of interests and experiences—as an advertiser, a CIA agent, an amateur historian, a tourist, a culture collector, a quasi missionary—his tactics included everything from rigging elections to using "black operations," starting a rumor campaign based on local vampire legends, overseeing Philippine presidential campaign songs, using slush funds to buy off political opponents, and orchestrating a fraudulent second coming of Christ. They ranged from creating civic action programs to organizing counterinsurgent hit squads. In one top-secret document from the 1950s, Lansdale described how he worked to get Filipinos to aid the South Vietnamese in the construction of their new country. Called Operation Brotherhood, the project included the construction of "a Filipino 'fish pond'" on a farm in South Vietnam near the 17th parallel, "a much talked-about symbol of what the free people of the world could do, word of it spreading through the communist north."[26] This seemingly benign effort to encourage fellow Asians to help each other combat communism (under the well-intentioned if covert guidance of a U.S. intelligence officer) dovetails with the academic theories involving modernization that became popular throughout the postwar era. Though he was no academic, Lansdale imbibed these theories championing nation building as a way to turn underdeveloped, postcolonial countries into models of anticommunist progress. Like many modernization theorists, he believed that Third World revolutions could be effectively managed by Americans if the leaders of these new countries accepted America's vision of the nature of development, which ranked societies according to a Western scale of achievement. Lansdale was by no means alone in his attraction to modernization theory—its ideas were acted upon with equal fervor by civilian and military leaders and remain central to understanding why the United States intervened in Vietnam[27]—but he put these ponderous theories into practice with a creative flair derived in part from his advertising background and in part from his observations of local folklore.

Despite Lansdale's advocacy of modernization theory, he also championed a warrior's approach to defeating communism. Although he always acted in advisory capacities and was thus never directly responsible for military action—the bombing campaigns, Agent Orange defoliation, the ordering of troop movements—he did orchestrate ruthless covert actions and even advocated the assassination of political leaders. For example, another top-secret memorandum that he wrote in 1962 as chief of operations of Operation Mongoose, under the heading "THE CUBA PROJECT," reads: "Basically, the operation is to bring about the revolt of the Cuban people. The revolt will overthrow the Communist regime and institute a new government with which the United States can live in peace."[28] Lansdale considered everything from fire-bombing Cuba's sugar crop to manufacturing photos of an obese Castro to discredit him among the Cuban people. As Operations Brotherhood and Mongoose both suggest, Lansdale's methods varied from his community-grounded efforts to foster economic growth to his fundamentally antidemocratic skullduggery. His ability to mesh a genuine interest in the peoples and folklore of indigenous cultures with a relentless zeal to remake those cultures along modern American lines, while remaining oblivious to the sometimes appalling contradictions between the two approaches, remains the key to understanding him and the world view he represented. How and why his efforts initially succeeded in the Philippines and later failed in Vietnam and Cuba form the chronological arc of this story.

IN TRADITIONAL BIOGRAPHIES an individual's life is chronicled against a backdrop of historical events so that the history is seen only through a prism of the subject, one that invariably distorts the relationship of the individual to much larger forces. So much is known about Lansdale that my central purpose is not to write that kind of chronological narrative. Nor have I a desire to write a "pathography"—to use Joyce Carol Oates's term—of his personal foibles or moral failings. Conversely, if larger, impersonal forces dominate a biography, an individual's choices and actions may be viewed as simply a footnote to the history of broad structural change; Arthur Schlesinger Jr.'s plea that "the Vietnam story is a tragedy without villains" is symptomatic of this perspective.[29] One risk of this approach is that it can absolve individuals of moral responsibility for their actions. As Daniel Ellsberg put it in defending his leak of the Pentagon Papers to the *New York Times* in 1971, "To see the conflict and our part in it as a tragedy without villains, war crimes without criminals, lies without liars, espouses and promulgates a view of process, roles and motives that is not only grossly mistaken but which underwrites deceits that have served a succession of Presidents."[30] I would argue further that there is something missing in reconstructions of the past that relegate individuals to positions as mere pawns of capitalism, imperialism, or colonialism. To lessen the role of individuals to this extent becomes a process of erasing history.

I have tried to balance the two approaches by using Lansdale's life and character to tell the story of American expansion abroad during the Cold War while documenting the instances in which this individual's attitudes and actions had powerful consequences for the trajectory of that historical narrative. More than biography, then, this book should be read as a work of cultural mythography, its main subject being American Cold War culture and the complex ways in which Lansdale both embodied and helped to shape it.

Neil Sheehan's declaration in his Pulitzer Prize–winning biography of John Paul Vann, *A Bright Shining Lie*, that "South Vietnam, it can truly be said, was the creation of Edward Lansdale" has been cited by a host of other historians as proof positive of the central (if still vaguely mysterious) role that this one CIA agent had in propelling America into the Vietnam War.[31] The authors of *The Pentagon Papers* employ a similar rhetorical flourish: "We must note that South Vietnam (unlike any of the other countries in Southeast Asia) was essentially the creation of the United States."[32] Although Lansdale's part was considerable, taking these statements literally places the entire responsibility for the birth of South Vietnam on the shoulders of one individual, providing too narrow an understanding of the situation. True, Lansdale went to South Vietnam in 1954 shortly after Ho Chi Minh's forces triumphed over the French at Dien Bien Phu, a victory that resulted in the partitioning of Vietnam into two sections. True, he oversaw South Vietnam's new constitution, spearheaded the election that solidified Ngo Dinh Diem's rule as its new president, and then convinced a wavering Washington elite to support Diem in 1955 during the Sect Crisis, when others—notably, President Dwight Eisenhower's personal friend and adviser General J. Lawton Collins and the U.S. ambassador to South Vietnam, Elbridge Durbrow—opposed this support. (In fact, evidence now exists that Lansdale spurred Diem on to initiate the battles against the sects that challenged his rule, as a way of maintaining his rule at home and support in Washington).[33] It is also true that he remained a key advocate of U.S. intervention in Vietnam, especially during the first year of the Kennedy administration.

Yet he was hardly alone in his enthusiastic promotion of South Vietnam; the list here is extensive. Most notably the "Vietnam Lobby"—including such influential (and politically disparate) American scholars, politicians, and religious leaders as Francis Cardinal Spellman, Supreme Court Justice William O. Douglas, the socialist Norman Thomas, and Senators Mike Mansfield and John F. Kennedy—wielded tremendous influence in shaping U.S. foreign policy.[34] Further, Lansdale's significance cannot be understood apart from the tumultuous religious and political divisions that racked Vietnam at the time, or from the history of America's long-standing relationship to colonial powers and to the colonies themselves. Finally, coming to terms with Lansdale's actions requires factoring in the role of the presidents, secretaries of state, and directors of the CIA who were giving him his marching orders.

Lansdale's overt and covert activities during the 1950s and early 1960s, though providing a unique window into American Cold War tactics, must be counterbalanced by the real limits to his power. He was effectively prohibited, for instance, from taking part in the crucial discussions during the fall of 1963, when the Kennedy administration decided that Diem was expendable, nor was he involved in the deliberations during the Johnson administration whereby U.S. forces were increased from 16,000 to the half-million mark by 1968. And when he went back to Vietnam in 1965 as a senior adviser to U.S. Ambassador Henry Cabot Lodge, his job was to run the burgeoning pacification programs in a country that was being overwhelmed by war. His greatest accomplishment during this time lay in his recording of Vietnamese and American GI folksongs. While these recordings have been used with tremendous insight by ethnographers, their historical appreciation was not what Lansdale originally hoped for; he saw them as a tool to better understand both the people he was supporting and those he was fighting.[35] This inability to wield power had the additional impact that by the time he began to write his memoirs in the early 1970s, his optimism about the nature of American foreign policy had darkened, and his politics had grown noticeably harsher. By 1979 his contribution of money to the staunchly anticommunist organization Young Americans for Freedom capped a lifetime of politics: Lansdale had gone from liberal anticommunist internationalist to supporter of archconservatives.[36]

But it is Lansdale the liberal anticommunist who remains the central concern of this book. Many were attracted to his knowing yet hopeful vision of a world remade by America. For instance, Walt Rostow, a national security adviser to President John Kennedy, used language suggesting that Lansdale's understanding of the Third World bordered on the omniscient: "He knows more about guerrilla warfare on the Asian scene than any other American. He had an extraordinary sensitivity and respect for the political problems of postcolonial nations and for the human beings caught up in them. No one had a better right to form an assessment of the situation in Vietnam and to have that assessment taken seriously."[37] And throughout Lansdale's papers one can find plaintive calls from midlevel American and South Vietnamese officials to "bring back Lansdale" to Vietnam because he alone was thought to understand the local history and culture. The fact that these countless acclaims were rarely acted on by senior Washington officials speaks to their eventual opposition and rising distaste for his policies and tactics, which often came to be seen as gimmicky or simply beside the point.[38] He becomes then at once important and yet not the classic "Great Man" around whom it is said that a history should focus.

MY FIRST TASK in understanding Lansdale's world was to study his own prolific writings, policy papers, diary entries, photographs, and tape recordings, as well as the body of literature amassed by those who wrote about him. I also interviewed people who knew him, read the secondary literature, and filed dozens of Freedom of Information requests with the U.S. government to learn about his covert actions for the CIA. Any study of Lansdale must begin with the two government publications that document his actions in detail: the internal history of U.S. decision-making toward Vietnam, published as *The Pentagon Papers* (1971) and the U.S. Senate's *Alleged Assassination Plots involving Foreign Leaders* (1975), commonly known as the Church Report because Senator Frank Church chaired the select committee investigating intelligence activities.[39]

After the release of *The Pentagon Papers*, journalists and historians peppered their accounts of the Vietnam War with stories of Lansdale's overseeing a group of CIA saboteurs who infiltrated North Vietnam and attempted to destroy Ho Chi Minh's regime by pouring sugar into the gas tanks of Hanoi's buses. And when Lansdale's efforts to destroy Castro's regime in the early 1960s became known during the Church committee's investigation in the mid-1970s, Lansdale was once again at the center of discussions over the nature of U.S. foreign policy. To some, he was Exhibit A proving that U.S. policy toward revolutionary Third World nations was simply a series of criminal actions; others applauded his efforts to challenge these communist regimes. But supporters and critics alike marveled at his exploits. Consider the following account by a witness before Church's committee:

> I'll give you one example of Lansdale's perspicacity. He had a wonderful plan for getting rid of Castro. This plan consisted of spreading the word that the Second Coming of Christ was imminent and that Christ was against Castro. . . . [Then] just over the horizon there would be an American submarine which would surface off of Cuba and send up some starshells. And this would be the manifestation of the Second Coming and Castro would be overthrown. . . .
>
> Well, some wag called this operation . . . Elimination by Illumination.[40]

Although some of these revelations simply defied rational explanation, Lansdale continued to have his champions (and he liked to brag that he was the only witness before the Church committee who didn't bring a lawyer with him). Even though the American people were just learning what the people of Southeast Asia or Cuba had known for some time about the extent of U.S. intervention in their societies, he continued to be seen by some as the man willing to oppose communism at all costs.

These two government publications also demonstrate Lansdale's stature in Washington in the 1950s and 1960s. Presidents and secretaries of state became fervent supporters, eager to listen to his new ideas for winning the Cold War in Southeast Asia (and later in Latin America, the Middle East, and even in Africa). President Kennedy was a particularly big fan of Lansdale's unorthodox methods in fighting communism. JFK loved new and faddish military ideas, especially ones that offered alternatives to increased bombing campaigns and more American soldiers in Vietnam. As David Halberstam wrote, "It was as if Brigadier General Edward Lansdale had been invented with the Kennedy Administration in mind. He was . . . a man deeply interested in doing things in Asia the right way, the modern way."[41] Lansdale also came to be seen as someone the Kennedy brothers valued: a tough guy who was also a liberal anticommunist. As Aleksandr Fursenko and Timothy Naftali note in their history of the Cuban missile crisis, "To the extent that John and Robert Kennedy gained reassurance from a man's man, Lansdale and the solutions he proffered were extremely satisfying."[42] The sheer number of bizarre schemes considered or enacted by Washington to defeat communism during this time suggests the success with which Lansdale had ingratiated himself with key figures and was able to influence governmental policy. The fact that presumably rational people often advocated policies that today appear ridiculous highlights the skewed frame of reference generated by Cold War ideologies.

It is a testament to Lansdale's renown that so many writers have viewed him as central to an understanding of the nature of U.S. foreign policy. These include both Cecil Currey, whose flattering biography presented Lansdale as an extraordinary man who could have achieved an American victory in Vietnam, and Richard Drinnon, whose harsh narrative features Lansdale as a central villain in the shaping of American imperialism.[43] More than anything, the chasm between these two portrayals of Lansdale reveals the extent to which each writer's own stake in the politics of the period colors his view of the facts. Other accounts of Lansdale's efforts abroad tend to reproduce one another's snapshots of the man. Stanley Karnow's first-rate *Vietnam: A History* (1983) notes that although Lansdale's role has been exaggerated, he was nonetheless an all-purpose CIA agent who, after successfully destroying a communist rebellion in the Philippines, was then dispatched by the Eisenhower administration to do likewise in South Vietnam. Karnow sums up with economy and force: "Lansdale counted on psychological warfare techniques that resembled advertising gimmicks. He also exuded a brand of artless goodwill that overlooked the deeper dynamics of revolutionary upheavals, and he seemed to be oblivious to the social and cultural complexities of Asia."[44]

Lansdale is characterized in a remarkably similar fashion in dozens of other academic and journalistic studies of the Cold War. This repetitive tendency among historians has the uncanny effect of making him a recurring shorthand for the more bizarre CIA operations of the period more than an appropriate subject of historical study. These countless brief references accomplish little more than a further inflation of Lansdale as a Cold War celebrity because they convey his actions as a stereotypical CIA agent without subjecting them to much critical or historical analysis. Perhaps because he was such a charismatic figure, people who knew him, as well as historians, can't seem to resist describing him in the fantastic language of hack journalism. For example, Robert Dean's recent *Imperial Brotherhood* is a nuanced view of the role of gender as it intersected with American Cold War strategies. Yet when Dean considers Lansdale, he says that "MONGOOSE operated in secret, with a domestic political payoff awaiting a successful result from the actions of Lansdale's swashbuckling guerrilla-spy-gangster myrmidons: the murder of Castro, or the collapse of his regime."[45] Conversely, the CIA's William Colby held Lansdale in such high esteem that he called him one of the world's ten greatest spies, the unconventional warrior par excellence, unafraid to take extreme risks in defense of American interests.[46] Regardless of their politics or point of view, then, one constant is the colorful language that writers have used to describe him.

Contemporary journalists established a precedent for attributing to Lansdale qualities and accomplishments far beyond those he actually achieved. Some employed the figure of Lansdale to reassure the reader that "our man in Asia" was on the front lines of the Cold War, single-handedly fighting communism while escaping yet another assassination attempt by communists and their agents. For other journalists, Lansdale represented the high-level conspiracies that manipulated governments according to the edicts of the CIA. Even those who knew him were not immune to these impulses and often wrote of him in almost mythic terms.[47] Still others found him to a rarity among Americans abroad: someone who actually listened to the Vietnamese. In a nationally televised interview with Walter Cronkite in 1971, Daniel Ellsberg (who had worked with Lansdale in Vietnam in the mid-1960s) described with extraordinary force the American institutions and the Cold War mind-set that had created the Vietnam debacle. When Cronkite asked him whether there were any heroes to emerge from the Pentagon Papers, Ellsberg responded: "Never in those cables or estimates, I think, outside of memos by a few people, General Lansdale being one, will the public find . . . a Vietnamese leader described with concern, friendship, respect, or evaluated in any terms other than as an instrument of American policy."[48] Ellsberg later suggested that reading up on the life and times of T. E. Lawrence would provide clues as to who Lansdale really was. This comparison was by no means unique: because of Lansdale's personal involvement with the people and folklore of Southeast Asia, others too found the British adventurer the key to understanding him.

By the 1970s, two different visions of Lansdale thus coexisted and competed: (1) the "good" Cold Warrior who understood the danger that communism posed to the West and was ignored or prevented from shaping policy, and (2) the "bad" CIA agent who publicly championed democracy for all while covertly engineering actions that resulted in the killing of people who did not share his vision. Both renditions turned Lansdale into a prop for a particular narrative of the nature of the Cold War, and conflicting views continue in the battle to determine his legacy. After his death, articles and editorials in the *New York Times*, the *Washington Post*, and even *Soldier of Fortune* and the John Birch Society's publication the *New American* chose one or the other of these positions on Lansdale and on the nature of American foreign policy.

Interpreting such varied political and cultural responses to Lansdale is a crucial part of this study. In addition to tracing his career as a Cold Warrior, I examined the legends, historical and fictional, that grew up around the man. Filmmakers and novelists in particular gravitated to Lansdale—actually to their "idea" of Lansdale—and added to the peculiar nature of his celebrity. The mere mention of his name invariably provoked a sharply opinionated response from those who were familiar with American foreign policy. Oliver North viewed himself as Lansdale's "protégé"; other historians have told me, and only somewhat jokingly, that he was America's "Darth Vader"; David Halberstam simply smiled when he learned of my project and told me that Lansdale was really nothing but a "hick."[49]

One of the odder encounters I had while tracking down individuals who knew Lansdale occurred at a 1992 Kennedy assassination convention in San Francisco.[50] Partly as a lark, and partly because my study includes Lansdale's actions during the Kennedy administration, I went to see what I would find at this decidedly nonacademic conference. On one level there were few surprises: a group of middle-aged males who knew an absolutely extraordinary amount about the events surrounding November 22, 1963, expressed their collective outrage at the sinister forces that had conspired to kill Kennedy. The atmosphere became a bit more heated when I challenged one presenter who made several disputable claims about Lansdale as the kingpin of efforts to depose Fidel Castro and argued that these in turn created the "blowback" that killed Kennedy. I protested that Lansdale was simply an officer who was following the edicts of John F. Kennedy, his brother Robert, and various other senior government officials.[51] The other conventioneers would hear none of this "academic talk," insisting instead that certain individuals, ones with black hearts, were responsible for both the assassination and the horrors of Vietnam that followed. To this audience, Lansdale epitomized the darkness at the root of American power, and no one talking about the larger history of U.S. foreign policy was going to dissuade them.

Lansdale's ability to straddle history and popular culture has long made him a favorite of those on the political margins. One of the most imaginative examples of this is "The Ballad of Ed Lansdale" at www.blackopradio.com, a website that bills itself as "the voice of political conspiracy research." Here in this retelling of American foreign policy through the prism of conspiracies, sound effects, and heavy metal guitars, is a feverish six-minute history of Lansdale and his role in toppling governments. At one point "Lansdale" sings:

> From a long line of Cover and Deception
> I've rewritten history
> You won't find my name in any school books
> Even to my brothers, I'm a man of mystery
> Cloak and Dagger, Fun and games
> Done with C.A.R.E., it's all the same
> With a blank check book from Uncle Sam
> I was the best, I was the man
> I'm a fixer, I'm a plumber, I'm a cover up man . . . I'm all three!
> But my biggest and best was November 1963.

The discussion of "November 1963" is, of course, an insider's fanciful reference to Lansdale's orchestrating the assassination of President Kennedy.[52]

The continued faith of such conspirators that Lansdale could wield such dark power led me to ask myself why these people viewed him that way and, further, why so many Americans share varieties of this conspiratorial vision of their government. To be sure, this is by no means a new phenomenon; Richard Hofstadter charted it in his 1967 essay collection *The Paranoid Style in American Politics*, documenting with fascination and dread the "heated exaggeration, suspiciousness, and conspiratorial fantasy" that have marked American political thought since its founding.[53] As the conference demonstrated, the vision of history as the work of a cabal of men shows no sign of abatement. In a way, then, my study became the flip side of the conspiratorial best seller about the Kennedy assassination by the New Orleans district attorney, Jim Garrison. His fevered exposé, *On the Trail of Assassins: My Investigation and Prosecution of the Murder of President Kennedy*, has since become a central text for Kennedy conspiracy buffs, or, as they prefer, "assassination researchers." Garrison's story of how dozens of people were involved in the greatest of conspiracies was of course earnestly discussed at the convention. More important, I recognized that I was on a similar trail of a figure from our recent past, with the coda that I needed to appreciate both the world of historical archives and the broader cultural spectrum—including popular magazines, films, novels, and conspiracy conventions—that would help to explain this individual and his place in history.

The passion of the JFK conspiracy's true believers brought me to see that the traditional historical approach was incomplete; documents can give us at best a partial answer to the aura that surrounded Lansdale and the way others saw him. A second approach, examining what our culture has made of Lansdale, meant sifting through nontraditional perspectives and analyzing the host of fictions and fantasies that have attached themselves to his name. In other words, I needed to examine the actual history of Edward Lansdale but also to study how and why people have used Lansdale to explain and to stand for the very nature of the American mission abroad. It is this combination that best explains the American attempt to remake Southeast Asia during the Cold War. Tackling this dual project required me to consider not only portrayals by academics such as Currey and Drinnon and by journalists who knew Lansdale in the Philippines and Vietnam but also the work of popular writers and artists who put Lansdale-esque characters in their works of art. This group includes such luminaries as Norman Mailer, Joan Didion, and Ward Just.

The one portrayal that has informed all others however, achieving an enduring and widespread explanatory power, is in Graham Greene's novel *The Quiet American* (1955), whose title character succeeds in bringing death and destruction to the people of Vietnam—but with the best of intentions. Alden Pyle has been assumed by subsequent writers, by a broader public, and by Lansdale himself to be based on Lansdale. Even though Greene claimed no such intention (see Chapter 6), his portrait of a destructive do-gooder abroad was so accurate and powerful in exposing America's self-deluded mission that it shadowed Lansdale for the rest of his life. It also prompted subsequent writers to build from Greene's depiction, for he portrayed in stunning fashion the ideological certainties that the real Lansdale did take with him into Asia. Even though he had other Americans in mind when creating the character, Greene captured Lansdale's idealism and blindness better than anyone else. If only for this reason, *The Quiet American* remains a remarkable explanation of the origins of the Vietnam War.

A more recent reference to the mystique of the Lansdale legend occurs in Oliver Stone's movie *JFK* (1991). Here, an individual who bears an uncanny resemblance to Lansdale (though identified only as "General Y") is intimately involved in the conspiracies surrounding the assassination of President Kennedy; in Stone's funhouse vision of Cold War America, he is the master manipulator CIA agent who, after attempting to assassinate Castro, joined with other rogue elements within the government to kill Kennedy because the president was threatening to pull the United States out of Vietnam and thus to end the very Cold War that gave life to these warriors. Without question, Stone's depiction is a stunning vision of a behind-the-scenes Cold Warrior at work in the heart of the chaos, quietly pulling the strings that set in motion "black ops" (covert missions) throughout the world. Although "General Y's" face is mostly seen in shadows or hidden behind objects, thus shrouding his true identity, his physical trademarks are still readily if only briefly apparent. Glimpses of his mustache (when all other military personnel in the movie are clean-shaven), his aviator sunglasses (worn even in dimly lit rooms), and his well-known smile while informing "Colonel X" that he is being sent to the South Pole in order to allow the massive conspiracy to proceed—these make "General Y" a particularly sinister rendition of the mysterious Lansdale persona and, in the hands of an agit-prop director like Stone, a very effective one.[54]

In addition to these influential fictional portrayals, a host of hack writers have found it next to impossible to resist Lansdale's charms. For "old Asia hand" journalists he became a stand-in for America writ large; he provided the pithy quote and the heartfelt monologue about why America was in Vietnam; and his dashing looks and "good-time Charlie" approach to life offered a contrast to the many staid bureaucrats and gray military men who inhabited Washington and Vietnam. Half-fanciful, half-journalistic accounts helped to establish Lansdale as the true American adventurer and transformed him into a Cold War celebrity. Consider this statement from Fulton Lewis Jr., a journalist/gossipmonger: "I have a special memorandum from a close and trusted friend of mine—himself an Oriental—who has just come back from Saigon and who is in the professional intelligence field, and while his identity must be kept confidential, I think his report is interesting and significant. Here is what it says: . . . 'The Vietnamese have let it be known in the White House that they prefer, above all others, General Edward Lansdale.' "[55] Later writers described Lansdale as a "lone wolf operator," the "kingmaker," and an agent provocateur. Lansdale's own "wink-wink, nudge-nudge" response to questions about his activities only added to their interest. His charismatic appeal, wit, and unshakable faith in America's political and economic system became favored descriptive elements in such diverse cultural outlets as pornographic magazines, popular entertainment guides, and movies, from which millions learned of him and the ideas that he propagated.

This fascination with Lansdale was by no means limited to Westerners. Filipinos nicknamed him Colonel Landslide after his assumed role in manipulating their ballot boxes, and Vietnamese called him the phoenix for his legendary ability to reappear repeatedly in their country. Prince Norodom Sihanouk of Cambodia cast himself in a series of movies in the 1960s in which he triumphs over and usually kills an American CIA agent called "Lansdale." Even with their radically divergent histories and cultures, Southeast Asians seemed to view Lansdale in the same mythic ways favored by Westerners—as the missing link between disparate Cold War events. As a composite, these portrayals—Southeast Asian or Western, isolationist or interventionist, left or right—create a shape-shifting aura that reflects Lansdale according to each writer's political or cultural agenda. It is this lasting effect that defines him as a pure product of twentieth-century Americana. By the time of his death, Edward Lansdale had become a commodity to be used and abused at will. A telling summation of his life came from one of his brothers, David Lansdale. Shortly after reading *In the Midst of Wars*, he wrote that "a review of the *Pentagon Papers* makes it pretty clear to me that you were involved in activities that could make another completely parallel story."[56]

One of Lansdale's favorite authors, John Le Carré, wrote about the Cold War in a way that crystallizes the effects of such parallel lives upon a person. Le Carré's protagonist, George Smiley, gets at the essence of spies like Lansdale when he recognizes in *Tinker, Tailor, Soldier, Spy*: "It is a habit in all of us to make our cover stories, our assumed personae, at least parallel with the reality. . . . The more identities a man has, the more they express the person they conceal. . . . Few men can resist expressing their appetites when they are making a fantasy about themselves."[57] In many ways Lansdale embodied that description. Each of his series of "cover stories"—Cold Warrior, advertising man, CIA agent, historian, missionary, and tourist—provides a parallel reality, a slightly different way of understanding his life, his motivations, and the times he lived in.

THIS BOOK takes up the perspective allowed by each of those cover stories as a means of explaining Lansdale and his Cold War, and it examines the array of cultural responses that contributed to his celebrity. Only by looking at the composite provided by these varying perspectives can we find the true expression of the person and understand the character of his world.

The first five chapters sift out the various layers of American intellectual and cultural thought that came to create that world. Chapter 1 explores how the advertising field that Lansdale worked in before World War II affected his tactical outlook as a Cold Warrior, particularly when he operated in Japan and in the Philippines. Using everything from pithy slogans to media manipulation, Lansdale promoted his vision of U.S.-Asia relations while inspiring confidence in himself as the central proponent of those relations. Chapter 2 analyzes his less successful use of these publicity-based strategies in Vietnam and in promoting himself back in America.

Chapter 3 details Lansdale's missions as a CIA agent, what his goals were, how he operated in Southeast Asia, and the ideological certitude about the Cold War that led him to oversee a host of covert operations. Chapter 4 considers Lansdale's use of "history"—American, Southeast Asian, mythical—to market his notions of how the Philippines and Vietnam should develop along American lines. His ideological assumptions about the nature of history were what prevented him from perceiving the authentic quality of the revolutions sweeping throughout post–World War II Southeast Asia and from understanding why these people resisted American power and culture.

Chapter 5 examines Lansdale's ideologically complex role as an explorer of Southeast Asia. In marked contrast to most Americans, who stayed close to American bases and their creature comforts, Lansdale relished the opportunity to travel and spend time in the remote areas of these countries. He brought to his CIA missions abroad the zest of both a tourist and an ethnographer, camera and tape recorder always at hand, eager to learn everything possible about the cultures in which he operated, both from a genuine interest and from an understanding of the strategic value of that knowledge. Equally, he saw himself as something of a goodwill ambassador for the United States.

The last two chapters look at the variety of cultural perspectives that developed around Lansdale. Chapter 6 explores the construction and reception of him as a celebrity, particularly in Graham Greene's *The Quiet American* (1955) and William Lederer and Eugene Burdick's *The Ugly American* (1958)—and their respective Hollywood movies. Chapter 7 continues this analysis by studying the impact on his celebrity aura of fiction and media images, from Norman Mailer's depiction of him as a CIA agent with "hollow eyes" to journalistic accounts and a myriad of films and pulp novels inhabited by Lansdale-like characters. Together, these chapters show how modern American culture and the celebrity-making apparatus worked in positioning Lansdale as an iconic Cold Warrior.

The epilogue considers the results of Lansdale's efforts for the peoples of

Southeast Asia. The current political instability, poverty, and devastation in sections of this part of the world cannot, obviously, be attributed to the work of one man. Nevertheless, his fervent efforts to remake Southeast Asia in America's image came at a heavy price to those countries—and cost Lansdale himself dearly as well.

1

Confidences

Everybody should advertise while they are alive. . . .
The man who does not advertise is a dead one, whether
he knows it or not. . . . Life is too short for you to hide
yourself away mantled in your own modesty.

—Elbert Hubbard, editor of the *Philistine*, addressing
a meeting of advertising agents in 1911

HERMAN MELVILLE'S *The Confidence-Man* (1857) foregrounds the Cosmopolitan, the Devil, a stranger "in the extremist sense of the word." He urges his wares upon the unsuspecting and the cynical alike, including a cripple who is busy selling confidences himself. The cripple's guilt-inducing tales of being a veteran of America's war against Mexico, however, are no match for the strategies of the Cosmopolitan, who in the guise of an herb doctor proclaims his ability to cure the cripple of his many afflictions with the Omni-Balsamic Reinvigorator. The cripple, though wary at first, becomes even more seduced by the idea of this product:

> "Stay, stay! *Sure* it will do me good?"
> "Possibly, possibly; no harm in trying. Good-bye."
> "Stay, stay; give me three more boxes, and here's the money."
> "My friend," returning towards him with a sadly pleased sort of air, "I rejoice in the birth of your confidence and hopefulness. Believe me that, like your crutches, confidence and hopefulness will long support a man when his own legs will not. Stick to confidence and hopefulness, then."[1]

The cripple's dream of a magical recovery remains as steadfast as his physical condition remains unchanged.

Melville's troubling meditation on the quintessentially American search for immediate cures extended beyond the routine confidences involved in the buying and selling of bogus goods; his real concern was for the feeble and malleable nature of the human soul. It is the very power and richness of the word "confidence," used by Melville to such devastating effect, that has since fascinated critics of his work. Consider the historian Jackson Lears's scrutiny of this word: "'Confidence,' in this broader context, is another name for hubris: to have confidence is to believe that the experts know best. The confidence man asks his dupe to accept specific product claims as well as the myths of human centrality and power supporting those claims."[2] Melville's exploration of grifting can do double duty by licensing another reading, one that sees the wishes and wish fulfillments played out on a nineteenth-century steamer as equally revealing during the Cold War. For it was beliefs in anticommunism and market economies, coupled with deeply held beliefs in ideas of progress, that provided the confidences America used to bargain with the rest of the world after World War II.

A key orchestrator of these joint military and commercial efforts during the Cold War was Edward Lansdale. He knew well the power of combining American belief systems with the persuasive forces of money and military strength. Among the many roles he adopted was the classic confidence man selling his therapies from Southeast Asia to Washington. His world was one where bargains were to be had, money for elections procured, protection from the communist hordes insured—but always for a price.

The starting point for Lansdale's confidences begins with his work in advertising in the 1930s. "I hated people who told lies about products, and I refused to do it," he later said, declaring that he would support only quality goods and services.[3] Perhaps this explains why he eventually left the field and went into the military to serve as an intelligence officer. In any case, Lansdale was thoroughly middle class in mores and comforts, but he yearned for more. Born in Detroit in 1908, he grew up in a fervently religious home: his mother was a Christian Scientist and his father a Presbyterian. The family subscribed to the work ethic in all its varieties. Lansdale attended UCLA during the Great Depression, majored in journalism, joined a fraternity and became its president, performed as an extra in a dozen or so Hollywood films, and was the editor and cartoonist for the college humor magazine, *The Claw*.[4] He was the classic Big Man on Campus, and (as a friend recalled) his ability to "work on" people was apparent to all: "he had the facility for encouraging people to do what he thought would be good for them."[5]

To pay for school, Lansdale produced cartoons and ads for local companies and later left UCLA to work in advertising in Los Angeles and San

Francisco. His artistic ability and quick wit helped him succeed in this burgeoning field, and he soon came to work on the accounts of some of the
largest companies on the West Coast: the Wells Fargo Bank, the Union
Trust Company, Levi Strauss.[6] One of Lansdale's early advertisements,
which included a photo of himself, used tactics designed to appeal to the
local culture. Wavy, bold letters grabbed the attention of potential retailers
of the Wellman corporation's product line by proclaiming: "WHO'S THE
'HERO OF THE WEEK'?" The gap between the literal products—coffee, green
beans, marmalade—and hero-promoting images calls attention to the dual
force of the ad. The copy makes use of the aura of radio, talent scouts,
Hollywood "stars" and "scriptwriters" to publicize the products. At the same
time, it engages in selling Americana, war preparedness, and a model of
heroism:

> America loves its heroes. You do. Your customers do, And, so do we! In fact, we
> have known of so many unsung acts of valor in California, that we have decided
> they shall no longer go unrecognized. Now Wellman, Peck & Company, Cali-
> fornia's largest manufacturing wholesale grocers, will send "hero scouts"
> throughout California in search of unsung heroes. Script writers and radio stars
> will present a thrilling dramatization of the week's outstanding act of bravery
> . . . after which the hero will receive the specially designed Wellman Valor
> Award medal.
>
> Also, Guest Chefs from California's famous restaurants will appear during this
> epochal series of broadcasts and suggest new uses for Wellman "Flavor Famous"
> Foods . . . to help you help your customers.[7]

Leaving aside the "epochal" nature of this campaign, in which heroes and
consumption are conflated, the historical context is clear. It was written in
March 1941, when the Great Depression and World War II were the great
issues in American lives, and "heroes" (and then soldiers) were needed. In
announcing its search for "unsung heroes," the advertisement champions the
American values of patriotism, bravery—and consumption. At the same time
it offers the consumer a vision of an ideal and hero-laden America. These
tactics are exactly those later employed by Lansdale in his government career
when he helped to establish American interests in postwar Southeast Asia.[8]

Long after Lansdale had grown tired of being an advertiser back in the
United States, he continued to transplant the ideology behind the "hero of
the week" ad campaign to his search for leaders in Southeast Asia. Writing
in 1965 to a longtime friend, the journalist Robert Shaplen, he emphasized
his strategy of selling people and ideas through the marketing first of Ramon
Magsaysay in the Philippines and then of Ngo Dinh Diem in Vietnam:

"Incidentally, I'm amused that you saw so little similarity between a save in the Philippines and a save in Vietnam. Somebody had to do the strategic planning, keep Washington firm enough on backing the play, and ride herd on the tactical implementation while building up a local national hero. In both instances, Asian Communist subversive insurgents took lickings—the only time the U.S. has been able to do so."[9] American Cold War interests became the product line embodied in the discovery and marketing of these "local national heroes."

In promoting this mixture of hard and soft sell, Lansdale recognized all too well its heady and long-term effects. He used the publicizing strategies of advertising and the "logic" of consumption to override the complex histories and varying political contexts in Southeast Asian countries and to drive them toward an ever more desirable and unattainable goal. He knew it would not be enough to enforce American military control over these countries' politics or simply to import the ideology of capitalism as a universal good. Rather, the package of attributes that Lansdale hoped to graft onto these cultures combined the attraction of American money and goods with a universalized system of cultural values and revolutionary democratic ideals. It is at this juncture that the power of advertising is most apparent. As the cultural critic Christopher Lasch has argued, "The importance of advertising . . . does not lie in its manipulation of the consumer or its direct influence on consumer choices. The point is that it makes the consumer an addict, unable to live without increasingly sizable doses of externally provided stimulation."[10] In advertising the "magic" of American capitalism for Southeast Asians—in seeming to create cultural bonds and common goals where none had existed—Lansdale became at once the best consumer and the greatest addict of his own advertising maneuvers.[11] He can be seen, then, as a devotee of Americana who passed on his faith to his various consumers in Washington, the Philippines, and Vietnam.

This intermingling of advertiser and military officer is how many came to define Lansdale, and countless Cold War dispatches thus shaped their stories about him. Having been an intelligence officer in the ROTC program in college he tried to reenlist immediately after the Japanese attack on Pearl Harbor in 1941, working alternately for the army's intelligence branch (MIS), the Office of Strategic Services (OSS), and later the air force on behalf of the CIA. In pursuing his military career, Lansdale frequently called attention to his advertising background. On his army application form, for instance, he sold himself to the government by noting that he had "written several movie scripts, directed & produced two, did camera work on one— for commercial films used by advertisers."[12] He also stated his interest in the field of military intelligence, which led to his being recruited by "wild" Bill Donovan, then head of the OSS, who sought a winning personality coupled with a keen sense of American interests. Later, Lansdale reminisced about his years as a World War II intelligence officer with tremendous nostalgia: "They kept using me to go out getting new information and meet new people all the time, which seemed to be my forte . . . The Army had great demands for information and we were trying to satisfy those as well. So I was sort of the handy man [for both OSS and MIS]."[13]

The advertising, marketing, and public relations that figure in Lansdale's history became stand-ins for the larger forces of consumer culture operating in this period. Just as advertising agents laid claim to the modernizing of America, Lansdale the advertiser joined post–World War II attempts to spread "the good news about progress," to bring modernizing forces to the rest of the world, particularly to those parts threatened by communism.[14] The embedded ideology of "progress" propelled much of American foreign policy and was inherent in modernization theorists' prescriptions for remaking the Third World. Michael Schudson's analysis helps to explain the relationship between modernization and consumption: he documents how advertising's power of endlessly generating desire is tied into notions of progress. In fact, Schudson argues that advertising "does not claim to picture reality as it is but reality as it should be—life and lives worth emulating. . . . It always assumes that there is progress. It is thoroughly optimistic, providing for any troubles that it identifies a solution in a particular product or style of life."[15] The historian Roland Marchand also refers to advertisers as "missionaries of Modernity."[16] For Lansdale, the coupling of a consumerist ideology with the modernizing ethos was completely naturalized by the consolidation of his two careers. Yet if the advertiser's application of the ideals of progress and the promise of future fulfillment was questionable in the American context, it became exponentially so when Lansdale and others promoted this ideology of abundance—backed by American power—to the cultures of Southeast Asia.[17]

Relating consumer capitalism and modernization theory to the nature of U.S. foreign policy, Emily Rosenberg's *Spreading the American Dream* (1982) details how American businessmen in tandem with State Department officials used advertising when "invading" a new country. State Department interests and Lansdale's influence in Southeast Asia were always mediated by companies such as Coca-Cola and Standard Oil, which were equally bent on converting everyone to the American way of consumption as progress. The similarity of Lansdale's strategies to those of the American businessmen described by Rosenberg signals his participation in the larger project of making

Southeast Asia into a market. In this sense, he took part in a long tradition of American influence abroad, beginning at least with the nineteenth-century American missionaries who went to China and "sold" American ideologies and religions. Lansdale's delight in peddling Americana became a reality only because it was underscored by the economic and military power at his disposal and by the prices he exacted for American-based confidence. Given this backing, Lansdale was even more successful in Southeast Asia than earlier Americans had been in China and Europe.

Further, advertising became for Lansdale a game of cover-up just as much as of disclosure. One of the hallmarks of his career was his constant hedging about his relationship to the intelligence community. In his military file he wrote, "I organized and operated the Positive Intelligence Branch during WWII."[18] He kept the title purposely nondescript, to prevent prying individuals inside and outside of government from learning that he was employed by the MIS and OSS. In this dual and unusual wartime capacity, he worked from a desk in San Francisco training agents before they were sent into enemy territory.

This was the first position in which he applied the skills he learned in advertising, and he did so against the Japanese. One episode is particularly revealing. In 1943, Lansdale focused on ways to reduce morale among Japanese troops, and the result was a document titled "From the Serpent's Mouth," specifying "Japanese proverbs which may be turned against Japan":

> The Japanese, like all Orientals, love proverbs. Their literature—and their daily conversation—are interlarded with them:
> — "The reputation of a thousand years may be determined by the conduct of one hour."
> — "One meal without rice mars domestic happiness for a week."
> — "The man who makes the first bad move always loses the game" (Remember Pearl harbor!).[19]

This effort, however fascinating and subtle, exhibits a blinding naiveté regarding the complex forces that might motivate another culture. Yet Lansdale's culture-based approach was strikingly in contrast to the standard contemporary American depictions of the Japanese as subhuman and even insectlike.[20] At the same time, his tactics depended upon assumptions of cultural superiority. "Tokyo Rose" may have produced ridicule among American servicemen, but in Lansdale's view, comparable attempts to outwit the Japanese could triumph only because the enemy was simpler, more malleable, more primitive. His ad campaign then seems to have been designed more to reassure Americans that they were going to win the war than to mislead or dismay the Japanese.

As public information officer of the U.S. Army in the Philippines after
World War II, Lansdale continued to use his skills in ways that reflected his
earlier advertising experience. For instance, he wrote to his fellow army
officers what they needed to take into account in order to have the Philippine
people support U.S. policies in Asia:

1. It is time we changed our thinking about our public relations. We have been
   on the defensive. Sharp criticisms by the press, in the past, have caused us to
   adopt a policy of answering attacks against us. . . . [N]ews items were seldom
   complimentary to the U.S. Army.
2. Now is the time to take the initiative. The past PRO's [public relations offi-
   cers], Colonels Chester and Hindle, spent much effort to make friends with
   local journalists. These journalists are now sympathetic towards the U.S.
   Army. Many are good friends. . . . It is up to us to give them good news that
   is worth newspaper space. If we do this, we will have their active, constructive
   help.[21]

This advice can be seen as relatively innocuous, an enthusiastic young man's
prescription for improving his country's image, yet underlying it is another
of his exchanges of confidence: selling images and ideas by providing journalists with "good news."

To be sure, Lansdale did not spend all his time writing upbeat memos
explaining how the army could persuade journalists or U.S. government
officials "to get on the team." His central task in the Philippines involved
defending U.S. interests in its former colony, and he relished this job as
much as he keenly appreciated the power he wielded. Perhaps his greatest
promotional campaign followed his "discovery" of Ramon Magsaysay, the
proponent of American interests who rose from relatively unknown congressman to appointment as defense minister and then election as president
of the Philippines in 1953.[22] The dimensions of this campaign encompassed
both Lansdale's real affection for Magsaysay and the American military and
commercial dominance of the Philippines. As a result, the relationship between the two men was a lopsided one. Lansdale frequently described the
warmth of their friendship by declaring, "We were so close that we thought
and spoke of each other as 'brother.' Our relationship was so deeply personal
and involved shared risks to such an extent that I find it extremely difficult
to discuss with anyone who wasn't there at the time."[23] Yet Lansdale did not
always hide his disdain for what he perceived as Magsaysay's cultural limitations, calling him "Superstitious. Believed in the ghosts and ghouls of the
provinces. Angry with me when I started to scoff. Told of how he had seen a
'kafri' when a boy in Zambales. The 'kafri' is a gigantic black man ('kaffir'?)
who strides the countryside at night. You can tell he's there, when the tall

grass stirs in the night wind, the moving grass showing his rapid, otherwise invisible strides."[24]

It may very well be that Magsaysay, originally a car mechanic who favored Hawaiian T-shirts and the rumba but also a superior military strategist and politician, was superstitious or continued to place credence in the stories from his youth. Lansdale's comment, however, constructs Magsaysay as the primitive child of the relationship who needs direction and a dose of reason. This outlook was no doubt helped by Magsaysay's intense willingness to be "America's Boy." As Lansdale noted to fellow American officers in a top-secret memorandum, "He wants to be associated more closely with Americans, for political as well as personal reasons, and I believe that he is wise in this judgement of the reactions of Filipinos," and that "he would like to have the U.S. fly him in a U.S. aircraft from the Philippines, so that he would become most closely identified in the Philippines as a friend of the U.S."[25] A photograph of Lansdale serenading Magsaysay to sleep with a harmonica gives an indication of this relationship at work, yet it was not always so harmonious; when Magsaysay once sought to give a speech that had been written by a Filipino (instead of one of his American handlers), Lansdale reacted with rage, actually hitting the presidential candidate hard enough to knock him out. Lansdale later said this was simply a case of two "brothers" arguing: they were so close that he simply forgot protocol. What he did not address was the obvious fact that he, along with many other Americans, was keenly aware of American power in this political relationship and was ready to quash any attempts to alter that power relation.[26]

Another example of this influence can be found in a memo Lansdale wrote to State Department officials concerning the upcoming Philippine elections in 1961. With typical Lansdale bravado he challenged their diplomatic prowess: "Is the Department of State ready, willing, and able to undertake the task in time to have a beneficial effect on this November's election?"[27] There appears to be no hint of irony in his discussion of the active U.S. involvement in another country's electoral process. Historians, though, would eventually learn that Lansdale had ready access to millions of American dollars provided by the CIA to influence Philippine elections in the previous decade.[28] But even more startling than his access to secret funds to help bring Maysaysay to power is Lansdale's CIA after-action report, "The Philippines Election, 1953." In this top-secret document declassified in 2000, Lansdale (using his code name "Geoffrey Villiers") informed the CIA of his team's actions in gleeful detail. Typically, he built into his report a narrative of excitement and bombast: "Why did Kugown [the CIA code name of their group] become involved in a Philippine political campaign in 1953? In brief, it was because we saw no other ready solution to the defeat of Communism in the country." Their successes, he declared, were multiple, concrete, and historic, as the election sparked "a social revolution which would have delighted Thomas Jefferson." He also detailed the means by which he helped set up a newspaper to champion Magsaysay. The report ends with a self-revealing sentence: "It was a privilege to work with my fellow Kugowners and to give the lie to the current adage that the white man is through in Asia. Hellsfire, we're just starting."[29]

Lansdale's covert activities aside, Magsaysay brought to Filipino politics a number of qualities deemed essential for a political candidate in the recently independent Philippines. He was militantly anticommunist in a country wracked by a civil war between a weak government and a communist guerrilla organization; he was fervently nationalist and did not have the political stigma that marked other officials of having collaborated with the Japanese during the war; and he was relatively honest, especially in contrast to the former president, Elpidio Quirino, whose involvement in graft and kickbacks was legendary. American media picked up on these attributes; *Time*'s 1951 cover story of Magsaysay, "Cleanup Man," included the header, "Magsaysay of the Philippines: 'I will send my own father to jail if he breaks the law.'"[30] Magsaysay also presented himself as a politician in the American model. Richard Nixon, for one, commented on his "pure animal magnetism . . . whenever he appeared before a crowd" and related that Magsaysay had told him (when Nixon was vice president): "Everywhere in Asia people look at the Philippines and realize that American values are being tested here. I feel that if we can succeed here in bringing prosperity and freedom and justice to our people, our example and through us the American example will be a powerful magnet for others in this area and in other parts of the world as well."[31] As this speech indicates, Magsaysay was exactly the sort of individual whom Lansdale and the U.S. administration would choose to govern the newly independent country. By elevating Magsaysay, Lansdale helped ensure that the Filipino leadership would champion the continuation of U.S. military bases in the Philippines.

Important to an understanding of U.S. policy in the Philippines was the way Lansdale "sold" Magsaysay to the American and Filipino journalists and the American public. In one of Lansdale's most successful endeavors he oversaw the production of and then blanketed the islands with campaign literature, including a "Magsaysay is my guy" button and the recordings in a big-beat format of "The Magsaysay Mambo" and "The Magsaysay March." The second song is a particularly instructive blend of Filipino popular culture as it existed in Manila (urban, literate, with English as the common language, and directly mimicking American tastes and fashions) and a political platform conducive to U.S. interests:

> *We want the bell of liberty*
> *Ringing for us once more;*
> *We want the people's will to be*
> *Free as it was before!*
>
> *We want our native land to lie*
> *Peaceful and clean again;*
> *We want our nation guided by*
> *God-fearing honest men!*
>
> *Men who'll serve without the nerve*
> *To cheat eternally;*
> *Who'll do the job and never rob*
> *The public treasury!*
>
> *Only the man of destiny*
> *Our need will satisfy;*
> *This is the cry for you and me;*
> *We want Magsaysay!*[32]

Lansdale oversaw the production and dissemination of this song.[33] With pride, he recounted to his CIA superiors in his after-action report of the presidential election of 1953 that his allies had silenced a policeman who threatened anyone who sang it; they "made the policeman strip to underwear and join in singing this political Mambo." And to help Magsaysay supporters who feared that the election was going to be stolen, "we passed them information on the techniques of sabotage and 'accidental' murder; 'kill a few and you don't have to kill thousands.'" Finally, Lansdale told how he set up a meeting between all senior American officials and Magsaysay in a "safe house" where the candidate "was warned by Spruance, Lacy, Villiers, and Lanbock not to take irresponsible action. Magsaysay promised that he wouldn't."[34]

The inverse of Lansdale's selling of Magsaysay, was buying him and his associates. In one of the many interviews Lansdale later gave about his time abroad, he casually told the following story (which the interviewer recounted in third person):

Lansdale operated with very little money. His mode of operation was to gain the confidence of the Filipinos and to persuade them to take the necessary actions to promote Magsaysay, and to do this to help their own country and not to help the United States. However on one of his trips to Washington, Allen Dulles [director of the CIA] offered Lansdale 5 million dollars to finance the CIA operations in the Philippines. Lansdale was uneasy about this amount of money and asked if he was supposed to buy votes with it . . . He did finally accept one million dollars, which was delivered to him in cash in a suitcase by another CIA operator in the Philippines . . . Lansdale knew [then President Elpidio] Quirino personally and did not hate the man. However, he had no qualms about destroying him in order to get Magsaysay elected President.[35]

There is also a sparse document from an official in the Philippine Department of National Defense (written in 1951 and partially declassified by the U.S. government in the 1990s). The official is presumably Ramon Magsaysay, but the entire memorandum reads as if it had been dictated by Lansdale. Here, the "Philippine Government" offers Washington a wish list of goods:

FUNDS FOR PSYCHOLOGICAL WARFARE:
1. Request $500,000 from U.S. (MSA [Mutual Security Agency], or any other agencies) for conduct of psy-war [psychological warfare] in P. I. [Philippine Islands]
2. SUGGESTED CONDITIONS:
    1. Check to be drawn in favor of Secretary Magsaysay, not P.I. government, on an unofficial basis. . . .
OTHER REQUESTS IN ORDER OF PRIORITY:
1. 60 sound trucks,
2. 36 still cameras (35-mm),
3. Printing press,
4. 30 movie projectors w/acc. (16-mm).[36]

Having U.S. funds go directly to Magsaysay set the stage to increase his power in relation to other Philippine officials. The U.S. government, and Lansdale, had identified him as the centerpiece in American efforts to defeat the guerrilla organization that was challenging the Philippine government (the Huks; more on them below) and to bring a modicum of political and economic stability to the former colony. This document also points to the simple fact that although Magsaysay may have been incorruptible, half a million American dollars used to promote him and his army surely explains some of his success.[37]

Lansdale also solicited contributions for Magsaysay's presidential campaign from the larger American corporations doing business in the Philippines. Among them was Coca-Cola, whose local director breezily admitted to his board that "Ed made me an Eagle Scout, so I gave money to the Magsaysay campaign." Of course, Coca-Cola and other companies furnished election funds for reasons beyond Lansdale's "old boy network." Businesses with global ambitions understood the necessity of maintaining an American presence on the islands, and the company's inroads into the innermost regions of the Philippines suggests its rationale for funding Lansdale.[38]

Journalists who understood a good story were quick to describe the Lansdale-Magsaysay relationship in the most colorful of ways. Richard Hughes reported in 1957 in the *Sunday Times* (London) that "Magsaysay was discovered, tutored and skillfully built up as national leader by one of Washington's cloak-and-dagger operators, the mysterious and powerful Air Force Colonel Edward Lansdale."[39] Particularly concerned that Hughes's reporting did not become the favored line by other journalists, however, Lansdale responded to the article by emphasizing Magsaysay's manliness and understanding of political power. "You who know the Filipinos so well know that there are some real men among them. Magsaysay sure was one of them," he wrote to one friend.[40] This version of manliness, of course, sidestepped the issue of American of political power and security interests.

So blatant was Lansdale's motivation in spinning stories about his candidate that Magsaysay's opponent, Elpidio Quirino, "outed" Lansdale as a CIA agent, and reporters often greeted him with "How is the agent of American imperialism?"[41] CIA Director Allen Dulles was clearly concerned about Lansdale's growing celebrity when he wrote to the U.S. ambassador to the Philippines, Admiral Raymond Spruance, "Both State and ourselves willingly accept your judgment with regard to the return of our mutual friend for a further tour of duty, and I just have word that this has now been cleared with the Air Force. It is important that he realize the delicacy of his position and that he conduct himself with extreme discretion."[42] Yet, Lansdale's activities were so widely known in the Philippines that the local press took glee in reporting his every move, even as he continued the polite fiction of being only an air force historian.[43] In one case the contrast between Lansdale's public statements and private actions led the *Philippine Saturday Mirror* to question General Joseph Harper's declaration that the United States was a "disinterested bystander in the political campaign and the coming elections. At the same time [the] JUSMAG (Joint U.S. Military Advisory Group) Chief disowned the alleged consorting of Colonel Ed Lansdale 'with a certain candidate.'" The Philippine journalist ended his story by declaring that "General Harper's statement . . . does not allay our suspicions."[44] And years after Magsaysay's death, William Stevenson, U.S. ambassador to the Philippines, told an interviewer, Dennis O'Brien, of the unique friendship between the Philippine president and a CIA agent:

> STEVENSON: The CIA felt responsible for having made Magsaysay President and having helped him through that famous colonel whose name escapes me at the moment, he ultimately went over to . . .
> O'BRIEN: Lansdale?
> STEVENSON: Lansdale . . . He, as part of the CIA, had helped Magsaysay win.[45]

Perhaps the most damning account of Lansdale's actions involving Mag-saysay came from one of his closest friends, Peter Richards, a British expa-triate who lived in the Philippines and may have had dealings with the British intelligence unit, MI-6[46] In 1982, Richards wrote to Lansdale (referring to him in third person, as he often did):

> I always maintain that, in his day, Lansdale could have placed my houseboy on the throne, if that had been desired and he had been correspondingly instructed to do so.
>
> The Magsaysay operation, which involved the *active* cooperation of the New York Times, the Philippine American Chamber of Commerce in New York, Washington Post, Fortune Magazine, Saturday Evening Post, the Cosmopolitan Magazine, Reader's Digest, Los Angeles Herald, San Francisco Chronicle, The US Embassy (Manila), . . . and Time & Newsweek, was driven to success by Lansdale's brilliant management and control of timing.
>
> I am still wondering whether the first interference, without which the second interference would not have been provoked, did more harm than good. I am referring to the 1949 election before which Lansdale said to me "we must not under any circumstances allow Laurel [Jose Laurel, a Philippine politician who had worked with the Japanese during World War II] to be elected." He used "we" and referred to the elections in an independent nation![47]

Richards's summary of Lansdale's influence in promoting Magsaysay's cam-paign for the presidency becomes a tribute to the impact of Lansdale's ad-vertising charisma.

One example of the American press's support for Magsaysay can be found in a Sunday supplement to the *New York Times*, featuring Magsaysay on the front page with a list of his political and military accomplishments.[48] The most stunning instance may be an article by S. A. Schreiner Jr., a writer for the popular *Parade Personality*. His "Ramon Magsaysay: Our Best Friend in Asia" portrayed Magsaysay as a democracy-loving tough guy who carried a gun but still took communion and who spoke to *Parade* of "the enlightened nature of America's rule over the Philippines and . . . the many contributions made by the United States to our progress and advancement. . . . America's colonization of the Philippines was not harsh or oppressive. . . . On the con-trary, the United States trained our people in democratic government, built roads and schoolhouses in our country and tutored us in the ways of modern technology and medicine." Schreiner concluded this paean to colonialism by noting: "Like the boy in the classical American success story, Magsaysay started out poor, worked his way through college and climbed the ladder of business success . . . An Horatio Alger hero, Magsaysay preaches an honest, simple life."[49] The content and tone of the article suggest a Lansdale-inspired confidence, especially in emphasizing that the best way to beat the guerrillas was by expanding democracy and instituting land reform.

The group that Lansdale helped defeat, the Huks (Hukbo ng Bayan Laban Sa Hapon, or People's Anti-Japanese Army), had at the height of its power 15,000 guerrilla fighters and up to one million supporters. It also had a history fairly typical of postwar nationalistic and revolutionary movements, especially after it changed its name to the People's Liberation Army and incorporated socialist and Marxist ideology into its goals.[50] Although the CIA's internal analysis noted that "the appeal of the Huks has been based on the legitimate grievances of tenant farmers," this awareness did not prevent the United States from viewing them as a threat to its national security interests.[51] As noted by John F. Melby, a State Department official overseeing Philippine relations during this time, "They didn't really know much about what Marxism was all about . . . But [our mission] was to do what had to be done to save the Philippines from its own follies."[52] This Manichean vision of the Cold War informed U.S. foreign policy and downplayed the history and origins of the Huk movement—a movement, after all, that had formed in 1930 to fight for greater economic and political democracy within the Philippines and, during World War II, took up arms against Japanese imperialism on the islands. In one of the more bitter ironies of this period, the Huks, in their struggle against the Japanese, viewed the Americans as allies because they saw the United States as anti-Japanese and the leading antifascist and anticolonial power in the world. These mutual interests were made clear in a letter sent by a U.S. military officer to the Huks after they helped to rescue an American flier: "It is desired to extend to you [Luis Taruc, leader of the Huks] and the men of your command the thanks of this office in behalf of our American forces for the cooperation and assistance given by you and your command in the recovery and return to the American forces of Captain Frank C. Hogan, U.S. Army Air Force and William Robinson, an American citizen."[53]

After the war the Huks continued to press for political, economic, and social changes, and when these were rejected, they ultimately took up arms against the Philippine government then in power, which had the backing of General Douglas MacArthur and the United States. When Huk members were arrested and jailed after they won congressional elections in 1948, their motto changed from "land for the landless" to "bullets not ballots," indicating their growing frustration and radicalization.[54] Huk literature was filled with proclamations that the Philippines had become so intertwined with and corrupted by U.S. colonization since the Spanish-

American War of 1898 that reform would accomplish little. Yet even with episodes of murder and kidnapping on their record, the Huks may well remain the single most gentle revolutionary organization in history. Led by Luis Taruc, a man whose favorite magazine was *Time* and who was released from prison by Philippine president Ferdinand Marcos decades later, the Huks advocated the need for gradual land reform and often adopted a parliamentary approach to initiating changes in the Philippines. As Taruc told a journalist after his capture, "I had been bitten by the bug of social reform and I could not cure myself of the itch."[55]

These contradictions and possibilities eluded Lansdale. As he represented them, the Huks formed a part of the communist monolith imperiling the world: "So ironclad is their grip and so feared is their power that the peasants dare not oppose them."[56] Later less impassioned analysis of the Huks and Taruc would appear, including a 1993 investigation by the Foreign Area Studies Program at American University (under contract to the Department of the Army), which concluded that "the rebellion's main impetus was peasant grievances, not Leninist designs."[57] But at the time such detailed determinations were effectively silenced under the rush by Washington to confront all forms of communism, both real and imagined. (The classic response by Dean Acheson to the situation in Vietnam—"Question whether Ho as much nationalist as Commie is irrelevant. All Stalinists in colonial areas are nationalists"—would be accepted by all administrations.)[58] Perhaps Lansdale understood that his language and construction of the Huks was hyperbolic, yet he also understood the need to create a more fearsome enemy than actually existed. He was well aware that his real claim to power and influence resided with those who read his reports in Washington.

Throughout Lansdale's time waging war against the Huks in the Philippines (1950–53), he employed a variety of methods ranging from folksy sing-alongs to textbook "black operations" against the guerrilla organization. His most infamous counter-insurgency scheme, as he recounted to a group of military officers, played upon the general Filipino fear of vampires. First, his psychological warfare team moved into a village:

> Rumors were spread, in markets, barber-shops, and other public places—in segmented anecdotes which a listener would finally put together for himself. The stories were based upon the reputed saying of a noted soothsayer in Ilocos Norte, an old lady who had predicted the death of President Roxas. She was now predicting that men with evil in their hearts would be the victims of the local and terrifying vampire. The Huk jungle area was named as the locale in the noted soothsayer's prediction. A man would be foolish to believe this—but then, who knows? Roxas hadn't believed her and look what happened to him.

> This story was planted all one day. When the Huks came . . . the last man [of their patrol] was silently grabbed by the [government] patrol. When the Huks were out of the vicinity, the captured Huk was held down, two holes punched in his throat, held up by the heels, and drained of blood. The body was carefully placed back on the trail. The returning Huks found the body. The vampire evidence was compelling. The Huks deserted their strongly held jungle area before dawn.[59]

Is this true? Perhaps. Or maybe it was just a good yarn celebrating Lansdale's actions; he repeated the episode, though in an abbreviated fashion, in his memoirs. In either case it is typical of Lansdale's partial grasp of the belief systems that motivated Filipinos. It features his orientalizing view of their superstitions and his ignoring of the specific basis of these beliefs. Because the Huks operated in mobile units as part of their guerrilla tactics, this operation may have amounted to nothing more than the death of one Huk. What is certain is that this story became part of the legend of achievement created by Lansdale's own advertising and marketing techniques back in Washington and in the field.

Another of Lansdale's advertising schemes involved having the Philippine army enter a Huk village and post pictorial propaganda on every hut. This particular counterinsurgency tool had its origins in Lansdale's understanding of the uses of history as well as the power of imagery: "The name of this technique, 'the eye of God,' reminded me of the ancient Egyptian practice of painting watchful guardian eyes over the tombs of the pharaohs. The painting was stylized to give the eye a baleful glare to scare away grave robbers. Recalling its appearance, I made some sketches until I recaptured the essence of its forbidding look . . . At night, when the town was asleep, a psywar [psychological warfare] team would creep into town and paint an eye on a wall facing the house of each suspect. The mysterious presence of these malevolent eyes the next morning had a sharply sobering effect."[60]

In addition to images, Lansdale used sound to advance his campaigns of counterinsurgency and to play upon traditional Filipino folklore and superstitions. In one instance, Lansdale and his lieutenant, Napoleon Valeriano, engineered a plan that involved having a Filipino army unit capture

> a Huk courier descending from the mountain stronghold to the village. After questioning, the courier, who was a native of the village, woefully confessed his errors in helping the Huks. His testimony was tape-recorded and made to sound as if his voice emanated from a tomb. The courier was killed. His body was left on the Huk-village line of communications. Soldiers in civilian clothes then dropped rumors in the village to the effect that the Huks had killed the courier. The villagers recovered the body and buried the Huk. That night army patrols infiltrated the cemetery and set up audio-equipment which began broadcasting

the dead Huk's confession. By dawn, the entire village of terror-stricken peasantry had evacuated! In a few days, the Huks were forced to descend the mountain in search of food. They were quickly captured and/or killed by the army unit.[61]

This story is so bizarre that it provides another testament to Lansdale's ability to sell his tactics to Filipinos and American military officers. Confessions that met with death, voices from the grave that were clearly unnatural to even the most sheltered peasant, the use of advanced Western technology as a way for these very same peasants to reject Huk politics—these were the tools that Lansdale almost gleefully claimed to wield to establish victories over the Huks.

Lansdale was never just a "money man," even though his language was infused with notions of economic prosperity and power. The key for him was the art of persuasion, of eliciting confidences: "Each individual, in effect, was a gold mine if the interviewer was a good miner and knew how to go after such things," he said later, reflecting on the art of successful interrogation of captured guerrillas.[62] At times his belief in the value of interrogation called for a dramatic object lesson. Once Lansdale went out on a military patrol with Filipino soldiers who, after one battle, captured, killed, and then cut off the head of a Huk prisoner. An infuriated Lansdale grabbed it from the soldiers and began to ask it questions about the nature of the Huk organization. Receiving no answers and getting angrier and angrier, he slapped its face until the solders thought he had lost his mind: "Colonel, Colonel, it is dead. It cannot talk to you." "No, you stupid son of a bitch!" Lansdale replied. "Of course, it can't! But it could have, if you hadn't been so fornicating stupid as to sever the head from the body." He then threw the head on the ground in disgust.[63]

These episodes highlight the intermingling of counterinsurgency practices and the power of advertising principles and, in turn, complement the poet Vachel Lindsay's 1915 observation that "American civilization grows more hieroglyphic every day. . . . [T]he advertisements in the back of magazines, on the billboards and in the streetcars, the acres of photographs in the Sunday newspapers make us into a hieroglyphic civilization far nearer to Egypt than to England."[64] Lindsay's critique of the pervasive imagery of advertising and its juxtaposition of modern and ancient forms of communication seems to have been adopted wholesale by Lansdale. He worked in ingenious ways to establish links between an industrialized consumer society and largely illiterate peasant societies, then transformed these links into weapons and sought to understand these societies only to the extent that he could control them within the larger field of American Cold War interests.

As fantastic as these methods may now appear, they seemed to have worked—at least, American observers came to think so. At a 1963 Rand Corporation symposium on how the United States triumphed in the Philippines, Lansdale's "eye of God" technique was discussed at great length. Although there was no independent testimony confirming Lansdale's account, military officers in attendance viewed it as a model psychological warfare ploy for defeating an enemy "on the cheap." Other governments combatting internal threats were encouraged by Lansdale and the Philippine military officers who worked with him to adopt this kind of technique because of its simplicity and cost effectiveness.[65]

These examples become even more sinister when seen as case studies of a successful ad campaign in which one targets the audience and then markets a product through knowledge and fear. In a Filipino critique of the infamous vampire tale in 1986, Hilarion M. Henares Jr., whose column for the *Philippine Daily Inquirer* was titled "Make My Day!" (à la Clint Eastwood's Dirty Harry character), exclaimed that the story

> makes Filipinos vomit. Lansdale would never dare desecrate the body of a white American . . . But not the Filipinos, who are dung, who are of an inferior race, and whose bodies may be desecrated, drained of blood and left to rot in the jungles. . . . It was Lansdale and the CIA who taught our armed forces that they have license to torture Filipinos who are enemies of Americans. The water cure, the electric cattle prod, the high voltage electrodes applied to testicles and nipples, the coke bottle forced into the vagina, the rubber hose and the pliers, are all techniques taught to our soldiers by US Special Forces. Now the same techniques are used by the rebels. We Filipinos devour each other fighting America's holy war . . . It was Lansdale and the CIA who manipulated our press, . . . our elections, . . . our government. . . . And they still do.[66]

Henares's response to Lansdale's tactics underlines their horrific implications from a Filipino point of view and the role they could play in the development of anti-American sentiments.

Not all of Lansdale's methods were so gruesome; they often included moral suasion and a language of reform. He introduced the classic American pep talk into his conversations with Filipinos, proclaiming that "democracy is a light bulb—and the people are the current." Yet to whom was Lansdale addressing this homily? Certainly not the Huks; their war was as much against the United States as it was with the Philippine elite. The landowning classes would not have responded to calls for more democracy either; they must have thought such speeches rather quaint, given the view of events from their estates. Nor could Lansdale's light bulb message have possibly reached or impressed the peasants, whose notions of American-style democracy were tenuous at best—and who, more often than not, did not even have

access to electricity. Only someone like Ramon Magsaysay, whose supporters made up the Filipino middle and working classes, would have responded
favorably. They believed that their country's true interests lay with the U.S.
presence in the Philippines and that it was crucial to follow the American
lead in prosecuting the war against the Huks.

Like any good advertiser, Lansdale realized that he must understand his
audience and made continual efforts to penetrate what he saw as "the mind"
of his enemy. Of the Huk leader he wrote: "Luis Taruc, the 'Supremo,'
fascinated me. I had met him several times, including once when he visited
Manila in 1946 after being elected to Congress (but wasn't seated), and knew
members of his family and many of his friends." This remark demonstrates
the contradiction between Lansdale's real fascination with Taruc and his
continual efforts to create slogans that would vilify the Huks and and their
leader. He attempted to probe Taruc's psyche in order to understand how
and why this gentle man had become a "savage" revolutionary, but he did so
only from an American viewpoint. It is not that he and other Americans were
blind to the economic privation and political corruption that were rampant
in the Philippines—on the contrary, Lansdale was often outraged at the
chasm that existed between the haves and have-nots—but he simply could
not understand why American ideals were not embraced by all parties and
then implemented in a reform-minded spirit. He could glide therefore over
the more unsavory qualities that marked American-Filipino relations and
instead concentrate on second-guessing Taruc.

Lansdale's curiosity about Taruc included an interest in his archenemy's
private behaviors, including his poetry: "romantic verse to the women in his
life which I read unashamedly whenever I could get my hands on copies, in
order to understand him better. He was a passionate man. Also, I had noted
the delivery of law books to Taruc when he was hiding out near Mt. Pinatubo
and had heard that he had taken up legal studies in his spare time. Under
other circumstances, he might have become one of those citizens we look
upon as a 'pillar of society.' "[67]

In marked contrast to Lansdale's attempts to understand the complexity
of Taruc's background and beliefs, his marketing of Taruc and the Huks as
the communist enemy reduced them to a series of catchphrases and jingo-
isms. In a two-part op-ed piece for the *Christian Science Monitor*, "Art of the
Guerrilla War," Lansdale proclaimed:

> The Huk guerrilla force was organized in squadrons and led by a Supremo, Luis
> Taruc. The military, including the Supremo, was under the tight control of the
> Politburo. Political indoctrination was carried on at schools hidden in the jun-
> gles and hills, the so-called "Stalin universities," in troop units by political com-

missars, and through the use of "self-criticism." This continual political indoctrination, coupled with "iron discipline," turned a movement which had started
out with an old-time Robin Hood and agrarian Socialist flavor into a tough,
ruthless force that had hope and intent—by mid-1950—of winning the Philippines by 1952.[68]

Within this "history" of the guerrilla movement, the intricacy of Taruc's
position converted him from Robin Hood to Stalin with breathtaking swift-
ness, reducing a complex situation to a simple idea that could be dramatically
communicated to a Western audience. The extreme shift in Lansdale's description of the Huks from well-intentioned outlaws to well-drilled agents
of communist terror sought to undermine the workings of Marxist ideology
as well.

This inflammatory rhetoric denied the coherence and purposefulness of
the Huks' aims—qualities that Lansdale was actually in a position to appreciate—but it garnered American economic backing. Magsaysay's success in
achieving reform of the Philippine army was undoubtedly helped along by a
Lansdale-inspired "Peace Fund." Lansdale was not shy in detailing this success either; in *Orient* magazine he extolled their joint efforts as a way to
provide Magsaysay with funds to buy loyalty from allies and pay potential
foes not to join the Huks. In his memoirs, Lansdale wrote about reformed
Huks who began to work as carpenters on behalf of the Philippine government: "They won a competitive bid and soon were boasting to other pris-
oners that they had started making a profit and that 'capitalism' was both
exciting and rewarding."[69] His assessment of the fund is notable partly because of his nuanced understanding of the trade in confidences and because
of the apparent divergence between his public statements and his covert
operations.

Another of Lansdale's promotional strategies, the Economic Development Corporation (EDCOR), was designed to give land to Huks who agreed
to stop fighting and surrendered to the government.[70] With great fanfare,
Huks were photographed as they put down their guns and joined this government program. "It was a smash hit," Lansdale later noted.[71] As if a further
layer of advertising were called for, these episodes were staged in the presence of American journalists, becoming classic "pseudo events," even though
EDCOR actually resettled few former guerrillas. The key to any such policy
always lay in its publicity, as Lansdale later made clear to American officials
considering doing the same in Vietnam: "While EDCOR was really a U.S.
plan, the Filipinos were led into thinking of it and developing it for themselves; thus, as something of their own, they carried it out with great spirit
and were given all the credit afterwards; the Americans concerned had a

'passion for anonymity.' The idea was carefully introduced to Filipinos and developed in informal bull-sessions (held in my house over the breakfast table or in coffee klatches)."[72]

At the same time, Lansdale spent considerable energy denying stories of his efforts at furthering American interests in Southeast Asia. Typical was the way he wrote about his involvement in the Philippine elections in the draft version of his memoirs: "Some were convinced that I expended vast and clandestine sums of money which somehow purchased the loyalties and affections of patriots abroad. This is a shabby bit of illogic and untruth, since the best in any man is never for sale for money." Later, he revised his story: "Yes, there was money poured into the campaign against the Huks in 1950. As I recall, there were about two million pesos, amounting then to nearly a million U.S. dollars, given to the Philippine Secretary of National Defense as his discretionary money, to be used in meeting the contingencies of the campaign. This money came from the Filipino people and was raised in a Community Chest style of fund-raising drive headed by Vice President Fernando Lopez."[73]

Despite Lansdale's denials of American-funded support for Magsaysay, stories circulated of his involvement in attempted blackmail. Years later he received a handwritten note, unusual for its frankness about his past activities: "I used to send your peso check to the confidential address somewhere in the P.I. Only you and I knew the details then. . . . I am in trouble; or might I say, trouble was brought to me."[74] In a not too subtle manner the writer of this document was trading on his knowledge of Lansdale's past deeds as a way of extricating himself from a current problem. Such an effort suggests the limits of shared confidences and the ease with which they can degenerate into simple blackmail.

Whatever the success of these efforts to refashion the Philippines, at times they became something of an intellectual bind for Lansdale. On the one hand, he described himself to a Filipino friend as "a Liberal anti-communist." On the other hand, his identification with liberal aims became problematic: a State Department official complained to his superiors that Lansdale's advocacy of a more "liberal" use of napalm in fighting the Huks was counterproductive to winning this guerrilla war.[75] These multiple uses of the term "liberal" signal more than just a pun; as numerous histories of U.S. foreign policy have detailed, the word can encompass divergent sentiments. It may also begin to explain why defeating the Huks and later the communists in Vietnam was viewed as a necessity by American policymakers throughout the Cold War period. Moreover, the term highlights Lansdale as a true believer in the Cold War. He even saw the use of terror and violence as a legitimate way to further America's goals against the communist menace. (To this day, stories—uncorroborated—circulate about Lansdale's methods of extracting information from Vietcong guerrillas and tossing them out of helicopters if they were uncooperative.)[76] He championed the contras in Nicaragua and the Salvadorian government during its brutal civil war in the 1980s, sanctioning the use of violence in order to achieve anti-communist goals.[77]

Yet, as an advertiser, Lansdale advocated more genteel acts of counterinsurgency, preferring persuasion and salesmanship to the death and torture favored by some military men. In order to understand this facet of his character, one needs to consider how advertisers and public relations managers themselves thought of their profession during the period when Lansdale was learning his trade. For example, public relations guru Edward Bernays, the nephew of Freud, juxtaposed the power of propaganda with the role of advertisers in the modern world:

> The conscious and intelligent manipulation of the organized habits and opinions of the masses is an important element in democratic society. Those who manipulate this unseen mechanism of society constitute an invisible government which is the true ruling power of our country.
>
> We are governed, our minds are molded, our tastes formed, our ideas suggested, largely by men we have never heard of. This is a logical result of the way in which our democratic society is organized.[78]

Though Bernays is cheerily cynical about corporate elites trumping governmental power in their ability to manipulate the public, he generally thought of the advertising network as a positive feature on the American landscape. Precisely because of his ease at joining together such words as "manipulate" and "democracy," (Bernays would later be an adviser to the U.S. Information Agency), his observations are helpful in explaining Lansdale's notion of the power of advertising. Compare the following statement Lansdale made before American military officers in 1959: "The liberty of individual man, expressed in our Declaration of Independence, is spelled out in our Constitution—particularly in the Bill of Rights—that every one of us military men have sworn to uphold. This is our really precious, fundamental political belief. If we are gradually strengthening peace by helping so many nations and people preserve freedom, we must do so in the *spirit* of our own most precious beliefs as a free people—and practice what we believe! This is our bond of brotherhood with free men, with men striving to be free, everywhere in the world."[79] Here he deftly intertwines the freedom of the individual with the attempt to inspire other nations and peoples to practice American constitutional beliefs. His behind-the-scenes efforts to mold others constitutes precisely the "unseen mechanisms" that Bernays had in mind.

Another significant figure in this history of advertising is Bruce Barton, the quintessential publicist and author of numerous "self-help" books. In his immensely popular *The Man Nobody Knows: A Discovery of the Real Jesus* (1925), he transformed Jesus into a modern businessman with a winning personality, one who was "the most popular dinner guest in Jerusalem!" For Barton, Jesus' ability to get along with people was the key to his being able to make the big sale: "It is said that great leaders are born, not made. The saying is true to this degree, that no man can persuade people to do what he wants them to do, unless he genuinely likes people, and believes that what he wants them to do is to their own advantage. The secret of Jesus' success was an affection for folks which so shone in his eyes and rang in his tones, that even the commonest man in a crowd felt instinctively that here was a friend."[80]

Again, comparisons can be drawn between Barton's sense of empathy and civility as corporate strategies and Lansdale's reflections on the roots of his power among the people of Southeast Asia:

> I have a very bad ear for languages, and I have a very bad tongue for them. But having spent many years among foreign people who don't know English and only picking up a few rudiments of a foreign language, I've had to depend a great deal on a look of empathy, a physical look, and an ability to try to communicate without words—acting out things, and somehow or other getting the touch of one human being with another. I don't know what you would call it, but people respond to smiles, to an interest in their well being, even if you can't speak their way. If you've got a look that somehow or other they can read, why you can communicate with them.[81]

Lansdale's lessons learned in the field included (along with such aphorisms as "the poorest of an insurgency is from an office desk") a thoroughly Bartonesque remedy for selling a product that might not be universally understood by the potential customer: "A good smile is a great passport. Use it!"[82]

The basis for Lansdale's methods lay in a combination of Barton's power grid and Bernays's network of civility and human connectedness. He was able to make friends at a moment's notice and had a deep-seated belief in the necessity of bombarding his consumers with a sustained message from all possible angles. In this respect he echoed the philosophy of J. George Frederick, who in 1925 proclaimed, "The Advertising man can mass the thousand and one methods of advertising into a concentrated volume of appeal that will make the people absorb his thought as though through the air they breathe, and as naturally."[83] Of course, the process of unraveling these methods can only begin by acknowledging that radically different examples of American power are always at the disposal of the advertiser: Levi jeans and

B-52 bombing raids may both be exponents of American power, though they have little else in common. Yet for Lansdale, the differentiation was strategically minimal; he used a variable combination of subtle communication and violent force in conceptualizing the American role in Southeast Asia, with apparently no sense of the contradictory implications. In a speech to U.S. military officers, he instructed them with an example of military-civilian relations:

> The outstanding one which comes to mind for an American is the Philippines, where U.S. combat soldiers started teaching the three R's to Filipino children just before the turn of the century, and the U.S. War Department established the fine public school system of free education. Much of the noted Filipino resistance in WWII against the Japanese invaders, the close comradeship with the American military, came from a shared devotion to the cause of liberty, which we mutually had learned young . . . Just remember this. Communist guerrillas hide among the people. If you win the people over to your side, the Communist guerrillas have no place to hide, you can find them. Then, as military men, fix them . . . finish them![84]

Any standard history of the early period in American-Filipino relations documents the extraordinary cruelty inflicted by American soldiers upon Filipinos: water torture, concentration camps, the burning and looting of villages.[85] Yet in Lansdale's idealized vision these are replaced by Americans as goodwill ambassadors teaching "the three R's."

More than a hundred years after Melville created his confidence man, the 1960s culture critic Norman O. Brown set out to explore many of the same issues in a nonfictional format and through a very thick Freudian lens. Although he did not directly allude to Melville, Brown found his own confidence man prowling throughout dysfunctional societies, both old and new: "The Devil is the lineal descendant of the Trickster and Culture-hero type in the primitive mythologies. The Trickster is a projection of the psychological forces sustaining the economic activity of primitive peoples."[86] For Brown, "the Devil" was another name for capitalism, and in this respect his work bears an eery similarity to the nineteenth-century world observed by Melville. The figure of the Trickster becomes a way to see the hand of Edward Lansdale at work during the Cold War. Obviously, Lansdale was no devil simply because he saw democratic capitalism as the surest path to salvation for the people of Southeast Asia. But those who objected to or deviated from his cause and his methods eventually found themselves at odds with him—and with United States policy.

2

Selling America, Selling Vietnam

Go out and sell goods that will make the world more
comfortable and more happy, and convert them to the
principles of America.

—Woodrow Wilson addressing the Salesmanship Congress,
1916

HOWEVER CENTRAL the idea of progress may be to the workings of advertising, its projection of an ideal future is always mingled with a nostalgia for a recreated past. The art critic John Berger dissected these connections, pointing out that when advertisers design publicity, "they never speak of the present. Often they refer to the past and always they speak of the future." Berger's argument about the way the past is mythologized and decontextualized in order to project the advertiser's desired vision of the future ties into Lansdale's continual use of a mythical past and an idealized future to further U.S. goals in the Third World. Berger provides a useful way to think about Lansdale's strategy when he argues that advertising "proposes to each of us that we transform ourselves, or our lives, by buying something more."[1] This is precisely what Lansdale did when he marketed ways for people of the Third World to buy into the American Dream, or when he asked Washington officials to invest in his unique ability to comprehend the peasant mind. Just as he wielded the art of publicity in the Philippines, he used consumer goods and the power of consumption in waging his Cold War campaign for America in Vietnam.

Lansdale's awareness of the power of consumer goods to inspire specific desires and to project visions of an American-style future had already been

49

put to work in the Philippines. For instance, he had brought Americana to Filipino children by showing them Walt Disney cartoons. Delivering a fantasy about American consumer culture became a way for him to introduce to the Philippine people the goodness of American values, as becomes explicit from this 1946 passage in his diary: "When all the kids were inside the unpainted and slightly creaky prefab which the men have fixed up into a club, we showed movies, . . . a lot of mickey mouse and donald duck cartoons. As kids will in any country, these little Filipino orphans ate it up, inching their way along the floor until they could get right up to the screen where all these funny characters were."[2] Lansdale saw the cartoons as a cross-cultural medium that drew in the Filipino children through a universalizing American product. They were fascinated by this aspect of the culture, and wanted to be part of it, without fully understanding its workings or cultural codes. This passage offers a vivid image of a culture in the act of being colonized once again, with its children attracted to the great illuminating light of the movies, as of Western civilization. (It also echoes the famous scene in Preston Sturgis's 1941 film *Sullivan's Travels*, when Depression-era prison inmates are led into a church to watch Mickey Mouse cartoons.) Lansdale's belief in the uplifting power of Hollywood becomes evident here, just as his vision of the Philippines appears largely shaped by Hollywood-esque assumptions about the cross-cultural sameness of responses to the wonders of technology and the desirability of American-style entertainments.

That vision was predicated on an awareness of the power of American goods upon those who did not have them. In an extremely remote village Lansdale took a picture of Filipinos near a country store on which was emblazoned the sign "Drink Coca-Cola." American ideology and power had permeated this corner of the world, and neither Lansdale nor presumably the Filipinos missed this particular message. The photo is important for another reason: it was taken when Lansdale was out on a military patrol with Magsaysay and his Filipino armed forces, attempting to search out and destroy Huks. For Lansdale, the rewards of capitalist culture functioned as another kind of weapon in his arsenal of confidences.

His certainty that American culture was fundamentally right for all other people never seems to have wavered, even as he realized at times that the deep-seated economic problems faced by the vast majority of Filipinos were being exacerbated rather than improved by the semicolonial relationship that existed between the Philippines and the United States. He could envision only the benefits to Southeast Asian peoples of becoming more American— of adopting an economic system based on market principles, a political system opposed to communism, and a culture composed of movies, television, and magazines that were distinctly American. And although the legacy left behind by Americans in the Philippines was one primarily of corrupted political mechanisms and an economy beholden to commodity prices for rice, coconut, and other raw materials, when Lansdale left the islands, he retained complete confidence in the power of publicity. "I'm afraid the Huk campaign just wasn't given adequate photo coverage," he said of his years of waging this guerilla war.[3]

Nor did this absence of "coverage" deter his ability to market himself to Washington policymakers. Secretary of State John Foster Dulles's 1955 account of a top-level policy discussion highlights Lansdale's perceived indispensability.

> The President [Eisenhower] said that at his commencement General Hobbs had again spoken to him at considerable length about the situation in the Philippines. He felt that Magsaysay needed someone like Colonel Lansdale to consult with; that he was inexpert in politics and was badly harassed by people like Recto [Claro Recto, a Filipino politician]. I said we recognized Magsaysay's dependence; that [State Department official William] Lacy had had that kind of relationship with him, but that we had sent Lacy to Korea in the hope of developing a similar relationship with Syngman Rhee. I said that Lansdale was now in a position of special responsibility in relation to Premier Diem.[4]

In short, thanks to Lansdale's perceived successes in the Philippines, he was now seen as indispensable to waging and winning the Cold War throughout Asia. That he had oversold some of his efforts and conjured up a few of the results become secondary; his name had become indelibly linked to defeating a communist movement and stabilizing the political and economic system of a former colony. By 1954, Lansdale would be off to Vietnam to invent a country. Joseph B. Smith, for one, noticed this trajectory. In his tell-all memoir of his years in the CIA, Smith wrote, "The United States' fateful engagement in Vietnam began in Manila in the early 1950s, not in Saigon in the early sixties. . . . The same Americans and Filipinos who created the Magsaysay administration in Manila created the Diem government in Saigon—Ed Lansdale and his team."[5] This was clearly overstating the case—there were many others involved in the origins of the war—but the fact remains that Lansdale was associated with both battles and in a unique way that called attention to his exploits. By offering the Vietnamese a version of the American dream, the ideology of capitalism conflated with the lure of technological progress and consumer abundance, Lansdale hoped to turn the communist tide in this region. As Lansdale knew from previous experience, Americans responded endlessly to advertising's unreal world of limitless pleasure and fulfillment, to the world of abundance that advertisements always promised and never completely supplied. By offering these same promises of abundance to others overseas, he hoped to inspire a desire that only America could seemingly fulfill.

WHEN LANSDALE first arrived in Vietnam in June 1953, before the defeat of the French by the Vietminh, he was basking in the glow of his successes in the Philippines. "The things I did that were so strange in Vietnam," he said in 1984, "were really the things that the US Army did when they first fought out in Asia in the Philippines. And they won the Philippines. . . . Very successful. They'd started the public education system, public health, and things to benefit the people and let them grow. Take care of themselves. . . ."[6] He went to Vietnam as part of an American mission led by General John W. "Iron Mike" O'Daniel, whose purpose was to survey the French efforts at combatting a guerrilla war. Lansdale admitted that he knew next to nothing about this other Southeast Asian country: "The only book I could recall having read about the area was 'Man's Fate' by Andre Malraux. . . . I felt that I was journeying into far places of mystery."[7] He also began to learn French, indicating both his investment in this mission and his sense of the best way to communicate with the centers of power there. His overall impression of the country during the First Indochina War would foreshadow his actions for years to come: "The people were strikingly different from the Filipinos, but the guerrilla methods of the Communists were all too familiar."[8] At this time he worked with the French in combatting the Vietminh by developing clandestine operations and psychological warfare programs. Apparently, his one disruption of this alliance between the United States and a colonial power was a prank in which he photographed French intelligence officers in the nude and then sent the photos back to the CIA.[9]

It is of note that even before the French were defeated at Dien Bien Phu, President Eisenhower received advice at a national security meeting that the CIA director, Allen Dulles, "should develop plans, as suggested by the Secretary of State, for certain contingencies in Indochina." These included sending American agents to Vietnam to frustrate Vietminh efforts. And so Lansdale returned to Vietnam on June 1, 1954, at the behest of the Dulles brothers.[10] The difference between Lansdale's first two missions to Vietnam could not have been greater, since the fall of Dien Bien Phu and the ongoing Geneva conference had considerably altered U.S. policy toward the former French colony. Chester Cooper, a high-level CIA official, succinctly noted this change: "The Central Intelligence Agency was given the mission of helping Diem develop a government that would be sufficiently strong and viable to compete with and, if necessary, stand up to the communist regime of Ho Chi Minh in the north."[11] Thus, Lansdale was authorized by the Dulleses to do far more than survey the political and military situation. Rather, he was to refashion South Vietnam—known as Free Vietnam at the time—into a stable anticommunist state. Furthermore, he was instructed to stay clear of any actions that would seem to help the French maintain control; U.S. policymakers already envisioned a Vietnam without the baggage of French colonialism.

Lansdale's notoriety had preceded him, and he often spoke of the tensions that existed between his orders and those of the French as they jockeyed for position in their former colony. From his perspective he was an American revolutionary and, as such, found much to dislike about the way the French treated their former colonial subjects. Lansdale recalled that the French "weren't too sure that they wanted me anywhere near them, because I was first of all an anti-colonial, I'd made that very plain."[12] In interviews and in his memoirs Lansdale told stories of how the French constantly sought to smear him and his efforts. As he said to his friend the journalist Robert Shaplen, the French hatred of him was such that their "daily wish was that a truck would run over me," because in his eyes they deserved to lose this colonial war. Lansdale also developed an equally passionate dislike of the French and did not hesitate to tell interviewers about French involvement in the thriving Indochinese drug trade.[13] At the same time, Lansdale was aware that his continual efforts to convert everyone and everything were not always effective. He spoke of not only French but American officials who were not nearly as enthusiastic about his policy recommendations as Allen Dulles was: "I gathered that both [American and French officials in Vietnam] harbored the romantic notion that I was taken to be a secret agent who had used the O'Daniel mission as a cover for gate-crashing my way into Indo-China."[14] This statement is noteworthy for the sheer audacity with which Lansdale sought to manipulate others into accepting his version of events. He was, after all, writing to a journalist who by this time clearly knew of his association with the CIA.

Undeterred by what other bureaucrats or journalists thought of him and his actions, Lansdale went on to play an immense role in creating and maintaining the new regime headed by Ngo Dinh Diem in South Vietnam. His efforts were directed toward two fronts: persuading the American public to support Diem and gathering forces in South Vietnam to support Diem. On the American side, he worked with the likes of Cardinal Spellman and Michigan State University's political science department (in particular, Wesley Fishel) to create a pro-Diem press. Other individuals helping with this effort included Senator Mike Mansfield and Supreme Court Justice William O. Douglas, who, after meeting Diem for the first time, described him as "revered" by the Vietnamese people. These individuals and a host of other influential Americans formed the American Friends of Vietnam (AFV). Members of this most influential private organization to support South Vietnam in the 1950s and 1960s spent considerable time touting the merits of Diem, even when his flaws became increasingly obvious. Their initial successes were noteworthy: they sold the American people the idea that a small, fledgling country fighting communist aggression deserved unequivocal American support. As one of Lansdale's trusted aides recalled, "Ed was low-key but he could always convince people. . . . God! The way Ed explained the situation in Vietnam. If we gave up, all of Asia would go down the drain. It was just remarkable . . . Of course he was an advertising man, a salesman, very soft-spoken, very quiet, very smooth."[15]

In a typical effort to promote his candidate, Lansdale wrote to Diem in 1960 suggesting ways that the South Vietnamese leader could improve his image in Washington: "Talking with Madame Nhu [Diem's sister-in-law] about your problems in Vietnam reminded me once again of the problem of getting an honest picture of your accomplishments and needs to the U.S. government and people. You still need much more help on this than is being done at present. As you know, I have long believed that you need a good, private American public relations firm to help you." Lansdale went on to recommend the firm of King and Maheu Associates in Washington, D.C., as the key to solving Diem's public relations problems on the American front.[16] He also tried to generate an interest among Americans in all things Vietnam-related. Among other things, he worked with State Department officials to create a "sister city" relationship between Vietnamese villages in the Strategic Hamlet Program and cities in the United States that were to adopt them.[17]

The most detailed example of Lansdale's efforts at selling Vietnam can be seen in a 1961 memorandum titled "The Village That Refuses to Die." This top-secret missive to President John F. Kennedy involved a Chinese community transplanted to the tip of southern Vietnam by relief agencies and headed by a Catholic priest, Father Hoa.[18] These northern and Catholic "outsiders" were eager and effective props in the war against the Vietcong and were accordingly championed and armed by the United States. Kennedy was so taken by the story that he had Lansdale's report declassified; it was then published in a May 1961 *Saturday Evening Post* as "The Report the

President Wanted Published," written by "an American officer." The memorandum and the article are nearly identical, with Lansdale's trademark breathless prose surrounding his feel-good story of defeating communists in Vietnam. He described a battle between these villagers and the Vietcong: "The settlers fought back, mostly with Boy Scout stones and knives (many of the men had been Boy Scouts—a number of them saluted me with the three-fingered Scout salute, the only one they know)." In describing the villagers' love of freedom and hatred of communism, Lansdale went on to remark that "the troops [the armed villagers] have two hours of indoctrination every day, in the village or out in the field. This is based upon news from Voice of America. . . . The subject [for discussion one evening] was 'What Freedom Means.' Each soldier was having his turn to tell what it meant to him, and his remarks were then discussed by the group. From the way their eyes lighted up when mentioning this, freedom is very precious to them, personal—not just a word in a book or oratory. They were anxious to borrow USIA [United States Information Agency] films."[19] This is a bizarre affirmation of the nature of freedom, given that it mimics the straightforward use of "indoctrination" and the communists' penchant for "self-criticism" (a hallmark of Maoist efforts to maintain unity among revolutionary guerrilla organizations), plus the fact that these declarations took place under the watchful eye of Lansdale, an American military officer. By championing the methods favored by his enemy, Lansdale really succeeded only in neutralizing the central differences between the two political systems. Further on, in both memorandum and article, he compared these villagers to American settlers fighting off Indians.

This story caught the eye of a young Sacramento TV reporter, Stan Atkinson, who contacted Lansdale about the village and its anticommunist battles. He was then flown out to Father Hoa's village, where he filmed a documentary titled "The Village That Refuses to Die." His documentary is notable for its unflinching examination of the poverty of Vietnamese peasants even as it remains resolutely anticommunist. If possible, the mingling of government-sponsored policy and reporting was even further blurred when the film was financially supported by Desilu Productions (the Desi Arnez and Lucille Ball company) and narrated by Stan Atkinson himself. In one scene the camera pans over a series of CARE packages and then shows an apparently choreographed battle between the villagers and the Vietcong, followed by the burning of a VC flag. One of the cruel ironies of the documentary is that even with all of its heavy-handed praise of the villagers of Binh Hung—their goodness as opposed to the sheer evilness of the communists—the one time that viewers actually see a member of the Vietcong is when the camera lingers on a captured woman and her children, desperately poor, who look identical in every way to the villagers.[20]

Lansdale promoted the documentary and showed it to a variety of audiences. In 1964, scheduled to give a speech titled "Guerrilla Warfare" at the Council of Foreign Relations in New York City, he asked to screen the film beforehand so that the makers of foreign policy and the Wall Street bankers who would attend his talk could get a flavor of the battles taking place in Vietnam by viewing "the most graphic portrayal of the spirit of countering Communist insurgency I have ever seen." He was informed that members had already seen it.[21] Lansdale continued to extol Father Hoa, however, and later that year Hoa received the Ramon Magsaysay Award from the Rockefeller Foundation for outstanding service in Asia.[22] The portrayal of this one village was soon being disseminated throughout American culture, including perhaps its oddest placement in the comic strip *Buz Sawyer*, which featured "The Village That Refuses to Die" and Father Hoa in a story line. The marketing of this village to Americans and to Vietnamese was such that, according to Lansdale anyway, it was singled out for "abuse" by communist publications because of its anticommunist vigor.[23]

As he continued these marketing efforts on the home front, Lansdale also placed a premium on becoming Diem's American confidant. This policy undoubtedly stemmed from his similar and successful relationship with the Philippine president, Ramon Magsaysay, and from his belief in focusing publicity for national campaigns on the personality of leaders. Diem's extensive knowledge of Magsaysay and the fact that he "kept an autographed portrait of Magsaysay in his study (though the two men had never met)," suggest Lansdale's insistence on the parallels between the two leaders.[24] For Lansdale, personality became the defining measure of the worth of one's life and the basis on which to sell a politician to his constituents even as the relationship that developed between himself and the other man led to a series of self-destructive, addictively interdependent acts, with each increasingly needing the other to maintain his own power.

When Lansdale met Diem for the first time in 1954, he gave him a memo headed simply "Notes on How to Be a Prime Minister of Vietnam," which laid out a plan that would create a Western-style democracy in South Vietnam with its twin goals of fighting communism and improving local living conditions. Though the memorandum remains classified, Lansdale spoke about it elsewhere, leading the historian William Conrad Gibbons to conclude that it "tended to characterize the American approach to Vietnam during the entire course of U.S. involvement in the Vietnam War." (When later asked by Gibbons how he formulated the ideas in the memo, though,

Lansdale simply said, "These were Vietnamese views that I tried to pass along to him."[25] Modesty aside, Lansdale's statement points to his view of himself as a conduit between Diem and his own people as much as between the U.S. government and Diem.) In one of the more comical if convoluted moments in this whole episode, Diem explained that he could not read the English copy very well, so he handed the document and his eyeglasses to the American translator, who had not brought his glasses with him. As luck would have it, Diem's glasses were the same correction as the interpreter's, and Lansdale's memorandum was finally read to Diem in French. "Thus it was that I became acquainted with Ngo Dinh Diem," Lansdale recalled, and from that moment on the two men formed a special bond that lasted until Diem's assassination in 1963. Shortly after their initial meeting, Lansdale moved into Diem's presidential palace and had his own bed there, solidifying his claim of importance—and replicating a tactic he had used successfully with Magsaysay.[26]

Just as Lansdale's stature and influence in Washington were tied to Diem's ability to solidify power, whenever Diem feared for his political life, he would cable Washington to have Lansdale immediately sent back to Vietnam, believing that Lansdale alone understood the problems he faced.[27] Lansdale's unwavering support of Diem, however, led key individuals in the Kennedy administration to see him as having a clouded perspective on the nature of the war and on Diem's ability to govern effectively. (Diem's government had, for instance, in addition to wholesale arrests of anyone thought to challenge his rule, banned dancing).[28] Shortly before Washington sanctioned a coup against Diem in the fall of 1963, Lansdale was asked by Kennedy if he would go to Vietnam and try to get Diem to separate himself from Nhu, Diem's megalomaniacal brother. According to Daniel Ellsberg's account, Kennedy added, "But if that didn't work out or if I changed my mind and decided that we had to get rid of Diem himself, could you go along with that?" Lansdale replied, "No, Mr. President, I couldn't do that. Diem is a friend of mine and I couldn't do that." Kennedy thanked him, and the conversation ended. Later, Secretary of Defense Robert McNamara was furious at Lansdale for refusing an "order" from the president, and Lansdale never again had any real influence on U.S. decision-making policy regarding Vietnam.[29]

Lansdale's continuing support of Diem naturally grew out of their long relationship and the simple fact that he—as much as any other American— had had a direct role in Diem's rise to power. Lansdale and organizations such as the American Friends of Vietnam used every conceivable facet of Diem's life to promote him both to his own people, to American policymakers and journalists, and to the American public. Among other things, they had Diem portrayed in a heart-rending cover profile in *Time* during the Sect Crisis of 1955 when his presidency was most in peril and U.S. policy was in flux over the degree to which it should support him.[30] A year later the *Saturday Evening Post* chimed in with this breezily ethnocentric defense of Diem's government after he had quashed national elections: "the Red time bomb failed to go off as scheduled because the promised elections were cancelled by the anticommunist Chief of State in South Vietnam, a man with a name Americans find almost impossible to pronounce: Ngo Dinh Diem."[31] Diem's own publicity machine created and marketed a glossy (and unintentionally self-parodying) publication titled *The Special Magazine Commemorating Two Years of President Diem's Government*, apparently produced within a political vacuum, since there was no particular audience who would have responded to its glowing portrait of Diem. It assumed a fair amount of knowledge about recent Vietnamese history, overlooked Diem's widely commented-on autocratic ways, and belabored the point that he was the George Washington of his country. Its political propaganda included songs written in honor of Diem with lyrics such as, "He is back and everyone gets a share in his affection. . . . We firmly believe that he is immortal," thus blending instant history with Vietnamese myth about the "immortal" status of the emperor.[32]

Later on, Lansdale publicized the Vietnamese movie *Fire and Shadow* as a way to instill anticommunist sentiments. He wrote to an American officer of the Foreign Service Institute that it "tells the story of a Vietnamese youth who fights in the Communist Vietminh ranks for his country's independence. He becomes disillusioned with the Communist cause and joins a group of other disenchanted people escaping to freedom in South Vietnam. There are French-Vietminh combat scenes, a love story, the cruelty of Peoples Courts imposing land reforms, and the harrowing escapes. When first shown in Vietnam in 1956, it brought the Vietnamese audiences up shouting patriotically in the theaters."[33] Lansdale recalled that he had shown and narrated the film in the Pentagon and that a Filipino version had been made as well. He did not discuss the extent to which the film was cross-culturally successful.

One of Lansdale's more genteel methods of promoting Diem involving remaking him into a man of the people—no small task, since he thought of himself as a mandarin ruler, was eccentric and shy, favored white uniforms even while campaigning in the marshy Mekong Delta, and maintained a thoroughly ascetic life. To Lansdale, the last of these qualities needed to be amended so that whispering campaigns about Diem's sexual orientation could not gather steam:

> I remember trying to get him married, because he was a bachelor. I asked about the girlfriends he knew when he was growing up. Yes. There was one girl he had been very much interested in. . . . I made him promise he would call on this girl, take her for a boat ride down the Perfume River. . . . When he came back, I said, did you see her? Well, he replied, I went by and looked at her house but couldn't get up enough nerve to go to her door. Imagine. This man was president of his country. He was number one. He could have gone with armed guards and broken his way in if he wanted to. But with all that power, he was a shy, modest sort. This is the man I knew.[34]

Time, even as it championed his efforts to combat communism, also commented on Diem's "girl problems," and his personal habits as well: "He long ago pledged himself to chastity; he is so uncomfortable around women that he has none on his personal staff and he once put a sign outside his office: WOMEN FORBIDDEN. . . . [S]ometimes at formal receptions he handles his chopsticks like a coolie, shoving bowl to mouth and shoveling. He likes to hunt (duck and tiger). He may erupt into sudden violence. Considering someone he dislikes, he will sometimes spit across the room and snarl, 'dirty type!' "[35] Clearly, Lansdale, *Time*, and Washington would have preferred a virile, manly president waging war against communists—again, along the model provided by Magsaysay. Diem, though, remained obdurate. Vice President Lyndon Johnson, among other Westerners, continually had to combat an alienated Western view of Diem. He settled on simply proclaiming Diem as the "Winston Churchill of Southeast Asia."[36]

In addition to his publicity portfolio for Diem, there is a great deal of evidence that Lansdale was busy employing such other means to support this regime as financing alliances between Diem and his former opponents to help solidify the president's political base. Lansdale vigorously denied that he did such sordid things, but *The Pentagon Papers* tells a different story: Lansdale's covert intelligence organization, the Saigon Military Mission (SMM), was authorized by the CIA to "secretly reimburse Thé Lien Minh's forces [former Cao Dai General Trinh Minh Thé's guerrilla forces, known as the Quoc-Gia-Lien-Minh], which moved into Saigon and acted as Diem's palace guard in October [1955]."[37] Lansdale's own secret report about his activities as head of the SMM confirmed that "at Ambassador [Donald] Health's request, the U.S. secretly furnished Diem with funds for Thé, through the SMM."[38] Bernard Fall's history of these events is particularly exacting (and damning): "To be sure, the fact that exceedingly generous amounts of American currency were available to bribe key sect leaders was of some importance [in achieving America's and Diem's success]. . . . Diem bought the Cao Dai 'General' Trinh Minh Thé—mastermind of the messy Saigon street bombings of 1952 so well described in Graham Greene's *The Quiet American*—for $2 million; another Cao-Dai 'general,' Nguyên Thanh Phuong, for $3.6 million (plus monthly payments for his troops); and a Hoa-Hao warlord, Tran Van Soai, for $3 million."[39] At the time, though, Lansdale continued the polite fiction that these sworn enemies of Diem's rule simply put down their guns for the good of the South Vietnamese nation.

Lansdale again applied his advertising expertise while working on the grandly named Operation Passage to Freedom. Also known as the biblically inspired Operation Exodus, this effort in 1955 was widely covered in the American press as an example of U.S. efforts to help hundreds of thousands of Vietnamese refugees flee from North Vietnam to South Vietnam.[40] Readers learned that once the North Vietnamese refugees completed the journey, they were given "'welcome kits' of soap, towel, and toothpaste, and tins of milk labeled 'From the people of America to the people of Viet Nam—a gift.'"[41] Publicity was mounted on all fronts to support American actions in this former French colony. The International Refugee Committee became deeply enmeshed in these affairs, and its chairman, Leo Cherne (a former intelligence officer), established a public relations program to support the refugees and the government of South Vietnam, cabling like-minded officials: "IF VIETNAM GOES COMMUNIST ASIA LOST. [U.S. Ambassador to Vietnam Donald] HEATH OTHERS BELIEVE VIETNAM MUST BE SAVED AT ALL COSTS.˙. . . . . KEY TO VICTORY ONE HALF MILLION ANTICOMMUNIST REFUGEES FROM COMMUNIST NORTH NOW BEING MOVED US NAVY PRIVATE SHIPS AIRCRAFT ETC."[42]

What the American people did not know at the time was how Lansdale and his CIA team were expediting these matters—including their ad campaign in which the slogan "the Blessed Virgin Mary is going south" was broadcast in Catholic areas of North Vietnam. Still another gambit had Lansdale promising five acres and a water buffalo to every relocated refugee—echoing the "forty acres and a mule" promised to former slaves during the Reconstruction era in American history. Although this plan was not enacted, the historian Seth Jacobs has found that the United States did provide "$89 for each refugee in a country with an $85 per year capita income," clearly an economic impetus.[43] But even those efforts paled in comparison with Lansdale's coup de grâce: dropping leaflets showing a map of North Vietnam with a series of concentric circles emanating from Hanoi. This not too subtle suggestion that Hanoi was a potential target for an American atomic bomb attack—less than ten years after Hiroshima and Nagasaki—showcased Lansdale's multifaceted ways of marketing American power.[44] The result was that tens of thousands of North Vietnamese abandoned their homes, often following their parish priests to new towns in the South and, not incidentally, creating an instant political base for Diem, a Catholic, in an overwhelmingly Buddhist country.

Lansdale was equally determined to make other Asians aware about this emigration from communist territory. Working with a Filipino production company, he helped raise 1.5 million dollars to produce a film that was "a love story taking place during the evacuation."[45] In another publicity stunt, he had his team produce false astrology almanacs that foretold bad things for those in communist areas: "The almanac became a best-seller in Haiphong," he proudly recalled. (The existence of such almanacs was later confirmed by interviews with team members and research by the journalist Neil Sheehan).[46] Through such promotional efforts, Lansdale manipulated the very real religious and political impetus mobilizing this movement and highlighted his own role in advancing American security and commercial interests. He later recalled with pride that "the refugee flow from the north had impressed US policymakers I know very much, because this was (as I recall) about the largest movement—mass movement—of people in modern times . . . [and] the fact that this many were moving was a real influence on US policy at the time."[47]

The larger goal of this transfer of people was not only to create a political base in the South for Diem but also to discredit North Vietnam as a free and open society. At the same time, Lansdale developed Operation Brotherhood (OB), a project designed in the 1950s whereby Filipinos would provide medical assistance to the South Vietnamese. Its goal was simple: having Asians from different countries working together (though under the covert auspices of the United States) would lend the new government of South Vietnam an air of legitimacy in the eyes of other governments in Asia. Lansdale publicly depicted OB as a "happy and hardworking crew [which] had only one aim. They wanted to ease the suffering of their fellow Asians."[48] In a government memorandum, however, he emphasized a different side, calling OB "another private Filipino public-service organization, capable of considerable expansion in socio-economic-medical operations to support counter-guerrilla actions. . . . It has a measure of CIA control. . . . Their work was closely coordinated with Vietnamese Army operations which cleaned up Vietminh stay-behinds and started stabilizing rural areas."[49] The fact that the words "private" and "CIA control" are so easily juxtaposed in the same document offers a glimpse into the world inhabited by Lansdale and others, one that simply elided such contradictions. Later, Lansdale wrote in a history of OB: "The students must be taught community and group organization, cooperatives and marketing. The ideological implications must be subtly interwoven into these courses. . . . The cost of equipment and supplies could be properly presented to US manufacturers with the golden opportunity of demonstrating their products in areas of the world that are hungry for technological improvement. This opportunity would certainly give a decided advantage to the first comer."[50]

Operation Brotherhood made for great anticommunist theater, but it was not terribly successful. As Gloria Emerson noted in her caustic postmortem of the Vietnam War, "The Philippines did not become an important anti-Communist force in Vietnam; the Vietnamese did not at all trust other Asians manipulated by the Americans."[51] Yet despite this failure, Lansdale succeeded in propelling the United States to support his vision of the political composition of South Vietnam.

In these efforts to establish and publicize South Vietnam, Lansdale found an ally in Tom Dooley, the celebrated Catholic doctor who worked in Vietnam and Laos. As Dooley's biographer, James Fisher, pointed out, "In one of his many inspired moments Lansdale recognized in Tom Dooley—the young go-getter he kept hearing so much about—an almost too perfect conduit between the suffering Catholic pilgrims [in North Vietnam] and the straight-shooting, wise-cracking American journalists and pundits both in the country and back home who knew a human interest story when it fell into their typewriters."[52] While ministering to these immigrants, Dooley staged numerous publicity campaigns calling American attention to their plight as victims and railing against the evils of communism. Equally, both Lansdale and Dooley understood that the real substance of their work also involved exporting Americana to Asians through every possible venue. As Dooley explained it to his mother when he was about to leave America for Indochina, "We must make our American dreams Asian realities."[53]

In 1955 Diem rewarded Dooley with the newly founded state's highest honor, the "Officier de l'Ordre National," for his work with refugees. The proclamation read, in part: "It gives me great pleasure and it is a honor for me to speak in behalf of my people. They have asked me to award you recognition for the outstanding work you have done for the past ten months in the refugee camps in Northern Viet Nam. You are well known and beloved by my people. In the resettlement areas here in Saigon the name of the 'Bac Sy My' [doctor] Dooley is well known." What Dooley did not realize was that Lansdale had typed up that text and then asked Diem, the "Catholic Mandarin," to read it before presenting Dooley with his citation. Lansdale understood the potential host of uses in promoting the "jungle doctor" back in the United States as well as in South Vietnam. It was an inspired piece of advertising.[54] Dooley went on to write a best-selling potboiler of his time in Southeast Asia (the title itself, *Deliver Us from Evil*, indicative of his outlook) in which he described his efforts as a selfless model for promoting the wonders of American capitalism and American beneficence: "Rest assured, we continually explained to thousands of refugees, as individuals and in groups, that only in a country which permits companies to grow large could such fabulous charity be found. With every one of thousands of capsules of terramycin and with every dose of vitamins on a baby's tongue, these words were said: 'Dai La My-Quoc Vien-Tro' (this is American aid)."[55] For Lansdale's purposes Dooley's book amounted to a soft-soap sale for U.S. involvement in South Vietnam and for Diem's regime.

For a time, Lansdale and Diem were able to reciprocate each other's support. Diem moved into his "Freedom Palace" and made it a point to portray himself at every turn as a devout Christian. This religious observance helped him far more in the United States than it did in his own largely Buddhist country.[56] Who exactly was Diem's projected audience for his 1958 "Christmas Message of the President of the Republic of Free Vietnam"? It began, "Dear Compatriots, If to-day we unite to celebrate the birth of Christ, whether we are Christians or not, it is because the message He came to bring to the world is addressed to all, to all men of good-will."[57] Lansdale's return efforts to deepen the American commitment to South Vietnam emerged during the threatened overthrow of Diem in the spring of 1955. Support for Diem was being effectively sapped by a variety of Vietnamese groups, including gangster organizations such as the Binh Xuyen and those still loyal to the French. He was also being challenged by Americans such as General J. "Lightening Joe" Lawton Collins, who found him a president without a country and a man uniquely devoid of leadership qualities. On April 25, 1955, shortly before the civil war initiated by Diem against the sects Collins cabled back to Washington: "It would be a major error in judgement to continue to support a man (Diem) who has demonstrated such a marked inability to understand the political, economic and military problems associated with Viet-nam."[58] Lansdale disagreed vigorously with this assessment and continually pushed and plotted to maintain Diem's control of the government. Even during key moments of the attempted coup, when the United States was about to let the regime fall to factional forces, Lansdale set out to convince a wavering Washington elite that Diem must be supported and that he could successfully defeat his multiple enemies.[59] Lansdale later said that those enemies had so hated him that they "had a price put on my head for delivery alive so I could be slowly tortured to death (with torture details given to whet the appetites of prospective observers)."[60]

One eyewitness to these events was Howard Simpson, the press officer for the U.S. Foreign Service in Saigon. In his memoir he argued that one reason why Washington backed Lansdale's efforts was that "his cables were vibrant accounts of what he had witnessed during the Saigon fighting. The events and conversations he reported backing Diem's actions had an impressive 'I was there' quality," and these trumped the more staid diplomatic correspondence between government officials.[61] General Collins later remarked on the tension between his own efforts and Lansdale's: "The big mistake made frankly with respect to Lansdale and me was that there were two people supposedly representing the United States government. I [was] getting instructions from the president of the United States, and this guy Lansdale, who had no authority so far as I was concerned, [was] getting instructions from the CIA. That's all there was to it."[62] Years later, reflecting on his actions and their impact at home and abroad, Lansdale reflected also on his own rise to power: "I know it made a difference on the hill, because Mansfield was one of them—Senator Mansfield who was sort of in favor of: Let's not go too far here because of the very messy situation against Diem, and against the government, and with the French in, and the gangsters, and all of the obtuse elements around on the thing. But after Diem had come out on top, started to initiate reforms, and be very much the leader in those first days; then he said, "Well now, this is something we can deal with and the US can really help."[63]

Another example of Lansdale's manipulation of public response was his crucial role in the October 1955 Vietnamese election between Diem and the former emperor of Vietnam, Bao Dai. Although Bao Dai—living in France at the time—had declared it "illegal," the referendum went ahead, offering the populace two choices: "I support the deposition of Bao Dai and recognize Ngo Dinh Diem as Chief of State with the mission of installing a democratic regime," and "I do not support the deposition of Bao Dai and do not recognize Ngo Dinh Diem as Chief of State with the mission of installing a democratic regime." Lansdale's design of the paper ballots cleverly posed Diem "among a group of modern young people against a propitious red background," while Bao Dai "was portrayed in old-fashioned robes against an unlucky green background"—green signifying a cuckold within Vietnamese culture.[64] What he did not discuss were Diem's efforts at ensuring his own victory. These included putting loyal agents at the polling stations to oversee the election. One voter said, "They told us to put the red ballot into envelopes and throw the green ones into the wastebasket. A few people, faithful to Bao Dai, disobeyed. As soon as they left, the agents went after them, and roughed them up. The agents poured pepper sauce down their nostrils, or forced water down their throats. They beat one of my relatives to a pulp."[65] Diem won with 98.2 percent of the vote and, three days later, declared South Vietnam an independent republic and himself its legitimate president. Even the Pentagon found the victory too resounding and questioned its legitimacy. Not Lansdale, who found his methods perfectly suited toward achieving the greater good of establishing Diem's ascension to power.[66]

In 1956, though, the problem remained of the Geneva Convention's declaration for national elections. When the Dulles brothers asked Lansdale to stay on to help oversee the plebiscite between the North and the South, Lansdale calmly responded that since the communist regime was both illegitimate and unpopular, there was no point in holding a national election: "All I was saying was that I was sure the Communist leaders knew that they couldn't win this goal via the ballot box."[67] His decidedly undemocratic assurances were eagerly accepted by the Dulles brothers; they had no desire to pit Diem against Ho Chi Minh. This was one of countless examples of Lansdale's creating the Diem presidency and legitimating it first to the South Vietnamese and then to American policymakers.

Yet with each passing year, Diem's popularity decreased in part because of his hostility toward other religious groups in Vietnam. As the historian George Kahin noted, "If civil servants and army officers were not already convinced that 'at least nominal conversion to Catholicism' helped ensure advancement, they presumably were when, in 1959, Diem formally dedicated South Vietnam—with a population over 90 percent non-Catholic—to the Virgin Mary."[68] This combined with his notorious aloofness and his rejection of all advice save that of his brutal brother Nhu and his imperious sister-in-law Madame Nhu, increasingly alienated American political and military officials as well. Even earlier, during the Sect Crisis of 1955, Diem had challenged Lansdale to support him more fully and to worry less about the death of other Vietnamese compatriots. Lansdale's response collapsed the difference between a friend and a power wielder: "I told Diem to stop this line of talk. It was leading to a point where he might say something that would make me angry all over again."[69] Lansdale's awareness of what his "anger" might mean to Diem in terms of American support for his regime is clear, and eventually their relationship did suffer. One participant in these events, Tran Van Don, noted the change between the two men: "When I did not see Lansdale by his side any more, I asked Diem the reason for it. He answered, 'Lansdale is too CIA and is an encumbrance. In politics there is no room for sentiment.'"[70] Lansdale, in turn, grew increasingly concerned about Diem's rule. In a 1961 top-secret memorandum that greeted the incoming Kennedy administration, he noted, "I cannot truly sympathize with Americans who help promote a fascistic state and then get angry when it doesn't act like a democracy." This characterization of Diem and the Can Lao Party shows his disillusionment with Diem's ability to enact American-style reforms and, most important, wage effective battle against the Vietcong.[71]

What Lansdale never recounted publicly was that their close friendship became strained over another issue: the introduction of large-scale American military forces into South Vietnam. Diem, the mandarin anticolonialist, could not accept the use of foreign troops on his country's land, and no pleading or ingratiating on the part of an American, even an old military friend such as Lansdale, was going to change his mind. Lansdale, although regarded as the one American military official who agreed with Diem on this point, nevertheless did push at times for an increase in American forces in the early 1960s, thus challenging his own long-held belief that the war could not be won in this manner and that American force would succeed only in devastating Vietnam's civilian population.[72] Perhaps at the time he was trying to ingratiate himself with the new Kennedy administration, which wanted a more active American presence in fighting communism throughout the world. In any case, Lansdale's efforts in 1961, like the later ones of a myriad of American officials, failed to make Diem more responsive to American demands. The result was that the man whom Washington had put into power was now viewed within the administration as simply a growing liability in defeating communism in Vietnam. In the late summer of 1963, Kennedy and his officials sanctioned a coup against Diem, which resulted in his and Nhu's death in November.

One idea in particular, symptomatic of the gradually broadening gulf between Lansdale's approach and Kennedy's, highlights the reason other policymakers came to see Lansdale as capable of advocating only impractical suggestions. In 1961 he recommended that the best way to eliminate the Vietcong in one section of the jungles of South Vietnam was to deploy "human defoliation" of the hardwood forests: instead of using chemical defoliants, he recommended awarding a timber concession to a Nationalist Chinese firm that would employ veterans and arm them. Lansdale reasoned: "They might very well have to fight to get to the trees so they would clean up the Viet Cong along the way." General Maxwell Taylor, Kennedy's favorite military man and Lansdale's longtime political nemesis, had nothing but contempt for this particular plan and others suggested by Lansdale. Taylor preferred waging war without surrogates, employing America's technological superiority and ground forces. Lansdale's promotion of low-tech, moneymaking operations over firepower was rejected out of hand.

Another example of the differences between Lansdale and the Kennedy administration is even more telling. In 1963, when the self-immolation of Buddhist monks in protest of Diem's authoritarian policies received international coverage, relations deteriorated between Washington and Saigon. The Kennedy administration viewed Diem's brother, Nhu, a Sevengali-like figure, as a major impediment to easing the crisis. Walt Rostow's earlier assessment of Nhu as a fascist librarian was in many ways the most genteel of opinions at this date.[73] There was general agreement within the Kennedy administration that the key to maintaining the Diem government was to have Nhu removed from the presidential palace. When talk of coups began that summer, Lansdale advocated that instead of forcibly removing him, the Americans should "create a place for Nhu up at Harvard. . . . I said 'Kick him upstairs. Tell him he's an intellectual. Listen to him and give him a job there.'" This proposal, like so many others, was not taken seriously, and Lansdale recalled that John Galbraith, the Harvard economist and Kennedy's ambassador to India, "got mad" and said, "We don't do that at Harvard." Nhu refused to relinquish power and was assassinated during the coup against Diem in 1963. Meanwhile, Lansdale's penchant for unusual—even harebrained—schemes to achieve American victories became linked to his name and effectively placed him on the sidelines of American policy planning in Vietnam.[74]

NEVERTHELESS, LANSDALE'S promotional efforts still circulated on a myriad of levels within popular and elite culture, both American and Vietnamese, and were adopted by other government agencies, the press, and Hollywood. For instance, on September 27, 1963, the popular TV show *The Twilight Zone* aired an episode entitled "In Praise of Pip," starring Jack Klugman—one of the first examples of popular culture commenting on America's deepening involvement in Vietnam. After the Klugman character learns that his son has been seriously wounded in Vietnam, he looks into the camera and plaintively asks, "Where is Vietnam? . . . there isn't even supposed to be a war going on there, but my son is dying."[75]

Though the American public did not know this at the time, it was Lansdale who helped—through a variety of techniques, stunts, and plots that are classic public relations maneuvers—locate the answer to this question on their Cold War maps. In addition to appearances on public affairs television shows, he held high-level meetings with the editorial board of the *Reader's*

Digest in the early 1960s to promote his view that the United States must do everything possible to ensure the defeat of communism and to define how the magazine should depict the struggle. One of his suggestions: "The Readers Digest could make the man in an Asian rice paddy into a human being whom an American farmer could recognize and understand, could stress the great strength of our concept of man's Liberty when it comes to a toe-to-toe slugging match with Communism . . . and could help Americans recognize our own great political truths when they are alive in a foreign people, . . . a similarity Readers Digest should seek out behind the differences of skin pigmentation, alien languages, and strange dress."[76] There was a religious millennialism to his efforts here. He worked with one of the most influential American publishers to sell his vision of an idealized world where everyone would consider everyone else a brother, where progress would be the norm, and where democracy and free markets would eventually triumph over communism, provided the West was vigilant. It is this goal of working toward a better world that marks Lansdale as Cold War idealist.

As Lansdale used his advertising persona to instruct his fellow Americans about the nature of the Cold War, his "customers" were the American people, but his "goods" changed, depending upon the situation. When Cold War policy required public support of Diem and Vietnam, his goal was to ensure that South Vietnam received favorable press in the United States. At one point he wrote to one of Diem's top aides that the chief editorial writer of the *New York Times*, Robert Smith, was coming to Vietnam: "Since Smith has a great deal of influence in writing the editorials for this leading U.S. newspaper, I think it would be very wise for your boss to have a talk with him. . . . He can be a very staunch friend if you make friends with him."[77] Later, Lansdale provided the same type of advice to American journalists stationed in Vietnam. After they wrote pro-Diem articles, he reported back to the Eisenhower administration: "These mature and responsible news correspondents performed a valuable service to their country."[78] At no time did Lansdale's conception of democracy allow for the searching criticisms of Diem that began to appear in the American press in the early 1960s in the works of David Halberstam and Neil Sheehan. During the Kennedy administration, Lansdale met with the editors of *Life* to ensure their continuing support for Diem, even as his shortcomings were becoming ever more apparent. When they raised questions as to Diem's ability to win against the communists, he told these editors and with no hint of irony, despite his earlier role in elevating Diem to power "that they—and other Americans—were trying to play God, by trying to pick a leader for Vietnam."[79] For Lansdale, informing his audiences and selling his product were one and the same.

Enunciating the positive became crucial to Lansdale's promotion of confidences. "Let's not be anti-communist, let's be pro-freedom" became his common refrain when addressing Americans. Slogans such as these reflect the critical role played by Cold War rhetoric. Lansdale's advertisement for Wellman, Peck and Company (discussed in the previous chapter) exhibited a seeming gap in logic between the actual products and images of American heroism. Similarly, American leaders favored the language of "freedom" and "democracy," no matter how meaningless these words had become, to such words as "empire" or "intervention" in spelling out the goals of U.S. foreign policy to the American people. The operative word for policymakers was never "imperialism" but, instead, the quintessential liberal American ideology of "nation building" in the Third World: the creation of governments with sufficient social and economic strength and stability to resist communism. This policy envisioned postcolonial societies that were neither beholden to communist ideology nor dependent upon their former colonial regimes. Nation building was implemented in Vietnam soon after the fall of Dien Bien Phu in 1954, when the U.S. began overseeing the creation of Vietnamese military, legal, and educational systems all based loosely upon American institutions. The choice of language pinpoints one of the few distinctions between American and European constructions of imperial policy: Europeans had spoken openly and with assurance of their imperial mission to civilize the rest of the world, whereas American leaders chose a language intended to emphasize the alleged noninterventionist quality of their country's interests.

To understand Lansdale's actions, one must take into account his awareness of the power of rhetoric. Even when his promotional images were obviously idealized it did not matter; he had gotten the message out and his connection with it. On the most immediate level, the triumph lay in his ability to market his own glamor to others, and this became in turn a source of political strength. In one college student's impressions, "General Lansdale would make a great political candidate because he has such an enormous backlog of experience in American foreign affairs, speaks in a strong, quiet voice, and is good-looking in a craggy, 55-year-old way. He absolutely never turns from his main course: to resist tyranny in any form and carrying any name. The wild, adventure-story experiences he has had would certainly put most opponents at a terrible disadvantage."[80] Lansdale needed to sell himself as eagerly as others sold him to their constituencies. Magsaysay's and Diem's repeated calls to have Lansdale return to their countries and the circulation of stories, true and fanciful, heralding his successes and excesses were all crucial to his efforts to influence U.S. policy. The folklorist Bruce Jackson commented on the phenomenon whereby stories are never individually created: "No story exists out there by itself. The story takes life from two of us: the teller and the listener, writer and reader, actor and watcher, each a necessary participant in the creation of the space in which the utterance takes life, in which all our utterances take life."[81] The source of any particular story and its veracity, then, become of secondary importance.

Into this mix one must figure Lansdale's efforts to present himself effectively within the military bureaucracy. There is no question that he wrote detailed and impassioned reports to his superior officers about his accomplishments in the Philippines and later in Vietnam. And, contrary to some accounts, he always sought permission from these very same men whenever he embarked on one of his more imaginative schemes. As the quintessential military man, he recorded his appointments in military hours and favored a crew-cut hairstyle. His thank-you notes were prompt, always inspired, and voluminous. In this light, Lansdale becomes fodder for the sociologist C. Wright Mills's incisive critique of how the modern military man became a central character in "the power elite": "What will the future warlord do in the Pentagon, where there seem more admirals than ensigns, more generals than second lieutenants? He will not command men, or even for quite a while a secretary. He will read reports and brief them as inter-office memos; he will route papers with colored tags—red for urgent, green for rush-rush, yellow for expedite. . . . He will try to become known as a 'comer,' and, even as in the corporate world, somebody's bright young man."[82] What rings true of Lansdale in this description is the extent to which his advertising persona merged with his military office. In many ways he never differentiated between the professionalism demanded by advertising corporations and the expectations of the military-industrial complex.[83] As his immediate superior in the Pentagon, Roswell L. Gilpatric, remarked in a later interview, "Lansdale was sort of a man without a country—sure, he had an Air Force brigadier generalship, but he'd been outside the uniformed area so long that he really sort of went into gradual retirement as time went on. . . . Ed was, you know, a freewheeler, entrepreneur type of operator, and he would go around with an idea and sell it to somebody in the hopes that they would take him on as sort of project director."[84]

His self-promotion did not always work. One example was his attempt to sell himself as the next U.S. ambassador to Vietnam in January of 1961. He wrote that Ambassador Durbrow should be replaced as he was now "too close to the forest," presumably too entrenched in the diplomatic and bureaucratic world: "Our U.S. team in Vietnam should have a hard core of experienced Americans who know and really like Asia and the Asians. . . . Ambassador Durbrow should be transferred in the immediate future. . . .

The new Ambassador should be a person with marked leadership talents who can make the Country Team function harmoniously and spiritually, who can influence Asians through understanding them sympathetically. . . . This unusual American should be given the task of creating an opposition party."[85] Lansdale's hints about the "unusual American" who should be sought out and given the ambassadorship harks back to himself and, once again, to his original construction of the unsung American hero for Wellman, Peck & Company.

This memo, written just before the new administration came to office, was the beginning of the end for Lansdale's effective input into American policy in Vietnam. Though Walt Rostow brought Lansdale's recommendations to the attention of Kennedy, and Kennedy later hinted that he might want Lansdale's to be his ambassador to Vietnam, he was never appointed. Secretary of state designate Dean Rusk, among others, threatened Kennedy with his premature resignation if a former CIA agent were to be placed in charge of State Department operations in Vietnam. In a 1969 interview Rusk explained: "I personally did not think that a man like General Lansdale, who was basically a CIA type of operator, was the kind of man who should be freewheeling in Southeast Asia as an American ambassador. We needed someone who was a disciplined professional officer to take that post."[86] Kennedy was soon persuaded, and Lansdale found himself an outsider in the formulation of U.S. policy for Vietnam.[87]

His "freewheeling" ways, though, would serve him well when Attorney General Robert Kennedy chose him as Chief of Operations for Operation Mongoose, the $50 million campaign to overthrow the Castro regime in Cuba.[88] In fact, versions of Lansdale's indispensability continued well after his influence in Washington had abated. In one case, two Asian friends sent Lansdale a thank-you note after he wrote to recommend them for American citizenship. Their praise is typical: "You'd do swell in advertising, general!"[89] And in 1983 the aging Lansdale wrote to a friend: "Got a telephone call from the Philippine desk at the State Department. They were checking to make sure that I was here, not there. Said the Embassy in Manila had been getting a lot of enquiries about what I was doing in Manila. I gather that I was up to being my usual misbehaving self out there. Tsk . . . tsk."[90] Nor did his influence stop at his admirers. During the height of the Vietnam War, one of Lansdale's longtime cohorts, Bernie Yoh, wrote to him: "I asked my Russian friends to do a little research on what USSR have been saying about you and the outcome has been surprising. They call you the most dangerous man. 'Wherever he went, Communism disappears.' 'He stole our idea.' 'He took the revolution away from us.' etc. . . . They show 'fear' not disgust as toward others."[91] The point was reinforced at every turn that Lansdale's reputation preceded him wherever he went; Americans, Filipinos, Vietnamese, and communists, whether accepting or rejecting his methods, noted his ability to sell ideas. It seems everyone had a strong opinion about this man: fear of Lansdale, hatred of Lansdale, admiration of Lansdale—all these come into the mix of images he propagated.

Like all good advertisers, Lansdale would have understood Marx's analysis of the power of goods. Recall Marx's famous definition of a commodity: "A commodity appears, at first sight, a very trivial thing, easily understood. Its analysis shows that it is, in reality, a very queer thing, abounding in metaphysical subtleties and theological niceties."[92] For Marx, the modern world was explicable only through a language of commodities, and it was individuals like Lansdale who developed the art of selling refrigerators, American dreams, or Third World leaders to their own people and to Washington policymakers. For Lansdale, communism had to be confronted "by a better idea."[93] Just as General Electric's post–World War II slogan, "Progress is our most important product," connected to Eisenhower's political campaign director's statement that he "sold him just like soap," Lansdale constructed images of Magsaysay and Diem both for their fellow citizens and for Americans.[94] In so doing, he demonstrated that he understood the profound ways in which capitalism had redefined the economic and cultural relationships between peoples.

LANSDALE'S HISTORY may be envisioned as layer upon layer of confidence schemes mobilized by the power of publicity: Lansdale selling America and himself to Magsaysay and to Diem; Lansdale selling America and himself to the Dulles brothers; Lansdale appearing on television news programs or coordinating mass circulation articles selling the Cold War to the American public; Lansdale playing his harmonica or using the "eye of God" tactic to influence Filipino and Vietnamese peasants; Lansdale himself an advertisement for and consumer of the world of capitalism. In all these instances he was imaginatively reenacting what Bruce Barton deemed essential to the successful advertiser: "Reputation is repetition."[95]

Lansdale's use of advertising was put to the test many times in fighting the Cold War. His most spectacular failure, then, is notable because the very techniques that he used so successfully in the Philippines and initially in Vietnam failed when he tried to apply them in Cuba. The multilayered promotional schemes to eliminate Castro in Operation Mongoose (1961–62) were later succinctly characterized by none other than Secretary of Defense Robert McNamara as "insane."[96] These included having the CIA work with the public relations firm of King and Maheu Associates in Washington, D.C.—the same firm he had earlier recommended to President Diem to provide him with better U.S. press coverage. Working against Castro's Cuba, though, the firm became the conduit between the CIA and such organized crime figures as Johnny Rosselli and Sam Giancana in plans to kill Castro.[97]

In the driest of language, the Church committee later elaborated on how the U.S. government and the Mafia had come together to further their respective goals in Cuba: "Lansdale testified that early in the MONGOOSE operation he had suggested that working level representatives of the MONGOOSE agencies get in touch with 'criminal elements' to obtain intelligence and for 'possible actions against the police structure' in Cuba . . . Lansdale conceded that his proposal to recruit gangster elements for attacks on 'key leaders' contemplated the targeted killing of individuals, in addition to the casualties that might occur in the course of the revolt itself."[98]

The suggestion that criminals and gangsters be used as instruments of U.S. foreign policy is one reason that Operation Mongoose remains a notorious moment in the Cold War and was kept so top-secret. As Lansdale wrote in an "eyes only" memorandum to the highest officials in the government, "Any inference that this plan [Mongoose] exists could place the President of the United States in a most damaging position."[99] Lansdale, though, worked hard to make the "Cuba Project" a success. When it became known in the mid-1970s that he had explicitly recommended the assassination of Fidel Castro, he went to great lengths to deny his culpability, but the evidence on this point has been detailed by many. David W. Belin, executive director of the Commission on CIA Activities within the United States (commonly referred to as the Rockefeller Commission because it was chaired by Vice President Nelson Rockefeller) in the mid-1970s, recalled being told at first that Lansdale and the CIA were innocent of such plans. Then he came across an August 13, 1962, memorandum written by Lansdale: "It recorded highlights from a meeting in which a number of 'alternatives' were discussed. There was a space where four words were whited-out. Further investigation showed these words were 'including liquidation of leaders.' "[100] The historian James Hershberg has shown that a June 14, 1962, memorandum written by Lansdale discussed assassination as well. Although it contains a seemingly innocuous phrase—"this contingency is seen as a non-U.S.-initiated situation, similar to that rumored as being activated for mid-June 1962. U.S. actions are seen as including the use of U.S. military force"— Hershberg convincingly argues that this veiled and convoluted language referred to an anti-Castro uprising, to occur after the dictator had been assassinated by U.S.-sponsored forces or accomplices.[101] The most convincing evidence yet involving assassination is a March 16, 1962, Lansdale "memorandum for the record," in which President Kennedy and his national security advisers discussed implementing Operation Mongoose. Lansdale describes how Robert Kennedy proposed initiating a plot against Castro at a shrine being built to honor the memory of Ernest Hemingway in Cuba and notes, "we were in agreement that the matter was so delicate and sensitive that it shouldn't be surfaced to the Special Group [high-level government officials that oversaw covert actions] until we were ready to go, and then not in detail." In 2001 when this document came to the attention of Peter Kornbluh, a senior analyst at the National Security Archive and a specialist on U.S. policy toward Cuba, he said, "this is the closest thing to a smoking gun that has been declassified. Only assassination would be taboo for open discussion at the Special Group, which routinely planned sabotage, violence and chaos to undermine Castro."[102]

Lansdale also developed a convoluted plan that came to be known as "Elimination by Submarine." It involved a combination of submarines and fireworks, to be accompanied by a rumor campaign identifying the display as a portent of Castro's downfall.[103] When a witness before the Church committee described the failed operation under the joking pseudonym of "Elimination by Illumination," Lansdale denied sanctioning or even knowing about it; he wrote a series of letters to Senator Frank Church, the *Washington Post*, and the *New York Times* in the hope of squelching this story.[104] There remains, however, his October 15, 1962, top-secret memorandum titled "Illumination by Submarine" and declassified by the U.S. government in 1995: "Here is a concept for a psychological operation against Cuba which could be carried out by Defense, with exploitation by CIA. It would be effective if the operation were done after dark on 2 November, All Soul's [*sic*] Day, to gain extra impact from Cuban superstitions. The concept is: fire star-shells from a submarine to illuminate the Havana area at night.[105] What these actions—actually stunts—emphasize is that at this heightened stage in the Cold War no covert operation was dismissed out of hand.

To be sure, Lansdale was not alone in advocating fantastic anticommunist schemes. Among those who shared his enthusiasms was Richard Bissell, Deputy Director (Plans) of the CIA, who wrote to Lansdale in early 1961, "I certainly want to encourage in any fashion that I can a continuation of contributions from you on this subject."[106] The historian James Bamford has detailed the tactics of the Joint Chiefs of Staff at this time and their creation of Operation Northwoods, which "approved plans for what may be the most corrupt plan ever created by the U.S. Government. In the name of anti-communism, they proposed launching a secret and bloody war of terrorism against their own country to trick the American public into supporting an ill-conceived war they intended to launch against Cuba."[107] The Joint Chiefs also designed plans to blame Fidel Castro if American prestige were to falter in the all-important space race. Just before John Glenn became the first American to orbit the earth in early 1962, Operation Dirty Trick was concocted. Its goals were simple: "to provide irrevocable proof that, should the MERCURY manned orbit flight fail, the fault lies with the Communists et al Cuba." There was also Operation Good Times, which involved blanketing Cuba with faked photos of "an obese Castro" surrounded by beautiful women "and a table briming [sic] over with the most delectable Cuban food," to be captioned "My ration is different." (For reasons not clarified in the memorandums, the prints of Castro were to be made on sterile paper.)[108] And finally, the Joint Chiefs of Staff wrote to Lansdale of the need to reach back into history and recreate a " 'Remember the Maine' incident" as a way to rationalize a U.S. invasion of Cuba. "We could blow up a US Warship in Guantánamo Bay and blame Cuba," they wrote.[109]

Although the specifics of many of these operations were not known by the Soviets or Cubans, they were profoundly aware of the climate in which Lansdale operated on behalf of the U.S. government. Operation Mongoose—more than any other U.S. action—led in turn to Premier Nikita Khrushchev's decision to place Soviet nuclear weapons in Cuba as a way to protect the fledgling communist regime there from U.S. covert actions. And thus Mongoose led to the most dangerous moment during the Cold War, the Cuban missile crisis of October 1962.[110]

Lansdale remained undeterred by his lack of success in Cuba and blind to the effects of his actions. But though he continued working in a variety of different government careers, including a return to Vietnam from 1965 to 1968 with the rank of minister, his mystique began to wear thin. Diem was dead, and the war in Vietnam was larger than anyone had ever imagined. Eventually, Lansdale was relegated to giving pep talks to the different branches of the military. His earlier speeches had often been ironic, informative, even amusing, but these became increasingly strident about the need to fight communism. The man who had prided himself on his knowledge of the culture of the Philippines and of Vietnam, who often began lectures with music from these countries, was now asking, over and over, "Why are we in Vietnam?" For him the answer was the same one he had formulated after his first successes in the Philippines in the 1950s: America's selfless tradition, the evils of communism, and the need to maintain U.S. credibility abroad.

Though he was now shunted aside from making policy, Lansdale fared a bit better than William Harvey, the CIA operative with whom he had worked on the Cuba operations, who received a stuffed mongoose for his efforts.[111] Their failure does have historical antecedents, however, and points to some unholy continuities in American foreign policy. In the summer of 1916 the United States had sought to poison the Mexican revolutionary Pancho Villa by having two American agents administer poison in his coffee.[112] That plan also failed, and Villa's myth grew even larger once he had successfully challenged the Americans and their efforts to manage a revolution not to their liking.

3

The Power
of Secrets

We all have a trace of James Bond . . . in us. We would
all like to go on secret missions, known as *covert operations*
in CIA language. We would all like to be mysterious, with
a shirt marked "S" for Superman hidden beneath our
regular clothes.

—James Munves, *The FBI and the CIA*, 1975 (children's book)

"ED TOLD ME that he was never in the CIA." This simple statement, said
with a bit of a chuckle by Lansdale's second wife, Pat, is noteworthy for a
variety of reasons.[1] The disclaimer reflects Lansdale's cover as a U.S. Air
Force officer, which he maintained throughout his public career. Although
it is true that he was never an actual employee of the CIA, since he received
his paycheck from the air force, the document trail linking him with the CIA
is extensive and goes far beyond the odd yet instructive detail that although
he eventually rose in rank to become a major general in the air force, he
never knew how to fly a plane.[2] Given this evidence, it seems strange to find
that he preserved the air force cover with his wife and that she insisted upon
this polite fiction years after his death. The consideration of other contexts,
however, illuminates the parallel worlds Lansdale inhabited.

In a self-revealing letter to his biographer, Cecil Currey, written in 1985—
years after he retired from the U.S. government—Lansdale sought to down-
play his CIA involvement. It includes long passages of soul-searching about
his relationship with the agency, and concludes, "Therefore, it should be

said that I served part of my career as a military man as a volunteer on CIA duties. The period when this happened was only in a short span: 1950, 1951, 1952, 1953, 1954, 1955, and 1956."[3] His admission has an almost charming quality considering that few people still believed that he was the "innocent" air force officer he masqueraded as during his government career. It is also in contrast to the sense of bravado that Lansdale's name sometimes invoked when his relationship with the CIA came up among insiders. For instance, his superior officer in Vietnam related their first meeting in typical fashion: "Hells fire," wrote General Samuel Williams, "when I finally arrived in Vietnam I was greeted by Col. Ed. Lansdale, USAF, who told me he had a team of eleven CIA agents in the country."[4] And within the government Lansdale's background was no great secret. "I want to make it clear to this group that Lansdale is not going over there for us. Lansdale was with CIA for a long time, but he's retired now and this is not one of our operations," declared William Colby of the CIA at an interdepartmental meeting in 1965 in an effort to reassure his State Department colleagues that Lansdale was not returning to Vietnam with some secret agenda known only to the CIA.[5] Clearly, Lansdale occupied these double identities with ease, perhaps even to the point of becoming blind to their contradictions. In one of the odder, if comical, moments in its history, though, the CIA sent investigators in 1981 to the Hoover Institution, to which Lansdale had donated his papers; they combed through them for CIA-related material and took back to Washington a host of documents. In 2000, in response to my Freedom of Information request relating to Lansdale, the CIA sent me the records of its efforts to cleanse Lansdale's archives of CIA-related material—but the documents themselves continue to be classified.[6]

Lansdale had sought to cover his association with the CIA for years on end. In countless interviews and in his memoirs he liked to retell the story of how Secretary of State John Foster Dulles had sent him to Vietnam in the first place. Recalling the meeting in Washington, Lansdale wrote, "Dulles turned to me and said that it had been decided that I was to go to Vietnam to help the Vietnamese much as I had helped the Filipinos."[7] Yet it was Allen Dulles, director of the CIA, who first requested Lansdale to go, not John Foster. As noted in *The Pentagon Papers*, "Mr. Allen Dulles inquired if an unconventional warfare officer, specifically Colonel Lansdale, could not be added to the group of five liaison officers to which [French] General Navarre had agreed."[8] Lansdale's public emphasis on his State Department orders (which are strange, given that he was not a State Department employee), rather than his CIA connections, shows his determined efforts to write his cover into the annals of history.

His denials take on a curious quality in another way: his association with the CIA was the primary source of his power within the government. At the twelfth annual conference of the Military Government Association in 1959, where Lansdale was asked to speak on "cold war and civil affairs," his introducer let it be known that he felt "timid before such outstanding company as General Lansdale."[9] This reverential attitude stemmed from Lansdale's career in Manila and Saigon, one that marked him as a professional intelligence officer rather than a conventional warrior or diplomat.

It was a sense of awe paralleled by the State Department officials' intense distrust (with the exception of John Foster Dulles, of course), which dated back to the 1955 coup attempt against Ngo Dinh Diem, when Lansdale's back-channel reports to the Dulles brothers persuaded Eisenhower to support Diem. The astonishing thing here is that Lansdale's success was at the expense of other officials who believed Diem was a lost cause, that he was incapable of forming a viable government that could effectively wage war against the communists. From this point on, State Department officials never forgave Lansdale for his political interference against their policy recommendations and thereafter tried to hamper his efforts. Their distrust took on an unintentionally comedic quality when U.S. embassies in Southeast Asia urged Washington to prevent Lansdale from coming to their countries. Although these efforts at limiting his travel abroad were generally ignored, the State Department did ensure that he went under civilian cover. J. Graham Parsons, the American ambassador to Laos, for one, wrote that if Lansdale must come, "I think it would be wise if he were to wear civilian clothes."[10] Ironically, requiring him to wear the nondescript clothing of a middling bureaucrat only reinforced his image as an American spy in some quarters. This was not simply a case of another petty bureaucratic squabble triumphing over more serious policy discussions. Rather, Lansdale was believed to have been involved in past manipulation of elections in these countries, and there was fear that his very presence could initiate anti-American riots. In short, the aura of Lansdale as *the* CIA agent followed him everywhere and partially explains both his successes and his failures.

Beginning with the revelations of *The Pentagon Papers* in 1971, the process of unmasking and remaking Lansdale's history with the CIA—in which each new revelation or explanation calls attention to yet another cover-up—is central to understanding his Cold War battles. The history of the agency and Lansdale's professional trajectory both begin with a complex intersection of documented actions and events and end in a self-promotional public aura that reflects the power of the era's advertising culture. The very real political impact of Lansdale's actions on the lives of Americans and Southeast

Asians can never be disentangled from the CIA's imaginative and fictionalized place in American culture at that time. Thus, the story of Lansdale and the CIA is also the history of the public myths that surrounded and, to some extent, made them.

◈

THE INTERSECTION of Lansdale's advertiser persona and his career as a CIA agent becomes apparent in his flair and dramatic use of language in his CIA reports from Vietnam in the 1950s, which later became the favored narrative of how the CIA operates in the Third World. Although his actions were only part of the larger story of U.S. intervention in Vietnam, the revelations found in this multivolume study changed forever how both scholars and the public looked upon that intervention. Thanks to the conscience of Daniel Ellsberg, the American public had access for the first time to the secret world wherein the highest echelons of the U.S. government purposefully and deceitfully managed its escalating role in Vietnam. Part of the excitement surrounding the release of *The Pentagon Papers* stemmed from the American public's intellectual voyeurism concerning the way its government truly made decisions, not to mention a general weariness with "light at the end of the tunnel" proclamations regarding the state of the Vietnam War. When *The Pentagon Papers* was published in 1971 (one needs to recall that this was after LBJ, after Tet, and after the Cambodian invasion), these previously top-secret documents tapped into Americans' desire for truthful revelations after seven long years of war. Their simultaneous fascination and outrage with this inner history of the Vietnam War, and specifically with Lansdale's writings, was also deeply related to the power of secrets and their ability to shock and titillate through partial disclosure.

Among the mix of national intelligence estimates and action reports that made up the bulk of *The Pentagon Papers*, Lansdale's lengthy "Team Report" from 1954 and 1955 stood out, exuding a sense of Cold War excitement noticeably absent from many of the other documents. Here, in Lansdale's trademark mixture of modesty and shamelessness, was a Cold War adventure story, a "true detective" history of Americans in Vietnam:

> This is the condensed account of one year in the operations of a "cold war" combat team, written by the team itself in the field, little by little in moments taken as the members could. The team is known as the Saigon Military Mission. The field is Vietnam. There are other teams in the field, American, French, British, Chinese, Vietnamese, Vietminh, and others. Each has its own story to tell. This is ours. . . .
>
> The Saigon Military Mission (SMM) was born in a Washington policy meet-

ing early in 1954. . . . The SMM was to enter into Vietnam quietly and assist the Vietnamese, rather than the French, in unconventional warfare. The French were to be kept as friendly allies in the process, as far as possible.

The broad mission for the team was to undertake paramilitary operations against the enemy and to wage political-psychological warfare. Later, after Geneva [the agreement that ended the first war between the French and the Vietminh], the mission was modified to prepare the means for undertaking paramilitary operations in Communist areas rather than to wage unconventional warfare. . . .

It had taken a tremendous amount of hard work to beat the Geneva deadline, to locate, select, exfiltrate, train, infiltrate, equip the men of these two teams and have them in place, ready for actions required against the enemy. It would be a hard task to do openly, but this had to be kept secret from the Vietminh, the International Commission with its suspicious French and Poles and Indians, and even friendly Vietnamese. Movements of personnel and supplies had had to be over thousands of miles.[11]

The report is a testimonial to Lansdale's derring-do and highlights the curious character of a man who worked in the shadows but enjoyed the limelight. It combines modesty with ego: "We are thankful that we had a chance to help in this work in a critical area of the world, to be positive and constructive in a year of doubt."[12] Lansdale's "thankfulness" concerning the SMM, its goals and methods, did more than give his report a sense of moral closure. It allowed Lansdale to maneuver over the potentially tricky question of U.S. sponsorship of covert actions against North Vietnam, a country it had never declared war against, which violated the spirit if not the law of the Geneva agreement. To Lansdale and his superiors the larger war going on between the West and communism superseded all forms of diplomacy. His application of anticommunist ideology had the effect of turning his report into a Cold War tutorial through which he could instruct his intended audience in the comfort of their Washington offices on the perils that he and his team faced on the ground. No matter how questionable the task, Lansdale rejected the possibility of either doubt or despair about his methods, and he positively reveled in both the secrets he accumulated and those he dispensed to Washington elites.

Politically, the strength of the report lay in his keen understanding of his government audience. Lansdale as part showman, part lay minister, and part fixer-upper emphasized the variety of ways he was fighting the Cold War. He spiced up his tales of adventure and nation building with juicy tidbits, sure to capture the attention of staid Washington policymakers. He noted, for instance, in recounting his byzantine dealings with General Nguyen Van

Hinh (the pro-French Vietnamese Army chief of staff, who despised Diem), that the general's "mistress was a pupil in a small English class conducted for mistresses of important personages."[13] By sprinkling his account of political intrigue among South Vietnamese elites with mention of their dalliances, along with the comforting information that they understood the need to learn English (now that the French were being replaced by Americans), Lansdale was able to fuse titillating knowledge with his access to secrets. Within a short period of time, these same mistresses were reporting to Lansdale what the generals were thinking (and plotting against Diem). In this account, Lansdale becomes a mediator between two worlds, and once again spotlights his own accomplishments. Characteristically, he downplays the role of money as a source of his power; he always seemed more comfortable acknowledging moral authority than economic persuasion. The fact remains, though, that it was American dollars that funded allegiances among the disparate groups in South Vietnam, supplied weapons and matériel to these factions, paid for the Filipinos who came to Vietnam to train Diem's Presidential Guard Battalion, and of course set up the English classes where Lansdale could "turn" those mistresses for his intelligence uses. One such instance involved payments to Lieutenant Colonel Duong van "Big" Minh, an officer in the fledgling Vietnamese army. Lansdale remarked on his loyalty to Diem: "Here was a man who put duty before self. I discussed his money problems with Diem, and arrangements were made to transfer Defense Ministry contingency funds for his use." After this exchange, "Big" Minh helped Lansdale and Diem by attacking the Binh Xuyen.[14] None of this is discussed at any length in the report, but those who read it understood Lansdale's ability to provide economic support all too well.

Another side to Lansdale's CIA activities evident in his report was the SMM's effort to sabotage the nascent North Vietnamese economy. Its variety of "black operations" included inundating the countryside and cities of North Vietnam with leaflets detailing what the Vietminh "intended" to do once they gained control of Hanoi. With much pride, Lansdale reported that "two days later Vietminh currency was worth half the value prior to the leaflets." In perhaps the most celebrated of his "black op" events, the SMM team crept into North Vietnam to contaminate the oil supply in the bus depot of Hanoi. A certain Keystone Cops quality pervaded this operation, pointing to the fine line between cloak-and-dagger operations and black comedy: "The team had a bad moment when contaminating the oil. They had to work quickly at night, in an enclosed storage room. Fumes from the contaminant came close to knocking them out. Dizzy and weak-kneed, they masked their faces with handkerchiefs and completed the job."[15]

Given their amateur-hour sneakiness and destructive intent, such episodes became notorious once *The Pentagon Papers* appeared, yet their real impact is left open to question. Perhaps William Colby, director of the CIA in the 1970s, offered the most revealing estimation: "Lansdale was more symbolic. He was looking for the symbolism and the political effect of this, and not unreasonably. Some of his ideas are a little fey once in a while, but he did understand the basic political quality that was necessary to any continuing struggle." Colby went on to discuss with insight why these and other actions failed: "There is an inherent problem here, that CIA is an agency whose machinery works through secret channels. And you can't really win a war secretly."[16]

The most far-reaching event chronicled by Lansdale was the SMM's effort to spur the refugee movement of North Vietnam Catholics to South Vietnam. This transfer of populations profoundly altered the political situation in Vietnam, gave an immediate political base to Diem, a Catholic, and was viewed as a stunning Cold War victory back in the United States. The migration was no covert affair; it was discussed throughout the world's media and gave credence to the argument that when people had a choice, they invariably chose governments that were not communist. (This same argument would appear in the 1980s when Vietnamese "boat people" risked everything to escape the dictates of their country's communist government.) What the world's media did not know at the time is discussed with enthusiasm in Lansdale's report: his multilayered rumor campaign to help drive these Catholic refugees into South Vietnam. On one level, his efforts were unnecessary; many of the refugees, who had collaborated with the French and had little desire to live under the rule of communists, were only too happy to leave a regime that was actively hostile to their religious practices and past political allegiances. Predictably, Lansdale glossed over this point when reporting his success to Washington. His crucial goal was to build better relations between the fledgling state of South Vietnam under Diem's rule and a United States government that was neutral (and indeed hostile at times) toward Diem's gaining political power. To Lansdale, another major accomplishment was quelling political intrigues and potential coups sought by the Vietnamese military, headed by General Nguyen Van Hinh, against Diem. When "contention between Diem and Hinh had become murderous," Lansdale ensured that Diem would win the power struggle by sending Hinh's aides off to the Philippines, ostensibly to study antiguerrilla operations. Hinh himself left for France shortly thereafter.[17]

Nothing caused Lansdale to second-guess his involvement in internal South Vietnamese politics. His report consistently subsumes all the potential ethical issues of waging an undeclared war into the larger anticommunist struggle. In swashbuckling fashion, it also makes some questionable and unverifiable claims, among them that "one group of farmers and militia in the south [of Vietnam] was talked out of migrating to Madagascar by SMM and staying on their farms."[18] The idea that Vietnamese peasants were in the process of packing their belongings to travel on small boats thousands of miles to Madagascar defies belief. Who would take them? How would they be received? Yet these basic questions are simply ignored in a narrative presupposing that Lansdale could persuade anyone—peasants or presidents—toward the right course of action. Another example of Lansdale's mythmaking abilities shows up in Howard Simpson's memoir of his time in Vietnam in the 1950s; he recalled that "Lansdale flashed his all-knowing smile" when they discussed who had designed the false rumor that the Vietminh were torturing village children by rupturing their eardrums with chopsticks.[19] Whether or not any aspect of this story is correct, it indicates Lansdale's readiness to take credit for clever "psy ops" operations, however weird.

Overall, Lansdale's report reads like a boys' adventure tale, an updated version of Rudyard Kipling's *Kim*—a nineteenth-century novel that Lansdale spoke highly of and recommended to his team as showing the way a spy should operate.[20] How appropriate that Kipling's character Kim, who is of mixed parentage but raised as an Indian, becomes the "little friend to all the world," a chameleon who merges his personality and his very soul into the parts he plays, to the point of losing his own sense of identity. In an even more striking parallel with Lansdale, Kim is treated as the beloved friend of the Indian people, even as he worked for the British secret service and battled Russian enemies for the good of Western culture.[21]

The total impact of the 1971 publicization of Lansdale's report was far larger than any individual example suggests. In his hands the story of American involvement in Vietnam seemed more exciting and less bureaucratic to the American people than the dry revelations about presidential miscalculations and lies. His style of personalized storytelling suggests why the *New York Times* featured his report on the first day it began publication of the thousands of documents that make up *The Pentagon Papers*. Not surprisingly, Lansdale's narrative spawned countless speculations about intrigue and conspiracy: if one lowly colonel with a borrowed typewriter could change the course of history, then what were other midlevel officials of the U.S. government up to? Where were the supposed innocence and virtue that marked American policy abroad? Lansdale had achieved a place on the public stage where only Hollywood had gone before (be it James Bond or Maxwell

Smart): the American people now had an authentic face for their most mysterious of government agencies.[22]

Yet, the *New York Times*'s decision to publish may have been a bit more complicated than one editor spotting excitement in a story after having endured page after page of mind-numbing governmental jargon and bloodless statistical calculation of kill ratios. Lansdale figured as a political lightening rod, allowing the newspaper to glide over the more unsavory fact that the U.S. intervention in Vietnam, quintessentially liberal in origin, was something that the *Times* had initially supported. His report caused critics to focus their disapproval on one man's specific activities while paying less attention to the fact, made clear by *The Pentagon Papers*, that the interventionist policy in the Vietnam War had been weighed and calculated over a thirty-year period by five presidential administrations. As a flamboyant midlevel operator, Lansdale provided both a useful target for public outrage and a somewhat awe-inspiring glimpse into the inner workings of the CIA.

Without question, responses in the early 1970s were far different from the responses the report received within government circles in the 1950s. During the earlier decade it helped Lansdale immensely that his adventures had a ready audience of elites eager to hear about new and inventive ways to achieve Cold War successes. Additionally, the fact that his writing style blasted through the bureaucratic parlance favored by traditional policymakers furthered his fame in Washington and gave him access to secretaries of states, CIA directors, and even presidents who craved "action." Once he was back in Washington, however, the same qualities made him a target for those who believed that a Lansdalian approach to the Third World had its limits. His covert missions in Vietnam were by no means universally sanctioned by other U.S. officials. "In the spring of 1955," William Bundy—then a CIA analyst—told his biographer, "there was a colossal row about whether we should stick to Diem in Vietnam." Another CIA official, Chester Cooper, added, "There was a lot of controversy about Diem in that early period, both with his legitimacy and to whom was he really going to be answerable. He had a lot of patrons in this country, primarily in the Catholic hierarchy. But there were many people who felt that his connections with the true Vietnamese society were kind of thin over the years."[23] Unknown to these midlevel officials in the CIA, the decision to support Diem had already been made by others and implemented by Lansdale.

One typical critique of Lansdale's actions by Roger Hilsman, a key State Department official, told how Lansdale's earlier successes in the Philippines with Magsaysay had first caught the Kennedy administration's eye and led in turn to his being recommended for assignments elsewhere in Cold War arenas. Yet problems developed when more was learned about how Lansdale interacted with others: "Well, because Lansdale had been associated with that [the Magsaysay campaign], we figured that he was with it, you see. So we recommended him for jobs. I even put his name on a list for ambassadors once. The Pentagon continuously vetoed this. . . . They thought of him as . . . an eight ball, an odd ball. Later, I came to feel that he didn't really understand the problems the way I had thought he had. He's a guy who takes great delight in manipulating personalities. He's very much of a CIA type. But he had no influence."[24] This account is by no means unique. Lansdale spent his professional life seeking power, yet after his 1950s successes he was in continual battles with other bureaucrats who viewed him as someone whose unorthodox methods must be checked. He was also seen as a man who had his own or another agency's agenda in mind and was consequently untrustworthy. Critics found his policy recommendations impractical or inappropriate for winning the Cold War. One of his chief critics, General Maxwell Taylor, later declared that "Lansdale was an idea man, and he could turn out ideas faster than you could pick them up off the floor, but I was never impressed with their feasibility."[25] This is not surprising, considering that Lansdale once suggested to Taylor that among ways to disrupt the North Vietnamese economy, "one such measure might be the seeding of the Red River with a variety of water lily that really clogs up waterways and can make navigation almost impossible without extensive and continuous clearing operations. If seeded near the dams in the upper areas, this should have the blight gradually move down stream and eventually hamper the shipment of rice from the delta region."[26] Further, Taylor's caustic comments were sometimes echoed even by supportive policymakers, who, as Hilsman's comments suggest, may have found Lansdale's freewheeling, dramatic style as disconcerting as his CIA associations.

Lansdale's reputation as an "odd ball" may also have been fostered by his readiness to apply rhetorical shocks when working with other officials. In his first meeting with Defense Secretary Robert McNamara, he dumped a pile of old rifles from South Vietnam on McNamara's desk and then, as he wrote in the draft of his memoirs, "I introduced myself. Then I told him that the pile of weapons pointed up a moral that he mustn't forget as the U.S. Secretary of Defense. . . . [T]he most important thing for him to remember about Viet Nam was the fundamental need for something of the spirit, something of their own that the Vietnamese could believe in and defend, much more than the men, money, and material which were the customary solutions proffered by U.S. executives."[27] The astonishing aspect of this performance was not only that a military officer was daring to lecture the secretary of defense on the nature of the war in Vietnam but also that Lansdale had so misjudged his audience—a mistake he rarely made. Given McNamara's love of numbers and his belief that quantifying problems was the key to rational planning and decision-making, let alone his aversion to an emotional pitch, it was only to be expected that he found Lansdale's flair for the dramatic both counterproductive and amateurish. His disdain for the rifle stunt colored all their interactions thereafter: McNamara never again took Lansdale's policy recommendations seriously (including the one that he be made the new U.S. ambassador to South Vietnam). Nevertheless, Lansdale followed up his gun-dumping incident with a memo to McNamara detailing the "X" factor as the key to an American victory in Vietnam, "X" being the intangible spirit of the Vietnamese people and its interaction with American efforts in their country: "In Vietnam, we are up against an enemy who uses Mao Tse Tung's tactics. The text-book of imposing our will on enemy forces needs further interpretation. The real contest is to win over the people on the land, which includes protecting them."[28] Years later, when McNamara finally wrote about Vietnam, he apologized on every single issue, yet dismissed the legendary spy "as relatively junior and lack[ing] broad geopolitical expertise."[29]

Others, though, gravitated to Lansdale's sales pitch for winning Cold War battles because his ideas seemed so "new" and "modern"—words that reflected the way the Kennedy administration liked to see itself and the way it responded to foreign policy problems. When the new administration first turned its attention to Vietnam, Lansdale was already hard at work and wrote what Walt Rostow later characterized as an "ominous draft" about the situation in Vietnam, arguing that a communist triumph was inevitable without a more sustained American response.[30] Soon his ideas on achieving an American victory were being read by all the top policymakers, and he was asked to meet with the new president. Rostow summarized that meeting: "The President thanked General Lansdale for his memorandum and stated it, for the first time, gave him a sense of the danger and urgency of the problem in Viet-Nam. . . . The President asked what his estimate of the prospects was. Lansdale replied that the Communists regard 1961 as their big year."[31] It is a testament to Lansdale's assuredness and self-promotion that he never wavered or had second thoughts about his mission. Though the communists never achieved any sort of permanent victory in 1961, Lansdale was still considered a man who had the knowledge to achieve U.S. victories abroad. In his 1963 memorandum "A High-Level Look at the Cold War," he wrote to Kennedy and other senior policymakers that the United States needed "to find out the Communist strategic blueprint"—as if such a document existed even in the bowels of the Kremlin. He also asked whether "the Communists [were] planning to saturate the world economy with gold," and said that the government needed to develop a "school for political action" where recruits would be indoctrinated with U.S. goals and could read a "U.S. version of 'The Prince.'"[32]

These examples demonstrate Lansdale's dramatic flair and his determination to capture his audience's attention. His calls to arms were packaged for a quick sell within the government and then aimed toward consumption by the greater American public. They also suggest his essential faith in the U.S. mission to spread democracy throughout the world, even if doing so required "black ops." He was at ease with the contradictions between his public cover and his CIA role because he was in effect an American ideologue, someone who believed the biggest cover story of all. Yet Lansdale was also a manager of secrets and relished the power that such a position implied. In a December 3, 1962, conversation about Operation Mongoose, Lansdale hinted that he was receiving his orders from a higher up "they": "I asked what he meant by 'they,' but he simply repeated his statement with a smile," wrote Richard Helms, deputy director of the CIA. Either Lansdale did not think a lowly deputy director should be privy to such information or chose to cultivate an air of mystery. "They," of course, were President John Kennedy and Robert Kennedy, the attorney general. This constant tension between revealing and concealing became an intellectual high-wire act for Lansdale during more than four decades and while working for various U.S. government agencies.[33]

Lansdale's self-presentation as the keeper of secrets points to his awareness of the power of hidden knowledge, but it also suggests a consciousness of himself as a conduit between the elite policymakers and a public eager to understand American actions abroad. The cultural critic Michael Denning has written perceptively on the function of spies and spy stories as cultural mediators that served in part to take away the sting of imperialist failure to the home audience. His understanding of the ideological apparatus of spying is particularly astute: "And what is ideology if not a cover story so deeply lived as to be almost unconscious, that necessary cover story by which the individual steps into daily life and its collective webs of work, language, and sexuality?"[34] Although Denning writes about the British context, there are direct parallels with American constructions of the same phenomenon. The variety of Lansdale's cover stories, however, became the hallmark of an ideology so tangled in webs of deceit, fervent idealism, and the rhetoric of Cold

War patriotism that in the end they succeeded in covering up nothing but themselves.

Lansdale's lack of forthrightness concerning his occupation was one of the great common denominators in his life. In 1965, six years before the release of *The Pentagon Papers*, he appeared before the Senate Foreign Relations Committee in executive session to discuss the escalating war in Vietnam. He introduced himself to the chairman, J. William Fulbright, in the following manner:

> MR. LANSDALE: Senator, my name is Lansdale. I served in Vietnam in the very early period there, actually from 1954 through 1956, in the early days of Diem's regime, and then came back and served in the Pentagon as an Assistant to the Secretary of Defense.
> THE CHAIRMAN: Were you a General in the active service then?
> MR. LANSDALE: I am retired now.
> THE CHAIRMAN: Were you then?
> MR. LANSDALE: I was a Major General in the Regular Air Force, retired.
> THE CHAIRMAN: But I mean when you first served?
> MR. LANSDALE: When I was out there I was in the regular service.
> THE CHAIRMAN: That is what I meant.
> MR. LANSDALE: I was a Colonel in Vietnam.[35]

Here Lansdale was operating once again under the power of his secrets. His refusal to divulge his more hidden identity effectively challenged the authority of the senator from Arkansas, whose doubts about the Vietnam War were growing with every Senate hearing and would eventually lead to a political and personal break with President Lyndon Johnson. Yet Lansdale appeared undisturbed; to him, a Senate hearing was simply another venue in which to promote his vision of how a spy should behave and how the United States could win in Vietnam.

Lansdale's Senate testimony is noteworthy for other reasons as well. For one thing, it involved a detailed and generally accurate history of his relationship to U.S. policy in the Philippines and Vietnam during the 1950s. This was one of the first times (outside of the national security community) when Lansdale detailed his behind-the-scenes work of championing and solidifying the rule of Magsaysay in the Philippines and Diem in Vietnam, and also his political uses of covert CIA operations abroad. Since even his deliberate self-revelations remained classified out of fear that it might jeopardize his influence in other forums, how predictable for him to exclaim after divulging this top-secret history, "I sure hope this is kept in executive."[36] This performance also underscores Lansdale's belief that presentation style was as crucial as the substance of the message: he exhibited his passion and knowledge about Vietnam while simultaneously working to preserve the air of mystery that surrounded his image as a CIA agent.[37] Finally, for all of Lansdale's talk about the dynamic quality and inherent goodness of democracy, his comments before the Senate Foreign Relations Committee show his distinctly elite-based notions of American history: for him, powerful individuals not only make history but must ensure that their real actions are kept secret from the general public so as not to upset people or arouse their passions.

The Senate episode was by no means unusual. Lansdale's penchant for obscuring his identity was evident in his dealings with other government agencies. In August 1962 he was the administration's spokesman before a top-secret congressional hearing on the fashionable topic of counterinsurgency, which had many fans inside the Kennedy White House; other Cold Warriors, generally more conservative congressmen, thought of it as a fad. In this hearing these disagreements between conservatives and liberals degenerated into a series of hostile questions directed at Lansdale. While Lansdale eagerly championed counterinsurgency and its technological approach to dealing with Third World revolutions, he consistently refused to divulge his true identity—which proved this time to be a tactical error:

> Mr. Lansdale: I then served in the Philippine Islands towards the end of World War II, and stayed in the Philippine Islands and organized the Philippine Islands Intelligence Service.
>
> Representative [Daniel J.] Flood: Are you a desk chair commando, or were you actually in the field behind with the troops? Are you a guerrilla fighter, or a long-haired advisor to these people? . . . You are not a desk commando? . . . You have been up there and had your face dirty? You have been with troops? [Lansdale says that he was primarily helping Magsaysay but did go into combat areas].
>
> Representative [Albert] Thomas: Perhaps he might tell us about [his education, as he seems unusual].
>
> Mr. Lansdale: My education was at UCLA. I went into the service from advertising. I happen to like people very much. When I hit Asia I found a very great affection for the people who were facing the enemy there and their problems on the land. They seemed to respond very quickly. I suspect in the Philippine Islands I have perhaps one million people there that know me by name and I know most of them. Much the same over the mainland of Asia. . . . I was an English major in college.
>
> Representative Flood: What is he? I do not know what he is yet.
>
> Representative [George H.] Mahon: We can draw our conclusions. His work is with the Secretary of Defense.[38]

"One million people"? "We can draw our conclusions." The fictional quality that permeated this hearing room needs to be juxtaposed with the fact that the Kennedy administration had specifically instructed Lansdale to testify before Congress on behalf of counterinsurgency in waging the Cold War. Because Lansdale was its point man, the question remains: why did the administration's spokesman simultaneously give the appearance of frankness and refuse to identify himself before individuals who had the all-important power of the purse? The answer is never made clear, but it fits Lansdale's construction of his top-secret persona as giving him both the authority to speak on the issue and immunity from inquiring minds.

Equally important to this discussion is the recognition that Lansdale cannot be understood through popular cultural filters or clichéd representations of CIA agents. True, he favored sunglasses much of the time, which gave him a certain star quality, but he was not the spy of fiction: wearing a trench-coat, using a hidden camera, or decoding secret messages in invisible ink. He was in fact the polar opposite of James Jesus Angelton, the head of counter-intelligence in the CIA, who in the parlance of the intelligence community "looked for a coffin whenever he saw a bouquet of flowers." Lansdale's relaxed manner may be best summed up by the refrain with which he often ended personal letters: "Easy there tiger!"

At the same time, his pretext of openness became another of his covers, one that enhanced his mystique both at home and abroad. Deeply aware of the mutually contradictory images that came to be associated with his name, he played off them repeatedly; he once jokingly told a friend, "everybody thinks I'm an international spy."[39] Ultimately, both his CIA involvement and his maintenance of a cover became common public property. The following exchange was recorded in 1976 by a *Women's Wear Daily* reporter, no less: "'Well, if it isn't Mr. CIA,' said Kitsie Westmoreland, as she greeted Maj. Gen. Edward Lansdale at the Washington party to celebrate Gen. William Westmoreland's new book, *A Soldier Reports*. 'I don't think she should call him that,' complained Pat Lansdale. 'All our friends in the Philippines think he's with the CIA, and it's not true.'"[40] Such an interaction of fashion gossip with political and cultural revelation and cover-up suggests the extent to which the very transparency of Lansdale's "hidden" CIA identity had made it the ultimate of cover stories.

Outside of Washington, Lansdale's deep cover as an international spy took on broader implications. The daughter of an American serviceman in Japan recalled that even the act of looking at him proved to be a fascinating experience: "I was in Tokyo, Japan, between 1959 and 1961, and word had gone out through the Press Club that Lansdale was in town. We drove down to see Lansdale and he was showing up with Philippine characters who were known as his assassins—the ones he brought in from the Philippines. As a kid I was fascinated by him and his gun which everyone could see—unusual because no one in Japan had weapons. My father had identified him as a killer for our government. The whole idea of Lansdale and our government assassinating people struck me as shocking, weird."[41] In spite of this reputation Lansdale made extensive use of his American grin, a wink, and a hearty laugh and backslap to ingratiate himself or disarm potentially hostile Filipinos and Vietnamese—he performed the "friendly American," so to speak. A friend once noted his proficiency in relating to Filipinos: an "expert," he said, "allows as how our chum [Lansdale] was not exactly fluent in Tagalog but he had a way of sensing what was being said without knowing the words.'"[42] This was one of the most valued weapons in his arsenal and a key to his success. Military methods had their proper place, but they became counterproductive, he believed, if they were the exclusive tools used by American forces abroad. Of course, the friendly American with a gun and "assassins" might very well find people responsive to his winks and grins.

Being Lansdale, he also relished using these tactics to irritate those who would not work with him. The most notorious example, and a tale he was particularly fond of telling, involved the French chief of staff with whom he worked in Vietnam. This particular Frenchman found Americans in general and Lansdale specifically loathsome after the fall of Dien Bien Phu, when the American presence in Vietnam was growing at the expense of the French; he bitterly resented the dissolution of his country's empire in Indochina and sought to thwart the growing U.S. influence there. His continual efforts to hinder the working relationship between the French and Americans included—according to Lansdale, anyway—such petty responses as not showing up for agreed-upon meetings, spreading rumors about the behavior of Americans to "loyal" Vietnamese, and complaining about American efforts to seduce Vietnamese women. Lansdale responded to these attacks by acting as the loud, stereotypical Yankee: "I hardly endeared myself to him by my own behavior. I would put an arm across his shoulders familiarly and announce to those standing nearby in a grating American manner, 'This guy is my buddy. You treat him right, you hear?' This made him explode, angrily shaking my arm off his shoulders. I found out that he continued to believe the convoluted fictions about my bribing Vietnamese with huge sums of money."[43] That last sentence is uniquely Lansdalian: he calls attention to his notoriety, denies doing something that he did engage in, and then uses the accusations as a rationale for the poor French-American relations of that time.

Lansdale's choice of gifts to his Asian associates, materially valuable and deeply symbolic, became another tactic for purveying power through his friendly American persona. Typical was Lansdale's gift to Diem of a handsome desk ornament inscribed. "Ngo Dinh Diem—The Father of His Country."[44] Lansdale's steamroller approach to flattery, combined with his more traditional spying efforts, made him a very unusual and very effective CIA agent. To a great extent it was this combination of features that won him real power and a reputation for his handling of the Philippine and, later, Vietnamese people. His prowess abroad, rather than his less predictable performance in Washington, goes far in explaining the stature he achieved in both the Eisenhower and Kennedy administrations.

For a brief time Lansdale's stock rose very high inside the new Kennedy administration, precisely because of his image as both a successful secret agent abroad and an advocate of counterinsurgency. The personal regard of the president played a big role in this drama. Garry Wills has argued that Kennedy's intense enthusiasm for covert operations as a new and exciting way to combat communism led him to "admire the legendary counterinsurgent Edward Lansdale."[45] Lansdale responded favorably to Kennedy's message on the campaign trail (an effort to differentiate himself from Nixon): "I want an America that is not 'first, if,' not 'first, but,' not 'first, when,' not 'first, maybe' but 'first,' period. I want a world which looks to the United States for leadership."[46] Lansdale reciprocated the president's good will and sought to capitalize on it to further his standing within the new administration. In a 1962 lecture to fellow military officers titled "The Insurgent Battlefield," he proclaimed that "spurred by the personal interest of President Kennedy, the U.S. is discovering a new military term: 'counter insurgency.'"[47]

Lansdale's love of the great game of spying seems to have had a bigger hold on his imagination than even the power of J. William Fulbright's probing questions could shake. Perhaps this attraction to cloak-and-dagger intrigue was to be expected—he was an intelligence agent, after all, and did not share the vision of the Cold War favored by grand theoreticians like Henry Kissinger, who pontificated that all events needed to be looked at through a *realpolitik* prism. Lansdale vehemently disagreed with the kind of dictate favored by Kissinger such as his self-assured statement during Senate testimony that "one must not confuse the intelligence business with missionary work."[48] Actually, Lansdale saw these two vocations as intimately linked, and he spent much of his career working to bring them together. Very much the secular missionary, he idealized and championed American actions abroad. One of Lansdale's team members, Rufus Phillips, recalled that Lansdale had been "moved to a missionary attitude" by his actions in the Philippines and thought they would work in Vietnam as well.[49] The very idea of "America" resonated for him, even as he became increasingly conservative and despondent about the United States after the communist victory in Vietnam in 1975.

Yet to gain a real understanding of Lansdale's CIA history, with its complex mixture of manipulation, self-promotion, and idealism, it becomes imperative to see him as part of the CIA's larger Cold War purpose. Lansdale functioned very much within the structure of America's foreign policy after World War II, especially with regard to covert policy in Southeast Asia. In particular, the goals of the U.S. government in redefining its major adversary from fascism to "international communism," and then expanded to include the revolutionary/nationalist movements of the Huks in the Philippines and the Vietcong in South Vietnam, become crucial to an understanding of Lansdale's belief in and implementation of U.S. policies.[50]

ALTHOUGH THE CIA's basic charter in 1947 stipulated that it be only an intelligence-gathering agency, it came to be used by presidents as a private army and as a covert "state department" unencumbered by constitutional restrictions. President Kennedy, for one, told his national security adviser, McGeorge Bundy, "I don't care what it is, but if I need something fast, the CIA is the place to go."[51] It was these clandestine uses of the CIA to accomplish the more sordid deeds of U.S. foreign policy that propelled it into a terrain unlike that occupied by any other government office. Today, there is a tendency to ascribe to the CIA an otherness befitting an alien life force, to hold it responsible for everything from preventing true democracy in America to hiding the space aliens captured in Roswell, New Mexico, in 1947. Feeding these fantasies are occasional disclosures that the CIA did take part in what can only be described today as a series of truly bizarre efforts to frustrate the communist tide. Some of the ideas were simply silly, such as the "plan to fill balloon baskets with safety razors and other superior Western toiletries and let them drift downwind into communist zones where the standard of living was less comfortable."[52] But silliness soon degenerated into notions of wiring cats with miniature microphones, placing atomic weapons on the moon, and testing LSD on unsuspecting people to learn its mind-control possibilities not to mention operation MHChaos involving surveillance and suppression of Vietnam War protestors.[53] These schemes and countless others, referred to as the "Family Jewels," were itemized by Director James Schlesinger's internal investigation in 1973, which detailed every nefarious activity the CIA had engaged in, including its attempts to assassinate foreign leaders. Still, its effort to hold on to its secrets continued and approached the level of farce when in 1999, even after two years of learning the actual budget of the CIA (roughly $26 billion a year), a federal judge ruled in favor of the CIA to prevent such disclosures on the grounds that they "could reasonably be expected to result in harm to the national security and to reveal intelligence 'sources and methods.' "[54] The secret agency, one that more has been written about than any other government office, still attempts to cloak even such widely known details.

What accounted for all these policies and plans and fantasies was the overriding fear of communism and its threat not only to the United States but to Western civilization itself. True, the U.S. government sold the evils of communism in a host of cultural venues, yet policymakers remained fearful that this new contagion, labeled "red fascism," would spread throughout the world. Their fears were reinforced in the top-secret documents that became the internal foundations of the CIA, the most famous of which was written in 1947, the year of the CIA's charter. NSC-4/A is explicit about the rationale and methods for combatting communism: "The National Security Council, taking cognizance of the vicious psychological activities of the USSR, its satellite countries, and Communist groups to discredit and defeat the aims and activities of the U.S. and other Western powers, has determined that, in the interests of world peace and U.S. national security, the foreign information activities of the U.S. Government must be supplemented by covert psychological operations. . . . [T]he Central Intelligence Agency [is] the logical agency to conduct such operations."[55] In no uncertain terms, this document maintains that covert operations and secret agents will be central to American Cold War successes.

Another key document was NSC-68, written just before the Korean War in 1950. Whereas NSC-4/A focused on the need for an agency devoted to spying and subterfuge, NSC-68 argued for military-based responses to all perceived communist threats. It also served Secretary of State Dean Acheson's larger goal of having all branches of the U.S. government speak with one voice in regard to this new threat. As he recalled in his memoirs, "The purpose of NSC-68 was to so bludgeon the mass mind of 'top government' that not only could the President make a decision but that the decision could be carried out."[56] Further, the all-encompassing nature of the theory of containment plus the militarization of U.S. foreign policy as enunciated in NSC-68 allowed presidents to view any threat, anywhere, as an attack on the United States. Eisenhower's declaration in June 1954 that "we have got to keep the Pacific as an American lake" is symptomatic of this mind-set.[57]

Eisenhower elaborated these sentiments in a more nuanced way before a confidential briefing to Republican congressional leaders in 1954:

> Every individual is the center of the universe so far as that individual is concerned; in the same manner, every nation is the center of the universe in working out its own problems. Yet, in a general sense . . . it is correct to say that the United States is the central key, the core of democracy, economically, militarily and spiritually. Consequently in simple terms, we are establishing international outposts where people can develop their strength to defend themselves. Here we are sitting in the center, and with high mobility and destructive forces we can swiftly respond when our vital interests are affected. We are trying . . . with these programs to build up for the United States a position in the world of freedom of action. . . . [W]e cannot publicly call our Allies outposts . . . [but] we are trying to get that result.[58]

Eisenhower's meditation on American power is notable for its candor about the American role in the postwar world. Newly emerging states that chose to forgo entering into alliances with the United States or having American military bases on their soil were now to be seen as opposing American interests. This contradiction between sentiments and actions has led the historian Niall Ferguson to refer to American foreign policy as "the empire of denial."[59] Likewise, John Foster Dulles memorably rationalized American actions by declaring, "The principle of neutrality . . . pretends that a nation can best gain safety for itself by being indifferent to the fate of others. This has increasingly become an obsolete conception, and, except under very exceptional circumstances, it is an immoral and shortsighted conception."[60]

Although Lansdale's public proclamations were rarely so explicit, he operated in the Third World under these same assumptions; it was, after all, just such midlevel officials who spent their government careers working to transform these "outposts" into little Americas. The two NSC documents help to explain why Edward Lansdale was sent abroad. Though he liked to depict himself as a man who bucked authority and disdained all aspects of bureaucracy, he did not just wander into Southeast Asia and attempt to create governments to his own liking; he was directed to do battle with the perceived enemies of the United States. Regardless of how many people were killed by American actions, Dulles, Lansdale, and the entire national security apparatus saw only evidence of American successes or shortsightedness.

Dean Acheson wrote in *Present at the Creation* about the establishment of the Central Intelligence Agency by the National Security Act of 1947 in ways that were terribly prescient: "I had the gravest forebodings about this organization and warned the President that as set up neither he, the National

Security Council, nor anyone else would be in a position to know what it was doing or to control it."[61] The CIA became exactly what he feared: at some times it functioned to enact a president's private foreign policy; at others it worked almost autonomously. No one knew exactly what it was doing because its core purpose was to be a secret agency. Acheson's forebodings set the stage for the uneasy relationship between the CIA and the American interests that it was designed to serve. Lansdale's relationship to the agency further demonstrates the paradox of cover-ups and revelations that characterized its Cold War history. An adequate account of Lansdale's CIA involvement lies somewhere between I. F. Stone's declaration that 95 percent of the secrets in the U.S. government can be found simply by reading the small print in daily newspapers and the admission by James Edgington—an administrator in the Pentagon's Directorate for Freedom of Information and Security Review—that there were over three linear feet of classified documents involving Lansdale and his actions.[62]

Even should it be true that the CIA was simply a "BOGSAT—bunch of guys sitting around a table"—this quip cannot explain away its mythologized power.[63] The aura that surrounds it entices us with the promise of withheld secrets, yet no one revelation could accurately characterize the CIA or Lansdale's involvement with it. Their mutual histories inhabit an uneasy terrain between fact and fiction, between documented and undocumented actions, and within the shifting status of public images.

In this unstable borderland, the early discussions of agency policies and actions are illuminating. In 1954 a three-part friendly exposé in the *Saturday Evening Post*, "The Mysterious Doings of the CIA," and another piece of fluff called "Allen Dulles: America's Master Spy," in *Cavalier*, dramatically extolled the agency.[64] In these officially sanctioned writings one sees a breathlessness about the CIA, an excitement about the external dangers it had to confront, and an uncertainty about whether it was up to the task. Like Lansdale's own top-secret writings, these narratives sought to reassure both the American people and Washington policymakers that someone in the government was on the job fighting the communists in far-off lands. Both also played on the relationship between the keepers of secrets and the inquisitive audience. They served the additional purpose of acclimating the American people to an ever increasing need for a national security apparatus. Lansdale excelled at this sort of agency promotion in his official capacity as a member of "The Company" (as insiders referred to it) and devoted his career to cheerleading their efforts abroad.

By the mid-1950s the CIA came to be seen as critical to maintaining

American power yet not as stodgy as so many other government agencies. The CIA's "coolness" enabled it to cross the line between the gray flannel suit and the black leather jacket. It was not subject to mass conformity, not the passive victim of modern America then being critiqued by such social critics as William H. Whyte in *The Organization Man* (1956), not taking orders from Mamie Eisenhower. Nor were its agents Beats playing bongos and swilling cheap red wine late into the night. The CIA had a mission, and its cultivated allure, its mystery, was carried beyond media reports by its top officials, many of whom led socially prominent, hard-drinking, womanizing, adventurous lives. Evan Thomas's social history of the CIA, *The Very Best Men*, argues that these confirmed Cold Warriors really enjoyed partying as much as they enjoyed fighting the commies: "At one of his frequent stag dinners at the Alibi Club, [Allen] Dulles leaned over to Lloyd Emerson, a junior staffer in the DD/P [Deputy Director for Plans], and asked, in a conspiratorial voice, 'Do you read the society pages? Young man, that's where I get a lot of valuable information. You should read it every day, to get the beginning of things.'"[65] This mingling of mystery and media, rumor and reality, would reach its nadir when President Kennedy inquired whether Lansdale was America's James Bond.[66]

What the public writings about the CIA highlight is the incestuous and corrosive mix between the government and the media that developed during the Cold War years. Clearly, that War could never have been waged so long and with such fervor without the media's active participation and docile acquiescence to the ideological goals defined for them by the government. The fact that the American public simultaneously respected, feared, and approved of the CIA's actions until the 1970s was the result of one of the most successful promotions undertaken by the U.S. officialdom. In a 1954 profile of the CIA, for instance, the *Saturday Evening Post* told its readers: "So if size, cost and secrecy were the sole criteria for gauging the success of CIA, the country could sleep soundly tonight in the assurance that we have the right answers to Russian scheming."[67] And as John Heidenry observes in his history of the *Reader's Digest*, the subjects of anticommunism and sex were the perennial favorites in this most widely read of periodicals.[68]

Even former CIA agent Tom Braden's genteel exposé in 1967 tended to contribute to the CIA mystique. His article, "I'm Glad the CIA Is Immoral," may very well be the most provocatively titled piece ever to appear in the staid *Saturday Evening Post*. True, the CIA was by that time on the defensive within the government and anxious to bolster its image to the American people as a protective shield against communism. Braden's disclosures tended to support this task:

And so it came about that I had a chat with Allen Dulles. It was late in the day and his secretary was gone. I told him I thought the CIA ought to take on the Russians by penetrating a battery of international fronts. . . .

"You know," he said, leaning back in his chair and lighting his pipe, "I think you may have something there. There's no doubt in my mind that we're losing the Cold War. Why don't you take it up down below."

[With Dulles's approval, Braden did go on to design ingenious plans to combat communism.]

And then there was *Encounter*, the magazine published in England and dedicated to the proposition that cultural achievement and political freedom were interdependent. Money for . . . the magazine's publication came from the CIA, and few outside of the CIA knew about it. We had placed one agent in a Europe-based organization of intellectuals called the Congress for Cultural Freedom. Another agent became an editor of *Encounter*. The agents could not only propose anti-Communist programs to the official leaders of the organizations but they could also suggest ways and means to solve the inevitable budgetary problems. Why not see if the needed money could be obtained from "American foundations"? As the agents knew, the CIA-financed foundations were quite generous when it came to the national interest.[69]

This sort of confession is typical of the tales invoked by all who knew the hows and whys of the intelligence business. Although we must take Braden's word for it, since his conversation with Dulles was a private one, it shows how the CIA constructed and disseminated knowledge for the general public. The exposé itself was designed to amaze defenders and critics alike with the ability of a CIA agent to turn ideas into actions. Not surprisingly, Allen Dulles's *The Craft of Intelligence* included many such telling snippets, as did his *Great True Spy Stories*. Nor was the timing of Braden's history an accident: it came out precisely when the role of the CIA was finally being questioned by such establishment figures as journalists Walter Lippmann and Joseph Kraft. Braden's efforts can be seen as one way to regenerate the mythical aura of the agency as an institution central to saving Western civilization.

In fact, Braden's dramatic use of undocumented conversations was a format adopted by almost all ex-CIA agents when they wrote their own histories, whether their purpose was celebratory, confessional, or explanatory in nature. Individuals as diverse in their politics as Philip Agee and William Colby adopted the same heightened pseudorealist style in their personal accounts.[70] All these writers understood that their literary worth was measured in the marketplace by the quality and quantity of the secrets they shared with their readers. In this respect, Braden's and others' disclosures of how the national security state operated were predictable; the mingled wonder and fear they projected implied that the CIA could be anywhere and do just about anything. Even within the government, the CIA continued to have mythic qualities attached to it. Throughout the Watergate crisis, President Richard Nixon brought up the Bay of Pigs as the root of all of his problems. At one point he and H. R. Haldeman, his chief of staff, discussed Howard Hunt, one of the Watergate burglars and a White House consultant also involved in the Bay of Pigs:

> NIXON: This guy is a wiretapper. He's been tapping for years, hasn't he?
> HALDEMAN: I don't know. I don't know what he—he's a disguise type guy.
> NIXON: And deep cover.
> HALDEMAN: He writes dirty books.

Nixon went on to call Hunt especially dangerous because "he thought black."[71] With the president of the United States and his chief of staff spouting the kind of mindlessness favored in conspiracy-addled Hollywood films, in alternative press reports on the "true" nature of U.S. policy, and especially in barroom conversations, is it any wonder that the CIA would soon come under attack from so many different constituencies that it could not defend itself?

If the image-building propaganda for the CIA sought to deliver measured doses of carefully packaged pseudorealism to its audience, the 1970s disclosures and then attacks on the CIA, including *The CIA and the Cult of Intelligence* and *Uncloaking the CIA*, curiously replicated this phenomenon twenty years later.[72] In John Stockwell's depiction of the agency as a law unto itself, he still covertly dedicated his book, *In Search of Enemies: A CIA Story* (1978), to "In memory of TUBRAXEY/I." And the first sentence in Victor Marchetti and John Marks's denunciation of all things that bear the CIA imprint reads, "There exists in our nation today a powerful and dangerous secret cult—the cult of intelligence."[73] Leaving aside their literary mimickery of Marx's opening sentence in *The Communist Manifesto*, and the truism that if everyone knows about a secret it can hardly be one, the question remains, what did their disclosures about the CIA accomplish? On one level, because of their work and countless other investigative reports, we know today that CIA agents spied and assessed the communist threat, understood the nature and tenacity of the North Vietnamese far better than did other branches of government, and alerted the president to the Soviet introduction of nuclear missiles in Cuba. But they also spied on vast numbers of Americans, slipped LSD into the drinks of unsuspecting victims, attempted to kill a series of foreign leaders, installed such notorious Third World leaders as Colonel Carlos Castillo Armas in Guatemala and the Shah of Iran, engaged in gunrunning, and distributed opium to fund their "off the book" deeds.[74]

Much has been made of these covert actions, and there is a common belief that such airings of the government's dirty laundry led to a reformist spirit that cleaned up the intent and operations of the CIA. Yet an equally compelling reading of the exposés shows that they situated the agency in a dreamlike realm where its activities were still considered to be beyond the comprehension—and evaluation—of the public. This unreality is particularly destructive to the extent that it reduces truly horrific actions into something approaching a modern fairytale, with the "evil" CIA corrupting or wasting everything in its path and only occasionally being stopped by virtuous citizens. A classic portrayal of this kind appears in Don DeLillo's first meditation on the Kennedy assassination. In 1983 he wrote: "Espionage is well known to be a game, a maze, a set of mirrors. It is also big business, and this is a reason for people to sell secrets in the routine manner of a dealer moving Turkish rugs. Former members of the CIA seem happily occupied shipping explosives to Libya, torture devices to Uganda, military equipment to the Soviet Union. They don't call it the Company for nothing."[75] What these later works accomplish then—with Norman Mailer's novelistic rendition of this world in *Harlot's Ghost* (1991) being a more recent example—is a glorification of the idea of the CIA in the very act of revealing its corruption. The myth of the CIA as a destructive network of power came to inhabit the heart and soul of Cold War America just as deeply as did its previous image as the saving force of democracy.

Even taking into account the mythologies, it is important to restate that since the 1971 publication of *The Pentagon Papers* and the 1975 Church committee's report, a great deal has been unearthed about Lansdale and his actions in Southeast Asia and Cuba. We know in minute detail the Kennedy administration's multilayered efforts to assassinate Fidel Castro, beginning with the Bay of Pigs fiasco and ending with the multiple disasters of Operation Mongoose. As Lyndon Johnson observed after he left office, obviously feeling little compunction to guard his true feelings about U.S. policy or the Kennedys, "We were running a goddam Murder, Inc. down there."[76] The Kennedy administration's obsessive quest to destroy Fidel Castro was echoed by Edward Lansdale's voluminous top-secret memorandums on the subject, which exuded a high school enthusiasm for plotting ever more ingenious ways to sabotage the Cuban economy and assassinate the dictator. In 1962 Lansdale sent President Kennedy and other officials a recipe for death and destruction:

> *The Goal.* In keeping with the spirit of the Presidential memorandum of 30 November 1961, the United States will help the people of Cuba overthrow the Communist regime from within Cuba and institute a new government with which the United States can live in peace. . . .

> *Premise of Action.* Americans once ran a successful revolution. It was run from
> within, and succeeded because there was a timely and strong political, economic,
> and military help by nations outside who supported our cause. Using this same
> concept of revolution from within, we must now help the Cuban people to stamp
> out tyranny and gain their liberty.[77]

Lansdale clearly thought of himself as an American revolutionary in such a
battle; in a troubling sense this particular self-image seems to have been so
ingrained that it easily dispatched contradictory realities. Under the guise of
morality and based on a dubious reading of America's own revolutionary
past, Lansdale sought to initiate and then manage a war against a Third
World country. When his actions became public during the Church committee investigations, Lansdale went to great lengths to deny that President
Kennedy or his brother Robert had specifically asked him to develop plans
for an assassination, but he did tell one reporter that Robert Kennedy had
instructed him to develop "all feasible plans for 'getting rid of' Cuban Prime
Minister Fidel Castro." Lansdale went on to say that he interpreted this
assignment more broadly than the attorney general had intended. The
Church committee heard another report that Lansdale admitted he was "acting on orders from President Kennedy, delivered through an intermediary,
[and that his] job was to develop plans for removing Fidel Castro by any
means, including assassination."[78] Though the reporter stood by his story,
Lansdale vehemently denied saying this, even though the document trail
clearly indicates that he developed a host of plans to destroy the Cuban
government—including assassination.

Lansdale's advocacy of an interventionist mission in Cuba and Vietnam,
then, was not simply a matter of his moral compass somehow going askew.
He was acting according to the logic of a national security apparatus that
made careers for men like him and then cheered them on to create ever more
deadly and ingenious ways to implement their mission. Even when Lansdale
noted problems in an American client state—he once described Diem's government in the late 1950s as an emerging "fascist state"[79]—he did not deviate
from American foreign policy goals. To do so would have risked a loss of
power and thus his ability to change the very policy he was disagreeing with.

In ways neither Lansdale nor the CIA would fully understand or were able
to control, their respective efforts to wage the Cold War were responsible
for the deep level of political alienation that has been a hallmark of American
society since the Vietnam War—alienation triggered not just by the actions
themselves but by the seemingly unfathomable contradictions they represented. Here was a man who considered himself a true patriot—down to
raising and lowering the American flag in front of his house each day[80]—and

an agency whose very existence was supposedly dependent on waging battles against an implacable enemy of American freedom. This idealistic image combined with the tragic realities that resulted led to the decades of disillusionment and fantasy with which the CIA has been viewed since its actions became public knowledge in the 1970s. Critics have not been kind; Thomas Powers, for one, has found little to applaud about the CIA, and his series of rhetorical questions disposes of the agency's claimed effectiveness:

> How important to the outcome of the cold war were the . . . clandestine skirmishing, the spying and the counterspying, the black propaganda and hidden pulling of strings, the keeping and breaching of secrets during the forty-five years after the Soviet Union planted its armies in the heart of Europe at the end of the Second World War? In short, did the United States, which spent perhaps half a trillion dollars on intelligence since 1945, get its money's worth? . . . [T]he covert warriors in blackface caused much death and havoc in Southeast Asia, Cuba, and Central America but they did the US little apparent good in any of these places.[81]

Sentiments like this, combined with outright attacks as in Senator Daniel Patrick Moynihan's 1998 *Secrecy: The American Experience*, present a powerful case that the CIA as an outmoded institution needs to be shut down. Given this level of contempt by fully credentialed members of the establishment, it becomes deeply interesting to see whether the CIA can successfully reimagine and justify its mission especially considering its loss of credibility in the years since September 11, 2001.

4

The Perils of
a Usable Past

> For the spiritual past has no objective reality; it yields
> only what we are able to look for in it. . . . The past is an
> inexhaustible storehouse of apt attitudes and adaptable
> ideals; it opens of itself at the touch of desire; it yields up,
> now this treasure, now that, to anyone who comes to it
> armed with a capacity for personal choices.
>
> —Van Wycks Brooks, "On Creating a Usable Past," 1918

EDWARD LANSDALE was never in the first tier of policymakers, yet he
thought of himself as being at the forefront of those who explained the
intellectual basis for U.S. actions in the Cold War. This belief was reinforced
by reporters who found in him the government official who always had a
timely phrase or the aptly drawn historical analogy for current U.S. policy.
The journalist Frances Fitzgerald dug a bit deeper, surmising that Lansdale
was "no theorist, he was rather an enthusiast, a man who believed that Communism in Asia would crumble before men of goodwill with some concern
for 'the little guy' and the proper counterinsurgency skills."[1] This is a smart
assessment of the man but too restrictive. Lansdale very much thought of
himself as a Cold War theorist who provided to others, but especially to
Asians, a sense of the larger meaning of America and its battles against communism. Fitzgerald more accurately defined Lansdale from the perspective
of senior American policymakers as a capable tactician, someone who knew
the terrain and believed in the stakes, who was briefly considered indispen-

sable to waging the Cold War. In his memoirs Lansdale recalled his mission: "I was to go to Vietnam to help the Vietnamese much as I had helped the Filipinos."[2] These orders emphasized Lansdale's know-how and judgment but did not ask for a structural analysis of what that "help" might mean to America's Cold War policies.

Although the previous chapters depict a canny Cold Warrior willing to do just about anything to implement American policy abroad, Lansdale's public and private writings reveal other sides to his tactician persona. His writings are highly patriotic and melodramatic; at times a self-parodying quality marks them when he gets tangled up in historical analogies. But overall, they highlight his vision for America within a narrative of progress and virtue. They also reveal him as someone who sought to understand the power of history and its implementation through a country's foreign policy. He was an inveterate writer of everything from official reports, memoranda, and lecture notes to diary jottings, letters, and memoirs. His audiences were diverse; they included policymakers, students, and the general public in America and Southeast Asia. What is remarkable is how little he varied his pitch or his tone; he saw his Cold War message as so pure, so true, that little or no change was needed, whether he was addressing the U.S. president or a Filipino dockworker. In turn, many individuals or groups, struck by his fervency and call to arms, came to see Lansdale as "the prophet of winning."[3]

One of the ways that Lansdale sought to pursue American Cold War victories was through the use of history. At times he viewed history purely as a commodity, more often as a learning tool, but always as a "usable past" to be wielded as an ideological weapon. Time and again he argued that history was a key component of America's arsenal. Of course, Lansdale was by no means alone in the belief that tapping into the secrets of history could result in political victories for his country. The United States and the communists used every conceivable medium for advancing their respective agendas and ideas—in the American case, everything from the model kitchen so prominently displayed at the United States Exhibition in Moscow in 1959 (the site of the famed debate between Vice President Nixon and Khrushchev over the merits of capitalism) to the "selling" of abstract artists such as Jackson Pollock and Mark Rothko[4]—and history became for both blocs a key form of propaganda, a tool to motivate allegiance, to inculcate allies, and to locate nascent Western-oriented movements or communist threats in the recoverable past. Why Lansdale's uses of the past proved to be more persuasive in the Philippines than in Vietnam becomes a crucial part of this story. One of the reasons he would fail in Vietnam was that a series of Vietnamese intellectuals throughout the nineteenth and twentieth centuries viewed history in a similar ideological fashion but offered versions of their own past that competed with and eventually triumphed over Lansdale's version.

It needs to be emphasized that to focus on the world of ideas is not to ignore the very real history of economics and military force which propelled and enforced the rhetoric of men like Lansdale. His vision of himself as a policymaker and his multiple uses of history, however, further our knowledge of U.S. policy toward Southeast Asia by demonstrating the variety of ways in which an American empire was rationalized by Americans and received by Asians. On the surface, Lansdale's uses of history bear a striking similarity to the concept of a "usable past" associated with American intellectuals during the Progressive era. The concept has been explored by individuals such as Charles Beard, Carl Becker, and especially Van Wyck Brooks (who coined the phrase).[5] But unlike Brooks, whose approach to a "usable past" involved continual self-examination to prevent today's insights from becoming tomorrow's intellectual baggage, Lansdale reduced history to a series of truisms that could be endlessly used and reused. Regardless of his audience, Lansdale's histories were packaged in a way that provided reassurance to all who accepted his readings. They also promised to usher in a period of political democracy and economic growth similar to what the United States had achieved after its own revolution. His "usable past" became exactly what these earlier critics sought to avoid: a secular religion. For him, there was no change over time, no subtlety, no sense of irony when using or explaining the past. Even more important, his uses of history in the Philippines and Vietnam were never distinct from the control he possessed over American funding toward these countries.[6]

EDWARD LANSDALE never deviated in his beliefs about the Cold War, and when he died he was convinced that communism remained a mortal threat to U.S. interests. When his widow was asked what Lansdale would have made of the momentous changes in the world since the fall of the Berlin Wall, she answered with another question: "Now that there is no more communism, or Soviet Union, what would he do now? His life was based on it."[7] One possible answer is that Lansdale might have rested a bit easier by ascribing this victory to one of his most cherished beliefs, the redemptive power of history. The starting point for this faith in the power of history to educate others can be found in his own family history. He often spoke of an ancestor who was killed in the Pacific islands in the late nineteenth century while fighting for the expansion of the American empire; they were "overrun by pursuing natives," wrote Lansdale. He noted that his mother, born in the newly independent state of California, had recalled what life was like during the last of the Indian Wars; that his father, born in Virginia, had been a Civil War buff; and that a signer of the American Constitution may have been a distant relative.

In the late 1960s when Lansdale began to prepare his memoirs, he wrote and rewrote a number of episodes detailing how he came to love history. The drafts of the memoirs provide a relatively uncensored view of his beliefs compared with the published version, which left out many of the stories and names of his associates.[9] One section begins with his reading of the American Revolution and its effect on him:

> Among the books on the shelves at home was a set bound in green suede leather. The set was a collection of writings from the American Revolution complete with the leaflets by Tom Paine and Sam Adams, the jaunty humor of ballads pointed against the day's mighty authorities . . . and the clear essays of political logic that gave an ideology to our revolutionary movement. I read and re-read these volumes at an early age. . . . The essence of what I learned about the American Revolution then has stuck with me through the years. I believe in the statements of the Declaration of Independence about men being "endowed by their creator with certain unalienable Rights" and in the practical rules of the "Bill of Rights" for assuring them. The ideas of the American Revolution are too close to the truths men seek universally to be penned in by the shores of the United States. . . . These are precepts for a man to live by, even two centuries later.[10]

This passage is repeated in various forms throughout his writings and indicates Lansdale's idealized view of the American Revolution, which became the basis for his all-purpose ideology; as an adult he even typed out for his own personal reflection a copy of the Declaration of Independence.[11] The remarkable aspect is that the stories he learned as a child about this eighteenth-century conflict in North America were later exported, wholesale, to twentieth-century Asia.

For Lansdale, the American Revolution was the "good" revolution, clearly opposed in his mind to communist-led instability and revolt. This reverence was not unique to him; both conservative and liberal Americans have viewed this eighteenth-century event as distinguishing their country from the rest of the world, ushering in such modern concepts as the elevation of the rights of the individual, and institutionalizing such key liberal ideas as freedom of speech and freedom of religion. Of all forms of political upheaval, only the American Revolution was pure in their eyes, mitigating the chaos that often attended other revolutions. Lansdale, then, was only following in the intellectual footsteps of Woodrow Wilson, who as a young academic summed up these convictions in a commemorative address in 1889: "For us this is the centennial year of Washington's inauguration; but for Europe it is the centennial year of the French Revolution. One hundred years ago we gained, and Europe lost, self-command, self-possession."[12] Like Wilson, Lansdale saw the American Revolution as transplantable to other countries, giving his history lesson a relevance few historians would ever subscribe to, and one that far surpassed the comparisons drawn from the American experience by enthusiasts of Cold War modernization theory such as Walt Rostow.

This belief in the inherent goodness of the American Revolution explains why Lansdale, addressing American college students in 1964, could easily blend his reading of the meaning of 1776 with an appeal to wage the Cold War: "Let us start looking at Vietnam, and at Communist revolutionary invasions in other free countries, from the viewpoint of a Tom Jefferson, a Ben Franklin, a Sam Adams, a Tom Paine, our own great and practical revolutionaries. We need to go beyond being bountiful hardware merchants, bankers, and technical sophisticates—and start demonstrating again our kinship with the embattled farmers at Concord Bridge, with the plain-spoken burgesses at Williamsburg."[13] Lansdale's convictions were so secure on this issue that he did not feel the need to alter his message when addressing American foreign policy experts. At the Council of Foreign Relations he announced to a group of past and present policymakers: "I plan to tell a couple of stories to help guide you towards a deep truth. . . . This deep truth, when understood, can prove the key to helping our allies win." This "deep truth" involved retelling the fabled conversation between Ben Franklin and Tom Paine:

> FRANKLIN: "Wherever freedom is, that is my country."
> PAINE: "Wherever freedom is not, that is my country."[14]

Lansdale was so taken by this exchange that he returned to it in the preface to his memoirs. After writing, "You should know one thing at the beginning: I took my American beliefs with me into these Asian struggles, as Tom Paine would have done," he then recited the Franklin-Paine exchange and went on to exclaim: "Paine's words form a cherished part of my credo. . . . I feel a kinship with Thomas Jefferson. . . . I endeavored to practice my beliefs among embattled people abroad."[15] His embrace of America's Founding Fathers turned into a name-dropping riff that animated (and apparently comforted) Lansdale time and time again during his military missions.

It seems fitting that once Lansdale went abroad in the 1940s, he became a historian of communism as well. His image of communism was filtered through the prism of American history; like many Americans, he viewed it through the most threatening analogies from the American context, combined with fresh fears about the malleability of humans through psychological manipulation. Communist leaders were likened to Al Capone and his mob in Chicago, and the goal of communism was said to be the creation of an individual who was a "cipher of the state" and had "Pavlovian qualities." A typical Lansdale analysis of communism embraced this framework: "Americans have much to learn about the elements of "People's War" as fought by Asian Communists. At its heart, along with the applied behavioral psychology adopted from Pavlov, is the organizing of disciplined political structure based upon easily-grasped maxims. After twenty years of war, the Vietnamese had gained a deeply instinctive grasp of the truth, of the facts of life. The Communist words—even the words and material aid of our side— had become mere 'gimmicks.' Deeds, performed in the right spirit, were more important than slogans or merchandise."[16] The reference to Pavlov harks back to the Korean War and to beliefs in the communists' particularly fiendish ability to "brainwash" captured American GIs (shades of *The Manchurian Candidate*).

Another time Lansdale felt compelled to respond to a student who had expressed interest in communism: "I note you spell Communist with a lower case "c." I dropped this habit years ago. The capital "C" denotes the peculiar breed we struggle with today. They really aren't communists as the term was long used, such as in the experimental social communities in the U.S. The silverware on the tables in many U.S. homes were made by folks who originally thought of themselves as communists, the Community Silver folks. Nearly every U.S. state had such communists who followed early socialist creeds in seeking utopia."[17] For Lansdale, communism personified such as overwhelming evil that the question of means and ends lost any relevancy. He was a true believer in the Cold War struggle, and these statements give a chilling indication of why he supported America's intervention in Vietnam.

Later, Lansdale counseled President Kennedy in a manner that combined the virtues of American history with the religious truths of Christianity. In his 1963 memorandum "A High-Level Look at the Cold War," he once again emphasized that the American Revolution could be deployed to counter communist ideas. Additionally, he promoted the idea of reintroducing the Bible into the Soviet Union; this was the surest way, he argued, to make the USSR more "American."[18] In a sense then, God, like the Founding Fathers, could be appropriated by American policymakers as a justification for their actions. Eisenhower referred to the Cold War as a battle between the forces of evil and godliness (in 1954 he signed into law the addition of the phrase "under God" to the Pledge of Allegiance). Lansdale, in turn, advanced the ideals of the American Revolution to justify U.S. intervention in Cuba in the early 1960s.[19] These examples illustrate why he believed the United States had to assist the Philippines and South Vietnam in their own "revolutions"; to do nothing would endanger the very meaning and sanctity of American identity as he saw it. They also display the cheerleading quality that Lansdale brought to his role as an historian, as well as his continuing desire to personally shape U.S. policy.

Lansdale believed in this historical framework so much that at times it took on a transhistorical quality, as when he juxtaposed American history with his view of the aspirations and ethnographic potential of Southeast Asians. In one draft of his memoirs this merger became explicit: "I LIKE THE VIETNAMESE PEOPLE, HARD WORKING, FULL OF POETRY, MUSIC, AND EARTHY GOOD HUMOR, THEY SEEMED TO RECOGNIZE THIS LIKING IN ME AND RESPONDED. . . . I BELIEVE THAT THE AMERICANS AT CONCORD BRIDGE OR VALLEY FORGE WOULD HAVE RECOGNIZED THEM AS KINDRED SOULS."[20] A belief that America and Vietnam were spiritually linked led Lansdale to refer to Vietnam as his "home," a statement that takes on a curiously heartfelt if imperial tone. As he wrote to Diem in 1959 from the Pentagon: "I don't know if whether I am homesick for Vietnam or merely want to see if you ever tried on those red Hawaiian swim trunks, but anyhow I am thinking of you at this moment."[21] Lansdale invoked the same notion when he returned to Vietnam in 1965 and told a group of Vietnamese: "When Ambassador Henry Cabot Lodge asked me to join him on his mission to Viet-nam, I had the happy feeling that he was asking me to come back home again. Viet Nam and Vietnamese friends have been so much in my thoughts, so close to my heart, even while I was 10,000 miles away, that Vietnam truly seems like home again. So now I am home again."[22]

Together, all these statements about the American Revolution and Vietnam as a nascent America allow one to read Lansdale as a practical-minded devotee of the consensus school, the reigning historiographical method during the early Cold War years. Histories by Richard Hofstadter, Louis Hartz, David Potter, and Daniel Boorstin necessarily muted the conflicts from the American past, whether sectional, class-based, racial, or economic.[23] Furthermore, they were written to differentiate the idea of revolution from a Marxian analysis of class struggle, a form of change that Lansdale would spend his adult life studying in order to combat (it was said that he even memorized Mao Zedong's *Quotations of Chairman Mao*).[24] But although consensus histories were highly congenial to Lansdale's ideological framework, he applied ideas from these works wholesale and often ahistorically. Thus he himself could never be seen as a historian, but in many ways the consensus school's arguments gave him the apparatus he felt he needed to defeat communism. As he later wrote in a characteristically breathless manner: "I took these beliefs with me onto the battlegrounds abroad. . . . I even frightened some allies who saw in me a fool or a dangerous revolutionary or both. Yet, more than the hatred or the fright, I found a warm brotherhood with a great host of people who shared my beliefs in the principles of man's individual liberty. . . . I found an affectionate kinship with people I had once regarded as foreigners. We became strangers no longer."[25]

This remarkably self-revealing passage brings a number of Lansdale's "usable pasts" together. First, he made a self-conscious effort to deliver American ideology to everyone he encountered. Second, he used its tenets to establish what he believed to be a real rapport with leaders such as Ramon Magsaysay and Ngo Dinh Diem. Third, by making his reading of Asia understandable to Americans through these recognizable tropes of history, he commended those leaders to American elites. This last was especially important, since American policymakers often viewed Third World politicians, especially those who emphasized political democracy and land reform, as hardened communists even when they were not.[26] It must be acknowledged nonetheless that as much as Magsaysay may have been America's man, he was committed to enacting certain political and economic reforms that in other national contexts had invariably made Washington very nervous. Lansdale's public relations success here was to transform the foreign into the familiar.

Such efforts fit into a long tradition within American history. Since the time of the Puritans, Americans have invoked a history of moralistic absolutes as a way to teach, reprimand, or censure a particular audience. Another example of Lansdale's method appears in a speech to his fellow military officers in 1959, appropriately titled "Fundamentals for Americans," on the goals that Americans should strive for and the ideals they should take with them when they went to serve in a foreign country. He began by noting that at the end of World War II an American colonel and his Filipino assistant had access to all the money in the Philippine treasury but that instead of taking it, they "turned all of it over to the U.S. Army, to be restored to the Philippine National Bank. The Filipino told me later: 'There we were. All alone with millions of dollars worth of money. And, doggonit, that colonel made me an honest man.'" Lansdale continued this homily by telling his audience, "we all get the feeling that this is *right*—*right* not only in the sense of what the world expects from Americans—but *right* within the spirit of our own American heritage, of what we expect from ourselves." And then, with one of his classic rhetorical flourishes, Lansdale launched into a lecture on the nature of the American Revolution, characterizing it as "enduring ideology, not corn" (that is, not corny).[27]

Each of Lansdale's history lessons emphasized the commonalities between Americans and Asians. In a lecture to students at Tufts University in 1968, he proclaimed: "Those who have participated in our own [New England] town meetings would find much that is familiar in the way Vietnamese villagers manage their own affairs." He continued the comparison by emphasizing that the Vietnamese man in the street "would have handled himself well on our western frontier," thereby conflating attractive visions of Vietnamese town-hall democracy and a pioneer spirit.[28] In 1968, Lansdale resorted to instances of social turmoil from the American past to make the Tet offensive understandable to his audience and perhaps to himself as well: "It was a gangster epic on a colossal scale."[29] To Ellsworth Bunker, the American ambassador to South Vietnam, Lansdale explained the meaning of Tet by making an allusion to Shays' Rebellion and Washington's response to that challenge to democracy in the eighteenth century.[30] In both cases, though, the implications of describing the Tet offensive as a mob action legitimized the American side of the battle by transforming the event into a "Cops and Robbers" narrative. One month after the Tet Offensive, Lansdale wrote a detailed memorandum to the U.S. ambassador assessing its impact. It is a bleak analysis, and one sees Lansdale's inability to counter the popularity of the Vietcong. He was struck, though, by the U.S. recapture of the city of Hue. He believed that this victory, and the raising of the South Vietnamese flag above the Citadel in the city, could become South Vietnam's "'Remember the Alamo', 'Remember the Maine', 'Remember Pearl Harbor.'" Later he argued that the slogan "Remember Hue" could be used in songs, postal cancellation marks, and used by President Thieu on all occasions.[31]

A particularly revealing example of Lansdale's efforts to remake Asia into America appears in a memo he wrote to John D. Rockefeller about his desire to set up an annual award in honor of Ramon Magsaysay after the Philippine president's death in 1957: "It is useful to peer behind the screen labeled 'the inscrutable Orient' or 'the mysterious East' and see the Asian man as Magsaysay saw him. Oddly enough, this is the same man whom Jefferson saw and wrote about in our Constitution. He is the same man who was Lincoln's friend. Magsaysay saw his fellow man as an individual endowed by his Creator 'with certain unalienable rights.' . . . His decision to run for President in 1953 was based upon the American revolutionary doctrine of changing the government when it 'became destructive of these ends.' "[32] (One wonders if Jefferson or Lincoln, let alone Ho Chi Minh, would have worked with a foreigner and CIA agent, as Magsaysay and Diem did, one who provided large amounts of money for a presidential election or a new campaign to defeat his country's adversaries.) As this passage shows, history often became a remedial tool for Lansdale to remind Americans of a forgotten heritage. To him, the perils of forgetting American history were as severe as the dangers of subscribing to communist tenets. The fact that his understanding of American history was at best naive and at worst wrong is beside the point; the rhetorical impact of his historical analogies often had the intended effect. It is of interest that immediately after Magsaysay's death the CIA instructed the officer who replaced Lansdale in the Philippines to "find another Magsaysay."[33]

Particularly in the Philippines, Lansdale's efforts built upon the half-century of American imperialism that preceded him. An American-based school system set up for Filipinos had, for instance, punished schoolchildren who spoke Tagalog; English was the only language allowed in the classroom.[34] Tapping into this history, Lansdale described the system as yet another example of U.S. efforts to improve the lives of the average Filipino, especially in comparison to Spanish rule. Additionally, he stressed that the Philippines would someday be an independent country; that is, it would be remade into a young America. But to remake the Philippines effectively after the devastation of World War II, Lansdale needed one individual to turn his histories into concrete actions. He found the perfect protégé in Ramon Magsaysay who eventually became president of the Philippines with the resolute help and outright manipulation of Lansdale. Lansdale's major concern was to promote Magsaysay in both the Philippines and the United States as a true Filipino nationalist, and from all American accounts, at least, Magsaysay embraced this project as well. He enjoyed telling people that "when I was a boy, I always remembered the way I saw our American pioneers of this country."[35] Other Americans noted Magsaysay's love of American history and capitalized on this phenomenon with enthusiasm. Admiral Felix Stump, for one, recalled:

> Well, President Magsaysay always was friendly toward the United States. He was a patriotic Filipino, no doubt about it. But I was surprised, after he had been President for some time, to go into that great, big room there in Malacanang, which is the Presidential Palace in Manila, and see hanging up around the walls paintings of American Governors-General, like Taft and General Wood. . . . It was most impressive to the senior military officers of SEATO when we had a SEATO meeting during the Magsaysay regime to go in there and see the pic-

tures of Americans hanging up around this beautiful large reception room, the
biggest room, in the Malacanang.[36]

Such recollections could be something of a double-edged sword, allowing
President Magsaysay the Filipino nationalist to be seen as Magsaysay the
American puppet.

Lansdale enhanced the value of Magsaysay's reputed fascination with
Americana by combining a reformer agenda with his histories; a "usable
past" was, after all, only as good as its effect in motivating people into action.
The reformer in Lansdale was never more obvious than when he spoke of
how he and the newly elected president worked together. At times his reformist zeal gave way to an explicitly imperialist view of the structure of their
relationship: "Each night we sat up late discussing the current situation.
Magsaysay would air his views. Afterwards, I would sort them out aloud for
him while underscoring the principles or strategy or tactics involved. It
helped him select or discard courses of action."[37] More important than the
self-aggrandizement exhibited by Lansdale here, however, is the suggestion
that he imported his American histories as a way to manage present-day
Philippine politics. Further, the tutorial relationship depicted was particularly attractive to American policymakers and the general public as well.
Even *Time* magazine commented, when describing the elections in the Philippines, "It was soon no secret that Ramon Magsaysay was America's boy.
For a time, U.S. Colonel Edward Lansdale of the U.S. Air Force took a desk
in Magsaysay's Defense Office, became virtually his mentor and publicity
man." But to prevent *Time*'s readers from drawing the inappropriate conclusion that Americans might be controlling the candidate, the article added
this caveat: "U.S. officials were worried by Magsaysay's open and unabashed
exploitation of the friendship, but not Magsaysay."[38]

Lansdale's views were deeply steeped in the history of America's civilizing
mission among the Filipino people. The long-standing ties between the
United States and the Philippines date from 1898; the history of the Spanish-
American War and the colonization of the country that followed was a history that all were aware of. In his 1940s journal entries, Lansdale wrote of
his intense hatred toward the Japanese alongside his high regard for Filipinos; his respect for those who had fought with the Americans during World
War II to free the Philippines from Japanese control was deep and profound.
When he described those who were captured by the Japanese, the narrative
merged a dramatic storytelling style with the quintessential American touchstone: "Many of the Filipinos were tortured . . . until they were just broken
lumps of bleeding flesh. Still most of them managed to gasp out 'God Bless

America' just as they died. I wonder if Irving Berlin ever knew that his corny tune was given so much dignity by these martyrs."[39] Whether or not this actually happened, the story reveals that even while extolling the courage of another people, Lansdale could not envision a culture independent from America, for to be "American" was by definition the highest attribute to which a culture could aspire. In Lansdale's view, then, the people of Southeast Asia only wanted what Americans could selflessly provide—and he was to be the major conduit.

Lansdale's immense successes in the Philippines can be measured by the extent to which Magsaysay and his fellow officials mouthed Americanisms back to him, and with an earnestness that perhaps surprised even Lansdale. In his memoirs, Lansdale recounted a conversation with Ramon Magsaysay's brother, Jesus Magsaysay, as they walked toward the Lincoln Memorial. Jesus said to Lansdale: "I never knew before why Americans helped other people. Now, I think I understand. You are too shy to tell us. What you really mean to do—want to do—is to share something of your spirit with others."[40] No doubt those sentiments were exactly what Lansdale hoped for (the "shyness" notwithstanding), as Jesus probably knew quite well.

It is important to keep in mind that Lansdale did far more than just preach, since as a CIA agent he engineered numerous covert operations to defeat nationalist or communist movements throughout the Cold War. Yet his vision of history was so idealized that it enabled him to intervene in the affairs of other countries for reasons he liked to describe as simple altruism. This rhetoric also allowed him to proclaim American goodwill even during the height of the Vietnam War, when civilians were dying by the hundreds every week. He was, then, simply echoing Woodrow Wilson, justifying intervention in another country with an ideological single-mindedness that assumed its own high moral principles. As the historian Walter LaFeber has argued, Woodrow Wilson "eloquently clothed the bleak skeleton of U.S. self-interest in the attractive garb of idealism."[41] Comfortably situated within the history of American liberal internationalism, with Wilson as the intellectual godfather of its ideas, Edward Lansdale can be seen as both the eager recipient of that heritage and a man who sought to implement Wilson's ideas throughout the world.

Lansdale's uses of history had their limitations, however, and no one appreciated this better than his other Asian "student," Ngo Dinh Diem. As he had done in the Philippines, Lansdale took his histories with him to Vietnam in the 1950s and mobilized them in the effort to defeat communism. But this approach, which had worked well in the Philippines, failed in Vietnam, a country which had a powerful tradition of resisting the imposition of foreign systems, including other people's histories. In short, Lansdale had no malleable history to tap into in Vietnam when he tried to impart the rhetoric of democracy to a people who, unlike the Filipinos, knew little about America or its ideals.

Lansdale's actions in Vietnam disclose the cultural insensitivity of a man who consistently believed that he knew the "Asian mind" and demonstrate his intellectual closeness to the colonial mentality he continually spoke out against. His pushing American analogies upon Diem in the face of repeated failures reveals his attempt to erase Vietnamese history and replace it with decontextualized myths of the American past. When Diem continued to resist these efforts, Lansdale only tried harder to defeat communism by implanting Americanisms among the people and leaders of South Vietnam. For instance, in Diem's 1954 "Report on the First 100 days" of his presidency, the language—indeed, the very typewriter upon which this document was written—seems to have come from none other than Lansdale. Evoking President Franklin Roosevelt, Diem proclaimed: "I pledge myself personally to deal with the needs and just demands of our people." He also used such stock American political phrases and FDR-isms as the imperative to confront "fear" and the need for "progress." Elsewhere, Lansdale had Diem mouth words that eerily presaged John F. Kennedy's tone and memory: "A thousand days from now, we want a nation of free men," and "Our greatest national asset is our *youth*." Lansdale encouraged Diem to declare his support for such classic liberal principles as increasing government spending on education and establishing a ministry responsible for veteran affairs. The speech ended with a dramatic call to arms: "But the most important aspect of Communism is that Communism is ANTI-GOD . . . WITH HEAVEN'S WILL VICTORY IS OURS."[42] Both the style of delivery and the political platforms advocated by Diem can be read as Lansdale's idea of what a Vietnamese Great Society should be.

Lansdale's pen also seems to have edited the Vietnamese constitution, fixing the grammar, tightening the language, and generally making it into a document Americans might appreciate.[43] He even brought to South Vietnam from the Philippines a lawyer friend who had a background in constitutional history to help construct this document.[44] The problem here, of course, becomes one of legitimacy—with the Diem administration being appropriated by American ideals—and of grafting two disparate political philosophies upon one constitution. The Vietnamese as a people and as a nation were being rhetorically displaced by Lansdale's efforts and recreated as something more pleasing to American interests. Both Diem's speech and the new constitution are symptomatic of a profound intellectual disjuncture: Lansdale had Diem invoking the protocols of American history to make the case for what a modern Vietnam should become. One can only imagine what the Vietnamese intelligentsia who despised Diem thought of this, let alone the peasants whose relationship with Diem did not involve written proclamations.

Undeterred, Lansdale later wrote about Diem's response to these history lessons: "What Viet Nam needed in early 1956 was a George Washington, a leader above partisan politics who could guide the founding of the free political institutions so necessary to the survival of South Viet Nam. Diem needed to be George Washington. . . . I told him as much, urging him to so comport himself and so handle Viet Nam's affairs that he could earn the title of 'father of his country.' (I must have held this measurement up to Diem too much, because one day he burst out, 'stop calling me papa!')"[45] This account illustrates Lansdale's attempt to erase Vietnam's past, to begin the country again from a "year zero"—or perhaps 1776—with an American politics. Diem's response, if the narrative is accurate, suggests his recognition of the inevitable futility of attempting to graft American history onto Vietnam.

Lansdale's use of the past was highly ahistorical and decontextualized; he disregarded the profound differences that separated the American experience from that of the people of Southeast Asia. Further, his analogies became literally absurd when he tried to explain to Diem that Americans and Vietnamese were quite similar: "I found myself countering 'personalism' with reminders of the Vietnamese people's adherence to Confucian precepts. . . . I commented that Thomas Jefferson had read some Confucian principles shortly before he had written the American 'Declaration of Independence' and that these principles seemed to have strengthened his views of the nature of man as an individual."[46] But the ideology of personalism, which was central to Diem's political philosophy and subscribed to by Diem and his brother Nhu with a ferocious tenacity, fused the external hierarchy and authority of the Catholic Church with the embodied State (in the shape of Diem) and emphasized the direct infusion of both into the sphere of the individual's daily life. Personalism was, as the historian Edward Miller has pointed out, Diem and Nhu's "third solution," situated between the politics of communism and liberal capitalism.[47] Lansdale, too, sought a "third solution," but his involved creating a politics between colonialism and communism—that is, championing liberal capitalism. In the passage quoted above, Lansdale attempted to undercut the anticapitalist doctrine of personalism by invoking the older precepts of Vietnamese history and Confucianism, working to show a common origin for American and Vietnamese constitutional ideals. He could do so only by rereading Jeffersonian ideas as a new form of Confucianism. He thus distorted both American and Confucian principles of individualism in the attempt to graft American ideals onto Vietnamese history.

In attempting to intervene in this fashion, Lansdale was inadvertently confronting a tradition within Vietnam that revered history and all its applications. For many Vietnamese people, "history" was a defining feature used to locate themselves in relation to their families, their villages, and their definitions of Vietnam as a country. The forms of Vietnamese spirituality intertwined with a reverence for the past were different from the reformist religiosity and Puritan language favored by Lansdale. Alexander Woodside, a historian of Vietnam, has viewed this aspect of Vietnamese history as central to an understanding of the dynamic of the modern Vietnamese revolution. He argues that history provides one of the tools through which the Vietnamese sought to create new forms of "organized communities" to combat their country's enemies.[48] His insights build upon those of the most noted of scholars of Vietnam, Paul Mus, who argued that "the Vietnamese consider the creation of new communities not as political acts but as spiritual ones."[49] These descriptions of Vietnamese politics can be viewed as highly romantic but powerfully unifying national visions.

Among examples of the Vietnamese use of their own history (not Lansdale's) as a motivational tool is Ho Chi Minh's "Letter from Abroad," written in 1941 to his fellow Vietnamese. Adopting the same uses of history that Lansdale favored—mixing pedagogy with political exhortation—he wrote:

> Since the French were defeated by the Germans, their forces have been completely disintegrated. However, with regard to our people, they continue to plunder us pitilessly, suck all our blood, and carry out a barbarous policy of all-out terrorism and massacre. . . . Some hundreds of years ago, when our country was endangered by the Mongolian invasion, our elders under the Tran dynasty rose up indignantly and called on their sons and daughters throughout the country to rise as one in order to kill the enemy. . . . The elders and prominent personalities of our country should follow the example set by our forefathers in the glorious task of national salvation. . . . Let us unite together! As one mind and strength we shall overthrow the Japanese and French.[50]

Here, Ho the communist fused his political goals with his nationalist sentiments. In the end he was successful—or, more accurately, his uses of history eventually attained a more widespread response than Lansdale's.

An even starker example of the uses of history within Vietnam is provided by Vo Nguyen Giap, the communist general credited with defeating both the French and the Americans. Fifteen years after the unification of Vietnam, he told the American journalist Stanley Karnow, "Marxism also seemed to me to coincide with the ideals of our ancient society, when the emperor and his subjects lived in harmony. It was a utopian dream."[51] Vietnam was and continues to be a country whose history is steeped in wars against foreign occupiers. North Vietnamese Prime Minister Pham van Dong, for instance, enjoyed telling Western journalists that "our history is a history of struggle."[52] Giap's and Ho's "usable pasts," fusing the discrete ideologies of Marxism and Confucianism with the ideals of nationalism, thus proved far more durable than Lansdale's imported versions of Tom Paine and John Adams. The fact that the American forces had overwhelming firepower resulted only in the greater destruction of Vietnam. Giap's forces should not be underestimated either, since by the end of the war Vietnam had the fourth largest army in the world. A key element in Giap's success, however, was his call for national unification, which appealed to a popular belief deeply rooted in the version of Vietnam's past that he offered. Although, in the end, the military options of both sides may have determined the outcome, one cannot underestimate the more persuasive and influential uses of history and propaganda employed by the communists.

One of the reasons Vietnamese communists triumphed over Lansdale and the Americans, then, is that they placed a greater emphasis on what their own intellectual forebears had written. In particular, such early nationalists as Phan Chu Trinh and Phan Boi Chau were central to this process. They had sought to construct a new vision of Vietnamese nationhood in the late nineteenth and early twentieth centuries, and the communists eagerly adapted their writings to later political struggles.[53] Although they often espoused very different liberation tactics (Chau believed in revolutionary monarchism; Trinh was an antimonarchical democrat), both greatly influenced the thought of Ho Chi Minh.[54] It is ironic that the communists later embraced many of their prescriptions, given that both Trinh and Chau cited American history in suggesting ways to triumph over colonialism. Chau's political tract "Idolizing Beautiful Personages" glorified George Washington, though his history of America was somewhat distorted; one episode involved Washington's covert tactics in becoming a soldier in the British army so that he could learn their methods and later defeat them. Trinh's epic poem on American and European history, "Rare Encounters with Beautiful Personages," employed highly romanticized literary conventions along with fanciful history to persuade his countrymen to rebel against the French:

In the past, when the American people first flocked together, they initiated liberty here [Philadelphia], in group discussions. Heroes were leaving their impress on the rivers and mountains of their homeland, it was truly the year 1774. . . . [F]reedom was increasingly engraved upon the hearts of the people. . . . Old mothers forgot their hardships, and shedding tears, they urged their sons to charge directly onto the battlefield. . . . Washington had to endure a period of bitterness, remnants of his soldiers formed an army and deployed themselves at Erie, the weather was brutally cold. . . . Rolling up his flags, and holding his mandarin's badge of office in his mouth, Washington cut through the Delaware River and destroyed the English in a frightful battle. From that point on his military prestige echoed like thunder on all four sides.[55]

Had Lansdale been aware of these writers, he might have had more success, for although they used the same stock images of America, they did so for very different purposes. Instead of trying to meld his histories into local tradition, Lansdale tried to superimpose his version upon a Vietnamese government whose claim to history, let alone legitimacy in the eyes of its citizens, was extraordinarily shallow. Again, Alexander Woodside's insights are worth noting: "Trinh was in effect serving as a cultural broker, attempting to introduce the thought and action of Western revolutions to Vietnam in ways that the Vietnamese upper classes could comprehend."[56]

It is true that Lansdale did imitate one intellectual tradition used by Vietnamese intellectuals such as Phan Boi Chau: he too sought new ways of making history into a usable product that might provide answers to the problem of colonialism. His efforts in Vietnam were distorted because his knowledge of Vietnamese history was as ideologically shaped as was his version of American history. Even when he cited key events in Vietnamese history, he always sought to assimilate them into his morally uplifting narratives of democracy. He used everything that he learned to emphasize the virtue of America and viewed anything that deviated as needing to be remolded accordingly. In contrast, these Vietnamese intellectuals sought new ways to create a modern, unified nation from its ancient roots, not the creation and sustenance of a new state dependent upon the dollars and desires of another country.

Ho Chi Minh understood this point all too well. When he declared Vietnam independent from the French in 1945, he invoked history, and American history at that, to describe the triumph over colonialism and to initiate a communist state. He began by proclaiming to all Vietnamese:

All men are created equal; they are endowed by their Creator with certain unalienable Rights; among these are Life, Liberty and the pursuit of Happiness.
This immortal statement was made in the Declaration of Independence of

the United States of America in 1776. In a broader sense, this means: All the peoples on the earth are equal from birth, all the peoples have a right to live, to be happy and free.[57]

Eyewitnesses to this event have commented that these words resonated in Hanoi as surely as they had in eighteenth-century Philadelphia. Given that American officers were sharing the dais with him, Ho was clearly courting American support at the time, yet these words spoke to a universal dream of human rights, one that seemed to transcend capitalism or communism. Universalism may also account for Ho's decision to use these words as he announced the creation of the Democratic Republic of Vietnam. Ho Chi Minh and his fellow communists, ruthless at eliminating other political groups and closing off alternative paths of liberation from French colonialism, had acquired an effective mantle of history which they made use of to achieve their goals. And the Vietnamese found other ways of placing themselves in this "usable past." Consider the North Vietnamese artist Quach Phong: "The soldiers would ask me to draw their portraits in case they died. It was a kind of historical evidence of them. This way they thought they would have a tiny part of history."[58]

Until 1968, Lansdale remained convinced that if the United States stopped the mass killing of the Vietnamese and concentrated on the more important but less glamorous task of "nation building," the Americans could triumph in Vietnam. He remained convinced that if the Vietnamese could only be drawn into America's "usable past," success would be theirs, and America's as well. Yet even Lansdale, the liberal reformer and enthusiastic exporter of Americana, knew by then that U.S. policy was fatally flawed. And by 1972 he was reduced to writing, "Think of what would have happened in Vietnam if the practical ideas from our own Revolution had been applied there—by our side, not the enemy's."[59] It was only a matter of time before South Vietnam collapsed under the weight of its illegitimacy, corruption, and authoritarian practices. The uses of American history did not play a terribly important role at this moment. In a draft of an introduction he later wrote for a collection of essays on the Vietnam War, Lansdale maintained that America's failure stemmed from a lack of passionate commitment: "Maybe we forgot to get mad in Vietnam. . . . TJ [Thomas Jefferson] would have hated them [Vietnamese Communists].[60]

Of course, Lansdale was by no means alone in his efforts to direct Diem according to American edicts; other Americans acted in a similar fashion. Lansdale's immediate superior, General John O'Daniel, commander of the U.S. Military Assistance Advisory Group, Vietnam (MAAG), had daily access to Diem during 1954–56. His attitude was even more imperial than Lansdale's, as his eulogy for Diem in 1963 made clear: "I think of the many times that I handed Diem . . . an idea of mine on a piece of scratch paper, without any heading or signature and how a week or two later the idea appeared as his own in his own written orders and in the Vietnamese language."[61]

O'Daniel and Lansdale never pondered what effect American military and economic aid might have on Diem's claims to legitimacy or the fallout from using American dollars to force Diem to reconsider a particular question. Lansdale could even tell a Harvard audience in 1957 that Diem was a man to be supported because he had once said (to a group of Americans), "The most precious thing that Vietnam received from the United States was the phrase: Give me Liberty or give me Death.'"[62] It appears that Diem had learned how to manipulate his American friends for his own necessary purposes. With each passing year, however, the relationship between Diem and the Americans deteriorated. Each American ambassador insisted that Diem must reform all facets of South Vietnamese society if American aid were to continue. When Diem did not comply, their inducements turned to threats, and he was eventually overthrown in an American-sanctioned coup in 1963.

In attempts to counter this unraveling of diplomatic ties to Vietnam, Lansdale enlarged his historical repertoire. He began to use the history of World War II, the "good war," with its clearly defined enemies and its clearly understood message of why Allies were involved, writing to Diem in 1961, "Your country needs you to rouse spirits right now, the way Winston Churchill did for Britain at a dark hour." He went on to discuss ways that Diem could strengthen his government, including instituting "two strong political parties."[63] Leaving aside Diem's relationship to democracy, World War II was seen quite differently by the Vietnamese than it was by Filipinos. Although Filipino collaboration with the Japanese, especially by the landowning classes, had been extensive—beginning with the first postwar Philippine president, Manuel Roxas (installed by General Douglas MacArthur)— many Filipinos had fought with the Americans in their united efforts to defeat the Japanese. In contrast, the only Vietnamese who might have responded to Lansdale's idealization of World War II and Churchillian imagery were two political organizations that both Diem and Lansdale were deeply committed to defeating: the communists and the Cao Dai sect. It was, after all, the Vietminh who had worked with the American OSS to recover American pilots downed in China and in Indochina; perhaps Lansdale knew that the OSS had rewarded Ho's efforts by making him OSS Agent 19, code-named "Lucius"[64] And the Cao Dai sect had sought to place Churchill in its pantheon of saints upon his death—along with Charlie Chaplin, Victor Hugo, and Joan of Arc.[65]

The overwhelming problem for Lansdale was that Diem was not in the least interested in creating a modern, democratic political system. Notwithstanding his opposition to the former emperor, Bao Dai, Diem sought to recreate the lineage of the Nguyen dynasty, which had been disrupted by the French and by the chaos at end of World War II. When Neil Sheehan drily noted that Diem's "one concession to modernity would be to call himself a president," he summed up the problem succinctly.[66] Even more conservative journalists found Diem wanting—the influential columnist Joseph Alsop, for instance, argued that Diem was "wholly out of contact with reality"[67]—but not Lansdale. Both personal loyalty to Diem and sheer ideological conviction frequently led him to levels of hyperbole that suggest he too was "out of contact with reality." Before a group of Yale students in 1964, he exhorted his audience to take part in Cold War battles throughout the world. Action, not reflection, was his message here, and the dangers of communism became his motivational tool in emphasizing the need for American commitment: "The time right now is 0400 hours, tomorrow morning. Today is over there [in Vietnam]. . . . If brave and dedicated people keep on buying an opportune tomorrow, and yet another tomorrow, and still more tomorrow's tomorrows then they are buying the potentially most priceless commodity of all—*time*—time in which the future of Vietnam will be decided."[68]

Despite Lansdale's overwrought language, his earnestness shines through in this speech. His real belief in his declarations always generated new supporters for him and his Cold War cause, often leading to something akin to a fan club. Perhaps the most extraordinary example was their belief that only Lansdale could help forestall the overthrow of Diem in 1963. One of his protégés, Rufus Phillips, argued in the summer of 1963 that Lansdale was the only man who could save Vietnam. In a telegram to the State Department he portrayed his mentor in quasi-superhuman terms:

Subject: Recommendation for Immediate U.S. Action: . . . I specifically recommend that an urgent request be made for the immediate temporary assignment here of General Lansdale, to serve as an official personal advisor to President Diem. . . . [T]here is no other American, regardless of position or rank, who can evoke the same response from the President or in whom he has any comparable degree of confidence. I can also attest that there is no other single American . . . who enjoys the same degree of confidence and respect from almost all Vietnamese officials, as well as members of the political opposition. . . . [O]nly General Lansdale's presence will give us [a] reasonable chance at this point of advancing U.S. interests here. . . . Our attempts to influence the situation through normal channels seem unsuccessful. General Lansdale, as many of us can attest, repeatedly demonstrated his ability to cause President Diem to act in accordance with high U.S. policy, when all other appeals, whether official U.S., or those of his family, were unavailing. . . . I most emphatically recommend the immediate assignment here of General Lansdale.[69]

The next day Phillips sent a copy of this telegram to Lansdale and added: "I realize this is unsolicited by you and you may not approve, but it is the only thing I can think of to get us out of the mess we are now in." Phillips would soon make the same recommendation directly to President Kennedy. Yet for every official who wanted to unleash Lansdale, there was another who felt certain that containing him was necessary. These partisans tended to cancel each other out, and Lansdale remained without power. More than thirty years later, though, Phillips's heartfelt recollections of this period and other personal accounts retained an overarching thesis: "We believe that if U.S. decision makers had sought and followed the advice of experts like General Lansdale . . . the massive introduction of U.S. combat troops, beginning in 1965, might never have taken place."[70] Here again one sees Lansdale the individual endowed with superhuman qualities, since the idea that one and only one man could have prevented the horrors of the war and the eventual failure of the United States remains fantastic.

Not only Americans but Vietnamese engaged in this hero-making process. Tranh Van Dinh wrote to Lansdale in December 1963 to let him know that "my last meeting with President Ngo Dinh Diem was less than 24 hours before he was assassinated. During the meeting he was talking about you. He did not believe that you were retired, having as you know, the highest esteem and appreciation of your abilities."[71] Lansdale later told an interviewer that in Diem's last conversation with U.S. Ambassador Henry Cabot Lodge, he had pleaded, "Please get Ed Lansdale back." Lansdale went on to intimate, none too subtly, that because Lodge did not acquiesce to Diem's wishes, America was doomed to lose in Vietnam.[72]

Lansdale's assuredness and his enthusiasm for using history to wage an ideological campaign made him an influential figure among the broad spectrum of American policymakers and journalists. For instance, I. F. Stone, the noted left-wing iconoclast, wrote to him: "We disagree I am sure very deeply but I recognize the idealist in you, and I am sure I could learn a great deal in talking with you." And the noted chronicler of presidents Theodore White began a letter, "Dear Ed Lansdale (I hope you will let me call you 'Ed')" and went on to beg forgiveness for having earlier questioned his authority on the history of communism and the nature of "people's war" in Asia.[73] Both journalists were responding to his supposed influence in Washington and were eager to cultivate his friendship.

ALTHOUGH LANSDALE continued to have his supporters—one columnist referred to him in 1965 as the "tweedy, pipe-smoking man with a kitbagful of bombshell ideas"[74]—by the early 1970s his disciples had become increasingly rare. When they sought Lansdale's advice, he could think of no better option than to support Nixon's "Vietnamization" policy. This policy was designed to send the South Vietnamese even more American aid, minus American troops, yet to increase the bombing of North Vietnam that made large sections of it resemble a moonscape. That "Vietnamization" had its roots in Lansdale's efforts from the 1950s points to one more cruel irony generated by this war.

What Lansdale never understood was that his benevolent view of nation building—a program that he initiated and that went to the heart of America's intervention in Vietnam—was the underside of the "search and destroy" missions that he later decried. By the 1960s his "usable past" was less than useless; it had become simply the basis for a massive war by America. Though Lansdale remained blind to this outcome, the sociologist C. Wright Mills explored the use of such an ideological apparatus to characterize other peoples. In an essay written at the same time that Lansdale was managing Vietnam's revolution from the Pentagon, Mills declared: "Every man, to be sure, *observes* nature, social events, and his own self: but he does not, he has never, observed most of what he takes to be fact, about nature, society, or self. Every man *interprets* what he observes—as well as much that he has not observed: but his terms of interpretation are not his own; he has not personally formulated or even tested them. Every man talks about observations and interpretations to others: but the terms of his *reports* are much more likely than not the phrases and images of other people which he has taken over as his own."[75] Lansdale never understood the limits to a "usable past," let alone its potentially destructive consequences; as a result, he never appreciated the variety of ways through which largely peasant societies and their histories could be interpreted. To him, the precepts supplied by American history were stable, not propositions requiring constant revision when applied to new contexts. This obliviousness, shared by a host of other Americans, helps to explain why the American commitment to Vietnam had grown from a few advisers when Lansdale first arrived in 1954 to over half a million soldiers in 1968, when he left the country for the last time.

Perhaps it is only fitting, then, that Lansdale the historian ended by re-placing history as the source of future truth with a kind of soothsaying. So discouraged did he become about the absence of an American victory in Vietnam that the drafts for his memoirs include language that is quite liter-ally apocalyptic, with the "fall" of Vietnam foretelling the end of the world: "We, the people, are in the midst of a long, long war. It may be the longest war in the history of mankind. It may even be the last war that men ever wage on our earth, since visionaries have told us through the centuries that we would reach such a time of universal conflict and that it would have a final, awesome spasm of pain and travail called Armageddon, after which there would be eons of peace."[76] He also cited the words of fortunetellers he had known in Vietnam as hard evidence that history might come to an end in the year 2000 A.D.; in doing so, he dramatized the dangers of history when, colliding with superstition and myth, it becomes history as revelation. Thus, the man who used fortunetellers' stories as a way to fathom and then manipulate the Asian mind became the historical prisoner of those same stories.

Major General Edward Lansdale, retirement photo, 1963. *USAF*

"Hero of the Week" promotional campaign from Lansdale's early career as an advertiser, with Lansdale himself pictured on the far left. The ad champions the virtues of patriotism, bravery, and consumption—all of which Lansdale would later emphasize in his Cold War endeavors. *Lansdale Papers, Hoover Institution*

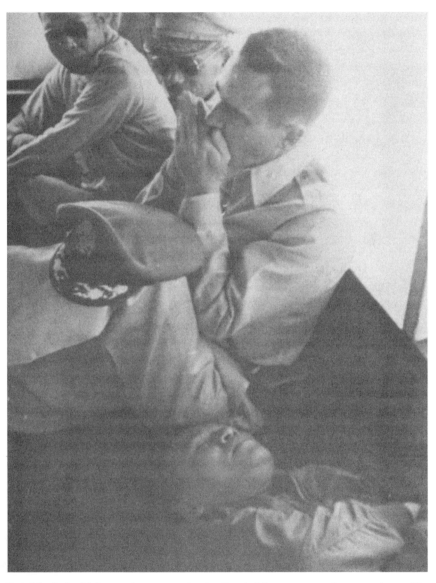

Lansdale playing his harmonica next to a sleeping Ramón Magsaysay, 1952, in a scene that testifies to the intimacy of their friendship. Lansdale reported to the CIA at the time: "He [Magsaysay] wants to be associated more closely with Americans, for political as well as personal reasons, and I believe that he is wise in this judgment of the reactions of Filipinos." *Lansdale Papers, Hoover Institution*

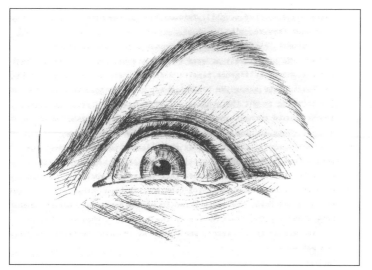

The "Eye" leaflet used by Lansdale as a counter-insurgency tool in the Philippines. Philippine Army troops posted these drawings in villages suspected of harboring rebel Huks to suggest the omnipresent government surveillance. *Rand Corporation*

Photograph taken by Lansdale while accompanying a Philippine military patrol in the early 1950s. For Lansdale, the spread of capitalist culture, symbolized by the Coca-Cola sign in the center of this provincial Filipino village, was no less important than military operations in the promotion of American democracy. *Lansdale Papers, Hoover Institution*

Lansdale as tourist at Angkor Wat in the 1960s. Cambodian Prince Norodom Sihanouk believed that Lansdale's leisure activities were simply a cover for his efforts to organize a coup against Sihanouk's government, as detailed in his memoir, *My War with the CIA*. *Lansdale Papers, Hoover Institution*

Landing supplies (rice & carrots) from the
Lekoku-Maru at Funakura, Nakano-shima for
malnutrition cases. Suwanose in distance.
Taught these fishermen to sing "Roll Me Over"
when they rowed ashore.

Kids meeting us at Funakura. Taught them
that Americans said "hello" by saying
"my papa, Major Lansdale" when any
Americans visited the island in the future.

Images from Lansdale's photographic journal during his post–World War II mission to Ryukyu Islands, an archipelago stretching between Japan and Taiwan. His handwritten notes reveal an ethnographic turn of mind mixed with frat boy humor. *Lansdale Papers, Hoover Institution*

This formerly classified photograph from the 1960s shows a U.S. official with a Vietnamese astrologer. Lansdale wrote numerous memos to his superiors about the uses of astrology, convinced that it provided helpful insights into local perspectives and beliefs. *Lansdale Papers, Hoover Institution*

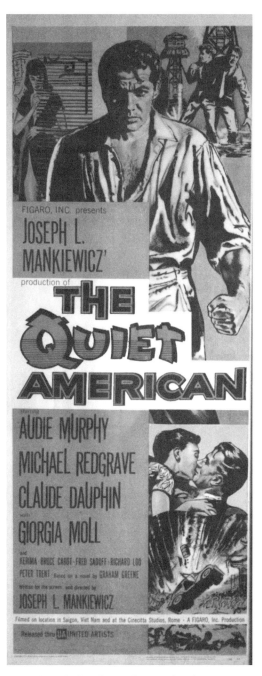

Poster from the first film production of Graham Greene's
novel *The Quiet American*, 1956.

Indicative of how images of the "Orient" were conflated when Hollywood looked to the East, this 1963 movie poster for *The Ugly American* juxtaposes Thai and Chinese architecture while depicting student rebels wearing Japanese bandanas.

In 1986, a year before his death, Lansdale met with a group of individuals intent on waging the Cold War in Latin America. Left to right: Andy Messig Jr., Executive Director, National Defense Council; Lansdale; Medardo Justinano; Maj. Gen. John Singlaub, U.S. Army (Ret.); Lt. Col. Oliver North, USMC (Ret.). North, a controversial figure in the Iran-Contra scandal of the mid-1980s, described himself as "Lansdalian" and, according to the *Washington Post*, "was already Lansdale-ized when he reached the NSC." *Lansdale Papers, Maxwell Air Force Base*

Flyer distributed by a group of Vietnam veterans, known as "Ed Heads," who believed that if American authorities had only listened to Lansdale, the U.S. would have triumphed in Vietnam.

VISIONARY VIETNAM VETERANS

presenting

The Edward Geary Lansdale Fan Club

Edward G. Lansdale was the first, and perhaps most relevant, American advisor to the people of South Vietnam.

Lansdale dedicated his life and his work during the 1950's to help sow the seeds of democracy in Southeast Asia: first in the Philippines, then in the infant republic of South Vietnam. Hated by some, highly respected by others, at times labeled as "The Quiet American" and "The Ugly American", and recently called one of the ten greatest spies in history; all spell one thing: controversy. The work of this controversial person must now be examined for greater clarity and relevance in the continuing effort to transplant democratic institutions in the East. For Lansdale, the formula for success was to give as freely of our Nation's democratic ideas and values as of our economic aid and military assistance.

We can only keep our freedom strong by sticking to the great beliefs and principles that are our heritage.

— E.G. Lansdale

For more information, contact
The Visionary Vietnam Veterans
Veterans War Memorial Bldg., Room 101
San Francisco, California 94102

Photograph taken near Dealey Plaza in Dallas on November 22, 1963, allegedly showing Lansdale (back to camera) passing a group of hobos suspected of involvement in the assassination of President Kennedy. In the film *JFK* Oliver Stone recreated the same scene, with Lansdale thinly disguised as General "Y," orchestrating the Kennedy assassination. *National Archives*

5

Gazing at the Third World

The people stared at us everywhere, and we stared at them. We generally made them feel rather small, too, before we got done with them, because we bore down on them with America's greatness until we crushed them.

—Mark Twain, *The Innocents Abroad* (1869)

IN A 1957 episode of the popular television program *See It Now*, opera singer Marian Anderson was featured on a U.S. government-sponsored goodwill tour of Vietnam.[1] The ostensible purpose of this TV segment, hosted by America's premier journalist, Edward R. Murrow, was to highlight the ways in which the United States was promoting civil and human rights around the world. It was also intended to demonstrate U.S. concern for the impoverished nations, in stark contrast to America's communist adversaries with their economic and political "iron curtains." Yet all did not go as planned. Anderson was greeted in Saigon with flowers and serenaded by a group of schoolchildren with the American folksong "Getting to Know You." As they sang, the camera cut to the children's feet showing them valiantly tapping to the unfamiliar beat. To Anderson's evident surprise they sang it within the traditional Vietnamese song structure so that it sounded unlike any version she, or the TV audience watching back in America, had ever heard. The resulting melding of two cultures was a less than perfect fit. The scene was both striking and plaintive. Marian Anderson smiled throughout the performance and applauded politely, even though the

Vietnamese version clearly offered a defamiliarizing glimpse of her own culture's folksongs.

This one small instance suggests the host of questions raised by the cultural encounters between Americans and Vietnamese during the Cold War. How do we experience another culture? How do we translate its symbols and hierarchies of meaning into something intelligible to ourselves? In turn, what can we learn from the encounter about our own cultural assumptions, made visible through the eyes of another? These questions, which continue to haunt the entire discipline of anthropology and its quest for accurate representations of others, confronted Edward Lansdale in Southeast Asia. What separated his experience from Anderson's was his deeply held conviction that we are fundamentally all one culture—shaped by American ideals of democracy and prosperity—and that the vast historical differences between these worlds could be melded, ignored, or overcome by the American can-do work ethos. He never winced, as Anderson appeared to do at times, when the meeting of cultures seemed to be ineffectual or even forced. He simply plowed ahead, convinced that he would transform everyone he encountered with the gospel of Americana. Doubts about the impact of American mores, let alone the untranslatable foreignness of foreigners, never entered his vocabulary or his writings.

In conceiving of and augmenting his military missions in this way, Lansdale was operating loosely within the frameworks of post–World War II tourism and pre–World War II anthropology. In this curious mix of attitudes he was the modern tourist who slings a camera over his shoulder in order to gaze upon the locals and record his own "I was there" participation in foreign cultures, even as he was documenting his experiences anthropologist-fashion and cataloguing the people and terrains he encountered in detailed and purposeful ways. The underlying logic of Cold War politics led him beyond the guileless curiosity of the tourist. When Lansdale traveled abroad, gazed upon exotic locales, and catalogued his experiences, he was working both within the structures of imperial espionage and as a sightseeing member of the leisure class. The extent to which he was aware of this dual role is open to question: he spent an equal amount of time recording in diaries and letters to his family back home the people, fish, and fauna that he encountered as in sending classified reports to Washington detailing the political conditions in these same countries. Both frames of reference were at work in his friendly interchanges with people he met, in his efforts to transform the foreign into the familiar, in his flirtations with "going native" so as to fully experience and fully infiltrate the inner workings of another culture.

Unlike the French—whose travel narratives and fiction about Indochina are filled with "a sense of inaccessibility, of the remote and incomprehensible nature (to a Westerner) of Vietnamese society"[2]—Lansdale was confident that he could mingle in and understand these foreign worlds with ease. To be sure, Lansdale was by no means alone in this attitude. As the historian Robert J. McMahon has argued, many American Cold War policies involved deliberate efforts to "recast the face of Southeast Asia in an American image."[3] And though Lansdale was certainly aware of cultural differences, he simply thought they could be overcome. Here was a man, after all, who decided one day to go out into the jungles of the Philippines with the stated purpose of looking for Huks in order to get to know them better by engaging them in conversation. Later, he wrote of this episode: "My hiking into the provinces to talk to guerrilla leaders was merely to illustrate the point that even peasant leaders, isolated from much of the world, subscribe to ideals or principles familiar to us . . . and with which we can work as Americans."[4] His sheer audacity in believing that the Huk guerrillas, who were intent on purging their country of the very Americanism he championed, would engage in dialogue speaks to his crazed courage but also to his cultural blindness. The tale is even more revealing when one considers that Lansdale was relaying this account to U.S. military officers. His notes from this period also illustrate his underlying belief in combining military muscle with other approaches: "Why shoot a man if you could talk him into surrendering?"[5] He convinced himself and seduced others into believing that America's Cold War mission was not only a good sell but also a natural fit for those living in the Philippine rain forests or the Vietnamese delta.

Lansdale's efforts to normalize the foreign should be understood within the broader context of his character and his genuine delight in cultural differences. Although his primary concern was always the defeat of communism, he also went to Southeast Asia to observe, to drink in new experiences, to have fun, and to escape the doldrums represented by a desk job back in the States. If there was one common thread through the way Lansdale lived his life, it was that he rejected the regular, the monotonous. Like classic American adventurers (whether Lewis and Clark, Huck Finn, or Peter Fonda and Dennis Hopper in *Easy Rider*), he relished the excitement of lighting out for new territories with mixed motives and an openness to personal risk. He never saw himself as a man who would be satisfied within the buttoned-down managerial culture and the life of a suburban dad that would await him if he left the U.S. military. Here was a man, thoroughly middle class in orientation and a solid proponent of American ideologies, who went to the Philippines and later to Vietnam to experience something he felt was missing in modern America with its rules and regulations, who sought out new experiences and took pleasure in the exotic—courtesy of the American military.

Although the Philippines and Vietnam were by no means classic tourist destinations at this time, he went to these exotic locales carrying with him the devices that any modern tourist would carry along. And by the time of his final departure from Southeast Asia in 1968, he had accumulated hundreds of photographs and made dozens of reel-to-reel tapes documenting the folksongs of the people he encountered. He kept a detailed journal from his time in the Philippines in the 1940s and for the next twenty years wrote intermittent reflections about his life there and in Vietnam. In many ways these artifacts tell us as much about how he viewed his actions as the score of top-secret documents he produced. There are photos of him mugging for the camera at Angkor Wat, being the life of the party at a friend's villa in Vietnam, with Magsaysay sporting identical Hawaiian shirts symbolizing their brotherliness. Lansdale meshed these fun-loving activities and his military duties with apparent ease, though the contradictions between them now seem astounding and unreconcilable. For instance, in a 1963 meeting with fellow military officers, Lansdale was blunt when discussing the relative strategic or administrative value of a given territorial objective: "Even a resort area is fine if it is an easy victory."[6] Lansdale the gazer was naturally always looking for that "victory." Thus, his interaction with the people of Southeast Asia always involved a doubleness of purpose even when it seemed to be characterized by the naive cultural arrogance and blundering goodwill of Twain's American innocents.

In addition to this tourist's zest, Lansdale became equally avid as a collector and ethnographer of the Asian cultures in which he traveled. At times his notes sound like those of a nineteenth-century anthropologist, combining personal and professional interests with full-hearted support for the needs of empire building. He also delighted in noticing what was striking or beautiful or simply strange about the world of Southeast Asia and in bringing these tales of wonder and enchantment to American policymakers. This practice is something that the anthropologist Clifford Geertz deplored among his colleagues as well when he referred to anthropologists as those who "hawk the anomalous, peddle the strange" and are "merchants of astonishment"—a phrase that also applies to Lansdale's operating strategy.[7] He saw himself as the expert who could achieve Cold War victories because of his knowledge of different worlds. He once described for Robert McNamara the sights he would see when he went to Vietnam and, at the same time, not so subtly reminded the secretary of defense of his own past successes there: "Long An is Saigon's vegetable garden and is the direct route to Vietnam's major rice production area; if food is the way to a man's heart then Long An is the way to the Vietnamese heart. . . . [After the projected defeat of communists] the "bamboo telegraph" will spread the word among the people in a way that will be believed. It will give them hope . . . as when President Diem was considering proclaiming himself Chief of State in 1955, with the backing of the Armed Forces after victory over the sects, he quickly recognized the truth of my advice to hold elections and let the people decide."[8]

In another memorandum, Lansdale detailed the meanings of various colors for the Vietnamese people: "*White*: color of mourning, also of purity, peace," could be potentially used in a future psychological operation.[9] That he sent this brief to the incoming American ambassador to South Vietnam in 1965 is indicative of how seamlessly and consciously he melded his keen observations of other cultures with the interests of his military career. Moreover, his canniness about how cultural knowledge could be used to win the war was appreciated. Ellsworth Bunker, the U.S. ambassador to South Vietnam from 1967 to 1973, noted Lansdale's deep-seated impact on the pacification programs being implemented by the United States at that time. Lansdale was, he said, "an adviser on the local scene—which he knew, I suppose, perhaps better than most of us, most of the people who were there; he'd been there longer—and I think the native culture, psychology, and so forth."[10] As Lansdale understood, his presumed insider's knowledge of various cultures increased his value within policymaking circles. Throughout his career he deployed his genuine fascination with Filipino and Vietnamese cultures to make larger diplomatic and military points to his American superiors. His goal, he said, was simple: "to know places and peoples and what was going on there and what made them tick and the economies, the value of life and structure of societies."[11]

Lansdale described himself through and against changing notions of what it meant to be an American in the Third World. His unique melding of his role as a CIA officer with that of a tourist adventurer sheds light on the nature of postwar American tourism as a casual interaction between two cultures through their citizen-representatives. His actions also help to show the ethnographic impulse of this period as it was recast to become a weapon in the American battle against communism. He traveled throughout Southeast Asia as a tourist but equally as an American proselytizer, an explorer, a missionary, and an amateur anthropologist, and these multiple roles and the attitudes they engendered reveal a great deal about both the man and the cultures in which he operated.

◆

THIS FACET OF Lansdale's history began during World War II, when American intelligence services were assigned the duty of providing information on Japan's newly expanded Co-Prosperity Sphere. Since the U.S. government found itself with desperately little knowledge of Japan's military capabilities, Lansdale, as an intelligence officer, was sent out across the United States in search of people who possessed knowledge of Southeast Asia and could provide clues as to where Japan might launch its next military strikes. He relished this job. Getting out of the office and interviewing specialists about the people and conditions throughout Asia provided the excitement that he craved: "I interviewed folks who had been in foreign areas, such as scientists, geologists, ichthyologists, and others. We would sort of mentally take them through their experiences in these countries . . . [and they would] tell us about the people they knew and the conditions as they were when last seen and so on . . . Each individual, in effect, was a gold mine if the interviewer was a good miner and knew how to go after such things."[12] Intermixing his military duty with an unorthodox, people-centered approach to operations paid off here. He would contact someone in an esoteric field such as ichthyology (the study of fish) and tease out information that might be put to military use, such as harbor configurations and other geographic elements. These encounters also made him knowledgeable in a range of subjects that would provide a common ground for his interactions with various people he would later meet in Southeast Asia. Lansdale's account of his meeting with the ichthyologist—which he repeated many times and in many different places—reveals his conscious enjoyment of the quirkiness of seeking out such a specialized academic but also suggests a canniness about how a larger, ethnographic understanding and interest could become his cultural capital once he was in the field or reporting to his superiors in Washington: "You'd have a map out and be filling in any details that you didn't have. You'd have your aerial photos and be doing, in effect, photo interpretation: What the hell is that square thing there or the squiggly thing or whatever? He'd usually know and fill you in on the details."[13]

Shortly after working on this assignment, Lansdale was sent on his first military mission abroad, where he came into contact with a broad spectrum of people from other cultures. His actions during this time were so freewheeling and unorthodox that it is difficult to attest to the accuracy of his testimony. For instance, in Indonesia the U.S. Navy used him to learn about the trustworthiness of Indonesian sailors working on Allied ships. This was considered an important matter, as there was concern that these sailors might rebel against their Dutch colonial masters and thus hurt the Allies' ability to move cargo and men throughout Southeast Asia. Lansdale's task was to get to know the Indonesian sailors whom he met in port and assess their motivations and loyalty toward the Allies. He approached his job with typical aplomb: "I had drinking bouts with them and at one of these I was rather exuberantly made a member of the Bartok tribe of Sumatra. The Bartoks . . . from then on kept me very well advised on what their plans were and also listened to me as I talked them out of having a strike and to continue on in the war effort until the day of victory when they could realize the four freedoms."[14] The notion that these colonial sailors' life-long quest for independence could be postponed simply by a few nights of carousing with one American first lieutenant speaks primarily to Lansdale's ability to persuade himself of his powers and to market himself in Washington. Yet even allowing for exaggeration, the account remains a representative example of his gift for getting along with people throughout the world and in all walks of life.

The most thoroughly documented example of Lansdale's love of foreign adventures occurred shortly after World War II. He was sent by the U.S. government on a reconnaissance mission to the Ryuku Islands, Japanese territory that neighbored the Philippines, where his official duty was simply to report if the islanders were harboring any enemy soldiers who had not yet surrendered. What distinguishes this mission from the countless others that the military authorized at the time was the sheer pleasure and excitement that Lansdale brought to the task and his efforts when recording his findings to turn the foreign into the familiar. His report detailed all aspects of the lives of the Japanese on this desolate island, including accounts of what made them happy or sad, what they ate, how they played—all the humanizing qualities that would make them knowable to his audience.

To a large extent, Lansdale's report reads like an Anthropology 101 study, with carefully indexed photographs and appendixes. Even in the classified portion, Lansdale transformed this routine operation into something of a travelogue, informing his superiors that he was reporting "the exploration of the little-known northern Ryukus Islands between Okinawa and Japan," and adding such pungent details as "travel was by the small Japanese wooden vessels Kee-mura and Tekeu-maru, as well as . . . by jeep . . . [and that] information for this report was gathered in hundreds of interviews of the inhabitants."[15] While Lansdale's basic military mission in the Ryukus was to analyze the extent to which any military clean-up actions might be required, his larger plans become apparent when one sees the vast quantity of paper this trip generated. Working only with a photographer and an interpreter, he made clear that he was already conceiving of his mission in an ethnographic framework: "This is a report of what U.S. Army, Navy and Air Force personnel have seen, heard and learned in the Northern Ryukus since the surrender of Japan." (In fact, he would use the same language of discovery when describing his efforts in the Philippines election of 1953, and the Saigon Military Mission and its "black ops" in North Vietnam in 1954 and 1955.) Individual Japanese are analyzed in unorthodox, scattered synopses: "Nata Iwachicko—(postmaster). Age—50. Although the post office looks like a pigpen, the postmaster is a bright, alert and helpful."[16] One can only imagine Lansdale's superiors reading this form of military intelligence and rolling their eyes at the mountain of extraneous details they had to wade through. But there is also an earnestness and a remarkable tolerance for the Japanese, given that they had been America's despised enemies just a few months earlier. In contrast to commonly held propagandistic views of the Japanese as cartoon characters or fiendish villains, Lansdale seemed to particularize the individuals he met and to delight in the daily rituals of their lives.

The perspective documented in Lansdale's official report offers a notable contrast to his account in a journal entry from this period, however. Describing his experiences at a 1948 geisha party he wrote: "All geisha games are aimed at getting the man to drink sake. I don't mind. Sake is strictly rationed and each cup meant one less for some Jap. I don't like Japs."[17] An obvious reflection of World War II attitudes, these private sentiments undoubtedly stemmed from Lansdale's particular outrage at the devastation he witnessed done to the Philippines by their Japanese masters. (Manila, in particular, suffered extraordinary damage during the war; also, the Bataan Death March had entered the lexicon as a crime against humanity.) It remains an interesting attribute of the man that his accounts from the Ryukus seem utterly devoid of this attitude. Either he was careful to separate his personal feelings from his professional life and reports, or, as seems more likely, these apparently opposing attitudes were simply reconciled in his mind. Without any hypocrisy, Lansdale would have seen a clear difference between this patriotic wartime hatred of the enemy and his lifelong embrace of a nonracialist universalism.

Perhaps prompted by this mix of attitudes, Lansdale crossed the line from his assigned role as military observer in the Ryukus to oversee the trial and conviction of the Japanese official governing the island. The official was charged—under what laws and by whom it is not exactly clear—of dereliction of duty to his fellow islanders: he had not provided them with the rice and other foodstuffs sent by the Japanese government and had, instead, sold the food on the black market, reducing the villagers to near starvation. Lansdale later recalled the desperate conditions he saw: "The people were very badly . . . undernourished, . . . eating grass and making soup out of grass. It was all they had." His sense of outrage was such that he took control of the foodstuffs and immediately gave them to the people. He then arrested the officer and set up a makeshift trial. According to Lansdale, the villagers flocked to thank him for his act of justice, and the local geisha girl gave him a pornographic handkerchief. Although the trial became something of a Western-style cowboy farce, with Lansdale daring the culprit to try to shoot his way out of the court, he exhibited real concern for these people. It was one of the few times he characterized the Japanese as victims rather than oppressors.[18]

As his Ryukus report makes clear, Lansdale recognized his main mission as military reconnaissance. But even at this early stage, and out of a keen personal interest, he was adding to his reports and his photographs extended stories and narratives of his time with the people he encountered in these remote islands. His photograph albums, clearly a source of pride, include dozens of snapshots with extended commentary below each one. Reflecting Lansdale's dual interests, they occasionally provide information that would interest his military superiors—"Only small boats can land at coast here" is a typical example—but there are also photos of the children, of the huts the villagers lived in, and of all the major village leaders.[19] With these photographs, Lansdale emphasized the human drama he always found in his work.

Although his report was of low priority to the military, given the current conditions on the Japanese mainland, it shows how he would later market his readings of Third World people to the American people, and in ways that were seductive, entertaining, and heartfelt. This modus operandi would continue throughout his career: he documented each of his encounters with passion, mingling a sense of the exotic with Cold War requirements. There are, for instance, photos that show Lansdale with Ilongot tribesmen in the Philippines on the island of Enchanto, Lansdale all set for the hunt with tribesmen, captioned, "men were fishing with spears."[20] In 1945 and 1946 he was very much the young GI on a great adventure in a strange and remote area of the world. As the cultural critic Susan Sontag noted, "Photographs furnish instant history, instant sociology, instant participation"[21]—and in the case of Lansdale, one can also add, an instant case study on behalf of the American government. Altogether, then, these photographs and reports document how Lansdale was merging the military requirements of the mission with a growing appetite for ethnographic observation, plus a kind of tourist's zest for the curious, the unusual, the foreign.

Even the restricted section of the Ryukus military report touches on Lansdale's taste for the dramatic (though why his psychological profiles of the village leaders needed to be kept secret is not clear), as in his pithy comment that the "head man" in the village "is a bright person with [a] psychopathic tendency."[22] But it is curious that many of these less than complimentary descriptions are quoted from the villagers themselves, indicating the trust (or powerlessness) they felt toward this American military officer.

Equally revealing are his "light moments" with the islanders. In 1948 the *Philippine Armed Forces Journal* reported an incident involving what Lansdale left behind in Ryukus: "On one tiny island he taught children, knowing as he did that other Americans would be soon following him, that the way to greet Americans was to shout: 'My Papa Major Lansdale.' "[23] This joke is not only of the macho fraternity variety but also comments on the inhabitants' misunderstanding of American greetings, suggesting how easily they could be duped. The Filipino enjoyment of the joke makes the additional point that a kind of hierarchy existed among colonial and defeated powers: the Filipinos enjoyed emphasizing that they surely would not have been taken in, as were the more "primitive" Japanese.

AFTER HIS JOURNEY to the Ryuku Islands, Lansdale settled into his career in the Philippines as a deputy intelligence officer. As his journals from 1946 and 1947 indicate, his keen interest in the details of the natural world and of peasant life became a defining feature of the way he constructed his military missions. There are photos of Lansdale sharing coconut milk with Magsaysay while tracking down Huks. There are even photos of Lansdale "going native," modeling a loincloth presented to him by a Filipino tribe. Examples from his journal show him integrating the cultural differences that he so celebrated in the Philippines into his CIA duties and tourist pleasures. In 1947 he wrote: "I went from hunting mudfish in mountain streams with Negritos to a diplomatic cocktail party in Manila, from beating around on the fringe of unexplored country where men are supposed to grow tails to cooking a 'California style' dinner for the Orendians."[24] (Johnny Orendian was the Filipino lawyer whom Lansdale later brought to Vietnam to write the 1956 Vietnamese constitution.)[25] He often appeared happiest when he got off the beaten path and encountered the people whose politics he was remaking: "I learned the joy of newly made bibingka for breakfast, made by sidewalk or market vendors in the early mornings in provincial towns" is a typical recollection from his time in the Philippines.[26]

Even Lansdale's accounts as a casual sightseer, however, become far from innocent, given the power relations on which they were based. Particularly his musings on his interactions with peasants demonstrate a classic Western perspective that interpreted cultures along a predicted continuum of social and technological development. Typical is a 1947 diary entry describing how he made contact with the Negrito people. His impressions have all the hall-marks of an early imperialist explorer enjoying his role as the "civilized" observer living among "friendly natives" of a less-developed country: "The fishing with the Negritos was in the Zambeles mountains. I'd been watching them use their little fish spears and wanted to try my luck, so I went wading after the mud fish, but didn't get one . . . In the morning . . . the Negritos rose up out of the ground as people do in the Philippines and watched me shave myself and go to the toilet and get breakfast. Ah me, has anyone ever been alone in the Philippines?"[27] It was from these early experiences, how-ever, that Lansdale developed deeper claims of intimacy with the people among whom he worked, particularly Filipino elites.

In a similar passage from his diary in 1946, his love of America and of the Philippines become easily conflated: "We entered the coconut country and my good humor came back, with the sight of green trees again, and the people walking barefoot alongside the road holding up big banana leaves in front of them as shelter against the rain and the puny little horses tied to trees next to the road to train them to not be afraid of traffic and a young kid on a carabao who let out a big whoop at the sight of me and then made the almost forgotten V sign with his fingers and yelled after me, 'veectory, Joe.'"[28] Here, Lansdale's good humor seems equally evoked by the experi-ence of the moment and by the reminder of World War II and the U.S. history of Philippine liberation from Japanese occupation (though not, of course, of the earlier U.S. occupation of the Philippines). Clearly, this pas-sage highlights the effects of colonialism and its distorting impact upon both Filipinos and Lansdale himself. Yet it also points to his nostalgic view of the Philippines, a place that became in his eyes simultaneously exotic and proto-American.

He saw in the Filipinos and later superimposed upon the Vietnamese a common love of good times and adventure, something almost innate in peo-ple from the Third World but missing in his friendships with more conven-tional Americans. If his love of adventure made him uniquely suited for his tour of duty abroad, his contentment in the Philippines had a very personal reason as well: he built a life there including a long-standing relationship with a Filipino woman (whom he married after his first wife died). In fact, throughout his time abroad Lansdale would often refer to the Philippines or Vietnam as his "home." In a draft of his memoirs he wrote, "I found a kinship with millions of people I had once regarded as foreigners. We became strangers no longer," and later added: "For years, I had simply thought of the Filipinos as people like myself, not as strange Asians to be bought and controlled by a foreigner from across the Pacific, but as warm-hearted comrades with whom I enjoyed being, with whom I shared nearly only [*sic*] of my major beliefs."[29]

These passages and many others testify to Lansdale's genuine and often successful efforts to establish a basis for kinship with everyone from complete strangers to sworn enemies to close friends. As he wrote in a draft of his memoirs, "My first step was always to observe, have sympathy for the people in the scene abroad."[30] He also held to his conviction that innate commonalities among peoples of the world always outweighed cultural differences: "At times I have had Americans or others with me as interpreters who were almost bilingual, or at least were rated excellent from a language school, and yet their empathy was flat. Some of them had picked up the manners of instructors or others, an outward show of superiority towards 'natives.' They were able to use the language far more readily than I ever was, and yet their manner caused people to freeze up. They lacked friendliness or something."[31]

Still, Lansdale's sense of kinship across cultures was always directed to the larger purpose of achieving American interests and of using the commonality lent by anticommunism. One reason for his extensive taping of Filipino folksongs mixed with political rallying marches was that he regarded music as a particularly revealing way of understanding the culture. His wife recalled, "When he went into a country the first thing that he liked to do was listen to the music, the folksongs."[32] Seeing in music a great basis for cross-cultural communication, he favored in particular that most portable of musical devices, the harmonica, his biographer noted. In conversation with his brother Ben, who had just returned from the Philippines,

> he asked Ben if he could remember any tunes he might have heard Filipino soldiers singing. When Ben could not, Ed pulled out his pocket harmonica . . . Ed played a couple of songs and asked if they sounded familiar. Ben confessed he had been listening to other things while on duty in the archipelago. "Since that wasn't part of my military duties," Ben later recalled, "I hadn't paid any attention. I wondered why he cared." Ed suggested that such things might be important. He wanted to understand and communicate with Filipinos and one way would be to know "their songs, something they hold dear to their hearts."[33]

Elsewhere, he mentioned the sociable atmosphere provided by the harmonica. In his diary he recalled entertaining U.S. officials with his harmonica playing and also described a party with Filipino military officers: "So we played while everyone sang, until I ran out of Tagalog songs to play. I had a bottle of gin with me. . . . [L]anguage was no barrier."[34] This image of a simple, all-American boy playing the harmonica appealed to others as well: William Lederer and Eugene Burdick made it a touchstone of their "Lansdale" character, Edwin Hillandale, in their best-selling novel *The Ugly American* (1958). This attractive portrait takes on a different cast, however, when one considers that Lansdale began a 1964 military briefing, titled "A Case History of Insurgency—The Philippines," by playing tapes of Filipino songs in order to provide a group of American military officers with information on waging guerrilla warfare.[35]

His ability to use perceived commonalities to influence people and institutions can also be seen as a key to his operating tactics. In his undated paper "How to select people for cold-war missions," Lansdale easily mixed the facility for making friends with his method for winning the Cold War:

1. Ability to earn friendship of people in country where peoples war is being waged—get invited into homes, with family (as in US, pot-lucks, even if family having TV-dinners, and not out to club or restaurant when family is just showing off or un-natural while "entertaining" self consciously or just plain lazy).
2. Dedication to US pol. principles and spiritual beliefs.
   [D]o things for foreign country that help greater good of U.S.—must ask natives do things for good of own country—US benefit in long run. Then have the grace to let others take the credit, whenever such encouragement is needed.[36]

The analogy he constructs of a Southeast Asian family meal with a TV dinner suggests the extent to which he believed in presenting the foreign within an American framework of images and customs. In this he was by no means unique: the anthropologist James Clifford has observed the phenomenon by which the traveler reproduces the topography that he thought to leave behind: "The 'exotic' is uncannily close. Conversely, there seem no distant places left on the planet where the presence of 'modern' products, media, and power cannot be felt. An older topography and experience of travel is exploded. One no longer leaves home confident of finding something radically new, another time or space. Difference is encountered in the adjoining neighborhood, the familiar turns up at the ends of the earth."[37] Lansdale did not simply seek out the familiar; he tried to integrate patterns of American history—his history—into his understanding of Southeast Asian society even as he helped to reproduce there the consumer-oriented, anticommunist institutions of twentieth-century America. The familiar "turns up at the ends of the earth" because individuals like Lansdale help to initiate or reconstruct it there.

Central to understanding these efforts is that Lansdale looked at the people he encountered with an eye toward making them understandable to a middle-class audience back in America. To do so, he realized that he needed to transform the American image of "them" from a kind of undifferentiated mass of darker-skinned primitives into a version of "us," people who wanted and dreamed of a world like America. As a former ad man, Lansdale knew that this was no easy sell. The differences were glaringly apparent to all. He also had to contend with traditional American views of the Philippines, cruelly summarized by the turn-of-the-century humorist Finley Peter Dunne when he said that most of his fellow citizens were uncertain as to whether the Philippines were "islands or canned goods."[38] And Americans knew so little about Vietnam that not even crude jokes were made about the country or its people until thousands of Americans were fighting and dying there in the mid-1960s. Given the vast gulf that existed between these two worlds, Lansdale's mediating efforts were not always successful. Recall, for instance, that President Lyndon Johnson's exclamation of approval at the February 1966 Honolulu conference toward his counterpart in South Vietnam, President Ky, "Boy, you speak just like an American," was meant as a compliment. Lansdale, though, was not deterred. Near the end of his government career he wrote to his old military commander, Samuel Williams, with an assuredness about what he perceived as his success in improving cross-cultural exchange: "I've tried to be a bridge between Vietnamese and Americans, Vietnamese and Vietnamese, and even Americans and Americans, to get them understanding one another and working in constructive teamwork."[39]

This effort to translate each culture into an assortment of understandable idioms turned Lansdale into something of a cross-cultural missionary. His mission entailed convincing Americans that the lands of Southeast Asia were simply potential little Americas and that these foreigners deserved our efforts and attention. One is reminded of Senator Kenneth Wherry, who exclaimed on the Senate floor in 1940 that American goals toward Asia were simple: "With God's help, we will lift Shanghai up and up, ever up, until it is just like Kansas City."[40] Lansdale shared these sentiments and believed that educating Americans about the commonalities between worlds was central to winning the Cold War. This process of educating involved more than simply being a walking and talking version of *National Geographic* (though Lansdale did refer to his World War II work in this manner). He had to contend with a host of Americans who could never see commonalities between themselves and Asian peoples, who found reducing "them" to stereotypes the natural thing to do. One result of his genuine interest in the real-life details of the Filipino and Vietnamese people and their cultures and histories was that Lansdale learned to despise the racism that permeated American speech at the time. This is why he appeared in so many venues "selling" the Philippines and Vietnam to Americans. From the article and then TV documentary of "The Village That Refused to Die" to calling Diem the George Washington of his country, Lansdale saw himself as the man who could bridge the cultural, ethnographic, linguistic, and historical differences that separated Americans from Southeast Asians. He used his gifts of empathy and his smile both to close the gap and to sell political and economic liberalism to all potential consumers.

Years later, recollecting his wartime work as an OSS officer, Lansdale acknowledged the intersections between military reconnaissance and ethnography: "Part of the work was almost like being an editor of the *National Geographic* magazine in that we collected photographs of not only airstrips and beaches for landings but also roads and bridges and more pedestrian types of geographic information. We also went into details on people who lived in places, their potentials for helping our troops."[41] *National Geographic* was, of course, the standard gateway for millions of Americans to the rest of the world. As Catherine Lutz and Jane Collins argue in *Reading National Geographic*, this popular magazine tells us as much about ourselves, as Americans, as it purportedly does about the rest of the world: "Generally speaking, *National Geographic* helped white, upwardly mobile Americans to locate themselves in a changing world, to come to terms with their whiteness and relative privilege, and to deal with anxieties about their class position, both national and international."[42] Despite a certain tendentiousness, their argument points to ways in which Lansdale conceptualized the world as a structural counterpart to America and as the raw material for reaching his goals and measuring his achievements. He anticipated the concerns of the father of containment, George Kennan, who wrote in 1949 that Americans needed to go "forth to see what we can do in order that stability may be given to all of the non-communist world."[43] Overlapping tourism with anticommunism meant that traveling the world became a form of waging the Cold War. It became the job, then, of every American citizen to demonstrate through every encounter with a foreigner the superiority of American-style capitalism and the openness central to its political ideology—the openness that made world travel (antithetical to communism, with its closed borders) possible. One obvious example of this sort of logic was Nixon's remark to

Khrushchev during the "Kitchen Debate" of 1959 that the Soviets might have bigger rockets but we had more automatic dishwashers. Lansdale echoed Nixon's glorification of American abundance with equal fervor.

In cultivating his persona as a representative American abroad, Lansdale also seemed to draw loosely on ideas championed by such anthropologists as Franz Boas, Margaret Mead, and Ashley Montagu in the first half of the twentieth century, ideas that had begun to generate a broad public interest. For instance, in 1950 and 1951 the United Nations Educational, Scientific, and Cultural Organization (UNESCO) brought together a number of prominent anthropologists, including Sherwood Washburn and Richard Leakey, to make a statement on the origins and nature of race and racial differences.[44] Although Lansdale was no intellectual—he found academics too elitist and removed from daily concerns—he was quick to pick up on popular theories regarding travel and cross-cultural relations. Like these anthropologists, Lansdale championed antiracialist thought and believed that investigations of another culture could have significant, positive political impact for all.

Among influential books touting antiracialist views was Ruth Benedict, *The Chrysanthemum and the Sword: Patterns of Japanese Culture* (1946), an outgrowth of her World War II work for the army's Office of War Information. Benedict's plea for greater cultural tolerance, for "a world made safe for difference," dovetailed with her then startlingly nuanced views of Japanese society. Together, her pleas and her specific argument about the Japanese deeply influenced Americans' conceptions of their former foe.[45] Lansdale sought to replicate her type of fieldwork in his own travels, frequently condemning those Americans who could see Asia only through the lens of race and the supposed social Darwinian hierarchies. He never seems to have adopted the racist epithets that came very easily to many Americans when describing Filipinos or Vietnamese. He characterized this liberal internationalist attitude during his official Air Force Interview: "To me people have always been people, and an individual has always been an individual regardless of the color of his skin or his race or his language." When asked why this was so, he simply responded, "I don't know what it is, I really don't."[46]

After the horrors of World War II and specifically the Nazi logics of racialist thought which culminated in the Holocaust, many other Americans recoiled at voicing racist ideas, and a broader cross-cultural sensitivity was gradually taking hold in the culture at large. At the same time that Lansdale was propounding racial universalism from the Philippines and Vietnam, an exhibit was making the same claims at home and receiving universal acclaim. *The Family of Man: An Exhibition of Creative Photography Dedicated to the Dignity of Man, with Examples from 68 Countries*, seen by more than nine million people over an eight-year period on tour from 1955 to 1963, argued through its photographs that all humans and therefore all cultures deserve respect and empathy.[47]

Franz Boas too, one of the fathers of modern anthropology,—following what he called "the ice-cold flame of the passion for seeking the truth for truth's sake"[48]—championed the idea that cultures could be observed, catalogued, and systematically described in relation to all others. Profoundly antiracist, he believed that a scientific method could lead to a broader understanding of other cultures and of our connectedness as humans. He despised the scientific racism so prevalent at the time yet still maintained an understanding of social development as a series of discrete stages from "primitive" to "civilized."[49] Interestingly, Boas had charged in a 1919 article, "Scientists as Spies," that a group of American anthropologists, ostensibly doing fieldwork but in reality working on behalf of the U.S. government, "have prostituted science by using it as a cover for their activities as spies."[50] Boas decried this unholy collaboration, but it continued and even prospered throughout the Cold War era. The American Anthropological Association, for instance, worked with the CIA in providing names of anthropologists who had knowledge of areas of mutual interest.[51] Lansdale, then, was acting like one of these academics. He observed with a real gusto the likes, dislikes, and habits of others but always on behalf of the American military and intelligence services. Although this approach may be seen simply as patriotic commitment, one can understand why critics of anthropology often regarded it as "the bastard of colonialism," or echoed Claude Levi-Strauss's observation that early anthropology consisted of "one part of mankind treat[ing] the other as an object."[52]

The question remains to what extent could Lansdale, the American, fully understand the culture and history of peasants in the Philippines and Vietnam? As Jeffrey Race has argued in his penetrating analysis of the Long An province in Vietnam in the 1960s, peasants from all economic strata share a resistance to authorities outside the established social hierarchies: "The general reaction to authority is a desire to avoid involvement, and 'long noses' automatically mean authority."[53] Since Lansdale would implicitly have fallen into the authoritarian category, everything he said or intimated, joked about or scowled at, would have weighed heavily on Southeast Asians' perceptions of him and his efforts in their countries. Furthermore, his quest to understand the nature of peasant societies, though genuine, was limited. As the work of Race and others suggests, peasant cultures are internally adaptive societies but are particularly resistant to outside influences. Peasants have traditionally not had the opportunity to migrate when their societies are

under attack; instead, they fight back. The long history of resistance to colonialism within Vietnamese history is a case in point.[54] Arguably, one reason
Lansdale was more successful in the Philippines than in Vietnam was that
Filipino society was so fractured by Spanish colonialism and by so many
centuries of imperial rule that it lacked the powerful tradition of resistance
to outsiders which mobilized the Vietnamese—and which Ho Chi Minh
tapped into as he worked to redefine (or update) the nature of Vietnamese
society. Lansdale's ignorance was a question not of racism but of depth: his
vision of the inherent commonality of cultures superseded the recognition
of such key differences.

LANSDALE'S ETHNOGRAPHIC encounters in Vietnam involved two distinct periods: first he was involved in a series of missions there from 1953 to
1956; then in 1965, during the height of the war, he returned with great
fanfare. As Stanley Karnow wrote in 1966, "On previous occasions he had
displayed an almost uncanny ability to drop into a strange setting, mix with
the people, understand the problem, recommend a remedy and assist in its
implementation. And he was at his best when he played a solo hand, person-
ifying American power for his native protégés."[55] Hence, a great deal of hope
attached to his return.

Lansdale did his best to champion his cause; he believed that his knowledge of Third World societies, learned first in the Ryukus and then in
greater detail in the Philippines and Vietnam, included ethnographic data
that could earn him power in Washington. Furthermore, he believed that
his unique knowledge of Vietnamese history and culture gave him the edge
over the communists, who were doctrinaire—indeed Stalinist—in their approaches. His writings detail the various political and religious organizations
thriving in Vietnam during the 1950s: the Hao Hoa, the Binh Xuyen, and
the Cao Dai.

He was particularly concerned with the Cao Dai political and religious
movement and its threat to American interests. This sect of a million strong
vied with the Diem regime as an alternative force in South Vietnamese politics in the 1950s. To Lansdale, any group that threatened Diem's leadership
must be either defeated or incorporated into the political platforms he was
devising, and to accomplish either result he had to understand it better. His
papers include detailed maps of the Cao Dai's Holy See and Temple, as well
as lengthy discussions of the history and tenets of the organization. One
memo argues that the sect might prove valuable as a kind of psychological

weapon against communism, and subsequently declassified documents disclose that he was exploring this possibility in top-secret discussions with the Joint Chiefs of Staff.[56] To help in achieving this goal during the sect crisis of 1955, Lansdale went to Cambodia, where the Cao Dai leaders were hiding, and bribed them not to attack Diem's forces. Like his earlier efforts in the Philippines, this approach was successful, which points to the real power of money and perhaps to the limits of anthropological investigation in waging Cold War victories.[57]

During his earlier missions in Vietnam, Lansdale recounted in classic tourist fashion such observations as "my first glimpse of the appealing dress of Vietnamese women, the *aodai*, with its satin trousers and fluttery overdressed buttoned to the neck but slit to the waist. It is frankly designed to catch the male eye. I noticed a stunningly beautiful Vietnamese girl sauntering along the walk before the hotel entrance, the satin of her trousers all agleam in the morning sunlight. She was being noticed by others, too. Interested males filled the windows of the coffee shop."[58] Like his earlier journals, Lansdale's notes detail specific scenes and individuals and are thus in stark contrast with the stereotypical summaries provided in standard CIA documents. Compare a 1960 CIA report on the physical appearance of the Vietnamese in a style that sounds as if it had come straight from a college anthropology text: "The typical Vietnamese is short, slim, of slight body build and olive-brown complexioned; and shows his Mongoloid heritage through a number of distinctive traits, such as the epicanthic fold of the eyelid." The report goes on to describe the Vietnamese people as "docile toward authority," "easily led in collective excitement," and given to "instances of individual violence and brutality."[59]

On his early visits, Lansdale spent time not only learning about the Vietnamese but also combatting the French, whom he had come to dislike during his initial 1953 post as an observer during the First Indochina war between the French and the Vietminh; he liked to say that they had tried to assassinate him at one point and even threatened his poodle. His methods for lampooning them included his response in 1954 when he learned of a brothel frequented by French soldiers:

> My tourist instincts aroused, I excused myself and made my way to the top floor [of a nearby hotel] where I could overlook the neighbors. En route, I saw the movie camera which was used for keeping a pictorial record of the journeys of General O'Daniel. . . . I took it along. From a top floor window, the neighbors presented a lively scene. There was a large courtyard surrounded by buildings which in turn were beehives of cubbyhole rooms. Several dozen girls were

in the courtyard, greeting with raucous laughter and wisecracks the soldiers who were filing in by the front gate. I fitted a telescopic lens on the camera, focused in on the scene, and then called down to the girls and troops below asking them if they would like to pose for a Hollywood talent scout. They laughed and went into vivid pantomime of their intentions towards each other, while the camera recorded the scene. I called thanks. They waved goodbye. I went downstairs, unobtrusively put the camera back where I'd found it, and finished my lunch. I wondered how a military briefing officer would describe the scene as he kept up a running commentary for viewers when the film of official visits was shown.[60]

Lansdale's reference to his "tourist instincts" is reminiscent of that popular figure in espionage fiction, the spy who poses as the innocent tourist. The passage also makes clear his thorough enjoyment in recalling the stunt.

Lansdale returned to Vietnam in the mid-1960s convinced that his knowledge and insights about the nature of Vietnamese culture could ensure an American victory. He wrote memos to the U.S. ambassador and fellow team members, as he had done in the 1950s, about the unique role of Vietnamese soothsayers and the "clandestine operational use of these persons"; about how geomancers work; and about his having been the only American present at a Vietnamese wedding.[61] He included in one report a top-secret photo of a Vietnamese astrologer plying her trade. Lansdale had written numerous memos to his superiors about the uses of astrology and apparently was truly fascinated with their "Eastern" ways. On his return from this initial tour he felt expert enough to assure Secretary of Defense McNamara and Ambassador-designate Henry Cabot Lodge in a 1963 briefing paper that they need not be fearful of the different, the exotic, that made up Vietnam: "*The Scene.* Looks alien, but is nation of small shopkeepers, small farmers, etc., who will fight for what they have—if given real hope. People have that unique Asian radar, quick to read your inner personality—whether you genuinely like them or merely putting on an act . . . Condescension, even minor, weakens influence. Vietnamese bathe frequently, are pleased when you do also. Really dislike a hug, an arm or shoulder, or back pat."[62] Such briefings accomplished little more than to provide a self-promotional exercise through which he could demonstrate his knowledge of how Vietnamese culture "worked."

Still, Lansdale's ethnographic fieldwork in his final tour of duty, from 1965 to 1968, took on a level of sophistication and insight that remains a model for capturing the music of men during wartime and documenting the culture they were fighting in. During that time he recorded hundreds of hours of tapes of Americans and Vietnamese who came to his villa. They sang a wide variety of songs, from old American ballads such as "Hang Down Your Head Tom Dooley" (a song from the Civil War) to recent Vietnamese folksongs that yearned for peace and an end to the war. Although this was not the reason Lansdale had returned to Vietnam, he turned his energies toward the project with real passion, and the thoroughness with which he compiled this series of tapes suggests a strategic attempt to tap into Vietnamese cultural traditions in a more powerful and immediate way. "I had hoped to catch some of the emotions of the Vietnam War in these folk songs and, with them, try to impart more understanding of the political and psychological nature of the struggle to those making decisions," Lansdale wrote to the Library of Congress when he bequeathed the collection to their archive.[63] Always, he sought to impress on American policymakers the subtlety and grace of Vietnamese music and culture, and to reorient Americans accustomed to thinking of Vietnamese as simply the communist "other" toward a sense of their cultural richness and variety. He played the tapes to visiting dignitaries and American delegations that came to visit him and sent them to a host of American officials—including President Johnson and then presidential candidate Nixon—in the hope that they would have a better understanding of the people against whom they were waging a war. Nixon's response to this gift is instructive of the limits of this entire enterprise. He wrote back to Lansdale, "I am especially happy to add your generous gift of Vietnamese folk songs to my collection and you can well imagine the delight of my two daughters when they heard them."[64]

In addition to this palpable lack of official interest, the failure of Lansdale's tapes to have the impact he intended may be partially explained by the traditional songs he chose to record, which tended to celebrate community events and express longings for a better future.[65] The political scientist James Scott, in his study of the various forms taken by the powerless to resist inequalities in their societies, has argued that folk traditions play a key part in this struggle. Scott uses an older Vietnamese folksong as one example of this phenomenon at work:

> The son of the king becomes king.
> The son of the pagoda caretaker knows only how to sweep with the leaves of
>   the banyan tree.
> When the people rise up,
> The son of the king, defeated, will go sweep the pagoda.[66]

Perhaps Lansdale's methods were not as thorough as they could have been or were hampered by his own unwillingness to hear the message of the songs.

In the end it seems that he became an anthropologist not of the Vietnamese but of the effects of American power upon the peoples of Southeast Asia. The tourism that he reveled in represented the first wave of an invasion force that was now killing thousands every week.

Lansdale's passion for cultural knowledge grew in intensity until at the end of his government career it seemed to subsume his political efforts and ambition. Just before he left Vietnam for good in 1968, a group of Vietnamese students came to say goodbye and play some of their country's songs with him. "That's just like Ed," another American official said when he heard about the farewell songfest. "He's feeling the pulse of the Vietnamese to the very last."[67] It is also clear that toward the end of his career he wanted to know Southeast Asians almost as much as he wanted to save them from the perils of communism. And when he failed, when the Vietnamese revolution triumphed and ushered in a unified communist government in 1975, the despair he felt never fully lifted. He had combined a nearly anthropological interest in the indigenous traditions and concerns of Southeast Asians with a passionate and fatal assumption that those traditions could only be leading in the direction of an American-style democracy. Lansdale thus became the epitome of American liberalism when it goes abroad, in its missionary zeal and its well-intentioned short-sightedness. In the draft of his memoirs he wrote two unusually perceptive questions that unfortunately he never returned to: "What was I leaving behind in Asia?" and "How does one intervene unwittingly?"[68] These questions are haunting. Because of Lansdale's efforts, the Vietnamese and the Philippine people are to this day living with the burden of his cultural history as well as their own.

6

Fictions of Quiet and Ugly Americans

> You must firmly remember that for us the most important of all arts is the cinema.
>
> —Vladimir Lenin

EDWARD LANSDALE was a Cold War celebrity. His fame perfectly mirrored a culture in which people live vicariously through their entertainers, athletes, and politicians. Although he was never accorded the public adulation offered to those Hollywood stars cast as defenders of American freedoms, or the attention paid a secretary of state pronouncing on the evils of communism, his fame was real. It can be attributed in large part to a series of writers who looked at Lansdale and saw a great story.

Though countless authors wrote about him, the core of his celebrity lay in just two novels: Graham Greene's 1955 *The Quiet American*, and William Lederer and Eugene Burdick's 1958 quasi rejoinder, *The Ugly American*. These, and the subsequent movies made of them, became central to the making of Lansdale's celebrity. The fact that one focused on a less-than-innocent American character while the other heaped praised on the brash American working abroad was of secondary importance. The drama of a go-getting American fighting communism through a host of unconventional methods trumped the actual story lines and ensured Lansdale's place in the popular histories of the Cold War.

Greene's supposed rendition of Lansdale remains of particular importance; his book has come to be seen as *the* novel that critiques the American intervention in Vietnam. The fact that it was written in 1955, ten years before American ground troops were sent in force, makes his work more prescient than he could have imagined. It offers a withering critique of U.S. actions abroad through a love triangle involving a jaded British journalist, a young Vietnamese woman, and an American enthusiast, Alden Pyle. There were some striking similarities between Pyle and Lansdale, and given Pyle's less than noble efforts in Vietnam, where people die because of his confidence in the American mission abroad, the portrayal made Lansdale despise the British novelist for decades. In fact, Greene and Lansdale would spend the rest of their years shadow-boxing over the novel and its politics. But although Pyle has been assumed by countless historians and commentators (and Lansdale himself, for that matter) to have been modeled on Lansdale, he was not. Greene spent the rest of his life denying the connection in all possible venues, and his official biographer, Norman Sherry, has gone to great lengths documenting the real man on whom Pyle was modeled: a relatively minor American official who worked in Vietnam in the early 1950s, Leo Hochstetter.[1] Moreover, Sherry found that Greene had already written the first draft of the novel before he briefly met Lansdale in the mid-1950s. Yet like so much about the nature of celebrity, Greene's denials concerning Pyle as Lansdale were drowned out by the far more intriguing tale of a British novelist and a CIA agent fighting their own personal Cold War. In ways neither could have appreciated at the time, Greene's novel created Lansdale's celebrity more than any single thing Lansdale actually did. One need only consider that after 1955 it is rare to encounter a story about Lansdale that does not refer to him as the "quiet American."

Greene's ability to dissect American intentions abroad remains of note, even if the book is not placed in the first tier by most Greene scholars. Set during the period surrounding the end of the First Indochina War and the beginning of American intervention, the novel begins with Greene's disclaimer that "this is a story and not a piece of history, . . . a story about a few imaginary characters." Yet this authorial bow is far from the whole story; in order to create a fiction from the perspective of a Western journalist, Greene himself spent considerable time living in and reporting from Vietnam in the early 1950s. His use of real incidents, beginning with the fall of Dienbienphu, and his incorporation of real individuals such as General Thé (the leader of the Cao Dai movement, who was championed by Lansdale) give substance and an authentic voice to his novel. This quality of "real" fiction, verging on the *reportage* method, lies at the heart of the book's success in depicting the country, but it also leaves open the question of whether we should read it as a journalistic account of the period or primarily as a fictional meditation on American power. Greene essentially wanted to have it both ways: a piece of nonfiction masquerading as a novel. In fact, Greene had been much more than a reporter or novelist; after he met Ho Chi Minh in the early 1950s, ostensibly for an interview for a piece he was writing about Indochina, he contacted British Secret Intelligence Service and described the content of their conversation.[2]

Without question, the book remains a searching critique for those interested in the deadly effects of American innocence on the people of Southeast Asia. In this light, its most famous sentence, "I never knew a man who had better motives for all the trouble he caused," continues to resonate today, even as it has become something of a literary cliché. The novel became a standard text for the antiwar movement, and its portrayal of the menace of American liberalism when projected upon other people has never been surpassed. Its influence on American reporters living in Vietnam in the early 1960s was particularly significant. David Halberstam recalled that he and many of his colleagues.

> used to sit in the small French cafes and talk about Greene's book. It seemed at that time . . . the best novel about Vietnam. There was little disagreement about his fine sense of the tropics, his knowledge of the war, his intuition of the Vietnamese toughness and resilience, particularly of the peasant and the enemy. . . . It was only his portrait of the sinister innocence of the American that caused some doubt, that made us a little uneasy. . . . The American Embassy public-affairs officer was particularly bitter about Greene's American: He called it an evil book, made worse, he said, because it was so effective, so slick.[3]

American readers were made particularly uneasy at seeing themselves through Greene's eyes. Shortly after Greene's death, Richard West, one of the "old Asia hands," wrote an extended obituary that openly revealed the effect of the novel upon his later work: "When I first made a TV film about Vietnam, in 1969, the director asked me to quote from Graham Greene's novel *The Quiet American*; I did, and later one of the TV critics wrote that I saw the country with a second-hand imagination."[4] In its testimony to the novel's persuasive power, this response and others like it added to Greene's well-deserved reputation. Some of the best passages reveal the skill with which the author depicted the people of Vietnam to Western audiences; he spoke of "the gold of the rice-fields under a flat late sun: the fishers' fragile cranes hovering over the fields like mosquitoes: the cups of tea on an old abbot's platform . . . the mollusc hats of the girls repairing the road where a mine had burst: the gold and the young green and the bright dresses of the south, and in the north the deep browns and the black clothes and the circle of enemy mountains and the drone of planes."[5] Such passages certainly benefit by comparison with the standard accounts of the time, in which "red Asian warlords" and the "Yellow Peril" inhabited Western versions of Asia. The reception of the novel, though, needs to be contrasted with its origins and ideological intent. Today one is struck by a number of themes downplayed by those who championed its anticolonial and anti-American qualities during the 1950s and 1960s. Central to this discussion are the contexts in which the novel was written, the ways in which supporters and critics alike used it during the Cold War, the themes Greene sought to project through the character of Pyle, and the diverse ways in which later commentators interpreted his work.

The genesis of the novel dates from Greene's dispatches from Vietnam as a correspondent for the *Sunday Times* (London) *Figaro*, the *New Republic*, and *Paris Match*.[6] In a 1952 series for *Paris Match*, Greene wrote about the First Indochina War in ways that are quite unexpected, even jarring, to those familiar with his famous novel and its supposed political positions. It seems almost inconceivable that Greene might defend any aspect of America— particularly the projection of its ideologies abroad—given his resolute anti-Americanism, yet he displayed sympathy for one of the mainstays of U.S. foreign policy after World War II, the much maligned domino theory: "The Indo-Chinese front is only one sector of a long line which crosses Korea, touches the limits of a still peaceful Hong Kong, cuts across Tongking, avoids—for the moment—Siam, and continues into the jungles of Malaya. If Indo-China falls, Korea will be isolated, Siam can be invaded in twenty-four hours and Malaya may have to be abandoned."[7]

Another feature of Greene's earlier writing which needs to be juxtaposed with orthodox readings of the novel is even more of a revelation for those who have constructed Greene as a man of the Left. In dispatches from Indochina he unabashedly promoted the virtues of colonialism, its importance to the West, and the need for it to endure over such passing fads as nationalism and communism:

> In the beginning the war may very well have been a colonial war (even if the Viet Minh fired the first shots), but the young [French] men who, with stubborn and ferocious determination, are doing the actual fighting in a hard climate against a savage and fanatical enemy, care little for the rubber plantations of Cochin China and Cambodia. They are fighting because France itself is at war

and firmly determined not to let its allies down *as long as humanly possible*. If we have criticized certain aspects of French administration in Vietnam we have not criticized France itself. France is the very young pilot in his little B26 bomber probing his way between a hostile mountain and a hostile jungle into a valley too narrow to permit him to alter course. France is the soldier up to his chest in a rice paddy, the nurse parachuted into an isolated post, and even the policy superintendent knifed in his bed by his trusted native servant. As for the future, England and America ought to remember that every human possibility has its limits. . . . The United States is exaggeratedly distrustful of empires, but we Europeans retain the memory of what we owe to Rome, just as Latin America knows what it owes to Spain. When the hour of evacuation sounds there will be many Vietnamese who will regret the loss of the language which put them in contact with the art and faith of the West.[8]

Green's subscription to a colonial mentality can be attributed to his desire to give his audience what they wanted; since "cultured" Frenchman believed in *mission civilisatrice*, he would put in a good word for it, now that it was under attack. This passage can also be read as Greene speaking from a peculiarly British understanding of the meaning and impact of colonialism over time—the impossibility of undoing the influence of one country upon another. Yet this generous interpretation has not been accepted by all critics; some believe that the traditional reading of Greene's work—modern tales of man's inhumanity to other men—must be revised in light of his defense of colonialism.[9]

If Greene was a defender of empires, however, why did he not take a more positive view of America's replacement of France in Indo-China? Why not support a new Western empire that was simply taking over from a dying one? Key British conservatives did exactly this and acted accordingly; as future prime minister Harold Macmillan commented in 1945, "These Americans represent the new Roman Empire and we Britons, like the Greeks of old, must teach them how to make it go."[10] For these British conservatives, it was time to pass on their knowledge, and clearly the American configuration of empire was more sympathetic to British interests than the Soviet rendition.

For Greene, though, the phrase "American empire" was not so much a reduction as a debasement of the very idea of empire. He explicitly argued that older European empires were worthy institutions, more virtuous than the Modern American configuration, whose sole purpose—other than denial—was to sell pop culture and Coca-Cola and to bring ever new notions of leisure and entertainment to other people.[11] To this American greed, Greene contrasted the ideals of former empire builders who wanted to bring

Enlightenment thought and culture to the eager, simple people of the Orient. The trajectory of his thought may explain why he could speak movingly about Saigon as "the Paris of the East" yet feel nothing but horror and disdain when it threatened to become an outpost of Washington. Consider, for example, the very first paragraph of *The Quiet American*, where Fowler (Greene's British protagonist) resignedly says, "I could see lamps burning where they had disembarked the new American planes." This phrase is repeated like a mantra throughout the novel and recycled in a more obvious manner very near the end when Fowler speaks of the inevitability of American intervention in Vietnam: "I walked down to the Majestic and stood a while watching the unloading of the American bombers."[12]

Another way to approach the problem of Greene and empires is to situate his views within an enduring strain of British Tory thought, with its historic antipathy to America and all things American; anything that opposed the United States needed to be supported (the "enemy of my enemy is my friend" syndrome). Greene was no Tory, but as a convert to Catholicism he energetically denounced anything that reeked of secular modernity, and America was the classic modern and secular state with its championing of democracy, the rights of the individual, and an absolutist belief in laissez-faire capitalism.[13] (Both friends and critics have regarded Lansdale as the quintessential American in just these respects.) For Greene, even the most humanitarian of American efforts played a part in its Cold War strategies. "Medicine's a kind of weapon isn't it," Pyle says at one point. One critic of Greene's work, W. J. West, has picked up on this statement: "The charge that Greene is making is clear: that in the guise of sending medical teams to help the local people the CIA was arming one small part of the complex political groupings." Greene continually wrote about the double-edged quality of American largesse: "It is difficult to feel so grateful when a gift is permanently stamped with the name of the donor. This is not the obtrusive spontaneous act of charity to which the poor are accustomed; the tents, the chicken coops, the packages of rations bearing the badge of American aid demand a kind of payment—co-operation in the Cold War. . . . The razors for hairless chins can be sold again perhaps (though to whom?) . . . and the white powder (that nobody tells them is milk and a few wily people may tell them is poison for their babies) can be spilt in the cracks of the ground and the tins scoured and used."[14]

The strength of Greene's anti-Americanism permeates any consideration of his work. Greene himself sometimes quite explicitly warmed to this subject. He once declared: "I have always felt ill at ease in the States. . . . [T]he terrifying weight of this consumer society oppresses me. . . . I will go to almost any length to put my feeble twig in the spokes of American foreign policy."[15] In an interview he said that Americans struck him "rather as the English abroad strike me. Noisy, and incredibly ignorant of the world."[16] There are, then, only so many possible readings for Thomas Fowler's internal dialogue about another American he is talking to: "He was like an emblematic statue of all I thought I hated in America—as ill-designed as the Statue of Liberty and as meaningless."[17] Even if one believes that Fowler is not simply mouthing Greene's anti-Americanism but projecting a response in keeping with his character, his visceral dislike echoes Greene's.[18] Indeed, throughout the novel, all things American are reduced to a series of caricatures and easy targets of ridicule. Even Alden Pyle's crew cut and puritan manner become stand-ins for the problems of American liberalism—and in British slang, "pyles" refers to hemorrhoids.

These obvious targets have led to many harsh critiques of *The Quiet American*. Terry Eagleton, though an avid admirer of the author, exposed the "style equals political commentary" approach favored by Greene and found it wanting. "Fowler's anti-Americanism," Eagleton writes, "is closer to a vulgar snobbery than to a shrewd analysis of the brutalities of U.S. imperialism, a fact which the novel itself seems significantly not to question." Another champion of Greene's work, Grahame Smith, found much wrong with this novel, calling it "tired," formulaic, and inhabited with one-dimensional characters. Smith is particularly scathing on the last point: he says of the Vietnamese woman whom Fowler and Pyle compete over that Phuong is nothing more than "an excursion into the world of Suzie Wong," and Pyle "remains cardboard throughout." Even Richard West's intellectual and emotional indebtedness to the novel did not prevent him from identifying hackneyed plot devices.[19]

Without question, the most scathing and entertaining critique of the novel came from A. J. Liebling in the *New Yorker*. He believed that the book was a case of "sour grapes" on the part of Greene, an "exercise in national projection" by an Englishman upset that the Empire had diminished. In addition to being a very funny review, it is also quite nasty; Liebling argues that Pyle is actually the prototypical *Englishman* abroad ("a naive chap who speaks bad French, eats tasteless food, and is only accidently and episodically heterosexual"), and Fowler a bad imitation of the American abroad ("Fowler is not a Hemingway hero by Hemingway, of course. He is nearer the grade of a Hemingway hero that occurs in unsolicited manuscripts"). Liebling then settles on calling Fowler, "Bogart-Fowler" through the rest of the review, in mocking reference to the classic American movie tough guy.[20]

Even though Greene consistently denied that he modeled the youthful, idealistic Alden Pyle after Lansdale, most commentators have assumed otherwise, given the number of similarities between the two. Even those who accept Greene's repudiation of any links between the two men cannot help drawing obvious parallels. Pyle is introduced in the novel as having "an unmistakably young and unused face," and Lansdale looked younger than his years. Pyle had a genuine desire to graft American institutions onto Vietnam—"He was determined . . . to do good, not to any individual person but to a country, a continent, a world. Well, he was in his element now with the whole universe to improve"—and this desire marks Lansdale through and through. Pyle was a true believer in the American Century: "You two," he informs Fowler about the British and French, "couldn't expect to win the confidence of the Asiatics. That was where America came in now with clean hands." Lansdale could not have said it any better. Finally, Pyle unshakably believed in and supported a "third force" within Vietnam: that is, a political system beholden neither to colonial powers nor to communist regimes. Lansdale was convinced that a "third force" was the key to attaining American Cold War victories.[21]

Of these parallels, the third force most closely links the two. It is in many ways the crux of the novel and illuminates why Greene spent a lifetime condemning U.S. foreign policy and why Lansdale became a real foe in Greene's political world. Greene did not invent the term "third force," but it became a catch-all phrase for any real or imagined independent political force wedded to neither communism nor colonialism. In Vietnam the term was used to distinguish such non-communists as General Trinh Minh Thé and the Cao Dai sect from Ho Chi Minh's communists and from the remnants of French colonialism. In the novel, the third force becomes linked with the optimistic self-projections of such Americans as Lansdale. Furthermore, Pyle's championing of a third force, both publicly in conversations with Fowler and covertly (Pyle supplies *plastique*, an explosive, also identified as "diolaction," to General Thé, who uses it outside a Saigon hotel), parallels Lansdale's concerted efforts to strengthen Thé's political and military power base. Fiction becomes fact in this case, for recently declassified documents disclose that Lansdale was promoting the third-force idea shortly after Greene wrote the novel. Lansdale was involved in top-secret discussions with the Joint Chiefs of Staff on the Cao Dai movement and on the possibility of using it as a psychological weapon against communism. In one memorandum Lansdale not only assessed Thé's charisma, political strength, and ability to sustain a third force within Vietnam but also deemed Thé crucial to achieving an American victory. It is worth keeping in mind that even after Thé's death (he was assassinated by either French or Vietcong forces in 1955),

Lansdale continued to attempt to remake Vietnam along third-force lines and to champion Thé's vision.[22] He later wrote to John Pratt, editor of *Vietnam Voices*, that "Graham Greene shares the French hatred for Trinh Minh Thé, who had one of their generals blown up (by grenade)," and thus tries to implicate the novelist (by two degrees of separation) in the death of the third force. What Lansdale did not add was his assessment of Thé as told to the journalist Keyes Beech at the time of Thé's death: "Oh, well . . . that's too bad. Trinh Minh Thé was a good man. He was a moderate, he was a pretty good general, he was on our side, and he cost twenty-five thousand dollars."[23]

To Greene, the propagation of a third force by Americans had a horribly corrosive impact upon the Vietnamese: it weakened and corrupted the Vietnamese political system, and made it increasingly beholden to American largesse. The most explicit critique of the third force in Green's novel appears in a scene between Fowler and the French Inspector Vigot immediately following the death of Pyle.

> "There it is on your shelf. *The Rôle of the West*. Who is this York Harding?"
> "He's the man you are looking for, Vigot. He killed Pyle—at long range."
> "I don't understand."
> "He's a superior sort of journalist—they call them diplomatic correspondents. He gets hold of an idea and then alters every situation to fit the idea. Pyle came out here full of York Harding's idea."[24]

Implied in this passage is a sense that Greene is meting out the form of justice most appropriate to those who preached the virtues of a third force to the Vietnamese, since Pyle is killed by the communists. It is of interesting that although historians and journalists have spent a great deal of time trying to establish whether Pyle was modeled on Lansdale, little has been done on the York Harding character. Like Pyle, he could easily have been based upon an American figure, someone like the popular writer Robert Payne, whose 1951 work *Red Storm over Asia* was widely read at the time. Payne spoke of how "an almost nihilistic opportunism became inevitable in all countries where a moderate 'third force' either failed to take power or found itself with no means of exercising its power." He also wrote that what was needed for the United States to prevail in the Cold War was "an extension of the social arm of America until it reaches the villages of Asia."[25] His warnings of a communist takeover of this part of the world fit the tone of the Harding character who so influenced Pyle.

When Fowler tells Pyle, "This Third Force—it comes out of a book, that's all," it is a moment that indicates Greene's own realism (or cynicism) about the practical applicability of the theory.[26] Another exchange between Pyle and Fowler allows Greene to explore the essence of America's mission in Vietnam, its illusions, and why it would inevitably be a disaster for all concerned. It also shows the growth of Greene's thought concerning the nature of colonialism and empires. Fowler tells Pyle:

> "Sometimes the Viets have a better success with a megaphone than a bazooka. I don't blame them. They don't believe in anything either. You and your like are trying to make a war with the help of people who just aren't interested."
> "They don't want Communism."
> "They want enough rice," I [Fowler] said. "They don't want to be shot at. They want one day to be much the same as another. They don't want our white skins around telling them what they want."
> "If Indo-China goes . . ."
> "I know the record. Siam goes. Malaya goes. Indonesia goes. What does 'go' mean? If I believed in your God and another life, I'd bet my future harp against your golden crown that in five hundred years there may be no New York or London, but they'll be growing paddy in these fields, they'll be carrying their produce to market on long poles, wearing their pointed hats." . . .
> "They'll be forced to believe what they are told, they won't be allowed to think for themselves."
> "Thought's a luxury. Do you think the peasant sits and thinks of God and Democracy when he gets inside his mud hut at night?"[27]

Fowler's last sentence sums up precisely what Lansdale and many Americans did believe after World War II—that peasants *did* sit in their huts and dream American dreams. On the basis of these assumptions, Pyle, like Lansdale, is able to rethink complex peasant societies as primitive reflections of American ideology; Vietnam in 1954 appears to him to contain the fertile yet still unformed foundations for a country based upon American principles. In this passage Greene is at his best in depicting the dangers of Americans practicing Cold War theory upon another people, and why the assumptions of Pyle are not only faulty but pervasively malignant.

Parallels between Pyle and Lansdale become even starker when one takes into account Lansdale's 1961 memo about the U.S. stake in Vietnam and its eery mimicry of Pyle's lecturing style: "If Free Vietnam is won by the Communists, the remainder of Southeast Asia will be easy pickings for our enemy. . . . A Communist victory also would be a major blow to U.S. prestige and influence, not only in Asia but throughout the world, since the world believes that Vietnam has remained free only through U.S. help. Such a victory would tell leaders of other governments that it doesn't pay to be a friend of the U.S."[28] Pyle is thus Lansdale to the extent that both sought to enact various nation building efforts in Southeast Asia that would have resulted in the refashioning of whole societies into American proxies. And Lansdale can easily be critiqued not only for acting imperially but for continuing to deny that he was doing so. In his mind his actions were benevolent, and the carnage caused by *plastique* or the perils of backing Diem against insurmountable odds were simply irrelevant to the ends he sought to achieve. Greene's "real fiction" is evident here as well: both Lansdale and Pyle pursued their conception of American idealism and the nature of American modernity regardless of its fatal consequences for so many of the Vietnamese people. Their concrete policies propelled Greene to expose acts of American "benevolence," as well as to explore their roots.

Partly because of their obvious similarities, efforts to settle this question of whether Pyle was based on Lansdale developed into something of a cottage industry. Drawn into the dispute, Greene and Lansdale each tried to outdo the other in rejections and denunciations. In a 1966 letter to the *British Sunday Telegraph*, Greene declared: "Just for the record, your correspondent . . . is completely wrong in thinking that I took General Lansdale as the model for *The Quiet American*. Pyle was a younger, more innocent and more idealistic member of the CIA. I would never have chosen Colonel Lansdale, as he then was, to represent the danger of innocence."[29] As his vehemence makes clear, Greene's goal was to bury Lansdale and his beliefs; he certainly wanted no part in making a legend of a man whom he detested. And the fact that this mistaken identity persisted only increased his anger. In 1975, he returned to the question in a letter to the same newspaper: "I grow tired of denying that there is any connection between my character Pyle in *The Quiet American* and General Lansdale, the American counter-insurgency expert whom I have never had the misfortune to meet. Pyle was an innocent and an idealist. I doubt whether your correspondent . . . would so describe General Lansdale. He should not refer in this way to a book which he has obviously never read, but I hope at least he will read this letter. Other journalists please note."[30] And in 1987 he denied the relationship once more, adding this little twist on the power of fame: "Of course he would naturally have known of my presence!"[31]

Greene's adamant denials can be taken at face value—except that he and Lansdale *had* met, as Lansdale recounted years later:

> The only time I ever saw Graham Greene, he was sitting on a hotel terrace with some French, in 1954, I guess it was. He was very close to the French. Peg and Tilman Durdin were a husband and wife writing team with *The New York Times*. . . . They were staying at the Continental Hotel. When I drove in there, some French officers were sitting out on the sidewalk terrace and Graham Greene was

with them. There was a sizeable group—30 to 50—and they started booing me. I wasn't very popular with the French. Graham Greene said something . . . and Peg stuck out her tongue at him and said to him, "but we love him." Then she turned around and gave me a big hug and kiss. I said, "Well, I'm going to get written up someplace as a dirty dog." So I guess I made his book. I had a french poodle at the time and he was with me, in the car with me, and they commented about the dog.[32]

Greene's account of how he came to write the novel describes an American model for the character of Pyle who was not Lansdale but bore some striking similarities:

The moment for *The Quiet American* struck as I was driving back to Saigon after spending the night with Colonel Leroy. . . . I shared a room that night with an American attached to an economic aid mission—the members were assumed by the French, probably correctly, to belong to the C.I.A. My companion bore no resemblance at all to Pyle, the quiet American of my story—he was a man of greater intelligence and less innocence, but he lectured me all the long drive back to Saigon on the necessity of finding a "third force" in Vietnam. I had never before come so close to the great American dream which was to bedevil affairs in the East as it was to do in Algeria.[33]

This recollection fits nicely with how one literary critic has analyzed Greene's method of writing: according to Judith Adamson, he "concentrated on particular incidents that caught his eye, adding to them by juxtaposing other points of view until the episode became visual metaphors for the history playing itself out before him."[34]

Lansdale himself seemed intrigued by the "Pyle as Lansdale" comparisons, however unflattering they may have been. According to one journalist, Lansdale laughed off the question, saying: "'I felt that Greene was anti-American. . . . Greene knocked him [Pyle] off in the first chapter."[35] Lansdale knew that his fame was partially linked to his characterization as the quintessential "quiet American," so his attempts to capitalize on this phenomenon seem only natural for a man who so avidly sought access to power. He understood the origins of his celebrity and marketed his notoriety to good effect. Typical was the 1960 address he titled "The 'True American,'" a not too subtle play on the novel's title, where he spoke about the state of U.S.-Philippine relations. He argued that a special person was needed to restore the relationship between these two countries, a "true" American, one who "emerges as a larger-than-life image: a person of integrity, with the courage of his convictions, with competence in some technical field, with devotion to getting things done, and with Christian affection for his fellow man." Lansdale's rhetoric was strikingly imperialist when he concluded,

"The whole climate of relationships can brighten to permit us to have a teamwork with Filipinos really consonant with a United States which is the leading nation in the world."[36] In other words, this "teamwork" involved the continuation of the American presence in and power over the Philippines.

Years later, when a correspondent again raised the question of "Lansdale as Pyle," weariness of the entire affair had clearly set in, and he responded, "I guess the most honest way to answer you is to say that I no longer care whether or not folks identify me with fictional characters." Yet in this same letter Lansdale could not resist taking another swipe at Greene: "Graham Greene once told someone, who later mentioned it to me, that he definitely did not have me in mind when he created the character, Alden Pyle. I sure hope not, since Pyle apparently unsexed himself by hanging around air-conditioned bathrooms."[37] Of course, nowhere in the novel did Pyle "unsex" himself. With little liking for the author who so unsparingly attacked everything he believed in, Lansdale perhaps decided that the best way to answer this attack was to question Greene's manliness and his choice of including homosexuals in his novels. As a "man's man," Lansdale could probably think of no better retort.

Of course, Lansdale was not alone in dismissing Greene's views of Vietnam and of America. The *Saturday Evening Post* found the British novelist's writings less than helpful in waging the Cold War; its editorial "To Get Rave Reviews Write an Anti-U.S.A. Novel" condemned Greene's "neutralist" politics. Playing off the same theme, the *New York Herald Tribune* proposed replacing the "ugly" and "quiet" stereotypes with "a gratifying number of United States Army officers and men who might be called, without flattery, the 'savvy' Americans."[38] More important was the enthusiastic acceptance by all "proper" American publications of John Foster Dulles's famous dictum on the immoral quality of neutralism when waging a Cold War. An "us" versus "them" attitude permeated almost all of Washington's actions during this period, and given the tenor of these times, Greene was clearly marked as one of "them," with the result that the American government amassed a forty-five-page security file on him.[39]

Two months after the Vietnam War ended in 1975, Herbert Mitgang (a member of the editorial board of the *New York Times*) reflected on Greene's novel and its larger impact:

> Now that it's all over but the writing I wonder if the bearded Hindu who owned the Salamath Book Center, toward the waterfront at the end of Rue Catinat in Saigon, will be able to stock Graham Greene's "The Quiet American" again. When I casually asked him for a copy one steaming night, during the height of the war's fury nearly a decade ago, a look of terror crossed his face. I tried to

reassure him that my interest was only literary and, no, I didn't work for any American intelligence agencies. With a smile of doubt, he said that he did not carry any books written by Mr. Greene—"especially not that one."[40]

The bookseller instead recommended a book about Vietnam subsidized by the Rand Corporation and Michigan State University's advisory group. The irony of being refused a fictional treatment of the CIA but offered a book that was funded by the CIA was not lost on Mitgang.

Throughout this entire convoluted history, the book endured and became a touchstone for those seeking to understand how and why America went into Vietnam. Even after the last U.S. helicopter had left South Vietnam in 1975, congressmen still looked to the novel as a way to understand the coming foreign policy problems. During a congressional hearing on why the CIA's intelligence about the North Vietnamese and the Vietcong had been so wrong, Greene's novel came up once again. At one point the following exchange took place between Congressman William Lehman (D-Florida) and William Colby, Director of the CIA:

> MR. LEHMAN: Just thinking back to some of the things I have read. I wonder how many of you gentleman ever read any of Graham Greene's books? Have you read "The Quiet American"?
> MR. COLBY: I have.
> MR. LEHMAN: Graham Greene . . . seems to have a conceptual understanding of the impossibility of understanding the motivations and what you called the capabilities of the armed services of that particular kind of culture. . . . I am just concerned about how can we possibly prevent the kinds of miscalculations, the misconceptualizing or lack of understanding of what is going on— the basic limitations of someone like this fellow Pyle, and Graham Greene, who is dealing from one culture into another culture without knowing what the hell he was doing.

In a convoluted way the congressman was speaking of Greene's ability to capture how different Eastern and Western cultures were, and to suggest the foolhardiness of U.S. intervention in the Third World. Mr. Colby, of course, tried to reassure the congressman that not only had he read the book too but that the CIA was able to see through the veil of other cultures, and that the United States was able to act (militarily and covertly) abroad.[41]

Whether there were winners or losers in this entire affair really depends on how one keeps score; almost every single book that mentions Lansdale prefaces his actions abroad by declaring that he was the "quiet American." Even Lansdale's official biographer assumed that he was the role model for the character, and Greene's denials are hardly ever noted.

An important part of *The Quiet American*'s legacy involved the novel's transformation into a movie, released three years later. In the process, a series of battles developed between Greene's efforts to preserve the political impact of his novel and the film director Joseph Mankiewicz's efforts to convert it into a story he preferred—not incidentally, an American Cold War story. Beyond the usual debates concerning artistic freedom and over streamlining a novel into cinematic form, Cold War exigencies played a crucial role and generated the more intriguing personal battle involving Greene, Mankiewicz, and—covertly—Lansdale. The end result was a movie that remade Alden Pyle along lines that were far more pleasing to American Cold Warriors but that Greene would never forgive.

Graham Greene once reflected on his writing style: "When I describe a scene, I capture it with the moving eye of the cine-camera rather than with the photographer's eye—which leaves it frozen. In this precise domain I think that the cinema has influenced me. . . . I work with the camera, following my characters and their movement."[42] This revealing comment not only suggests how Greene approached his work but also hints that *The Quiet American* was conceived with a movie in mind. Greene's prior work with films, notably *The Ministry of Fear* (1944) and *The Third Man* (1949), as well as the exotic locale of *The Quiet American* and the periodic appearance of Vietnam on the front pages of American and European newspapers, all support this interpretation. Yet Hollywood initially distanced itself from the novel; Greene's flirtation with the Communist Party in the 1920s, along with the book's politics, may have contributed to the delay of its appearance in celluloid form.[43]

It is impossible to understand the movie without realizing that it was a byproduct of the battles that raged in Hollywood during the Cold War, involving not only McCarthyism and the purging of the "Hollywood Ten" but the covert role of the CIA as well. More than any other branch of the U.S. government, the CIA recognized that the Cold War required influencing the "hearts and minds" of intellectuals and the middle class. The agency therefore worked to transform novels that had "neutralist" messages into pro-American movies. For example, the all-purpose CIA agent E. Howard Hunt purchased the film rights to George Orwell's *Animal Farm* and was involved with the 1954 remake of the film version of Orwell's *1984*."[44] The filming of *The Quiet American* was a bit more convoluted than those straightforward attempts, but as with Orwell's work, there was an active effort by the CIA to produce a rendition more in line with American Cold War efforts.

The starting point in this history is the relationship between two extraordinarily ambitious men, Lansdale and Joseph Mankiewicz. Mankiewicz not only directed the film but wrote the screenplay and produced it. One of the premier directors in Hollywood, he was justifiably famous for such earlier movies as *The Philadelphia Story* (1940), *The Ghost and Mrs. Muir* (1947), and *All About Eve* (1950). In Saigon the two men met and struck up a friendship while Mankiewicz was scouting for film locations. Mankiewicz found in Lansdale the perfect source for the host of questions he had about Vietnam, its people, the nature of the war. In turn, Lansdale found in Mankiewicz an American who could counter Greene in a way no one else had done. Greene's interest in seeing his book turned into a successful film included his sending unsolicited advice during the preproduction phase: "I do hope that the film does not depend on his [Mankiewicz] being allowed to shoot in Saigon itself. . . . There is nothing Eastern about Saigon except the passersby."[45] However, Lansdale's influence far exceeded this. The crucial document is a March 1956 letter in which Lansdale responded to a series of questions put to him by Mankiewicz. It is one of the most astonishing documents in all of his personal papers. Unlike the countless (and often ridiculous) documents that have been classified, and reclassified, or have simply disappeared, this three-page letter spells out the many efforts Lansdale made to promote South Vietnam to an American audience. For these reasons the letter deserves to be quoted at length, with the most intriguing passages italicized:

Headquarters
Military Assistance Advisory Group
Saigon, Vietnam

17 March 1956

Mr. Joseph L. Mankiewicz
Figaro Incorporated
1270 Sixth Avenue
New York, New York

Dear Mr. Mankiewicz.

During your visit to Saigon, I promised to send you answers to some of your questions about "The Quiet American." . . .

"The Quiet American" became a much sought after book in Saigon, so it took a little quiet larceny to obtain a copy long enough to read it. I have, and can see how it begs to be put on film. Also, I can see how your handling of the plot is thoroughly justified.

Trinh Minh Thé changed from Chief of Staff of the Cao Dai Army to Chief of the Quoc Gia Lien Minh, his "National Resistance Front," on 7 June 1951; as Cao Dai Chief of Staff . . . [he] received pay, arms, and other munitions from the French for the fight against the Vietminh. . . . His Lien Minh platform was pro an independent Vietnam and both anti-Vietminh and anti–French colonialism; these Lien Minh ideas strike a chord of memory of our own days prior to 1776, particularly of some of the ideas of our Committees of Correspondence.

The explosion in front of the Continental Hotel took place on 9 January 1952. One account of the incident states that the explosion was believed to be caused by a charge of approximately 20 kilos of French melenite (this explosive is commonly called "plastic" due to its plasticity) . . . [and] it seems probable that General Thé obtained it from the French Expeditionary Corps originally, since the French handled the supply of all munitions to our side. U.S. military supplies were handled by the French entirely in Vietnam.

General Thé claimed credit for this explosion via a broadcast over the National Resistance radio.

Since General Thé is quite a national hero for his fight against the Binh Xuyen in 1955, and in keeping with your treatment of this actually having been a Communist action, I'd suggest that you just go right ahead and let it be finally revealed that the Communists did it after all, even to faking the radio broadcast (which would have been easy to do).

So far, John Gates and the others have been unable to confirm the existence of "diolaction." All of us are convinced that this is a literary invention.

We discussed what sort of a job Pyle might have had out here. If he were out here on a foundation grant from some U.S. foundation, he could easily be doing a study of the government administrative system. At that time, the Vietnamese government was administering all territory not actively in the hands of the Vietminh, right up to the Chinese border in Tonkin. This government, of course, was subject to Vietminh action against it and, if a person such as Pyle should stumble into a Vietminh plot against it, it would be logical that he would be eliminated for endangering the plot or for knowing too much or even for revenge.

If there's anything else that we can do to help from here, please let me know. . . .

Sincerely,

EDWARD G. LANSDALE
Colonel USAF

p.s. Since writing the above, I happened to have a chat with a Vietnamese friend who was in Saigon at the time of the explosion and was in a position to know the facts. . . . According to him, General Thé used two bombs (duds) which the French had dropped on his forces during air attacks on Nui Ba Den (near Tayninh). He rigged each one up with a timing device and installed them in a sealed compartment in the gas tanks of two stolen cars, which were left parked in front of the Continental and the Prefecture. They blew up within seconds of each other.[46]

Lansdale's efforts at transforming the ideological purposes of a novel whose politics and tone he despised into a film he could enjoy and later use are apparent in this document.

In the italicized sections, Lansdale acknowledges General Thé role in the bombing that killed and wounded many but asks Mankiewicz to place the deaths at the feet of the communists. Also evident here is Lansdale's long-time interest in the uses of history, rendering a romanticized vision of America in 1776 into a justification for Thé's politics. It appears that novels were one thing, but movies were a far more important matter, given their popularity. The "hearts and minds" of the West were at stake and could not be lost because of one disaffected British writer.[47]

The results were as Lansdale wished. Mankiewicz remade the story and in fact sent the screenplay to Lansdale for his approval. Lansdale's response to the screenplay, through an aide, indicates how satisfied he now was with the movie version of the novel: "I am delighted to have received Mr. Mankiewicz' screenplay of THE QUIET AMERICAN. Colonel Lansdale has read it with interest and wishes to convey to Mr. Mankiewicz his appreciation of the script as well as his best regards." The CIA's interest in the film extended even beyond Lansdale's suggestions. Robert Lantz, a vice president to Figaro Inc., the production company that oversaw the making of the film, met with Allen Dulles before the film was made. Dulles apparently liked the idea of the film and how its message countered the novel's depiction of Americans abroad; he offered U.S. government assistance to make the film in Saigon.[48] A short time later the South Vietnamese government banned the novel and gave Mankiewicz complete cooperation in the making of his film; he received an official letter supporting him in this matter. To allay any doubts that a South Vietnamese bureaucrat might have, the letter specified that "the story of the film will be entirely different from "The Quiet American" by Graham Greene. [Mankiewicz] is anti-Communist, and aims at building up the future Republic of Viet Nam."[49] It was written by Vo Van Hai, a friend of Lansdale and at that time the Special Secretary of the Presidency of Ngo Dinh Diem. Once the film was completed Mankiewicz cabled Diem: "I hope you will be proud of the film and I look forward to showing it to you."[50]

There is a curious postscript to this affair. In relating the infamous bombing incident discussed by Lansdale in his letter to Mankiewicz, the novel makes no specific accusation as to its origins, yet Greene clearly believed the incident had been concocted to suit anticommunist interests. He would write later of his hunch: "The *Life* photographer at the moment of the explosion was so well placed that he was able to take an astonishing and horrifying photograph which showed the body of a trishaw driver still upright after his legs had been blown off. This photograph was reproduced in an American propaganda magazine published in Manila over the caption "The Work of Ho Chin Minh" although General Thé had promptly and proudly claimed the bomb as his own."[51]

Greene had no way of knowing of Lansdale's involvement in the movie version, and it is not known whether Lansdale was involved with the "American propaganda magazine" mentioned by Greene, but the entire affair has a Lansdalian touch to it. He had established an extensive network of anticommunist Filipinos working in Vietnam. Lansdale also helped organize the Eastern Construction Company, the Freedom Company, and Operation Brotherhood, using CIA funds to foster closer ties between Filipinos and Diem's new government in South Vietnam.[52] One can only imagine Greene's outrage if he had known that the cultural and economic network organized by the CIA in Southeast Asia included the making of this film.

Once the film was completed, Lansdale worked to make it a success back in the United States. His earlier efforts to have Pyle employed by an American foundation were realized—and then some—when the proceeds of the movie premiere went to the American Friends of Vietnam. The Pyle of the movie works for "Friends of Free Asia," an obvious reference to the American Friends of Vietnam. And after its premiere, Lansdale wrote to his friend and former boss in South Vietnam, General John W. O'Daniel, "I'm happy that you have been planning sponsorship of this picture by the American Friends of Vietnam. It's a natural association of ideas, with the way Mankiewicz treated the story. . . . I took the liberty of inviting a number of folks from practically all [Pentagon] departments, agencies, and services concerned with psychological, political and security affairs to attend the screening—and they all seemed to enjoy it as much as I did."[53] Key American policymakers and South Vietnamese officials attended, director Joseph Mankiewicz and the World War II hero and star of the film, Audie Murphy, were invited to join the organization.[54] Afterward, the Vietnamese ambassador to the United States, Tran Van Chuong, and his wife (the parents of Madame Nhu) hosted a party at the Washington Playhouse Theater celebrating the release of the film. The *Washington Post*'s society columnist recapped the highlights of the evening with typical fanfare: "Arriving guests at the theater were greeted by an Oriental dragon accompanied by masked musicians and dancers performing the centuries-old ceremony of the Orient to greet the lunar New Year."[55]

Tran and Lansdale communicated often on how best to help solidify the Diem regime both in South Vietnam and in Washington. A typical letter from Tran to Lansdale read, "I congratulate you for understanding the decisive importance of psychological factors against international Communism."[56] As Lansdale's earlier showing of Hollywood films to Filipino peasants demonstrated, he understood the power of movies in shaping perceptions of American efforts abroad. Greene too understood the power of the reworking and bitterly remarked, "Far was it from my mind, when I wrote 'The Quiet American,' that the book would become the source of profit to one of the most corrupt governments in Southeast Asia."[57]

Although Lansdale's part in remaking the book into a movie was unknown to the public at the time, almost all critics, viewing the film through the prism of the novel, saw that the real story was the changes that had been made to Greene's work, and most thought the changes were for the worse. The film does have its moments and, as one of only two films to be made in Vietnam during the 1950s, is quite good at evoking the color and rhythms of daily life there. Two scenes are particularly inspired. First, at the beginning of the movie the camera lazily follows a parade during the Tet celebration and then drifts away from the crowd of people to come to rest upon the dead body of Pyle. Second, the air of exoticism and mystery of the East is evoked by the camera's scanning of the interior of the Cao Dai cathedral and its wonders, making understandable one writer's comment that its architecture "would have dumbfounded Walt Disney." In fact, some of the scenes inside the cathedral were replicated in Rome, giving them a Vatican-like feel.[58]

Despite these effects, the film's transformation of the novel succeeded only in robbing it of its power. Scene after scene takes snippets of Greene's dialogue and either deletes the key phrases spoken by Fowler that serve Greene's politics or reworks Pyle's responses into something far more innocent and noble than the novelist would ever have allowed.[59] One of the most astonishing changes comes at the end of the film when, after all the tragedies that befall the characters, both renditions have Fowler's plaintive remark, "I wished there existed someone to whom I could say that I was sorry," yet the screenplay omits the first part of that line, in which Fowler comes to the decidedly upbeat conclusion that "everything had gone right with me since he had died."[60]

In the novel Fowler is reunited with Phuong, but when the film ends he has not only just learned that the communists have deceived him into helping them kill Pyle but is further humiliated by being rejected by Phuong. In other words, the communists make a mockery not only of his politics but of his manhood as well.

Among other alterations, the only drug addict portrayed in the movie is a communist character, whereas in the book, Fowler himself is addicted to opium. In one interview preceding the movie, Mankiewicz told a journalist that he sought to "mak[e] the American both more credible and truer to the earnest, hard-working, apolitical types that he had found in Indo-China." [61] In order to make the Pyle character seem more idealistic and innocent, Mankiewicz clears him of all connections to the CIA and to the bombing incident. Another difference is in Pyle's regional background: in the book he is from Boston, with all its associations with puritans and eastern elites; in the film version he becomes a rangy Texan spouting homespun truths. These changes display Mankiewicz's transformation of the multiple politics of the novel into a simple morality tale with goodhearted Americans on one side and cynical or damned Europeans on the other.

Many of the problems with the movie were attributed to Audie Murphy's weak performance as Alden Pyle; in fact, his weakness as an actor led Laurence Oliver to drop out of the project to be replaced by Sir Michael Redgrave. A man accustomed to acting in either westerns or World War II movies, Murphy did not possess the skills necessary to complement Redgrave's nuanced and polished performance as Fowler. The incongruity is particularly apparent when Pyle identifies a passage read by Fowler from *Othello*—this from an actor who always seemed far more comfortable around guns and horses than either people or books. Personal animosities between the two actors did not help matters. At one point Redgrave asked Mankiewicz to get Murphy to blink every now and then while Redgrave spoke his lines. Redgrave especially disliked Murphy's habit of always carrying a gun with him. In short, Murphy was simply out of his element (not to mention he had appendicitis during the making of the movie). After witnessing a Cao Dai religious procession that seemed moblike to him, he told a reporter: "The first thing I did was go to the nearest army post and draw a .45 and 500 rounds of ammunition, which I kept in my hotel room. The commies were only sixteen miles from Saigon at that time, and you never knew what was going to happen. I figured if they were going to get me, I'd give them a good fight first."[62]

The response of others to the same event is striking in its differences. Redgrave wrote in his diary at the time: "Only once did we see a sign of conflict. It was whilst we were shooting the scenes of the Indo-Chinese New Year. Placards borne aloft in a religious demonstration were suddenly turned around, revealing on their reverse side anti-Government slogans. When this was pointed out and interpreted for us, someone suggested we should have to cut those shots, or else reshoot them. "Leave them in," said Joe. An erudite, frequently witty man, he also cultivated a "tough guy" image. "What the hell? No one'll know what they mean.'"[63] The procession can be seen in the beginning and end of the film, making this movie more of a documentary than anyone had initially intended. Mankiewicz, though, was no fool; he wanted the anti-intellectualism and lack of refinement on the part of the actor who portrayed Pyle (who was Harvard-educated in the novel). Perhaps this is why he said that Murphy was "the perfect symbol of what I want[ed] to say." As his third wife Rose Mankiewicz explained it though, "Frank's first choice for the role was Montgomery Clift. Murphy was a hero not an actor," a World War II veteran with impeccable patriotic credentials.[64] The limitations of these credentials when it came to acting were noted by almost all critics. In one trade publication, "the box office magic of Audie Murphy's name" was cited as a prime reason the film was made, yet "Audie's personal virtues added to the many virtues of the character tend to make him a sort of male Tess Trueheart or a Y.M.C.A. secretary."[65]

Clearly, Mankiewicz wanted to portray an American who only wanted to help others and would never interfere in Vietnamese politics. In this respect Murphy was perfectly cast—he embodied both innocence and do-goodism—but he was not so much "quiet" as banal, especially given that he had to act against Redgrave as the worldly Fowler. Perhaps Mankiewicz's casting also had to do with his own view of Fowler: "I consider him the hero. He is right in all his political observations."[66] One wonders whether Mankiewicz really endorsed Fowler's anti-Americanism. Also, why would he go to the trouble of altering Greene's novel into something that might have been written by Lansdale yet allow Murphy's weakness as an actor to make Fowler the character the audience roots for. It remains something of a mystery and may suggest some ambivalence on the part of the director about altering the book and its politics. Or it could simply reflect the extent to which pressure was applied by Hollywood on behalf of casting Murphy.

Mankiewicz later said that he wanted Pyle to be like the Americans he saw in Vietnam at the time, "an idealistic bunch of kids . . . who couldn't set off a firecracker on the Fourth of July."[67] The fact that these "idealistic kids" worked in programs designed by the American Friends of Vietnam indicates once again how Lansdale and his connections with key members of the AFV (e.g., Wesley Fishel, Angier Biddle Duke, Harold Oram, Gen. John "Iron Mike" O'Daniel and Gen. Sam Williams) influenced the making of the movie. One AFV member wrote as the film was in production, "I think we have a very important ally in someone as bright and talented as Joe Mankiew-icz."[68] This alliance developed to the point that a member of Mankiewicz's production staff believed the director had been "brainwashed" by this orga-nization.[69] Although Mankiewicz suspected that Lansdale was with the CIA, his wife insisted that "Joe would never have bent for political reasons . . . he wanted to write it that way." Yet he was also aware that if the book's politics were not changed, the film would not be made because, as she noted further, "Nobody in Hollywood would listen at the time" to the making of a film that skewered American actions abroad.[70]

While there is a certain generic process at work within the film—its search for closure, both moralistic and literal, is standard Hollywood movie-making—the transformation and reduction of the novel, along with Mur-phy's feeble performance, inevitably led to mixed reviews. Pauline Kael wrote perceptively: "There are so many fine things in the film (especially Redgrave's portrait of a man whose cold exterior is just a thin skin over his passionate desperation) that perhaps you can simply put aside the offending compromises of the last reel. But for anyone familiar with the novel, that is nearly impossible." Bosley Crowther of the *New York Times* weighed in with a less harsh judgment, even as he noted the "curious" differences from the book.[71] The movie had its ardent champions, though, notably the French New Wave director Jean-Luc Godard. He passionately argued that it was one of the best films of 1958, though the extent to which he was being contrarian or deliberately absurd, one cannot know, given Godard's ap-proach to film and politics.[72]

Lansdale was far less concerned with how critics reviewed the movie; as always, it was the film's overt politics that were his primary concern, and he relished the way his vision had triumphed over Greene's story. He gleefully reported his triumph to Diem: "Just a little note to tell you that I have seen the motion picture, 'The Quiet American,' and that I feel it will help win more friends for you and Vietnam. When I first mentioned this motion picture to you last year, I had read Mr. Mankiewicz's 'treatment' of the story and had thought it an excellent change from Mr. Greene's novel of despair. Mr. Mankiewicz had done much more with the picture itself, and I now feel that you will be very pleased with the reactions of those who see it."[73] In other words, Lansdale's pupil Mankiewicz had done well: the movie faith-fully adhered to the American policy line regarding Vietnam. Indeed, when Mankiewicz had told his agent, Robert Lantz, "I will tell the whole story anti-Communist and pro-American," it was as if he planned to base the film upon Lansdale's earlier letter.[74]

To be fair to Mankiewicz, this was a very difficult period in his life; his wife at that time was deeply depressed and would eventually commit suicide. He later said of *The Quiet American* that it was a "very bad film I made during a very unhappy time in my life." Yet he also defended the politics of the movie by openly proclaiming that Greene had written the novel with its anti-American theme "in a fit of great pique" after the State Department refused him entry into the United States.[75] Mankiewicz vigorously denied that he tampered with the ending of novel for political reasons, but his explanation— "because in the book the motivation doesn't make sense about why he [Fowler] turned the American over to the Communists"—is quite unconvincing. Fowler's hostility toward American interests is both clear and easily understood by readers of the novel; equally, the novel is about much more than two men's jealousies over a women, yet it is these reductions that become central to the movie.

Not surprisingly, Greene was furious with these changes and thought of the film as "a complete travesty," "a real piece of political dishonesty. The film makes the American very wise and the Englishmen completely the fool of the Communists. And the casting was appalling. The Vietnamese girl Phuong was played by an Italian." When Greene returned to this subject a year later, if anything, his anger toward the movie had increased: "One could believe that the film was made deliberately to attack the book and its author. But the book was based on a closer knowledge of the Indo-China war than the American [Mankiewicz] possessed and I am vain enough to believe that the book will survive a few years longer than Mr Mankiewicz's picture."[76] There is a certain irony in these open hostilities in that Mankiewicz saw himself as very much an artist like Greene, something of a dissident within the Hollywood community. In fact, his views on Hollywood had far more in common with the ideas of Greene than of Lansdale. Mankiewicz elaborated on this attitude shortly after the movie had been made: "I left Hollywood because Hollywood happens to be located by what I consider the single most frightening phenomena of the American world, which is the city of Los Angeles and Southern California. There, I think, is the truly damaging part of it, the true threat to the American spirit and the American mind. Again, I think Hollywood had thrust upon it a great many of the evils that should be properly credited to Los Angeles, California—a place where I think it is still against the law to teach your children that the United Nations exists."[77]

Nevertheless, their differences aside, Mankiewicz shared with Lansdale an anticommunist liberalism which Greene despised but which proved a powerful force in influencing the direction of the arts at this time in America. The end result is that the film version of *The Quiet American* was not nearly as good as Mankiewicz's other works; his obituary in the *New York Times* did not even discuss it.[78]

Unlike Mankiewicz's troubles with the movie, Lansdale's efforts at remaking the novel appeared to be a Cold War success for the American government. Although his selling of his vision of America's role in Vietnam was successful in the short run, it cannot compare in longevity or cultural resonance with the impact of Greene's novel. Even so, in the larger context of the battles waged between political and cultural fronts during this period, the results of governmental interference in the arts in order to promote Cold War ideologies cannot be underestimated. It was men like Lansdale with their zealous sincerity who, by the late 1960s, helped to create a political and cultural climate of extreme skepticism about the role of the American government in Vietnam. This loss of faith in American institutions, which has its roots in the Vietnam debacle, extends into the present, in both politics and mass culture. It was a reflection of this broken rendition of Greene's novel that led Hollywood to remake the movie in 2001 with the young heartthrob Brendan Fraser playing the Pyle character and Michael Caine cast as Fowler. This version was far more faithful to the novel; a journalist on the film location noted that "verisimilitude is what the new rendition of the film is after. Phuong is played by a Vietnamese this time. It is also the most expensive movie ever made in Vietnam."[79] Yet this remake encountered problems as well. Because of heightened patriotism after 9/11 Miramax Films repeatedly delayed its release. "We were worried that nobody had the stomach for a movie about bad Americans anymore," said Harvey Weinstein, cochairman of Miramax.[80] Eventually, under a campaign initiated by Michael Caine, the film was released and did modestly well at the box office. Caine's performance as Fowler was easily as good as Redgrave's, and he richly deserved the Academy Award nomination for Best Actor. When speaking of the film, Caine captured the adventure of making the film in a communist country: "They closed down the entire center of the city for us. It was amazing. That's one of the benefits of dealing with a totalitarian government. And everybody there knew the book. Seriously. On every single street corner, there's a kid selling cigarettes, dirty post cards and 'The Quiet American.'" That Greene's book remains of interest over fifty years after its publication is proof enough that "Greeneland" continues to resonate.[81]

ANOTHER NOVEL, *The Ugly American* (1958) by William Lederer and Eugene Burdick, represented a "Lansdale" far more conducive to those who championed American Cold War interests. Written as an explicit warning to Americans that they were losing the Cold War because of their arrogance and ethnocentrism vis-à-vis the people and cultures of the Third World, this novel had a profound and lasting impact upon American public discourse. That it was poorly written, was filled with stock characters, and had no real plot other than anticommunist sensationalism was all secondary; it touched a nerve in many Americans and became a literary sensation because of its argument that the United States was blundering its way to defeat in the Cold War. Shortly after its publication it became a Book-of-the-Month Club selection and was serialized in the *Saturday Evening Post*. For seventy-two weeks it was on the *New York Times* best-seller list, and its cover blurb quoted the *Times* review: "IF THIS WERE NOT A FREE COUNTRY, THIS BOOK WOULD BE BANNED. DEVASTATING." The State Department, working with other agencies, commissioned a question-and-answer pamphlet as a way to respond to the host of charges made by the authors.[82] Soon afterward it was championed by Senator John F. Kennedy and in 1963 was made into a film starring Marlon Brando. The book has sold over seven million copies and is still used in college classrooms to show students how American foreign policy problems were discussed during that time.

This renown helped bring the novel to the attention of American pundits and politicians alike as a "how to" book—actually a "not how to" book—regarding U.S. actions abroad. Its influence was so far-reaching that the historian John Hellmann has argued that it helped spur later efforts by Kennedy to mobilize the country during his presidential administration: "Influential far beyond its very large readership, *The Ugly American* helped to create the atmosphere in which President John F. Kennedy would call for a national physical-fitness program, declare America's willingness to 'bear any burden,' found the Peace Corps, build up the American Special Forces, and emphasize new tactics of counterinsurgency to combat [the] communist 'people's war' in South Vietnam."[83] The novel was read as a repudiation of Greene's depiction of American efforts abroad even as it argued that the United States was losing the Cold War in these foreign countries. Although it shares with Greene's earlier work a critique of Americans living and working abroad, Lederer and Burdick's liberal, anticommunist politics led to a far warmer reception and a national soul-searching.

Lansdale figures in this history as well. He knew both the authors. In fact he knew Lederer so well that when Magsaysay requested President Eisenhower to send Lansdale immediately back to the Philippines to help in public relations matters, and specifically to counter the growing anti-Americanism in the country, Lansdale wrote to "The Director" (presumably Allen Dulles, director of the CIA) that Lederer should go instead.[84] Yet, what truly separates the politics of the two books is that *The Ugly American* was considered responsible criticism, not infected with "neutralist" thought, and sales of the novel were helped immensely by President Eisenhower's announcement after a long weekend at Camp David that he had read and enjoyed the book—a bit surprising, given that the novel was written and read as a liberal critique of Eisenhower-Dulles foreign policy. And although it was serialized in the conservative *Saturday Evening Post*, Democratic leaders championed the book because its criticism of the Eisenhower presidency seemed both responsible and patriotic. The Democratic leadership, like the novel, sought a more activist role for the U.S. concerning foreign assistance to Third World countries ("developing nations" was the term used at the time). In fact, Senator John F. Kennedy, after incorporating Lederer and Burdick's criticism into his overall presidential campaign strategy to "get the country moving again," rode the wave of fear, about falling behind the communists, into the White House in 1960.

The entire novel is set in dualities between "ugly" Americans—that is, good citizens who are not afraid to get their hands dirty and work with peasants—and "beautiful" Americans: the State Department officials who know little of the countries in which they work and alternately fear and despise those who are different from them. The Lansdale-like character in this case is the "ugly" Edwin Hillandale, an American military officer who is unique among the other American bureaucrats in that he works with, listens to, and—most important—respects the nationalistic sentiments of Asians. In turn, the people of Sarkhan, the mythical Southeast Asian country where the novel takes place, deeply admire the ideals of the United States and intuitively fear and hate communism. A simple equation has thus emerged: they want what he wants, and he wants what they want.

Because of Hillandale's convictions, he uses a variety of gimmicks and strategies to assist American and anticommunist forces. In the Philippines before coming to Sarkhan, he learns of a province controlled by the communists. Not content to let this matter stand, he sets out to undermine them in a most benevolent fashion: "When he arrived in the capital about half-past eleven, the people of Cuenco saw something they had never in their lives seen before. A tall, slender U.S. Air Force Colonel with red hair and a big nose drove into Cuenco on a red motorcycle, whose gas tank had painted on it in black 'The Ragtime Kid.' He chugged up the main street and stopped at the most crowded part. . . . After waving and smiling at everyone, he took out his harmonica and began to play favorite Filipino tunes in a loud and merry way. . . . Within about fifteen minutes a crowd of about two hundred people surrounded the colonel."[85] After a group sing-a-long—during which Hillandale convinces these peasants that he is as poor as they are—the Filipinos begin quarreling among themselves as to who can invite him to lunch. Since one of them owns a restaurant, "that's where the colonel went, with about ten Filipinos. They ate *adobo* and *pancit* and rice, and they washed it down with Filipino rum and San Miguel beer; and they sang many songs to the accompaniment of the Ragtime Kid's harmonica."[86] Hillandale's triumph is complete when over 95 percent of these citizens vote for the anticommunist candidate, Ramon Magsaysay, and his pro-American platform.

Magsaysay is the only character who is referred to without a pseudonym. Perhaps Lederer and Burdick used his real name to give the novel historical veracity, or considering that so few Americans had ever heard of Magsaysay, his name may have seemed to add an authentic "Sarkhanese"/Filipino touch. Although the novel begins with a classic disclaimer, "The names, the places, the events, are our inventions," the authors also describes it as the "rendering of fact into fiction." Even when fictionalized, the Orient functions as historical footage to be incorporated into American narratives of progress and anticommunism.

Typical of the self-reproducing quality of fictions such as *The Ugly American* was one journalist's later introduction of Lansdale to the newspaper's readers: "Lansdale has demonstrated a remarkable ability to establish personal relationships and mutual trust with Asians who more often than not look with suspicion on a Westerner. He swapped ideas over the breakfast table with Magsaysay. . . . Lansdale could induce the late President Ngo Dinh Diem, back in 1955 and 1956, to shed his mandarin-style dignity and go for a picnic in a Jeep—and Diem liked it. . . . Lansdale, however, denies that he rode around the Philippines on a red motorcycle bearing the inscription 'The Ragtime Kid.'"[87] Here, as with *The Quiet American*, Lansdale seemed to disavow his connections even as he conceded that maybe, just maybe, he was the inspiration for a famous fictional character. In fact, these fictional and journalistic descriptions of him are not really that fanciful; in a draft of his memoirs he wrote: "I had ridden a farm cart into town, playing a harmonica for the children along the road. Later, I had played a harmonica to accompany my friends and some fisherman in their singing around a night-time bonfire on the beach." Also in the draft, Lansdale fondly recalled a time in Vietnam when he was drunk and had insisted on playing the harmonica for all—but such carousing was tied to his supposed success in getting Diem to act more plebeian.[88] In that, he failed in no uncertain terms, even though he expended great energy in trying to transform Diem into a man of the people. Diem was many things, but hail-fellow-well-met was not one of them.

Among other parallels between Hillandale and Lansdale, one involved the uses of astrology as a Cold War weapon. In the novel, Hillandale, who had a degree from the Chungking School of Occult Science, ingratiated himself with the prime minister of Sarkhan in order to further American interests: "The Ragtime Kid and the Prime Minister closed the door of the study and stayed there for half an hour. What went on inside the study none of the other guests knew. But when the door opened, the two men came out arm in arm, and the Prime Minister was gazing up at The Ragtime Kid with obvious awe." Later, when Ambassador MacWhite asks Hillandale how he accomplished these feats, the colonel's response is classically Lansdalian: "It's very important for a palmist or an astrologer to know his man inside out."[89] When one journalist asked Lansdale if he, like Hillandale, knew how to read palms, Lansdale's responded in the only way he knew how—by simply perpetuating the fictions that surrounded his name: "'Well,' he said, with a slight smile that turned up the ends of his moustache, 'there's no question but that palmistry and astrology are important to many people in the Far East. I have used astrology in the past'"[90] Neil Sheehan also found evidence that members of Lansdale's Saigon Military Mission team members helped to write the phony astrological almanacs that Lansdale later employed to further American interests.[91]

Lederer later told Lansdale that the Hillandale character was actually a composite of Lansdale and Lederer himself, but most people have assumed otherwise. Almost every book on Vietnam or the Philippines that mentions Lansdale introduces him as being either Pyle or Hillandale or both, and Lansdale told interviewers that he considered those characters to have been modeled on himself.[92] Robert Kennedy, for one, after meeting with Lansdale, wrote in his diary that Lansdale was "the Ugly American."[93] J. Graham Parsons, the former ambassador to Laos, also reproduced these views when he referred to Lansdale as "a very able man who had a record of success in meeting difficult situations in a novel way, celebrated in *The Ugly American*, actually—that horrible book."[94] Perhaps most fittingly, in two separate interviews with Lansdale the interviewer miswrote Lansdale's first name as "Edwin."[95]

Friends of Lansdale also contributed to this process of fictionalizing him. One wrote to Lansdale and exclaimed: "Your letter to me has caused quite a stir in my household. Its arrival coincided with Marian's reading *The Ugly*

American. The combination was too much. She demands that I become ambassador to Burma *immediately!* . . . 'Just write Ed [she said]—he'll arrange it.' . . . I know *The Ugly American* is overdrawn and for a purpose. But the germ of truth is large and important."[96] The question of whether Lansdale may or may not have been Hillandale becomes lost under the general impression, continually reinforced by government officials, journalists, and friends, that he was in fact the "Ragtime Kid." Years later, he noted the dangerous influence that this fiction had upon Americans who went to war in Vietnam: some soldiers were so influenced by "Edwin Hillandale" that they decided to impersonate him and ride motorcycles into areas controlled by the Vietcong. According to Lansdale, these idealistic warriors, unable to differentiate between fact and fiction, were either captured or killed.[97]

THE MOVIE version of *The Ugly American* is remarkable chiefly for not having nearly such overdrawn plots and characters as the novel. A certain noteworthy subtlety surrounds the film, even though it has some of the absurd qualities that make Hollywood movies so ideologically transparent: a poster advertising the movie juxtaposed Thai and Chinese architecture and showed student rebels wearing Japanese bandanas, indicative of how the Orient and all its "mysteries" were constructed when Hollywood looked East. Yet in comparison with the novel's shallow vignettes and episodic qualities, the movie version, written by Stewart Stern and directed by George Englund, is far more coherent and in places even gripping. A linear narrative helps tremendously.[98]

Stern wisely compressed a number of secondary characters into one: Harrison Carter MacWhite, the U.S. ambassador to Sarkhan. Because he is the sum total of several characters, he shares both "beautiful" and "ugly" qualities. Since Edwin Hillandale, the "Lansdale" character, is part of the composite, it becomes difficult to identify specific characteristics. However, a Lansdale-like moment does occur at the climactic end of the movie. MacWhite is discussing the grand purpose of the Cold War and America's stake in combatting communism in the Third World in terms that Lansdale favored, with a sincerity and fervor that were trademark qualities of liberal Cold Warriors.

But MacWhite has been hit by the realization of his own and America's missteps. Additionally, he has finally comprehended that his political dogma made him partially responsible for the death of his close Sarkhanese friend, Deong, the man who championed the "third force" in Sarkhan. This scene deserves to be quoted at length. On one level it is, as film critic Richard Schickel has argued, a classic example of "liberal big-think" and social science fiction, but MacWhite also echoes Lansdale's trick of reformulating American Cold War policies in terms of the verities and virtues of the democratic revolution:

PRESS: Are we going to lose this country, sir?

MACWHITE (MARLON BRANDO): Well we never had this country.

PRESS: Mr. Ambassador, who killed Deong?

MACWHITE: The Communists. The Communists killed Deong . . . and a misunderstanding. . . ."

[*After this pause the press quiets down and acts as MacWhite's audience, akin to students in need of learning about the meaning of the Cold War. The press becomes then a stand-in for the movie audience.*]

MACWHITE: When I . . . said that a misunderstanding killed Deong I meant my own misunderstanding . . . see, Deong had a kind of passion that maybe all revolutionaries have. It's a kind of feeling that it is easy for us to misinterpret. We forget that the men who started our country had that same kind of passion that Deong had and that these other new leaders have. And unless we recognize their fight for independence to be a part of our own then we drive them to seek understanding in some other place.

PRESS: Are you saying that America is losing the Cold War because we are pushing these countries into the hands of the Communists?

MACWHITE: I'm not saying that. What I am saying is that we can't hope to win the Cold War unless we remember what we are for as well as what we are against.

[*MacWhite's wife looks approvingly toward her husband upon hearing this proclamation*].

I've learned in a very personal way . . . that I can't preach the American heritage and expect to be believed if I act out of impatience or sacrifice my principles for expediency. I've learned that the only time we're hated is when we stop trying to be what we started out to be 200 years ago.

Now I'm not blaming my country. I'm blaming the indifference that some of us show towards its promises.

[*Fade from MacWhite in American Embassy in Sarkhan to modern America and a superhighway and then focus on one house in a suburban community. Another fade to inside of house and its living room, where MacWhite is continuing to lecture, but is now seen speaking from the TV. As he continues to lecture, the family man walks into the living room, eating a piece of chicken.*]

If the Cold War disappeared right now the American people would still be in this fight against ignorance and hunger and disease because it's right. It's right. And if I had one appeal to make to every American it would be. . . .

[*Man turns off TV set; end of movie*].⁹⁹

This is a telling scene with its Lansdalian rhetoric about the meaning and uses of the American Revolution and its portrayal of the perils of American political indifference. And although MacWhite has recognized that his own actions caused misunderstanding, disaster, and death, he still feels comfortable broadcasting America's virtues to people who were no longer interested in listening to them—at home or abroad. This was to some extent Lansdale's fate as well. Like MacWhite, he never tired of interpreting for the American people the meaning of the Cold War, never deviated from his belief in the rightness of his cause, and remained convinced until his death that communism constituted a mortal threat to U.S. interests.

It was typical of the relationship between Hollywood and the government that the movie script was read and heavily critiqued by State Department officials, who did not care for its portrayal of policymakers as "beautiful" Americans or for its message about why the United States was losing the Cold War. Not surprisingly, it was the liberal contingent who were most outraged by the script. Key officials at the State Department, including Chester Bowles, and U.S. senators such as Hubert Humphrey, Birch Bayh, and Frank Church all objected to allowing the themes of the novel to be presented for worldwide distribution. Senator J. William Fulbright took to the Senate floor to denounce the making of the movie and urged the State Department to refuse to cooperate with the film's producers: "I have been told upon excellent authority that one of the producers of the movie said: 'This is our story line. Here is this lush shacked up with a Eurasian dame to whom he spills American secrets. . . . Translating this from Hollywood language, this means that the United States Ambassador to a Southeast Asian country is a drunkard who has a Eurasian mistress to whom he betrays secrets of our foreign policy."[100] Fulbright's analysis of the script was a bit off. Burdick and Lederer wrote that they had contacted Fulbright and "volunteered to take him on an *incognito* trip to Southeast Asia to see things for himself. He did not reply." In the same article they proclaimed that few American officials understood the true nature of the struggles in the Third World except "one U.S. Air Force brigadier general named Ed Lansdale [who] has pushed and struggled for a counter-guerilla capacity in Vietnam. . . . In our book, there is a Colonel Hillandale who argues for precisely these things. Any resemblance is purely coincidental."[101]

This entire episode demonstrated once again that the movie version of a popular book concerned Washington far more than did the novel itself. Later, Stern duly summarized the U.S. government's chief complaints:

1. Script makes Communists case better than Communists themselves. It will do great harm.
2. Script contends that U.S. has no interest in others and gives aid for selfish, aggressive reasons only.
3. Script supports the Communist "lie" and describes a U.S. policy which is contrary to the facts.
4. If the script did not dramatize policy but concentrated instead on showing Americans making errors which can be rectified, there would be no objection.[102]

There were thirty-one additional complaints in this list. With the support of Arthur Schlesinger Jr. and some further modifications to the script, however, the government allowed the movie to proceed.[103] Of interest here is that complaint 3 repeats 1 and 2 and that 4 seems to arrive at the real objection: namely, that State Department officials did not want American policy scrutinized by Hollywood. Instead, they wanted to continue the illusion that Americans acted on their own initiative and were not the mindless vehicles of government policy.

As important as Stern's script was—including the changes made to it after government complaints—it was secondary to the performance of Marlon Brando. In his memoir (of sorts), Brando barely discussed the movie other than to say, "In hindsight I now realize that the movie was also a metaphor for all the policies that led to Vietnam and the loss of 58,000 American lives, largely because of myths about the 'Communist conspiracy' and the 'domino theory' that sprang out of the heads of the Dulles brothers."[104] This lazy critique mirrors the effort he put into the acting, which remains the chief reason that the movie was so harshly criticized at the time of its release. Pauline Kael thought the movie so bad that it must be a send-up comedy. Andrew Sarris believed the movie was an egomaniacal project by Brando: everyone else in the movie acted so poorly that Brando could only look good in comparison. Both gleefully pointed to the absurdity of having Brando portray a State Department official.[105] Others were simply outraged at his salary: $500,000 plus 10 percent of the gross even as he said "the picture does not resemble the book."[106] Yet today Brando's performance seems quite diverting, especially in light of the self-parodic quality that characterizes his later work. In fact, the pleasures of watching *The Ugly American* today derive primarily from Brando's method-acting approach; his reaction to drinking palm whiskey for the first time involves mumbling and rolling his eyes at the same time, creating a small gem of a moment. Equally striking is the way the audience first sees Brando. Replacing the ripped T-shirt, motorcycle jacket, and trademark scowl that marked his persona in such classics as *On the Waterfront* and *The Wild One*, Brando here evokes a young Dean Acheson, sporting a pipe, vest, briefcase, and mustache to represent MacWhite's more "cultured" appearance.[107] The authenticity that the director sought is striking: President Kennedy's New York tailor was commissioned to provide the star's wardrobe. But all this falls by the wayside when we see Brando speaking "Sarkhanese" to a group of "know nothing" U.S. Senators. Viewers' complete inability to suspend disbelief and accept Brando as Acheson-like became a primary reason why the film failed.

Aware of the government's earlier objections, Stern's screenplay critiques the John Foster Dulles line of neutralism-as-immoralism in only the most genteel of ways. In this respect it replicates the novel's ideology fairly accurately and points to the limits of criticism available to liberals in the aftermath of McCarthyism. Although liberal perspectives may have offered a more nuanced view of Third World nationalism than conservative rantings about "the Asian peril," these critiques invariably championed modernization theory and the necessity for America to play a leading role globally, never entertaining serious discussion on the changing nature of imperialism in the postcolonial world. Again, the film's discussion of Third World nationalism must be contrasted with the conventional wisdom of the time, in which the term itself was thought to be either an oxymoron or a code word for communist revolution. It was exactly this sort of openness that originally interested Brando in the project.[108] Yet the movie, for all its liberal attempts to instruct the audience about the Third World, shared with conservatives a preference for viewing the problems of Southeast Asia through an American prism.

Although the film pays lip service—as did the book—to the limits and dangers of thinking that the rest of the world is just like America, in the end both renditions glorify modernization theory as the key to winning the Cold War. This theory was predicated on a scientific understanding of world historical development and argued on behalf of America's role as facilitator of this process. Working from the fields of political science, economics, history, and anthropology, a number of scholars began charting the process of social and technological development on a worldwide scale. Many were filled with a genuinely optimistic notion that "traditional" states with "stagnant" economies could be transformed into modern states with dynamic economic growth. This understanding of economic and political development became doubly powerful when it was coupled with the argument that the United States must ensure that these transformations take place as rapidly as possible; to delay was tantamount to surrendering to communist ideology and thus to world chaos. This mind-set is nicely encapsulated in historian Nick Cullather's assessment that "developmentese became the Kennedy administration's court vernacular."[109] Liberal academics and government officials such as Walt Rostow and Wesley Fishel, a professor of political science at Michigan State University, then worked to realize these goals in everything from flood relief and literacy campaigns to political intrigue and counterinsurgency efforts.

Modernization theory was so popular in the aftermath of World War II that it approximated the civil religion of liberal Cold Warriors. It held that American institutions, ideas, and technology not only could but should be transplanted into other areas of the world. It was touted not only as a new version of universal history but as one that seemed to offer solutions to two of the most vexing foreign policy problems facing the United States during the Cold War: how to ensure that the newly independent countries of the Third World would become integrated into a capitalist network of market relations and how to prevent these desperately poor countries from becoming communist.[110]

Rostow remains important to this discussion because he sought to write an intellectual antidote to Marx's *Communist Manifesto*. In *The Stages of Economic Growth: A Non-Communist Manifesto* (1960) he advocated building modern societies on counterrevolution and market economies and argued, furthermore, for wars with "just enough violence to be good sport."[111] Lansdale may have had his differences with Rostow even as he realized in the early years of the Kennedy administration that Rostow could provide him with access to power. Although both men remained convinced that American efforts to defeat the communists in Vietnam would not be easy, Rostow always favored technological and military solutions, whereas Lansdale endorsed "people" solutions.[112] They both believed that a U.S. victory was possible in Vietnam if enough will were put into the matter.

Fishel remains a fascinating figure as well because he was a professor with a cause: he headed the university's public administration program, which sold a practical application of modernization theory in Vietnam both to Americans and to Diem. A firm believer in systematizing the political, military, and social components of South Vietnam according to the tenets of this theory, Fishel poured his life into making Vietnam a successful test case. He first met Diem in 1951 and persuaded him to come and study in the United States. Later, he wrote about Diem in numerous American periodicals; he titled one article "Vietnam's Democratic One Man Rule" and worked with government officials, including Lansdale, to promote Diem as the man who could achieve this goal.[113] The process of transforming a nation, of making it into something altogether different from what it had been just a few years earlier, was an immense task, but Fishel approached it with passion and conviction. It was later revealed by former Michigan State University academics and in an exposé in *Ramparts* in 1966 that Fishel and others on his team who worked in South Vietnam were doing so on behalf of the CIA. Documentary evidence, wrote Warren Hinckle, showed that "the professors not only trained Diem's security forces but, in the early years of the Project, actually supplied them with guns and ammunition. In doing so, the East Lansing contingent helped to secure Diem's dictatorship and to provide the base and arms for the 'secret police' which were to make Madame Nhu and her brother infamous at a later date."[114]

Modernization theory permeates almost every aspect, every thought, even every camera angle of the movie. For example, the American-made highway—called Freedom Road—becomes a *leitmotif*. It was decided early in the making of the film that "THE ROAD" would play an important part; "it should be presented as a kind of recurrent visual signature throughout the film: a living, greedy and relentless being that shocks nature and man with its coming: a thing of power that cannot be turned aside or diverted from its blind and hungry destiny."[115] Though Stern does not acknowledge its imperial quality, his definition of the road seems to evoke the repressive nature of imperialism and its effects. Never mind that the only car ever seen on this shiny new thoroughfare is the ambassador's limousine from which the ambassador and his wife view, through the safety of their window, friendly peasants waving at them. The highway truly is a road that goes nowhere, yet it is lovingly presented in the film as the key to Sarkhan's development. When MacWhite single-handedly decides to change the highway's direction so that it goes straight into the heart of communist territory, the decision is based neither on necessity nor on the premise that the road has ceased to serve the commercial interests it was originally designed for but on the contention that its greater purpose is to go straight to the heart of America's enemies.

It may very well be that Lederer and Burdick, as well as Stern and England, were simply taking their cues from Lansdale on the question of this highway. He and other Americans were very much involved in pushing the development of roads in Southeast Asia to stress the anticommunist benefits they would produce. As Lansdale wrote at the time: "More first class highways such as 'Friendship Highways' are badly needed to link Bangkok with various ports of Thailand. . . . *Communist propaganda* has obtained tremendous results. It fools middle class people and also college students."[116] To be sure, Lansdale was not alone in linking Cold War messages with the importance of transportation projects; this was a very common approach taken by Washington in working out concessions from recalcitrant client states. When President Diem's authoritarian qualities proved too much for U.S. officials to support unequivocally, they wrote to their State Department colleagues for ways to correct the situation. The response is fascinating, reflecting Lansdale's thought on this issue and bringing together American power and ideology in an effort to motivate President Diem into being more democratic. The author of the State Department memorandum suggested having President Kennedy send a personal message to Diem in which he would first detail Diem's faults and then, as an aside, mention that America was, after all, paying his bills. The letter Kennedy eventually sent conveyed this point by referring to "the opening of the Saigon-Bien Hoa highway, the largest American economic aid project in Viet.-Nam."[117] But neither light- nor heavy-handed approaches did much to motivate "the last mandarin," a man who claimed direct lineage from Vietnam's great emperors. Diem eventually responded in a way sure to appeal to American technocrats even as he further dismayed American politicians: "All foreign observers who travel in the country are struck by the standard of living enjoyed by the mass of peasants: sewing machines, bicycles, transistor radio for each family in more or less comfortable circumstances, theater, movies in the most backward areas, motor boats on the innumerable canals, tricycle busses on all passable roads. And it is precisely in order not to interrupt this development program that we ask for supplementary aid to finance our war effort; otherwise we will be forced to make the tragic decision to abruptly cease all our social and economic progress."[118]

The communists too understood the power of American-built highways and responded in ways that were equal parts tragedy and black comedy. William Trimble, the U.S. ambassador to Cambodia in the early 1960s, recounted one deadly effect of planned American-supported highways—in conjunction with an improvement in relations between Sihanouk and Diem— upon all concerned:

> They were going to have a joint agreement to study the border, to outline the border which was ill-defined in certain areas—and it still is. The Chinese and Russians—I suspect the Chinese more than the Russians—got wind of the improvement that was taking place between Vietnam and Cambodia and in our relations with Cambodia. . . . So a bomb was delivered to the palace; it was a plastic bomb in a package addressed to the King [Norodom Suramarit] as a "present." It was delivered to one of the protocol officers in the palace who took it into the throne room. By coincidence, fortunately, just as it was about to be

opened the King, and Sihanouk, and the Queen went into the other room for some reason or another. The bomb went off, blew up several servants, and did quite a lot of damage, but the three of them escaped unharmed. With the bomb was a visiting card with the name of the Khmer-American Highway [Khmer-American Friendship Highway], obviously planted. Naturally, the Americans were accused of this thing. It was a pretty crude attempt because the card spelled the man's name wrong.[119]

Whether the communists were actually responsible for so ham-handed an operation—misspellings and all—cannot be ascertained. Partly as a legacy of colonialism, however, massive road building was rightly perceived as an imperialist intrusion. The real point of modernization theory is that its precepts became very much a Cold War counterideology, offering a market-based system of progress in opposition to Marxist theories of development. Yet it shared much with command communism, as both were rooted in the science and technology paradigm of the West.[120]

Both the novel and film versions of *The Ugly American* undertook to focus on a variety of faults in U.S. foreign policy. Their mutual goals were to correct these shortcomings in order to ensure U.S. successes in the Cold War. Clearly, Graham Greene's *The Quiet American* did not share in this intent, even though the film version of his novel did. Irrespective of politics or intent, the constructions of Lansdale-like characters in both fictions are surprisingly similar. In all cases, Lansdale emerges perceptibly as a vehicle through which the rhetoric of American power manifested itself in actualities such as the Khmer-American Friendship Highway, the distribution of plastic explosives, and the championing of Americanism to all. These fictional reflections would come to inform the way American policymakers came to view Lansdale as well. At the fateful meeting of November 3, 1961, when President Kennedy authorized Operation Mongoose, Robert Kennedy's notes include the following list of those who attended: "McNamara, Dick Bissell, Alexis Johnson, Paul Nitze, Lansdale (the Ugly American)."[121] The celebrity attached to Lansdale's name through this one novel had become power in and of itself.

7

The Half-life of Celebrity

> When he died, the event was a kind of explosion that went off silently, in minds and hearts; out of that explosion came many fragments, edging into the light, taking shape, changing shape again and again as the years went on.
>
> —Greil Marcus, *Dead Elvis: A Chronicle of a Cultural Obsession*, 1991

ALWAYS LURKING in and around the fictions of Edward Lansdale created by Greene and by Lederer and Burdick was his association with the CIA. Norman Mailer's massive novel about the CIA, *Harlot's Ghost* (1991), eerily reproduces and extends those earlier representations of Lansdale as the narrator describes him:

> The General is another matter. He delivers each one of his presentations with all the sincerity of an inspired salesman. He's an odd, tall man, who does not, but for his crew cut, look in the least like an Army general. In his fifties, he is mild, pleasant, soft-spoken, and not bad-looking—a long, straight nose, good dimpled chin, full mustache—but he has hollow eyes. I don't know quite what I wish to say here. They are not weak eyes, but they do not have any light in them. It's as if he is inviting you to enter some private hollow. I suppose I wish to say that he is the next thing to a hypnotist and seems to suck you right into the center of his concentration. Yet he is full of contradictions. He has to be sophisticated, but it doesn't show. He seems innocent.[1]

Mailer's intermingling of fact and fiction in this passage fuses Lansdale's physique with the ideologies he espoused. The mixture of gung-ho salesmanship, seductive hollowness, and an overall impression of innocence expresses better than any other image the essential contradictions of the man. How fitting, then, that Mailer, one of America's premier and most notoriously overdramatic of novelists, created a version of Lansdale more real than almost any that preceded his rendition.

Mailer's commanding style in his exploration of the many meanings of the CIA is augmented by his ability to make use of the rich material of images and fictions surrounding Lansdale. *Harlot's Ghost* is so closely tied to recently declassified documents and oral histories that it often reads as if it were a jaunty, even mischievous, internal history of the CIA by an ex-CIA agent, which sets this fictional work apart from journalistic depictions. Yet many writers before Mailer were struck by the symmetry between Lansdale's physique and his ideology. They too saw a correspondence between the facts of his life and their own fantasies about American power. So many constructions of Lansdale began to be circulated in the marketplace of American and foreign cultures that the real Lansdale in a sense ceased to exist. As Leo Braudy argued in his history of fame: "The audience that awards the famous the ultimate accolade of its attention is less interested in what they think they 'really' are than in what role they play in the audience's continuing drama of the meaning of human nature."[2] Images of Lansdale became the reality from which people imagined him and in the end created more facsimiles of the man.

The process through which Lansdale became "Lansdale" involved the construction of his Cold War celebrity through both American and foreign media representations. The degree to which he was fictionalized in these venues testifies to his dramatic appeal; even the most wooden of journalists realized that he made a good story. He was probably one of the few CIA agents whom the American people knew of *before* the revelations of CIA abuses made by the Church committee in the mid-1970s. In part, his renown was due to earlier appearances on the front pages of newspapers when his activities in Vietnam from the 1950s were detailed with the release of *The Pentagon Papers* in 1971. Consequently, when Lansdale was questioned by the Church committee in 1975, his testimony recreated his celebrity status across America. His responses to Senator Frank Church's questions and his involvement in the U.S. plots to overthrow Fidel Castro were detailed in forums both elite and popular. This was not your typical Washington news event, and Lansdale and the senators positioned their arguments on the uses of American power abroad and played to the cameras accordingly.

The revelations from the Church committee about the role of the CIA at home and abroad shocked the nation and led to numerous Congress-mandated restrictions on how the CIA was to function in a democracy. Assassination of foreign leaders, for instance, was thereafter explicitly banned by law. In all this tumult, Lansdale was singled out by the *New York Times* and the *Washington Post* for harsh condemnation, their editorials arguing that his efforts needed to be contained. The larger debate was over the very nature of U.S. foreign policy, but these battles highlighted the contested terrain surrounding Lansdale himself. Because he was seen as the CIA writ large, the process through which his celebrity aura was constructed sheds light as well on the changing status of the CIA both in fact and in public mythology.

THE HISTORY OF Lansdale's image dates from his time in the Office of Strategic Services (OSS) during World War II. Dozens of media portrayals of him built upon one another, each one familiarizing Americans with his fight against communism. These accounts invariably had Lansdale materializing at a moment's notice in Cold War hot spots—a floating quality pervades the descriptions—and finessing the situation through a mixture of string-pulling diplomacy and spy-master maneuvers. Even his friends thought of him in this idealized manner; as one friend wrote to him, "I was just figuring out whether you were in the Congo, Cuba, or in Laos."[3] Indeed, by the 1970s the very word "Lansdale" had become synonymous with all the veiled mysteries of the CIA—notwithstanding the role of James Jesus Angleton, the CIA counterintelligence chief from 1955 to 1975 who became famous for his paranoid fantasies of Soviet moles within the agency.

Lansdalian iconography extended into government circles as well. A State Department official once welcomed him to a top-secret session by noting that "the quickest, briefest introduction would be to say that he is the original Colonel Lansdale, famous or notorious, depending on your point of view."[4] This meeting, designed solely for career diplomats to hear Lansdale reminisce about his experiences in the Philippines, exemplified the "Lansdale" production at work. Even his team members in Vietnam thought of him in highly idealized ways. As Lucien Conein told him in early 1965, "You are the one they want. I wouldn't be Ed Lansdale for anything! Not today in Viet Nam! Don't you know how many people want you dead?"[5]

U.S. policymakers continually believed that Lansdale was capable of deeds he could not have done, and that he was operating in places where he could not have been. Even Allen Dulles came to believe a series of fantastic stories about Lansdale's power; despite repeated denials by the man himself, Dulles continued to speak of him as the expert on primitive cultures and the one American who spoke fluent Tagalog and Vietnamese and thus was uniquely equipped to handle the "natives." And John Foster Dulles opined, "Ed speaks all these different languages, stick him in a country and he immediately talks with people there." Lansdale vehemently denied this ability, reporting in his military file to the army in 1961, "I have only a smattering of Tagalog and Vietnamese," as well as French and Spanish. He often commented that all one needed when communicating with another person was "smiles" and "laughter."[6]

It is of more than passing interest that one of Lansdale's last disciples was Oliver North, the young lieutenant colonel in the Reagan administration who saw himself as a Lansdalian figure. " 'Ollie was already Lansdale-ized when he reached the NSC,' a source said" to a *Washington Post* reporter in explaining how a minor figure in the Reagan administration could have wreaked so much havoc in Washington, Iran, and Nicaragua. "By all accounts, North, a 'charismatic' Catholic, adopted the Lansdale ethos with almost religious fervor," the reporter concluded,[7] The connection between the two men becomes more complicated (and indeed more suspect) when one learns that through North, Lansdale met and worked with other key individuals involved in the Iran-contra scandal, including General John Singlaub. All these would-be Lansdales sought his guidance on how best to support the contras in the war against the Sandinistas in Nicaragua. To North, Lansdale was the older version of himself: a behind-the-scenes U.S. government employee who preached the gospel of "counterinsurgency" and "psychological warfare" as the tools necessary to U.S. triumph over Third World revolutionary and communist movements. That they broke numerous laws in the pursuit of this "higher good" was, of course, of secondary importance to these Cold War true believers. Oliver North's insistence that his fantastic and illegal guns- and drug-running schemes were somehow promoting democracy in Central America was reflected in his rhetorical skills, which mimicked Lansdale's acclaimed pep talks about the need to bring democracy to Southeast Asia.

Lansdale was well aware of the unpopular reception that his methods received in some quarters, but he seemed to revel even in his infamy. While chairing a Vietnam task force meeting in 1965, he began the session by announcing to the State Department representatives, "We will begin with a ten-minute session for you to say what a dirty bum I am."[8] Over the years, several U.S. government agencies objected to his being attached to them— even Pentagon officials distanced themselves from him at times—because his loyalties as a CIA officer always cast some doubt on his true allegiances and political intentions. The State Department deeply distrusted any association with him and at times referred to him as a "lone operator."[9]

Lansdale seems to have been caught up within the "Lansdale" vortex; even when he tried, he could not escape from the mythology his name invoked. In short, his CIA connections made him a marked man wherever he went, the "Lansdale" reputation simply overwhelming his ability to work within a bureaucratic environment, even when he wished to play by the rules. The most telling example is that when President Kennedy considered him for the U.S. ambassadorship to South Vietnam in early 1961, Secretary of State Dean Rusk threatened to resign if the appointment was made, saying that a former CIA officer could never represent the State Department; thus Lansdale did not get the post he had so desperately wanted and had maneuvered to achieve.[10] His lack of control over the images produced in his name emphasizes the impact his celebrity had not only on the American public but on his own career.

The diverse presentations of Lansdale as a Cold War celebrity can also be seen as manifestations of the expansive approach adopted by American foreign policy elites to explain the Cold War to a variety of social classes within the United States. Their efforts to instruct Americans about U.S. actions needed continual reinforcement and refinement, given the blatant illegalities and constitutional infringements their policies at times entailed. As Lansdale once noted in a speech: "The U.S. political warrior is actually extending the Pax Americana when he works effectively . . . [and doing so permits the] brilliant play of coordinated overt and covert actions, (often expressed as 'how do we hit 'em high while you hit 'em low')."[11]

The journalistic process through which Lansdale was represented and marketed figures powerfully in this analysis. Journalists not only reflected elites' views of him but also constructed their own versions of his mystique and disseminated those images to the American public. In 1968 the wartime correspondent A. J. Langguth wrote: "Solitary in his methods, disinclined toward bureaucratic empires, Lansdale has been a legend in Asia for almost 20 years, America's version of T. E. Lawrence."[12] Here Lansdale becomes by implication the new Lawrence of Arabia, the figurehead of Vietnam's revolution, perhaps "going native," perhaps becoming half-mad in his idealistic attempts to remake Southeast Asia in America's image. By contrast, an Associated Press writer observed in his generally positive "Gen. Lansdale: Mystery Man of S. Viet Nam" that factions within the State Department and the Pentagon referred to him as a "king-maker."[13] This depiction echoed Third World perspectives of Lansdale as a murky manipulator with all the power of the CIA presence behind him. South Vietnamese Premier Nguyen Cao Ky too found it appropriate (and vaguely humorous) upon meeting him for the first time to refer to him as the "kingmaker."[14]

In a three-part series in 1965, the journalist Richard Critchfield created yet another portrait, blending rebel with mystery man. Critchfield regaled his readers with hope that victory was possible, now that Lansdale was back "in country," and an allusion to Lansdale's intelligence past made it seem only more possible: "As he settles into his job as Machiavelli-behind-The-Prince to thirty-four-year-old Air Vice Marshal Nguyen Cao Ky, Lansdale becomes America's first full-fledged career revolutionary in Viet Nam," and "the Lansdale style is to remain largely invisible, a subtle, strong and firm American presence behind-the-scenes, prodding and thinking, acting as a catalyst on the Vietnamese political world, but never emerging as a clearly definable force."[15] In a similar vein, Jerry Greene, writing in the *New York Daily News* in 1961, presented Lansdale as a Western man who knew "the dirty digs" within Asia and used the wisdom of the Orient to further American interests. Lansdale appears more cynical here than in other renditions when Greene quotes his advice to U.S. Army officers on the importance of learning from Communist Chinese thought—not to create a better understanding but for more practical purposes: "The way to start defeating Chinese guerilla leaders and forces is to use the same cardinal principle—and to use it better."[16]

Within this spectrum of elite-to-mass versions of Lansdale, the most fantastic is by Phil Jeckyl (the name itself sounds like a pseudonym), who created a James Bond–like character for a pornography audience and described his daring exploits in fictionally graphic detail: "Lansdale always had a sense of humor. He chuckled. As he sat in the cab of the truck beside the Marine driver, he checked his GI 45 automatic and stood his Thompson submachine gun between his legs where it would be immediately available. He smelled trouble. That's why he was in China." Jeckyl also "recorded" the following conversation, just before Lansdale supposedly sneaked into China and took part in the first firefight of World War III: "'My name is Lansdale,' he'd introduce himself to various American diplomats and military personnel he'd come across, 'Major Ed Lansdale, Army Air Force.' Then he'd pull out identification which only the highest-ranking Americans would recognize as marking its owner top-drawer V.I.P."[17] (No doubt the author imagined Lansdale intoning his introduction in his best Bond-like British accent.) Although descriptions like this, suggesting connections both implicit and explicit between images of sex and fame, were not limited to pornographic magazines, this venue figured Lansdale prominently as an object of envy: the ordinary healthy American male not only desires the woman featured in the centerfold but also wants to be the man called "Lansdale." First he gets (to look at) the girl, and then, vicariously at least, he gets the commie.

Although such characterizations need not be taken literally, they do cast a revealing light on the versions produced by the more mainstream press, which also emphasized Lansdale's mythic qualities but interspersed their own breathtaking tales with actual historical data and quotations. For example, *Saga: The Magazine for Men* in 1967 devoted an article to Lansdale subtitled, "America's Deadliest Secret Agent." In a fanciful account (e.g., "Ho Chi Minh's order was succinct, 'Kill Lansdale at any cost' "), the author, Jack Lasco, mixes fiction with quotations from the *Economist* in portraying Lansdale as an important behind-the-scenes operator.[18] In another instance the syndicated columnists Rowland Evans and Robert Novak wrote in 1965: " 'Nothing happened in Saigon that Ed didn't have a hand in or know about,' an admiring Washington friend confides. 'He knows where all the bodies are buried.' "[19] Evans and Novak, like the pornography magazines cited above, foregrounded the racy thrills of Lansdale's adventures through their half-fictionalized accounts.

Similar features are apparent in an earlier article by the syndicated columnist Jim Lucas. In "Bad News for Red Warlords—Lansdale heads for Viet Nam," Lucas could hardly contain his enthusiasm upon learning that Lansdale was about to be "unleashed" by government bureaucrats and finally allowed to wage the Cold War in Vietnam as he believed it should be fought. In this rendition, Lansdale was being sent to Vietnam less as part of a team than as the lone American who could achieve victory against the communists. Lucas overlooks the fact that in this highly touted trip to Vietnam, Lansdale was part of a group headed by General Maxwell Taylor, and that the mission leaders were instructed by Kennedy to examine the deteriorating situation in Vietnam. As with other representations of Lansdale, Lucas's version highlighted his importance partly because doing so made a good story: "If there's any one American whose name rouses Asia's commies to fury it is Ed Lansdale."[20]

Lansdale often disavowed any similarities between the fictional spy James Bond and himself, but there was a certain self-promoting wink and nod quality to these denials, and they eventually became a standard component of articles about him. The Lansdale-as-Bond image peaked in a lengthy article (written in 1976 by Lansdale's friend David Martin) about William King Harvey, the infamous CIA agent who masterminded a successful tap of Soviet East German communications by tunneling under the Berlin Wall and later worked with Lansdale on Operation Mongoose. Martin has President Kennedy thinking of Lansdale as America's James Bond, while Lansdale not only politely denies the compliment but bestows the honor on Harvey instead.[21]

Given the media's idealized constructions of Lansdale and his impact on foreign affairs, it is not surprising that his attributes were later sought in the domestic sphere. As Raymond K. Price Jr. argued in "Bringing the Dream to the Ghettos," Lansdale's fabled powers of persuasion and ability to find solutions to nearly impossible situations were needed to combat the racial upheavals facing America: "Our ghettos, too, need a Lansdale," he wrote no doubt in reference to the 1967 race riots in Newark and Detroit.[22]

Each of these multiple representations of Lansdale built upon the next, adding additional layers to his celebrity and fame. The historian Leo Braudy has charted this process: "Throughout the twentieth century the popular feeling has grown that famous people were at once more real than we and less real: More real because of the heightened form of their reality, their images so huge in our eyes and minds; less real because that heightening promised constant availability to us and therefore a willingness to give up their private lives, to be invaded—since, after all, they were on show."[23] Lansdale and his actions (real or fanciful) were examined in so many forums that separating the realities of his life from the fictions became next to impossible. Articles about him appeared simultaneously in men's magazines and in the *Wall Street Journal*. He gave lectures at the Council of Foreign Relations while the Lansdale-inspired pulp docudrama "The Village That Refuses to Die" was airing on TV, illustrating his ability to market his vision of American interests abroad to a wide range of audiences.

The glamor that came to be associated with Lansdale's name played itself out in the cultural terrain in diverse ways. One was the formation of the Visionary Vietnam Veterans, or "Ed Heads," who believed that if only the United States had listened to Lansdale's wisdom, it would have triumphed in Vietnam. Lansdale was an agent of therapy for these veterans, providing a desired antidote for the tragedies produced by America's failure in Vietnam. The might-have-been theme is discussed in a more conventional manner by Zalin Grant in *Facing the Phoenix*, in which once again Lansdale appears as a man of unparalleled wisdom and knowledge about America and the rest of the world. A representative example: "Lansdale could form an immediate bond with another nationality. He had an indefinable quality that inspired trust and confidence among non-Americans."[24]

Together, all these images of Lansdale responded to and reproduced the collective fears within American society about the form and function of the Cold War. The exploits of one individual, sanctioned by Cold War ideology, coalesced into an American persona that seemed to provide solutions for the problems of the world—a world that had become increasingly less comprehensible and secure.[25] It is in this context that the fictionalization of Lansdale needs to be understood. Journalistic renditions suggest that in an age defined by the multiple threats that made up the Cold War, where the enemy was clearly defined yet real villains were strangely lacking, Edward Lansdale came to be seen in both popular and elite culture as America's number one man to fight for and protect America's interests abroad.[26]

Lansdale's fame abroad figures in this analysis as well. Communist media outlets generated such a steady stream of articles about him that he became something of a regular feature in the Soviet Union's *Pravda*. Soviet writers never seemed to tire of calling him "the American Spy master," and a typical entry fulminated: "Why is there an impenetrable mask on the face of this gentleman who is rubbing his hands? There are reasons for this."[27] The Vietcong also latched onto Lansdale as a representative of the evils of American power and often referred to him as a "spy chief." Even nonaligned governments reserved special terms for him: the Cambodian official newspaper, *La Depeche du Cambodge*, labeled Lansdale the "coup d'état specialist."[28] Revenge fantasies also figure in these constructions. Cambodian Prince Norodom Sihanouk produced, directed, and starred in a 1960s movie, *Shadow over Angkor*, in which he triumphed over and killed an American CIA agent called (what else?) "Lansdale."[29] And—at least according to one of his friends—both Syngman Rhee in Korea and Chiang Kaishek in China issued edicts prohibiting Lansdale from entering their countries. The fear that he might institute democratic reforms was clearly viewed as a threat to their dictatorial regimes.[30] Thus, Lansdale became a kind of force that must be contained. Whether the governments in question were communist or quasifascist, all seemed to view the very presence of Lansdale on their soil as harmful to their political interests.

These manifestations took on fantastic forms, including wish-fulfillment. There is the story of a group of Vietnamese Buddhists, most of whom could not speak English but who were still capable—at least in the hands of one American journalist—of "mouth[ing] Lansdalian phrases" of social revolution.[31] *Thoi Nay*, the South Vietnamese equivalent of *Reader's Digest*, meanwhile published an article on Lansdale titled "The Man Sentenced to Death by Ho [Chi Minh]."[32] Key South Vietnamese officials' affection and respect for Lansdale reached its apogee when they conferred upon him the title of "phoenix"; to them his power to emerge and reemerge to sustain anticommunist forces bordered on the mythic. The phoenix as a symbol of renewal takes on an element of pathos, however, in view of the extent to which

Lansdale became the embodiment of their hopes for a new democracy.[33] It also speaks to how these Vietnamese sought to curry favor with Washington—and Lansdale. The contrasting American, communist, and nonaligned portrayals show that they all manipulated images of Lansdale to suit their own purposes. As either champion or bogeyman, he could be used to give substance and a face to amorphous American ideals or, when the nature of U.S. foreign policy was to be demonized, to enemy attributes.

Given the multiple histories and representations of Lansdale, it is not surprising that he embraced his celebrity as a means to a greater end. He actively participated in this process not simply for vanity's sake (though he did revel in the spotlight), but as a way to gain access to the foreign policy establishment from the 1940s through the late 1960s. *Time* reported in 1966 that Vice President Hubert Humphrey was "an apostle of Edward Lansdale," and, showing his ability to bridge the political divide, his correspondence with Richard Nixon extended over a thirty-year span.[34] Lansdale used his fame to ingratiate himself with and then influence other powerful U.S. government officials as well. His effectiveness is well documented by the political and bureaucratic policymakers who viewed him as the man with all the answers—even after his retirement from government service in 1968. This view was epitomized on the eve of the Vietnam buildup in 1960 by a major general of the U.S. Army who wrote to Lansdale: "I have a saying which I have used many times in my conversation with both military and civilian people that all this country needs to win the Cold War is about thirty Edward Lansdales."[35]

Although he took part in his own mythmaking, at some point the sheer volume of images, fantasies, and wish-fulfillment narratives defied containment and individual control. By the time of his death, Lansdale's name had become attached to literally dozens of plots and plans. There were representations that made him complicit in multiple conspiracies to assassinate President Kennedy, in single-handedly maneuvering the United States into the Vietnam War, and in effortlessly bringing down the Marcos dictatorship in 1986. A surreal quality pervades many of these allegations; at their most reductive, the various "Lansdales" were designed solely for the political programs favored by their authors. Clearly, Lansdale himself orchestrated some of these profiles and was a creature of the media, yet his celebrity extended far beyond his real actions in the Philippines and Vietnam.

These examples portray Lansdale as somehow different from other government officials, even different from other CIA agents. All seemed to agree that he was capable of almost anything, given his celebrated role in defeating the Huk rebellion and his efforts at constructing South Vietnam. His fame, then, originated first in his own real efforts and very real events, which in turn inspired a multiplicity of images, personae, and narratives that fed off one another until they became self-propelling, and the Lansdale myth took on a life of its own. Public images of him—foreign or domestic, in mass-marketed magazines or high-brow interviews, journalistic or pornographic— all provided a mass of material from which fiction writers since the 1950s have crafted their own more coherent and enduring narratives. The development of fictional images surrounding Lansdale also stemmed in part from his rough, all-American good looks, which typecast him for the role of hero and adventurer. Second, his connection with the CIA only reinforced the aura of mystery that surrounded the man and his activities: there was always a good chance that the rumors and stories drifting back from those distant countries were true. Third, his extensive connections with key leaders in both America and Southeast Asia added to his cachet both abroad and in Washington. All these components contributed to the images of Lansdale and were then given narrative coherence and public exposure by a series of novels and films that focused on him as a prototype of the American cold warrior. And these fictional narratives in turn generated new images which were indistinguishably blended in journalistic and policymakers' accounts. All together, they fashioned the image of Lansdale that persists to the present day.

THE NOVELISTIC portrayal of Lansdale by the popular French writer Jean Lartéguy blends the journalistic "facts" of Lansdale's career into a cohesive fiction. Lartéguy's *Yellow Fever* (1962) represents Lansdale as Colonel Terryman, a sinister American confidant to the president of South Vietnam and his mercurial brother, Ngo Dinh Nhu. Working within a tradition of French *reportage* that uses fictions to support facts, the author keys Terryman's endeavors to those of Lansdale during the last months of French rule in Indochina. This portrayal is of note also because it veers into state-sanctioned propaganda: Lartéguy's hyper-French nationalism is apparent throughout the novel. Its defeat at Dien Bien Phu and the increased role of the United States in Vietnam were humiliating to France's vision of itself as a world leader and left the French very few options other than retreat. Lartéguy finds solace, then, in condemning the Americans whom he sees as having replaced the French role in Vietnam with little understanding of the responsibility this role entailed.

Little imagination is needed to see the American character Terryman as the stand-in for everything wrong with America and its foreign policy. He is introduced in a way befitting a conservative Frenchmen's almost hysterical view of the growing role of the United States in France's former colony: "Colonel Terryman had grey, closely cropped hair, a hooked nose and thin lips. He was wearing a light drill uniform with an open collar and because of a certain stiffness in his bearing he looked like a Prussian officer. Anger made him clench his heavy jaws." Even though this description appears to be the antithesis of Lansdale's laid-back style, much noted by other journalists, there are similarities between the Terryman character and the facts of Lansdale's life. The name itself is significant with "Terre" being French for "soil" or "land," thus a shorthand version of "Lansdale." Like Lansdale, Terryman is a promotional expert, an advertiser of American power who thinks of everything in terms of production values, even religion: "Terryman did not believe in God, yet he thought about Him sometimes, but always as a stage manager, for he reduced Him to precessions, church services, altars piled with flowers and the sound of organ music. He dismissed these untimely images from his mind: God did not yet need a publicity agent."[36]

At the point where he is introduced in the novel, Colonel Terryman is distressed, as was Lansdale (when he was writing his memoirs), over Diem's 1955 refusal to listen to his advice on the need to attack the Binh-Xuyen sect immediately. The fact that both Terryman and Lansdale eventually convinced Diem to initiate a battle against the "Vietnamese Mafia," who had long-standing ties to the French colonial government, suggests real parallels between the two figures. But for Lartéguy, Diem's success against the Binh-Xuyen left his beloved France with no power base and thus effectively removed the French from influencing policy in their former colony.

Lartéguy's depiction of this situation is unusual not only for its detailed chronicle of Vietnam in the 1950s but also in comparison with the images of Lansdale projected by the American media.[37] Lartéguy outstrips even the most cynical American portrayals, denuding his "Lansdale" of all idealism and focusing on his slick, self-congratulatory manipulations of Diem: "He was neither a remarkable Intelligence agent nor a specialist in political action, but a masterly stage manager. He could get hold of the most bigoted old scoundrel, the most inexperienced novice and, out of a gang leader, make a president of the republic; out of an odious and tyrannical old fogey, an all-powerful dictator." This Lansdale is ruthless and blinded by his complacency and his ability to wield American power. Most revealingly, however, Lartéguy exposes the seamy reality and the brutal power structure behind the images projected in the American media: "In Paris, in the Ministry for the Associated States [Indochina], there was a file on Terryman. But it was extremely incomplete, for it was based on press cuttings combined with a few garbled reports and padded out with pieces of Intelligence Service gossip.

The American was represented as a new Lawrence of Arabia, of questionable sexual habits since he was not known to have any woman in his life, brutal, uncouth and violently anti-French."[38] In creating this double-sided portrait, one side drawn from the American media and the other supplied by his own fevered homophobia and nationalism, Lartéguy appears determined to undermine the inflated celebrity that Lansdale had achieved within the American press; he summons up the American media in order to combat its effects.

The early representations of Lansdale-like figures, in Lartéguy's *Yellow Fever*, but also *The Quiet American* and *The Ugly American*, set the stage for a myriad of half-fictionalized portrayals. These include Mailer's *Harlot's Ghost* and also Joan Didion's description of the character Jack Lovett in *Democracy* (1984). Lovett, like Lansdale, was in Vietnam in the early days: "By May of 1955 . . . Jack Lovett was already in Saigon, setting up lines of access to what in 1955 he was not yet calling the assistance effort. In 1955 he was still calling it the insurgency problem, but even then he saw its possibilities. He saw it as useful." And, not surprisingly, Lovett exhibits many of Lansdale's qualities, though in a smarter, tougher way: "[Intelligence agents such as Lovett] are reserved, wary, only professionally affable. Their responses seem pragmatic but are often peculiarly abstract, based on systems they alone understand. They view other people as wild cards, useful in the hand but dangerous in the deck, and they gravitate to occupations in which they can deal their own hand, play their own system, their own information. All information is seen as useful. Inaccurate information is in itself accurate information about the informant."[39] Didion taps into the cultural constructions of the CIA and uses languages of control and identity that illuminate the mind-set exhibited by Lansdale, especially when he wrote up his after-action reports or detailed how his Saigon Military Mission had successfully planted falsehoods in North Vietnam.

Also, Didion understands the concealing power of a résumé in which job titles are simply another cover for the real purpose of an American intelligence officer:

> He never told me exactly what it was he did, nor would I have asked. Exactly what Jack Lovett did was tacitly understood by most people who knew him, but not discussed. Had he been listed in *Who's Who*, which he was not, even the most casual reader of his entry could have pieced together a certain pattern, discerned the traces of what intelligence people call "interest." Such an entry would have revealed odd overlapping dates, unusual posts at unusual times. There would have been the assignment to Vientiane, the missions to Haiti, Quebec, Rawalpindi . . . [And] there would have been blank spots. The military career would have seemed erratic, off track.[40]

Didion's description may also offer some insight into Lansdale's tight-lipped reticence as to whom he worked for, even when speaking to other government agencies; to offer information even to the very institutions that the CIA was constructed to serve might well have been a breach of just such an abstract and internalized code. From Lansdale's cover as an air force historian in the 1940s to his work in the White House as a consultant for the Food for Peace program in the 1960s, he too held job titles that seemed simply unreal and provide a revealing symmetry with the portrayal of Lovett.

Didion is clearly building on other novels and memoirs of the Vietnam War. She is indebted, for instance, to one of the classic reports, Michael Herr's *Dispatches* (1978). In this drug-soaked, rock-and-roll memoir, Herr too tries to come to terms with Lansdale: "Some people think 1963's a long time ago; when a dead American in the jungle was an event, a grim thrilling novelty. . . . There'd been ethnologue spooks who loved with their brains and forced that passion on the locals, whom they'd imitate, squatting in black pajamas, jabbering Vietnamese . . . and Lansdale himself, still there in '67, his villa a Saigon landmark where he poured tea and whiskey for second-generation spooks who adored him, even now that his batteries were dead."[41] Lansdale, a man who accomplished so much during his first years in Vietnam, was still someone to be revered.

There is also Ward Just's depiction of the ideologies embraced by Lansdale. His stunning novel *A Dangerous Friend* (1999) details the world of Americans in Vietnam in the early 1960s and with a keenness that no historical work has yet captured. Early in the novel the narrator observes: "My time was early days, when civilians still held a measure of authority. We were startled by the beauty of the country, and surprised at its size. It looked so small on our world maps, not much larger than New England. We understood that in Vietnam Americans would add a dimension to their identity. Isn't identity always altered by its surroundings and the task at hand?"[42] Though Lansdale is mentioned only once in this work, his experiences and views of Vietnam—and his obsession with nation building—form an undercurrent throughout the novel. His presence literally haunts and hovers over all the Americans who set foot in Vietnam and seek to remake it. Likewise, his efforts there help us appreciate what Americans were in the process of doing to Vietnam (and vice versa). More than any other Vietnam novel, Just's *A Dangerous Friend* provides a perfect complement to Greene's *The Quiet American*. It ends, as does Greene's work, with the unrelentingly bleak vision of American goods being unloaded en masse upon South Vietnamese airfields.

The most sinister—if brief—portrayal of Lansdale is in Oliver Stone's film *JFK* (1991). In this most explicitly political movie made by Hollywood in years, one that openly identifies and theorizes conspiracies relating to the assassination of President Kennedy, the Lansdale-like character "General Y" figures as a behind-the-scenes operator and a destroyer of Camelot. The power of this film is hard to overstate: it led to new congressional hearings on the assassination and the creation of the John F. Kennedy Assassination Records Collection in the National Archives. Countless editorials and op-ed pieces in American newspapers either decried Stone's irresponsibility or defended him with a religious-like zealotry. The power of the film went beyond the fact that it made millions aware of such theretofore obscure figures in the Kennedy assassination oeuvre as Umbrella Man and Babushka Lady. It crystallized what poll after poll has shown since 1963—that Americans believe some kind of conspiracy was at work that day and the U.S. government is preventing its citizens from knowing this truth. This is why one film historian has argued that "with the exception of *Uncle Tom's Cabin . . . JFK* probably had a greater direct impact on public opinion than any other work of art in American history."[43] To historians who toil in the "La Brea tar pits of cold war studies" it seems next to impossible to rehabilitate Kennedy, given all the evidence that has accumulated on both his political and military recklessness as well as his sexual caddishness.[44] But Stone's JFK is a man with an untainted past and a burning vision to end the Cold War and enact civil rights reform in America, and General Y becomes a key figure in the cabal opposed to Kennedy, the sinister CIA mogul whose nets of destruction forestall forever the new world that JFK envisioned.

Stone's history lesson has generated an extraordinary amount of commentary, ranging from Thomas Reeves's raving that the director was propelled by "an intense hatred of the United States" to Richard Heffner's declaration that *JFK* was really about "Stone's genius as a filmmaker versus the followers of Gutenberg."[45] Norman Mailer cannily described *JFK* as "one of the worst great movies ever made" because it is wrong on so many historical points yet draws in the viewer in a way that only a great film can.[46]

Lansdale is not named in Stone's rendition, but his presence as General Y, who oversees the government side of the assassination, is all too apparent for those familiar with the history of the CIA and the origins of U.S. involvement in Vietnam. Images of Lansdale flicker in and out the film, including a notorious photo possibly of him on the day of the assassination (more on this below), glimpses of him operating inside the Pentagon during the Kennedy administration, and stock footage of Americans that perhaps includes him with guerrillas in the Philippines. In an interview for the political/film journal *Cineaste*, Oliver Stone was asked about the connections between the real Lansdale and the fictional one seen in his movie:

> CINEASTE: *JFK* mixes facts with dramatic recreations and speculation. Would you say that the film's boldest leap of speculation is the somewhat veiled suggestion that General Edward G. Lansdale was one of the principal instigators of the assassination conspiracy?
>
> OLIVER STONE: No, we didn't get into the Lansdale business. That was suggested to me by Fletcher Prouty, who worked with Lansdale, but I never mentioned his name. There's no trace of Lansdale, really, unless you go back into Operation Mongoose. We tried to trace Lansdale's movements and one of our researchers actually came up with a scrap of paper that indicated there was a phone message from him in Fort Worth, Texas, on November 12th, about ten days before the assassination. I consciously backed away from the Lansdale business, but obviously it would have been somebody *like* a Lansdale, and that was the point.[47]

It may very well be that Stone found the parlor game of both hinting at and denying Lansdale's involvement in the conspiracy a crucial tactic for keeping the question open, though it seems likely from the interview that he himself was convinced of Lansdale's culpability. More important, the interview helps to make clear how Lansdale continued to figure as a representative figure for CIA misdeeds.

The outtakes from the movie, included in the printed version of the screenplay and in the "director's edition," make this even more explicit. In one scene, set a few years after Jim Garrison and Colonel X had originally met in Washington, they continue their discussion as to the role of the CIA in the Kennedy assassination:

> X: You never ask a spook a question. No point. He'll never give you a straight answer. General Y still thinks of himself as the handsome young warrior who loved this country but loved the concept of war more.
>
> GARRISON: His name?
>
> X: Does it matter? Another technician. But an interesting thing—he was there that day in Dealey Plaza. You know how I know? (*Garrison shakes his head*) That picture of yours. The hoboes . . . You never looked deep enough.
>
> General Y in photo: The idea for this scene has its roots in a story Col. Prouty has told many times that his former colleague, celebrated CIA man General Edward G. Lansdale, is seen from the back in one of the "hobo" photos.[48]

It is impossible to ascertain whether Lansdale, or Fletcher Prouty's version of him, was actually involved in this conspiracy. The primary clue is the photograph alluded to in the foregoing scene and shown repeatedly—if only briefly—in the final version of the movie. To my eyes, at least, the man with his back to the camera could be Lansdale, but even if this could be established, it would only prove that he was on the grassy knoll moments after President Kennedy was killed. Champions of Lansdale could easily counter that once again he was trying to thwart the assassination and arrived too late to prevent the tragedy. Of course, another conspiracy fan club believes that Lansdale was associated with no other than Lee Harvey Oswald.[49] It can be tempting to engage in this kind of speculation, but what such conspiracy scripts chiefly testify to is the self-propelling power of Lansdale's mystique. For other conspiracy buffs, countering this "history" with their own "facts" is half the fun. They revel in the mysteries of Lansdale's persona as a CIA agent, and his celebrity makes him the ubiquitous linchpin of their conspiracy networks.[50]

To understand our culture's endless fascination with these mysteries, consider Thomas Pynchon, America's most secretive of novelists. The following passage, although autobiographical, helps to explain the world of Lansdale as well: "I had grown up reading a lot of spy fiction, novels of intrigue. . . . The net effect was eventually to build up in my uncritical brain a peculiar shadowy vision of the history preceding the two world wars. Political decision-making and official documents did not figure in this nearly as much as lurking, spying, false identities, psychological games." Pynchon then goes on to ask a telling question: "Is history personal or statistical?"[51] He doesn't really try to answer it, because there is no answer, but the question helps to pinpoint the continual melting away of the line between fiction and nonfiction evoked by the passage. When millions of young American boys and girls read about, watched, and were taught how to imagine and confront America's enemies, it was inevitable that some might come to believe in this "reality" for the rest of their lives. Nor was the quality of projection limited to fantasists and those who were not in the know. Allen Dulles's penchant for intertwining fact and fiction led him to edit in his retirement a collection of his favorite spy stories.[52]

Of course, fantasies about the CIA have had a deep and enduring hold on Hollywood and have resulted in a host of films.[53] Although the most spectacular of these visions remains Oliver Stone's *JFK*, Wolfgang Peterson's *In the Line of Fire* (1993) is a notable entry in the list. On one level another attempt to come to terms with the meaning of the Kennedy assassination, and really just another reading of what has gone wrong with America since that tragedy, the film can also be seen as a visual rebuttal to Oliver Stone's *JFK*. It posits no secret governments or vast conspiracies, no confluence of the Real with the Re-creation; rather, one "wetboy" CIA agent (John Malkovich) duels it out against one old Secret Service agent (Clint Eastwood) in a spare but deeply laden exchange of phone calls, threats, and revelations. (Eastwood's spaghetti western topology also comes through as he once again defeats the bad guy, with the action simply transposed from the high plains to an elevator.)

Although stripped of the conspiratorial networks of knowledge and power that haunt *JFK*, *In the Line of Fire* alludes to the past misdeeds that the Malkovich character performed for God and country as an indoctrinated CIA agent and assassin. Tim Weiner, the *New York Times* journalist who covered intelligence affairs at this time, noted that the film originally had ideological roots similar to those of *JFK* but that the real "facts" became too hot for Hollywood directors not driven by Stone's vision (and access to money): "See—but don't believe—Oliver Stone's "J.F.K." he wrote. "Americans in general and Hollywood writers in particular need to believe in evil cells of secret government with the Government. In fact, such cells have existed. In a scene from "In the Line of Fire" that largely wound up on the cutting-room floor, Mr. Eastwood's world-weary agent mused that he was once detailed to protect Fidel Castro while the Cuban leader visited the United States—while, at the same time, the agency, in concert with the Mafia and on orders from the White House, was trying hard to kill Mr. Castro."[54] Allusions to such moments and to CIA-trained assassins gone ballistic have become self-referential Hollywood shorthand, and the unreal quality that pervades such stock images of the CIA has become deeply entangled in the public understanding and memory of the CIA.

There remains a question of simple believability when revealed truths exceed the fictions. Writing about more general events, Philip Roth noted that "the actuality is continually outdoing our talents, and the culture tosses up figures daily that are the envy of any novelist."[55] The fact that Roth wrote this in 1961 shows that he didn't know the half of it; how could he begin to guess that the CIA and the Mafia were already working together to eliminate Castro? By the 1970s, however, this narrative of governmental secrecy and betrayal was more easily understood than the urban riots, drug culture, and sexual revolution that soon followed Roth's pronouncement. The problem becomes not just the fictional nature of history but the inadequacy of anyone other than the fiction writer to convey the entanglement of event and myth, fact and fiction, that constitute America's post–World War II experience. As Norman Mailer put it in an interview:

"All my writing life, I've been writing fiction in order to make nonfiction believable to me. I wanted to make the C.I.A. believable to me. You hear about them trying to use depilatories to take off Castro's beard or trying to kill him with the

mafia—and that's a fact, but it's not very believable. I wanted to do this book [*Harlot's Ghost*] to make it believable to myself."
"But do you think America has in the C.I.A. a secret government?"
"Of course."
"And isn't that sinister?"
"It's worse than sinister—its unimaginative."[56]

Don DeLillo's masterly postmodern novel, *Libra* (1988), on the inner history of the Kennedy assassination raises the troubling question of how the CIA has succeeded in becoming a depository for the collective meaning of modern America. His declaration that "the CIA is America's myth. All the themes are there, in tiers of silence, whole bureaucracies of silence, in conspiracies and doublings and brilliant betrayals" is a view reproduced on countless conspiracy websites each day.[57] The CIA's mythic meaning has the capacity to replace the older myths of what America is, from John Winthrop's 1630 proclamation that "we shall be as a city upon a hill" to the historian Frederick Jackson Turner's 1893 thesis that the western frontier has made America uniquely different from Europe. DeLillo's understanding of changing national mythologies helps to illuminate Edward Lansdale's relationship with the CIA—and also how Lansdale came to view himself.

THE FINAL note in this history of image production remains the eventual impact of celebrity on Lansdale himself and on his career. When he returned to Vietnam in 1965, the American press immediately churned out a series of articles intimating that the United States was finally going to win the war there. Two typical responses:

> For the last month Saigon's booksellers have been unable to meet a feverish demand for two old novels until now gathering dust on their shelves, "The Ugly American" and "The Quiet American."

> Perhaps the most hopeful development lately is the return to Vietnam of General Lansdale, the Air Force officer who did so much to strengthen the political base of government against the Communist forces in the Philippines.[58]

Lansdale, of course, did nothing to dispel this view and granted numerous interviews with eager journalists desperate to write positive articles about America's effort in Southeast Asia.

The foreign press added an opposing viewpoint. In a typical critique of this return of Lansdale, the *Economist* dryly noted: "Mr. Cabot Lodge and General Lansdale, the recently returned American Ambassador to Saigon and his political pimpernel, are like two men coming back to the table to find that the same game is being played but the pack has been shuffled and the cards have lost their shine. The military problem is being taken care of, brutally but effectively. The political problem remains."[59] The more free-wheeling Philippine press alternately reveled in a brief stay by Lansdale in the Philippines and tried to take part in Cold War rivalries: "Don't look now, but Brig. General Ed Lansdale (of the late President Magsaysay's anti-Huk campaign days) was seen hovering around Malacañang Palace yester-day. With Lansdale in town from Saigon, what's up? As our recent Russian visitors would have said, Mir e druzba [peace and freedom]!"[60]

By the time Lansdale returned to Vietnam, journalists were using him as something of a literary dumping ground, interposing their favorite adjectives ("mysterious," "idealistic") in predictable stories featuring his exploits. The interpretations that emerged from both critics and supporters differed not only in the motives they assigned to him and the outcomes they connected to his actions but also in the very facts on which these stories were based. The climate of conditions in the Philippines and Vietnam, the nature of the enemy, the limitations within which Lansdale acted (e.g., one man's freedom fighter is another's terrorist) his level of awareness of broader U.S. goals all figured differently in each article.

Journalistic and artistic constructions of Lansdale's actions may have been as improbable or as malevolent as he believed his were benign, but their renditions had a staying power, for he was one of those proverbial individuals who were bigger than life. Currey's biography spends considerable time responding to the more fanciful accounts and concludes that Lansdale's actions in connection with Southeast Asia were essentially bureaucratic after his return from Vietnam in 1956. Yet Currey's book is viewed by conspiracy enthusiasts as the work of someone who has been taken in by the CIA, and—in the absence of logic or even a shred of evidence—they go on to claim they have "proof" that CIA agents were sent into bookstores throughout the country to buy up all copies of this "dangerous" yet (somehow at the same time) "duped" book.[61]

Lansdale was hardly an innocent in these matters, despite the aura of innocence that he projected. His fantastic memorandums in the early 1960s regarding Operation Mongoose, while detailed in their discussions of the damage the United States was to inflict upon the people of Cuba, have a bureaucratic Boy Scout quality and read today like some bizarre high school science project. In his infamous Saigon Military Mission after-action report of 1954, made public with the publication of The Pentagon Papers in 1971, Lansdale wrote of his and his team's efforts in a decidedly fictional way: "Each has its own story to tell. This is ours."[62] He then went giddily on to describe his team's efforts to destabilize North Vietnam—the newly formed Democratic Republic of Vietnam. If anything, these efforts of destruction—what Garry Wills later called "a schoolboy bent for turning whoopie cushions into weapons"[63]—establish that Lansdale always sought to be the Cold War celebrity he became. The fact that he achieved the celebrity he spent so long desiring should not obscure the other reality that came to be associated with him: he never escaped the images of him that arose in response to his fame. This duality is something that everyone who is famous, who enters into the American celebrity machine, has to contend with. For Lansdale, anyway, it overshadowed everything he did or tried to accomplish.

Epilogue

Southeast Asia after Edward Lansdale

> This understanding of a straightforward security threat is interwoven with another perception—namely, that we have our view of the way the US should be moving and of the need for the majority of the rest of the world to be moving in the same direction if we are to achieve our national objective. . . . Our ends cannot be achieved and our leadership role cannot be played if some powerful and virulent nation—whether Germany, Japan, Russia or China—is allowed to organize their part of the world according to a philosophy contrary to ours.
>
> —Secretary of Defense Robert McNamara to
> President Lyndon Johnson, November 3, 1965

"I PUT LANSDALE over there but nothing happened" was President Johnson's caustic comment to columnist Drew Pearson when Lansdale did not deliver the victory that proved so elusive to the United States.[1] After LBJ sent the fabled cold warrior back to Vietnam in 1965 to rework his magic and fashion a stable anticommunist state, Lansdale spent three more years in Vietnam, yet he, along with over 500,000 American soldiers, failed to achieve this goal. "Quite an unusual enemy we are up against," he wrote in 1966 to Henry Cabot Lodge, then U.S. ambassador to South Vietnam, when reflecting on the sacrifices the communists were making during the war.[2] The fact that Lansdale had personally been waging war against them for over a decade points to his utter failure to grasp the political nature of the Vietnamese revolution. His blindness toward the multiple strengths of the communists must be factored in with the continued dependence of the South Vietnamese upon the United States. Ward Just's assessment of "the Saigon government, that thin coat of paint on the listing hull," captures the artificiality of the American creation in a brutally honest way, one that Lansdale never could recognize.[3] Symptomatic of this problem was a 1966 meeting he had with Nguyen Can Ky, then co-leader of South Vietnam's government. "Prime Minister Ky called Ed in to ask for his advice. Ed pointed out that Ky should think of how he would look in the history books as the first Vietnamese to organize a truly honest election. He then passed Ky some thoughts on what he (Ky) might say."[4] The fact that Ky would solicit an American's opinion about how his own country should be organized speaks to Lansdale's extraordinary power of persuasion—and the power of America to elicit such a reaction from a client state. It also helps explain why the American intervention in Vietnam failed. Ho Chi Minh's forces needed no such lecture from their allies.

The disparity between the communists' and the South's abilities to wage war could be catalogued in a thousand ways. Whenever an American asked, "Why do 'they' fight so much better than 'our side'" the answer—the structural flaws within the South Vietnamese government, one that Lansdale helped create, versus the passionate commitment of the North Vietnamese and their ability to motivate generations to fight for a unified communist state—was self-evident. Lansdale, though, never gave up on his efforts. At another meeting he urged Ky to adopt a constitution, thereby giving his rule at least a democratic facade. Ky's response was telling: "I'm just thinking of you Americans. You want us to write a constitution and elect someone every four years. Like Marcos, huh?"[5] Unfazed by such responses, Lansdale continued his unflagging efforts to impose democratic ideals on a series of corrupt and authoritarian South Vietnamese governments whose leaders' relationship to democracy was at best of secondary concern to them (recall that Ky spoke with admiration of Hitler). And at another time Lansdale related to the U.S. ambassador a conversation with Nguyen Van Thieu, Ky's erstwhile colleague: "I asked about the composition of his Administration, if he becomes President. Thieu laughed and said, 'go ahead and give me a lecture about a "broadly based Government." ' He explained that 'this is what Americans talk to me about.'"[6] Lansdale's fanciful vision of democracy remained distinct from the true revolution taking place throughout Vietnam, regardless of Thieu and Ky's cynical understanding of the source of their own power.

If the South Vietnamese felt that they must endure Lansdale's pep talks, American policymakers had grown weary of them and of Lansdale's fondness for glorying in his past victories. In November 1967, John Roche, special consultant to the president, returned from Vietnam and wrote a report for President Johnson on his visit. In regard to Lansdale he spared no offense: "General Lansdale: essentially a public nuisance who has been waiting around in an alcoholic haze for the Second Coming of Magsaysay. Spends most of his time explaining to visiting firemen that if he had been listened to, the war would be over—and that he is responsible for whatever progress we have made. He should be kept in the United States and given a job that will keep him too busy to write a book." Johnson wrote on the bottom of the memorandum: "Call John and tell him I liked his memo very much."[7] Soon afterward, Lansdale was forbidden to meet with Vietnamese leaders. The times in which a National Security officer counseled the president of the United States to read a report by Lansdale had clearly ended. Journalists and midlevel officials still clamored to see him and continued to go up to his Vietnam villa and have a drink with this living legend, but he was now officially out of the loop, seen as an essentially harmless curiosity. Co Van Hai, general secretary of the Vietnamese Socialist Party, even sent Lansdale a Christmas card at the height of the war.[8] It is one of the cruelest of ironies that the only group that took Lansdale seriously at this time was the Vietcong. Upon learning that their foe was leaving Vietnam for good in 1968, their Liberation Radio exclaimed, "Suddenly Lansdale—A mythological personage in the flesh and blood of the United States, as he has been extolled by the U.S. Press . . . has been dismissed from his function as special assistant to Lodge. . . . [H]e has the determination of a brigand who had stained his hands with the Philippine people's blood. . . . [T]oday South Vietnam is no longer a place where archcolonialist Lansdale can display his talents."[9]

When Lansdale returned to the United States, he consoled himself by writing pieces about the war. His 1969 "Two Steps to Get Us out of Vietnam" in *Look* is indicative of the extent to which he was at war with himself, both sharing in a general loss of optimism about remaking Vietnam in an American image and retaining his missionary zeal for the larger anticommunist cause. The article sounds a note of defeat—"So now we are arriving at a time when the Vietnamese should be standing on their own feet and must do more for themselves"—but before long the zest of the true believer reemerges: "We must export the great ideas of man's liberty and help make freedom grow strong enough in the family of nations to be invulnerable to attacks such as the one in Vietnam."[10] Even in retirement Lansdale also kept a wary eye out for signs of communist aggression on the home front. The man who once delighted in bringing American movies to the peasants of Southeast Asia was now issuing warnings about communist uses of this pervasive art form to influence young Americans. In 1971 he wrote to an aide in the U.S. Senate's Internal Security Subcommittee that pro-communist films had succeeded in brainwashing the American antiwar movement: "I recall that, in 1963, I urged both the Vietnam Task Force at the Department of State and the National Security staff at the White House to obtain the help of Justice and the FBI in tracing down the source and delivery in the U.S. of the Viet Cong films being shown on U.S. college campuses."[11] This claim remains a marker of his understanding that his actions and rhetoric had failed. He was now taking part in the finger-pointing over who was to blame for the American failure in Vietnam.

A final assessment of Lansdale's Cold War career must also contend with his inability to acknowledge that the United States had lost in Vietnam. On May 1, 1975, when journalist Neil Sheehan telephoned him at his home to get his reaction to the fall of Saigon, he learned that Lansdale was there commiserating with a group of friends. When Sheehan asked Pat Lansdale what they were talking about, he was told, "They are trying to figure out how to save Vietnam."[12] This statement suggests equal parts tragic irony and delusion, given that the North Vietnamese tanks were even then driving through Saigon and Americans were fleeing in helicopters. Lansdale would spend the remainder of his years involved with various "revolutionary" movements that sought to liberate Vietnam from the grip of the Vietnamese Communist Party.[13] He also continued to seek a position of power in Southeast Asia. In 1977 he wrote to Averell Harriman, another of the "Wise Men" who had counseled presidents since Franklin Roosevelt, on the possibility of becoming the new U.S. ambassador to the Phillipines and emphasizing his personal relationship with President Ferdinand Marcos. There is no responding letter among his personal papers. At this late stage in his life, Lansdale's vision of the good that American intervention could bring to other countries' affairs had become something of a political liability.

This brief summary of Lansdale's post-Vietnam life provides some answers to the larger question posed by David Brion Davis in his exploration of American responses to foreign revolutions throughout history: "If we still cling to remnants of our old national messianic dream, we may ask why it is that a nation created by revolution, a nation whose first president ceremoniously received the key to the fallen Bastille as the "early trophy," in Thomas Paine's words, "of the Spoils of Despotism and the first ripe fruits of American principles transplanted into Europe"—why such a nation should become in time the world's leading adversary of popular revolutions."[15]

Lansdale embodied this contradiction and remained blind to it as well. He always envisioned himself as the perpetuator of American-style revolutions while simply discounting as inauthentic the actual revolutionary forces he confronted. The consequences of Lansdale's methods—his intertwining of capitalism's self-propelling force with a reformer's zeal for promoting a Jeffersonian vision of democracy as a revolutionizing force—and of America's attempt to remake Southeast Asia in its own image can never be fully measured, but an outline of their legacy becomes apparent in the subsequent histories of the countries involved.

The chaos and corruption left behind in the Philippines and Vietnam by years of American imperialist intervention and war provides a measure of the failure of those messianic dreams. Today, the Republic of the Philippines remains a deeply fractured society. The Filipino joke about its history, "three centuries in a Catholic convent and fifty years in Hollywood," is no longer very funny.[16] The legacy of Spanish colonialism combined with America's "benevolent assimilation" (President McKinley's 1898 phrase justifying U.S. control of the Philippines) has succeeded in making this country a textbook case for dependency theory. The CIA's *World Factbook* notes that over 40 percent of Filipinos live in abject poverty and that there is "uncontrolled deforestation in watershed areas; soil erosion; air and water pollution in Manila; increasing pollution of coastal mangrove swamps which are important fish breeding grounds."[17] Something has obviously gone wrong with bringing the modern delights of consumer capitalism to this country. Although the Philippines became independent on July 4, 1946, the continued presence and impact of the United States upon Filipino society is unmistakable. True, there is a thriving film industry, though it favors titles such as *I'll Exterminate Your Lineage, You're Worth Just One Bullet*, and its sequel, *You're Worth Just One Bullet, Part II*. These carnage outings help mitigate the daily terrors outside the movie theaters, where five-hour-a-day power blackouts are as common as the rumblings of Mount Pinatabo and where the proposed closing of the infamous Smoky Mountain garbage dump was met with widespread protests in the 1990s. Tony Santos, a forty-nine-year-old man who has spent twenty years scavenging in the dump as a way to support his wife and four children, painfully noted the contradictions and lack of alternatives he faced: "Where will I live, what will I do?" was his response when queried by a *New York Times* reporter about his predicament.[18]

It is not incidental to this modern horror story that U.S. corporations control almost every major industry in the country. Here the influence of American culture and its economic power dovetail. In 1990 the anthropologist Arjun Appadurai detailed the tremendous impact of American popular culture upon Filipinos, especially pop music: "An entire nation seems to have learned to mimic Kenny Rogers and the Lennon sisters, like a vast Asian Motown chorus." Given the artificiality of this cultural phenomenon, Appadurai considers this transplantation of Americana as creating a "nostalgia without memory."[19] This incisive and dismal critique of modern Filipino culture, where layers of colonization combine with a loss of sustaining identity, emphasizes the question, "Whose history?" The search for a defining political identity may begin to explain why the New People's Army, the communist guerrilla movement that replaced the Huks, and the more recent Islamic fundamentalist guerrilla organization, the Abu Sayyaf group, are potent forces in the political landscape.

The long history of American-Filipino relations is so entangled that the impact of American culturemakers such as Lansdale, although undeniable, is difficult to measure. The long-running status of the U.S. air and naval bases stationed within the country remained a classic case of this codependency. Until the eruption of Mount Pinatabo in 1991, at the end of the Cold War, destroyed one of the bases, they were considered of paramount concern to U.S. security interests in the Pacific. At the end of World War II the Joint Chiefs of Staff regarded the bases "not merely as outposts, but as springboards from which the United States armed forces may be projected" throughout Asia.[20] Although Filipino politicians often insisted in populist terms that the Americans must leave the Philippines or, better yet, pay more for the right to remain, Filipino leaders were keenly aware, as reported in the *New York Times*, that "the bases employ nearly 80,000 Filipinos, provide $1 billion a year to the economy and represent nearly 5 percent of the gross national product." These same officials were cognizant of another figure reflecting the troubled state of their society: 1 percent of Filipinos were applying for residency in the United States.[21] After September 11, 2001, a renewed urgency for U.S. protection, and with it the hope of generating jobs, swept the country. The journalist Raymond Bonner reported one impromptu gathering, some two thousand strong, of Filipinos who demonstrated for the return of the United States: "After two hours, the rally was over. It ended with a long line of men and women on the platform, many in baseball caps, including one with the New York Yankees logo, leading the demonstrators in a song. With their arms in the air, swaying, the demonstrators sang 'America the Beautiful.' All the verses."[22] This demonstration of allegiance to a foreign power brings to mind a warning issued by Emilio Aguinaldo, the Filipino leader who proclaimed Philippine independence from Spain and then fought the American "liberators" in 1899. Aguinaldo wrote in his *A Second Look at America*: "On the part of Filipinos . . . the mark

'Made in USA,' whether on an article of commerce or a way of life, is readily accepted by them as the best."[23]

The fragmentation of Filipino society is also directly related to the inept and corrupt politicians who have led the country since 1946. Even Magsaysay's efforts at reform—however halfhearted they may have been—were brutally undone by others, culminating in the hypercorrupt rule of Ferdinand and Imelda Marcos over a two-decade period that mercifully came to an end in 1986. The Marcos regime was fostered by a series of American presidents, as Raymond Bonner's *Waltzing with a Dictator* makes all too clear. The series of photographs Bonner includes in his work are particularly damming, including those of Nixon, Kissinger, Mondale, Schultz, Reagan, and Bush toasting the dictator or dancing with his wife. Marcos's overthrow appeared to usher in a new era, with Corazon Aquino and her yellow dresses symbolizing a fresh, clean start. She even revived the "Magsaysay Mambo" campaign song, apparently unaware of the extent to which Lansdale had concocted the song in an effort to sway Magsaysay's election.[24] Yet she accomplished little. Like her predecessors, she was simply incapable of narrowing the extraordinary gulf between the haves and have-nots and stemming the endemic corruption that grew out of economic injustice. American newspapers grew weary of reporting her constant battles to combat the rampant corruption spawned during the Marcos era. By the end of her term they concentrated instead on her libel case against a Filipino columnist who had written that during one coup attempt she "hid under the bed."[25] Her successor, Fidel Ramos, who had his own checkered past, faced the removal of the American bases—and thus American dollars—as an additional drain on Filipino society. And then there was Joseph Estrada, former president and tough-guy movie actor who rode his celebrity into office. He resigned in 2001 in order to avoid impeachment on a charge of general incompetence, along with accusations of extraordinary graft, perjury, and criminality (not to mention laziness). Almost as an afterthought, journalists noted that during this political crisis the peso had "fallen to its lowest rate in memory, less than 2 cents."[26]

The subsequent president, Gloria Macapagal Arroyo, must now contend with a host of issues, including the continuing political power of Estrada. A small Reuters article in 2002 indicated the problems confronting her government and her efforts to entice foreign capital to the Philippines:

> Thousands of workers and followers of former President Joseph Estrada marched on the heavily guarded presidential palace in Manila calling for the ouster of President Gloria Macapagal Arroyo. About 25,000 people took part, while 30,000 staged similar rallies in a dozen other cities. Elmer Labog, a labor

leader, said the president should be removed for "her sycophancy to foreign monopoly firms," which he said was reflected in "her promotion of globalization policies." He also accused her of violating the constitution by allowing hundreds of United States troops to hold counterterrorism exercises in the country.[27]

The one—bizarre—bright spot recently was the national pride many Filipinos felt when they learned that it was one of their college students who had created the "I Love You" computer virus in 2000 that crippled computer systems around the world—including the Pentagon's. "Yes, the Filipino can!" exclaimed the *Manila Standard*.[28]

In Vietnam the effects of the war remain ever present. More than 40,000 Vietnamese have been injured or killed by land mines since 1975. Compounding the devastation wrought by the war was an exploding population rate; by 2000, almost 40 percent of citizens were living below the poverty line, and the per capita income was only $2,100.[29] These figures illustrate why Vietnam remains one of the poorest countries in the world. Vietnam's Prime Minister Pham Van Dong summed up the problem: "Yes, we defeated the United States. But now we are plagued by problems. We do not have enough to eat. We are a poor, underdeveloped nation. *Vous savez*, waging a war is simple, but running a country is very difficult."[30] There are, though, hopeful signs that the current Vietnamese policy of *doi moi* (restructuring) may help bring some measure of economic growth and political freedom to the people. Vietnam has gone from the famine conditions of the early 1980s to becoming the world's third largest exporter of rice, after Thailand and the United States, and the fact that it now allows farmers to own their land shows signs of spurring economic development.

Despite Lansdale's convictions about the inauthentic and therefore necessarily catastrophic imposition of communist rule in this region, the Vietnamese Communist Party has maintained an enduring hold on the country. Whatever the government's faults today—and they are legion—it is absurd to deny the genuine struggles of the communists in overthrowing a colonial regime and an imperial overseer. One positive indicator among present-day authoritarian policies is that the Vietnamese leadership is now allowing some form of public criticism. Journalists and intellectuals must continue to tread carefully, however; they still flee Vietnam before speaking out if their critiques seem dangerous to the ruling order, and popular Vietnamese writers still find that their books cannot be published if, in whatever veiled way, they attack Vietnamese society and the communist leadership. As the August 2002 obituary of Vietnam's then leading dissident, Tran Do, noted, the government confiscated his memoirs and manuscripts because this "decorated Vietnam War veteran and former head of the Communist Party's ideology and culture department" had dared to call for the end of the Party's monopoly of power.[31] In short, the government's refusal to sanction real forms of *glasnost* leads to the conclusion that the Vietnamese leadership is not taking its cue from Eastern Europe or from the former Soviet Union; it is unwilling to step aside and allow others to organize Vietnamese society and politics.[32]

Yet even as Lansdale's reformist visions failed miserably when it came to understanding, let alone shaping, Vietnam's political future, he was prescient in foreseeing the powerful draw of American consumer capitalism. At the height of the war President Johnson declared, "I want to leave the footprints of America [in Vietnam]. I want them to say, 'This is what Americans left—schools and hospitals and dams.'"[33] In the new millennium the real footprint that America has left behind is the consumer culture that washes over the country in the inexorable logic of globalization. Japan, whose economic well-being once provided a rationale for American intervention in Vietnam, is now Vietnam's largest trading partner. Even in Hanoi, the imperative of globalization has impacted the city and its desire to welcome Westerners: "In what seems apt symbolism, the prison where [former POW later to become U.S. ambassador Pete Peterson] was held, the 'Hanoi Hilton,' is being partly demolished for a luxury high-rise, with some outer walls of the prison to be retained as a monument."[34] The world of business and tourism can also be seen in the completion of the Saigon Floating Hotel in Ho Chi Minh City, billed as a "hotel where one can do business," and indicates that the war is, for some at least, history. Among the most popular tourist sites in Vietnam are the tunnels of Cu Chi in which the Vietcong once lived and hid from American forces. Today on the streets of Hanoi one can still see the propaganda posters that exhorted the North Vietnamese to produce more, sacrifice more, and live more heroically—all in the name of achieving the successful fruition of the Vietnamese revolution—but today these posters must share space with billboards touting Coca-Cola, Federal Express, and a legion of other multinationals doing business in Vietnam. In fact, the revolutionary posters themselves have spawned a fledging industry of sorts: tourists can buy originals for $40 and prints for $10—part of Vietnam's "war tourism" packages.[35] The irony came full circle with a Guess Jeans ad campaign showing models in the same rice fields where Americans and Vietnamese fought and died. There was also a Ralph Lauren summer collection favoring a Southeast Asian motif, emphasizing that Eastern fantasies can still sell products intended for Westerners. Memories of Vietnam colonialism remain decidedly hip; its exoticism formed the backdrop for clothing designer Donna Karan's ad campaign featuring movie stars Jeremy Irons and

Milla Jovovich. Even more startling is the B-52 cocktail available in a trendy Hanoi eatery called the Indochine.

Stanley Karnow's quip that "the VC is being defeated by the VCR" has much truth to it, though it deliberately oversimplifies the process through which true revolutionary forces have lost impetus in Vietnam.[36] In fact, if Lansdale were to survey present-day Vietnam, he might feel that some of his Cold War aims had been achieved. What cannot be overlooked is Walter LaFeber's observation that "U.S., Japanese, and other transnationals rushed in [in the 1990s] to take advantage of cheap, disciplined labor. Indeed, the chance to exploit Vietnam's labor and emerging market was a central reason why relations with the former enemy had been established."[37]

All the same, it is a mistake to exaggerate the role of America's dissemi-nators of capitalism and democracy—embodied by figures such as Lansdale—in producing the inevitable end of the Cold War. As Garry Wills has astutely noted: "We never consider that other countries, freed from a colonial frame-work, must work out their own tribal and historical grievances without re-gard to us. If anything happens to the world, America must get the credit or the blame—we did not act, or we did not take the right actions. It never occurs to us that we are not all-important in the long-range tides of partic-ular peoples' histories. . . . The attempt at total control does not merely cor-rupt, as Acton said; it debilitates. It undoes itself."[38] Wills's portrayal of the hubris embodied in Lansdale's world view provides a reorienting outlook on America's role abroad and in doing so offers a lesson to the historian: only the Vietnamese can truly measure the costs of the "American War" within the broader sweep of their history.

We can better measure its impact on the American self-image and world view. For one thing, the Cold War and the clearly defined enemies it engen-dered have become the object of increasing nostalgia. "My official Cold War Recognition Certificate arrived in the mail the other day, signed by the U.S. secretary of defense—or at least his autopen. About time somebody showed a little appreciation for my role in toppling the Evil Empire." So begins Jerome Doolittle's amusing history of his very modest efforts during this period.[39] Congress has taken up the cause of remembering the Cold War as a way to increase local tourism. In January 2003, Representatives Joel Hefley (R-Colo.) and John C. Porter (R-Nev.) introduced H.R. 114, a bill to have the secretary of the interior identify and commemorate Cold War sites throughout the land. Using explicit analogies to commemorations of the Underground Railroad, these congressman propose including "nuclear weapons sites (such as the Nevada test site), flight training centers, manufacturing facilities, communications and command centers (such as Cheyenne Mountain, Colorado), defensive radar networks (such as the Distant Early Warning Line), and strategic and tactical aircraft." They have asked Congress to authorize $300,000 to fund this memorialization and as of August 2004, the bill is still pending.[40]

In sharp contrast to the war's direct impact upon Vietnam, Americans have generally explored its consequences from a distance, as if it were suitable for viewing only on TV or film.[41] Policymakers, though, have worried since the fall of Saigon that the United States must get over its "Vietnam Syndrome": that is, a hesitancy to use force to achieve its goals. President George H.W. Bush argued in his inaugural address of 1989: "That war began in earnest a quarter of a century ago, and surely the statute of limitation has been reached. This is a fact: The final lesson of Vietnam is that no great nation can long afford to be sundered by a memory."[42] Those remarks reflect how divisive the war has remained, then and now, and why each (potential) military action since has led antiwar activists to proclaim, "No more Vietnams." Despite its continuing presence as a political reminder, another phenomenon is the way the Vietnam War has been both erased and commodified. Consider, for instance, the popular roller coaster at Six Flags Great Adventure amusement park in New Jersey called "Rolling Thunder." How does one adequately explain to the average American teenager waiting in line to be thrilled by this ride that there is a history attached to this phrase, one of people dying and homes being destroyed by an army that was sent abroad to defeat communism?

Once again, Hollywood's myriad representations of the war weigh in to provide their own version of how America and its culture has thought of the war and the country where it was fought. From early representations in *The Quiet American*, to John Wayne's unintentional parody of American actions in *The Green Berets* (1968), through such classic 1970s extravaganzas as *Apocalypse Now* (1979) and *The Deer Hunter* (1978) to the very politically different Reagan-era films *Rambo* (1985, 1988) and Oliver Stone's wrenching *Born on the Fourth of July* (1989), the movies have portrayed the war in such a state of ideological flux that the only constant is the idea of Vietnam itself. In this respect Vietnam, the people and the place, has become both the marker of an American past and a symbol of cultural disillusionment. It is portrayed as a past episode in which Americans went either native or insane, in which soldiers were ostracized for not winning the war, and in which a country lost its innocence. Henry Kamm, the long-time *New York Times* correspondent, makes this point well in *Dragon Ascending*: "What would a Vietnamese make of a phrase that uses the name of his country to stand, not for his nation . . . but for a debacle in another nation's history?"[43]

While Hollywood continues to produce war epics such as Mel Gibson's 2002 bloody and nostalgic paean to warriors in *We Were Soldiers Once*, decidedly pro-American versions of the war must contend with alternative perspectives. At the Brooklyn Academy of Music's month-long film festival in 2002, "From Hanoi to Hollywood," showing everything from big-budget Hollywood movies to guerrilla newsreels, of particular note was one of the earliest Hollywood films about Vietnam: the crazed *China Gate* (1957). Starring Gene Barry, Angie Dickinson, and Nat "King" Cole, this potboiler of a movie by Sam Fuller remains both an over-the-top defense of French colonialism and as anticommunist an effort as anything Senator Joseph McCarthy could have wished for. What comes through in this and other films is that the Vietnam War was sold to Americans by both Washington and Hollywood. Further, in 2002 the National Geographic Society mounted an extraordinary photography exhibit, *Another Vietnam: Pictures of the War from the Other Side*, where for the first time Westerners could see photographs taken during the war by the communists and the determination of soldiers and civilians alike in fighting them. For the first time too the enemy was given a face in depictions ranging from a young Vietcong woman scanning the skies for American planes to a North Vietnamese makeshift operating room situated in a mangrove swamp.

Happily, there is increasing evidence that Vietnam fascinates Americans today in ways that have little to do with the war itself. The spring 2003 exhibition *Vietnam: Journeys of Body, Mind & Spirit* at the American Museum of Natural History in New York City was indicative of this evolution. The exhibit celebrated the variety of ethnic traditions and vibrancy of Vietnamese culture in the new millennium, rather than simply showing a place where America and Vietnam were at war. In fact, Americans hardly figured here, and the politics (and oppression) of the communist government were muted so that viewers could focus on the culture (though of course at the end of the exhibit was a gift shop that sold everything from conical hats to bamboo chopsticks and teapots).

Notwithstanding the long and tortured POW/MIA controversy and the 1992 presidential campaign scrutiny of Bill Clinton's efforts to avoid the draft, the normalization of United States–Vietnam ties marks the end of one era and the beginning of another. Clinton's visit to Vietnam in November 2000—the first made by an American president since the war—and his warm reception indicate both the sea change in relations between Americans and

Vietnamese and eager embrace of economic ties by the leaders on both sides.[44] This change in policy is not too difficult to fathom when one considers how Hoang Hon Thanh, a "man on the street," responded to the U.S. decision to end the embargo against its former enemy: "Me? I'm happy too. And I'm happy for a simple reason. Five years ago, I bought a Polaroid. Now that the embargo is lifted, I can finally buy some film for it."[45] Additionally, the Vietnamese inquiry into having the U.S. return to Vietnam and use the air and naval bases at Cam Ranh Bay ranks as one of the most startling if not bizarre events in the tortured history of this country.[46] At the very least, it signifies the Third World's continued jockeying for U.S. influence and money and explains why the term "imperialism" remains such a powerful and fluid concept.

Notes

Introduction

1. Eric Pace, "Gen. E. G. Lansdale Dies at 79; Adviser on Vietnam Strategy," *New York Times*, 24 February 1987, 1.

2. Recounted by Lansdale in Michael Charlton and Anthony Moncrieff, *Many Reasons Why: The American Involvement in Vietnam* (New York: Hill & Wang, 1978), 42. In his many retellings of this event, Lansdale frequently attributed both these exhortations to John Foster Dulles in order to preserve the polite fiction that he was not affiliated with the CIA. Yet Lansdale wrote in a letter to Allen Dulles, "Having had your courageous support in the good fight for so many years, I've been recollecting your many acts of thoughtfulness and real meaning. There are some wonderful experiences among them. Perhaps my finest memory is of your personal message of 'God Bless You' as I went into Vietnam in 1954 for dubious battle. It meant so very much more than all the orders and advice and instructions I received from others . . . God Bless you." Lansdale to Allen Dulles, 15 November 1961, Lansdale Papers, Hoover Institution on War, Revolution, and Peace, Stanford, Calif. (hereafter, Lansdale Papers), Box 37, #909. Dulles reciprocated the good-will: "I appreciated the outstanding services you rendered to our government and, in very particular, what you did in the Philippines and Vietnam during the period we were working so closely together." Allen Dulles to Lansdale, 21 November 1963, Allen Dulles Papers, Princeton, N.J. Box 37.

3. Edward Lansdale, *In the Midst of Wars: An American's Mission to Southeast Asia* (New York: Harper & Row, 1972), 102.

4. These preferences are deduced by looking at the books Lansdale donated from his personal library to the archives at Maxwell Air Force Base, Alabama.

5. Lansdale to Peter Richards, 19 May 1971, Currey Collection, Lutz, Flo.

6. David Chandler reviewed Lansdale's book in the *Journal of Asian Studies* 34 (May 1975): 856; Jonathan Mirsky in *Saturday Review*, 1 April 1972, 80; J. L. S. Girling in *Pacific Affairs* 47 (autumn 1974): 394–97.

7. To take but one example, well before Lansdale's actions as a CIA agent became publicized in the 1970s, the famed military correspondent Homer Bigart wrote in 1962 that Lansdale had been "the chief United States intelligence agent in Saigon" in 1955.

Homer Bigart, "Vietnam Victory Remote Despite U.S. Aid to Diem," *New York Times*, 25 July 1962, reprinted in *Reporting Vietnam, Part One: American Journalism, 1959–1969* (New York: Library of America, 1998), 66.

8. Cecil Currey, *Edward Lansdale: The Unquiet American* (Boston: Houghton Mifflin, 1988), xv.

9. Cited in Seth Mydans, "Asia's Wealth Ebbs, but Laos Is Too Poor to Care," *New York Times*, 1 January 1998.

10. "Film: Civic Action Seminar," 22 March 1967, United States Air Force Document Collection, National Archives and Records Administration II, College Park, Md.

11. Lansdale, *In the Midst of Wars*, 151–52.

12. Quoted in Lloyd Gardner, *Architects of Illusion: Men and Ideas in American Foreign Policy, 1941–1949* (Chicago: Quadrangle, 1970), 205.

13. The bombing statistic is cited in Walter LaFeber, "The Last War, the Next War, and the New Revisionists," *democracy* 1 (January 1981), 100.

14. Rudyard Kipling, *Rudyard Kipling's Verse: Definitive Edition* (New York: Doubleday, 1940), 321–23. The poem first appeared in *McClure's Magazine*, 12 (February 1899).

15. Jean Heffer, *The United States and the Pacific: History of a Frontier* (Notre Dame, Ind.: University of Notre Dame Press, 2002), 17–18.

16. Lucien Conein, interview by author, McLean, Va., 12 October 1992.

17. Leslie Gelb and Richard Betts, *The Irony of Vietnam: The System Worked* (Washington, D.C.: Brookings Institution, 1979).

18. Quoted in Raymond Hernandez, "Abbot Moffat, 94, Lawmaker and Then a Diplomat in Asia," *New York Times*, 23 April 1996.

19. George Kennan, "The Sources of Soviet Conduct," *Foreign Affairs* 25 (July 1947): 575.

20. U.S. Department of State, *Foreign Relations of the United States: 1950: National Security Affairs; Foreign Economic Policy* (Washington, D.C.: GPO, 1977), 1: 263, 237, 262–63.

21. Lansdale Papers, Box 9, #265; Box 10, #271.

22. Informal seminar by Lansdale at Harvard University, "Our Battleground in Asia," 19 June 1957, Lansdale Papers, Box 12, #296.

23. Lansdale to his family, 2 May 1955, Lansdale Papers, Box 4.

24. U.S. Senate, Committee on Foreign Relations, *The Situation in Vietnam, Executive Session of the Senate Foreign Relations Committee* (Historical Series), 7 January 1965, 89th Congress, 1st sess., 1965 (Washington, D.C.: GPO, 1990), 17:37.

25. Henry Luce, *The American Century* (New York: Farrar & Rinehart, 1941).

26. "Civic Activities of the Military in Southeast Asia," Anderson Subcommittee to the President's Committee to Study United States Military Assistance Programs (otherwise known as the Draper Commission) 13 March 1959, 6, in Lansdale Papers, Box 7, #239. Lansdale provides no evidence that anyone in the North even knew about these anticommunist fish ponds.

27. For a fuller discussion of these points, see Jonathan Nashel, "The Road to Vietnam: Modernization Theory in Fact and Fiction," in *Cold War Constructions: The*

Political Culture of United States Imperialism, 1945–1966, ed. Christian Appy (Amherst: University of Massachusetts Press, 2000), 132–56.

28. Program Review by the Chief of Operation Mongoose [Lansdale], 18 January 1962, U.S. Department of State, *Foreign Relations of the United States, 1961–1963: Cuba, 1961–1962,* (Washington, D.C.: GPO, 1997), 10:710.

29. Arthur Schlesinger Jr., *The Bitter Heritage: Vietnam and American Democracy, 1941–1966* (Boston: Houghton Mifflin, 1967), 32.

30. Quoted in "Pentagon Papers: The Secret War," *Time,* 28 June 1971. I am indebted to recent works concerned with Vietnam which have highlighted the role of the individual. Fredrik Logevall, *Choosing War: The Lost Chance for Peace and the Escalation of War in Vietnam* (Berkeley: University of California Press, 1999), emphasizes how the fatal combination of Lyndon Johnson's political ambitions and personal insecurities led to his widening of the war. Likewise, James Fisher, *Dr. America: The Lives of Tom Dooley, 1927–1961* (Amherst: University of Massachusetts Press, 1997), portrays the celebrated jungle doctor as giving a face to American efforts in Southeast Asia for millions of Americans in the 1950s.

31. Neil Sheehan, *A Bright Shining Lie: John Paul Vann and America in Vietnam* (New York: Random House, 1988), 138. Sheehan's book remains a model of methodological balance. With passion and grace he depicts Vann as the all-American boy who deepened America's involvement in Vietnam, conveys the complex relationship of the individual to the larger history of the American intervention, and integrates the larger structures of American policy with stories of those who implemented it. Not incidentally, Sheehan provides a great deal of evidence for Lansdale's influence on Vann in the early stages of American involvement. Of interest is that Sheehan's muted criticism of Lansdale in his book are not glossed over in his private papers. At one point he describes Lansdale as a "looney mystic," and in the margins of one of Lansdale writings, Sheehan exclaimed, "Lansdale was a knight of U.S. imperialism." Neil Sheehan Papers, Library of Congress, Washington, D.C., Boxes 28 and 71.

32. *The Pentagon Papers: The Defense Department History of United States Decisionmaking on Vietnam,* Senator Gravel Edition, 4 vol. (Boston: Beacon Press, 1971), 2:22. This is the edition cited unless otherwise specified.

33. The 1955 Sect Crisis involved Diem's initiating military action against the Binh Xuyen, a criminal gang that ran the brothels and gambling establishments in Saigon. With American assistance, Diem also bribed and neutralized the Hao Hoa and the Cao Dai, two popular religious and political sects with formidable militias. The fullest account of Lansdale's back-channel actions during the 1955 uprising is in David Anderson, *Trapped by Success: The Eisenhower Administration and Vietnam, 1953–61* (New York: Columbia University Press, 1991), 110–13.

34. Robert Scheer and Warren Hinckle, "The Vietnam Lobby,'" *Ramparts,* 4 (July 1965): 16–24. This article draws explicit parallels between the "Vietnam Lobby" and the more renowned "China Lobby" of the 1940s and 1950s. For a comprehensive discussion, see Joseph G. Morgan, *The Vietnam Lobby: The American Friends of Vietnam, 1955–1975* (Chapel Hill: University of North Carolina Press, 1997).

35. Lydia Fish, "General Edward G. Lansdale and the Folksongs in the Vietnam War," *Journal of American Folklore* 102 (October–December 1989): 390–411.

36. Lansdale Papers, Box 7, #236. Other conservative organizations that Lansdale became involved with in the last years of his life included the "United States Committee for Free Indochina" and "Accuracy in Media." Just before he died, he also had a detailed correspondence with the Army at the U.S. Army War College on low-intensity conflict (Lansdale Papers, Box 74).

37. W. W. Rostow, *The Diffusion of Power: An Essay in Recent History* (New York: Macmillan, 1972), 264.

38. A typical example of this distaste appears in a 1963 telephone conversation between John McCone, director of the CIA, and Secretary of State Dean Rusk: "M[cCone] said in that Agency there would be insurmountable problems raised re this man—no confidence at all in him and M could assume no responsibility for the operation." "Memorandum of a Telephone Conversation between Secretary of State and the Director of Central Intelligence (McCone), Washington, September 17, 1963, 12:01 pm," U.S. Department of State, *Foreign Relations of the United States, 1961–1963, Vietnam: August–December 1963* (Washington, D.C.: GPO, 1991), 4:241.

39. U.S. Senate, An Interim Report of the Select Committee to Study Governmental Operations with Respect to Intelligence Activities (hereafter, Church Committee), *Alleged Assassination Plots involving Foreign Leaders*, 94th Congress, 1st sess. (Washington, D.C.: GPO, 1975).

40. Church Committee, *Alleged Assassination Plots*, 142 n. 2.

41. David Halberstam, *The Best and the Brightest* (New York: Random House, 1972), 124.

42. Aleksandr Fursenko and Timothy J. Naftali, *One Hell of a Gamble: Khrushchev, Castro, and Kennedy, 1958–1964* (New York: Norton, 1997), 144.

43. Richard Drinnon, *Facing West: The Metaphysics of Indian-Hating and Empire Building* (Minneapolis: University of Minneapolis Press, 1980). In contrast to Currey's traditional biography, Drinnon's book is more difficult to categorize—part history, part meditation. His offhand and elliptical writing style allows him to quote almost any source as proof that at the core of American history and culture is an imperial ethos.

44. Stanley Karnow, *Vietnam: A History* (New York: Viking, 1983), 220.

45. Robert Dean, *Imperial Brotherhood: Gender and the Making of Cold War Foreign Policy* (Amherst: University of Massachusetts Press, 2001), 185.

46. Colby wrote about Lansdale in Richard Whittingham, *Almanac of Adventure* (New York: Rand McNally, 1982), 165.

47. Richard Critchfield, for example, wrote frequently about Lansdale and his book *The Long Charade: Political Subversion in the Vietnam War* (New York: Harcourt, Brace, 1968) was a chronicle of American miscues and misunderstanding of the nature of the war. If there was one hero, it was Lansdale, whom the book often invokes as the lone American who could see outside the fog of war. A more recent example is Zalin Grant's *Facing the Phoenix* (New York: Norton, 1991), a smart book that highlights the importance of the political nature of the war and why pacification programs were over-

whelmed by more conventional military methods. At the same time, it sanctifies Lansdale; he becomes an agent of therapy for Grant in his attempt to understand what happened to Americans and Vietnamese in Southeast Asia in the 1960s.

48. Ellsberg to Cronkite on the *CBS Evening News with Walter Cronkite*, 23 June 1971. A transcript of this interview can be found in Lansdale Papers, Box 23, #552.

49. North's admiration is documented in Marc Leepson, "The Cult of the Quiet American," *Regardie's*, November 1988, 86, and in Georgie Anne Geyer, "Lansdale's Lament," *Washington Monthly* 21 (June 1989): 44. The "Darth Vader" comment was made to me after I presented a paper on Lansdale at the annual meeting of the Society for Historians of American Foreign Relations, Bentley College, Waltham, Mass. June 1994; Halberstam's remark was made to me at the conference, "Cold War Culture: Film, Fact, and Fiction," Indiana University, Bloomington, February 1999.

50. "From Dallas to Watergate: Eyewitness Report," conference at Fort Mason Center, San Francisco, 6–7 September 1992.

51. The following document, declassified by the JFK Assassination Records Act in 1995, emphasizes my point about the chain of command and Lansdale's secondary role in formulating policy. On 19 January 1962 the chief of operations in the Deputy Directorate for Plans of the CIA, Richard Helms, wrote to the director of the CIA, John McCone, about a meeting he had attended concerning the "Cuba Project." Helms related that the attorney general had launched into an impassioned speech in which he said that defeating Castro carried "'the top priority in the U.S. Government— all else is secondary—no time, no money, effort or manpower is to be spared.'... the President indicated to the Attorney General that 'the final chapter on Cuba has not been written.'... the Attorney General directed those in attendance at the meeting [Lansdale and representatives from the Pentagon, Joint Chiefs of Staff, and CIA] to address themselves to [the Cuban Project] unfailingly.... He said, "It is not only General Lansdale's job to put the tasks, but yours to carry out with every resource at your command.'" In U.S. Department of State, *Foreign Relations: Cuba* 10:719–20.

52. www.blackopradio.com/lansdale_song.html. There is a long tradition of mixing this type of politics with music: for instance, the "Saigon Songfests" that Lansdale was involved with, which included former CIA men singing, "I've laid around / and stayed around / this old town too long / Summer's almost gone / a coup is coming on." In *Washington Post Potomac Magazine*, 23 February 1975, 4.

53. Richard Hofstadter, *The Paranoid Style in American Politics and Other Essays* (New York: Vintage, 1967), 3.

54. Apropos the overall style of the movie, Oliver Stone juxtaposed real film footage of American forces training anticommunist forces in the Third World with a "Lansdale" character operating in the Pentagon and in Dallas. Stone has acknowledged that his depiction of the Lansdale character is based upon information provided to him by L. Fletcher Prouty, a former member of Lansdale's team and later author of an influential conspiracy theory book, *The Secret Team: The CIA and Its Allies in Control of the United States and the World* (Englewood Cliffs, N.J.: Prentice-Hall, 1973). Since the release of the movie, Stone has also acknowledged that "Colonel X" is none other than

Prouty. Stone's address before the National Press Club, 15 January 1992, and Oliver Stone and Zachary Sklar, *JFK: The Book of the Film* (New York: Applause, 1992), cover these points.

55. "The Top of the News with Fulton Lewis, Jr.," 26 June 1964, was serialized in a number of papers and can be found in Lansdale Papers, Box 26, #603.

56. David Lansdale to Edward Lansdale, 8 March 1972, Lansdale Papers, Box 65.

57. John Le Carré, *Tinker, Tailor, Soldier, Spy* (London: Hoddert Stoughton, 1974), 200.

1. Confidences

1. Herman Melville, *The Confidence-Man: His Masquerade*, ed. Hershel Parker (1857, reprint, New York: Norton, 1971), 1, 86.

2. T. J. Jackson Lears, *Fables of Abundance: A Cultural History of Advertising in America* (New York: Basic, 1994), 101.

3. Quoted in Grant, *Facing the Phoenix*, 85.

4. Currey, *Edward Lansdale*, 3–8.

5. Cecil Currey, draft manuscript of *Edward Lansdale*, in Currey Collection, 32.

6. Currey, *Edward Lansdale*, 6–8, 15–16.

7. Lansdale Papers, Photography Section.

8. On America's multiple needs for heroes during the Great Depression, see Warren Susman, "Culture and Commitment," in his *Culture as History: The Transformation of American Society in the Twentieth Century* (New York: Pantheon, 1984), 184–210.

9. Lansdale to Robert Shaplen, 30 May 1965, Lansdale Papers, Box 40, #1111.

10. Christopher Lasch, *The True and Only Heaven: Progress and Its Critics* (New York: Norton, 1991), 518–19.

11. Raymond Williams has argued that "advertising was developed to sell goods, in a particular kind of economy. Publicity has been developed to sell persons, in a particular kind of culture." This point helps to situate Lansdale in a historical moment's publicity maneuver. Raymond Williams, "Advertising: The Magic System," in *Problems in Materialism and Culture* (London: Verso, 1980), 183–84.

12. Quoted in Currey, draft manuscript of *Edward Lansdale*, 51, based on U.S. Air Force personnel file for Lansdale.

13. Quoted in ibid., 59–60.

14. Roland Marchand, *Advertising the American Dream: Making Way for Modernity, 1920–1940* (Berkeley: University of California Press, 1986), 1.

15. Michael Schudson, *Advertising, the Uneasy Persuasion: Its Dubious Impact on American Society* (New York: Basic, 1986), 215.

16. Marchand, *Advertising the American Dream*, 84.

17. William Leach has elaborated on this point by arguing "American consumer capitalism produced a culture almost violently hostile to the past and to tradition, a future-oriented culture of desire that confused the good life with goods." In William Leach, *Land of Desire: Merchants, Power, and the Rise of a New American Culture* (New York: Pantheon Books, 1993), xiii.

18. Lansdale to the Adjutant General, Lowry A.F.B., Colorado, 15 December 1948, Lansdale Papers, Box 1, #2.

19. "From the Serpent's Mouth," 28 October 1943, Lansdale Papers, Box 31, #694.

20. John Dower, *War without Mercy: Race and Power in the Pacific War* (New York: Pantheon, 1986), analyzes with insight the origins and effects of these mutual misperceptions.

21. Lansdale Papers, 10 July 1947, Box 33, #733.

22. The relationship between Lansdale and Magsaysay continues to intrigue scholars. The standard view has Lansdale seeing in Magsaysay a pliable American tool; countless books depict Lansdale as a Svengali-like figure who persuades Magsaysay to think he is acting on his own or his country's behalf when he is really doing only what Americans think best. (Lansdale would never have used such language about their relationship, but he was not shy in pointing to his successes in working with Magsaysay.) Beginning in the 1990s, a revisionist interpretation began to develop. Richard Slotkin argues in *Gunfighter Nation: The Myth of the Frontier in Twentieth-Century America* (New York: Atheneum, 1992), 442, that "it was a serious mistake to see the Lansdale/Magsaysay partnership as a tutelary one. In fact, Lansdale and Magsaysay worked effectively because the relationship was balanced; and Magsaysay, as both a native leader and an expert on his own political culture, shaped the objectives and overall course of policy. Magsaysay was a genuine reformer." Slotkin goes on to describe the intelligence, integrity, and general acumen possessed by Magsaysay, all to make the larger point that people of the Third World were (and are today) not simply pawns or dupes of American policy. Likewise, Douglas J. Macdonald discusses American policy within a neo-conservative framework in *Adventures in Chaos: American Intervention for Reform in the Third World* (Cambridge: Harvard University Press, 1992) but asserts, "Though it was believed within the CIA, and by later critics of American policy, that Lansdale 'invented' Magsaysay, this is an incorrect, ethnocentric, and rather arrogant interpretation" (145).

Nick Cullather, in *Illusions of Influence: The Political Economy of United States–Philippines Relations, 1940–1960* (Stanford, Calif.: Stanford University Press, 1994), emphasizes that "the two men formed an association based on mutual career building" (101); that when they finally met in 1950, "Lansdale made it his business to advance Magsaysay's career, but . . . Magsaysay was already a leading figure in his own right" (100); and that one of the central reasons for his success was that "Magsaysay did not challenge his country's political system; he profited from it" (104). Although this work is the most sophisticated analysis yet of Magsaysay's rise to power, Cullather's larger argument about the "illusion" of American power within the Philippines needs to be contrasted with Raymond Bonner's *Waltzing with a Dictator; The Marcoses and the Making of American Policy* (New York: Vintage, 1988), which documents the horrific imbalance in power that characterized U.S.-Philippine relations after Philippine independence in 1946. Dana R. Dillon, "Comparative Counter-Insurgency Strategies in the Philippines," *Small Wars and Insurgencies* 6 (winter 1995): 292, adds the good point that "Lansdale leaves the reader [of his memoirs] with the impression, intended or not, that his personal relationship with Magsaysay was one of the most influential factors in the anti-insurgency strategy. Lansdale ignores events and activities such as the Bell Trade Mission, tax collection, economic aid, and others, not because they were unimportant, but because he was ignorant of them or how they affected the outcome of the war." Finally, Eva-Lotta E. Hedman situates their relationship within the larger one of American foreign relations where U.S. officials, beginning in 1898, tutored Philippine leaders in how the country should be run, politically and economically. This is a smart assessment and needs to be emphasized for any real understanding of this history. See her "Late Imperial Romance: Magsaysay, Lansdale, and the Philippine-American 'Special Relationships,'" in Richard J. Aldrich et al., *The Clandestine Cold War in Asia, 1945–1965*. (Portland, Ore.: Frank Cass, 2000), 181–94.

23. Lansdale to Jose Abueva, 5 November 1962, Lansdale Papers, Box 36, #817.

24. Lansdale Papers, Box 12, #295.

25. The phrase "America's Boy" occurs in "The People's Choice," *Time*, 23 November 1953, 37. Lansdale to Mr. Bendetsen and Colonel Sibley, 26 July 1956, Lansdale Papers, Box 35, #796 (declassified in 1990).

26. Bonner, *Waltzing with a Dictator*, 39. Lansdale casually related this information in an interview with Thomas Buell, 6 July 1972, Naval Historical Collection, Naval War College, R. I., 2–3. Buell went on to note: "Lansdale cited this as an example of his friendship towards Magsaysay and his at times unawareness that Magsaysay was a national figure. My own reaction to this story was that Magsaysay and Lansdale were two violent men."

27. Brig. Gen. Lansdale to the State Department, memo about the Philippines and their upcoming elections, 8 August 1961, Lansdale Papers, Box 48, #1352.

28. Bonner, *Waltzing with a Dictator*, 39; Stanley Karnow, *In Our Image: America's Empire in the Philippines* (New York: Random House, 1989), 15–16, 352–53; Cullather, *Illusions of Influence*, 108–15. Lansdale interview by Buell, 3, details Lansdale's access to funds and his statement that "he used no more than 50 or 60,000 dollars of the total amount" made available to him by Allen Dulles.

29. Geoffrey S. Villiers [Lansdale] to Director, KUBark, [the in-house name for the CIA], "The Philippines Election, 1953," 23 November 1953, in Edward Lansdale Collection, National Security Archives, Washington, D.C. (hereafter, Lansdale Collection). "Villiers," the agent's code name, is later identified as the individual who "captained the political-psychological team," and a number of clues point to Lansdale's authorship. For instance, in 1989 (that is, eleven years before this document was released), Stanley Karnow (*In Our Image*, 349) wrote that when Lansdale operated in the Philippines, he "signed his messages to Washington with the code name 'Geoffrey Villiers,' which he had taken out of a telephone directory." Additional evidence is that in an earlier memorandum about Lansdale's role in overseeing Magsaysay, the CIA referred to Lansdale as "Villiers" and spoke of his crucial role in furthering U.S. Cold War policies. (It appears that CIA protocols of protecting the identity of agents was extraordinarily lax at times.) Further, the breathless quality of the narrative is quintessential Lansdale; for example, "Villiers" digresses to include an idealized version of American history as justification for the CIA's actions during the election. Similar qualities can be seen in Lansdale's later memorandums detailing his covert actions in Vietnam when he formed the Saigon Military Mission in the mid-1950s (reprinted in

The Pentagon Papers). Finally, this document was found in Lansdale's papers, thanks to a Freedom of Information request.

30. "Cleanup Man," *Time*, 26 November 1951. In the article Magsaysay is further described as "a table-thumping, toe-tromping activist who would rather hip-shoot a gun at bottles tossed into Manila Bay than put away one of [President Elpidio] Quirino's famed two-hour breakfasts at Malacañan Palace, with pancakes, papaya and fried *lapu-lapu* (a choice fish)," 33. The cover art is noteworthy as it foregrounds a determined Magsaysay against a thick green jungle eerily clustered with peering red eyes.

31. Quoted in Richard Nixon, *Leaders* (New York: Warner, 1982), 289, 293.

32. Lansdale Tape Collection, Hoover Institution, Stanford, Calif., tapes #104 and 107; Lansdale Papers, Box 34, #753.

33. Fish, "General Edward G. Lansdale and the Folksongs in the Vietnam War," 396.

34. Geoffrey S. Villiers [Lansdale] to Director, KUBark, "The Philippines Election, 1953," 6, Lansdale Collection.

35. Lansdale interview by Buell, 3.

36. "Funds for Psychological Warfare," Lansdale Collection. This memorandum is on stationery of the Department of National Defense, Camp Murphy, Quezon City.

37. Even this sum is relatively minor in comparison with the total funds that the United States poured into the Philippines after World War II. See Karnow *In Our Image*, and Bonner, *Waltzing with a Dictator*, for a litany of financial dealings between the two governments.

38. Bonner, *Waltzing with a Dictator*, 39.

39. This article is in Lansdale Papers, Box 41, #1138.

40. Lansdale to Bert Talbot, 28 January 1958, Lansdale Papers, Box 41, #1138.

41. Cullather, *Illusions of Influence*, 115.

42. Allen Dulles to Spruance, 19 January 1953, Allen Dulles Papers, Seeley Mudd Library, Princeton, N.J., Box 60.

43. Lansdale, interview by Buell, 4.

44. "More or Less," *Philippine Saturday Mirror*, 7 September 1957, in Lansdale Papers, Box 1, #5.

45. William Stevenson, interview by Dennis O'Brien, 4 May 1969, 49–50, Oral History Collection, John F. Kennedy Library, Boston, Mass.

46. Pat Lansdale, interview by author, McLean, Va., 12 October 1992.

47. Peter Richards to Lansdale, Currey Collection, 27 July 1982 (original emphasis). Note: Richards often referred to Lansdale in the third person.

48. *New York Times*, Sunday supplement advertisement, 8 July 1956.

49. S. A. Schreiner Jr., "Ramon Magsaysay: Our Best Friend in Asia," *Parade Personality*, 12 September 1954.

50. The most comprehensive examination of the origins and strength of the Huks is Benedict Kerkvliet, *The Huk Rebellion: A Study of Peasant Revolt in the Philippines* (Berkeley: University of California Press, 1977), which downplays the role of the Communist Party in manipulating the Huks and focuses on their efforts involving land reform and other issues of immediate concern to the peasants. In contrast to Kerkvliet's

findings, Eduardo Lachica, *The Huks: Philippine Agrarian Society in Revolt* (New York: Praeger, 1971), portrays the Huks as a Stalin-inspired revolutionary movement. His discussion is so hyperbolic in places as to verge on black comedy; see especially Appendix A, "Ranking Huks and Awards for Their Killing, Capture, or Surrender," which carefully notes the pricetag of various Huk leaders.

51. The report continued, "As defense secretary, Magsaysay recognized this fact, but was able to establish only a token program to provide land for the landless." CIA, "Significance of the [1953] Philippine Election," *Current Intelligence Weekly*, 20 November 1953, Mori Database, Doc. 27363, Washington, D.C.

52. In addition to summarizing in a blunt fashion the nature of U.S. foreign policy, Melby was not shy in highlighting his own efforts in remaking the Philippines: "Out of the Philippine business, what Myron Cowen [U.S. Ambassador to the Philippines] and I developed was the belief that the only salvation for the Philippines was going to be to get rid of [President] Quirino. We selected Magsaysay as a logical successor. . . . We had a certain amount of very useful assistance from Ed Lansdale. He was with the CIA." John F. Melby, Oral History Interview, November 1986, 182–84, Harry S. Truman Library, Independence, Mo. In 1951, though, Melby praised Lansdale as a "veritable jewel" and said that "the amount of information he has about the Philippines is really staggering." Melby to Cowen, 7 March 1951, John F. Melby Papers, Box 8, Harry S. Truman Library.

53. Captain Harold F. Frederick to Luis Taruc, 28 January 1945, Lansdale Papers, Box 18, #424.

54. Although it is only a conjecture, one cannot rule out the possibility that the Huks' change in slogans was a Lansdale-inspired maneuver aimed at American policymakers.

55. Louis Taruc, interview by Antonio R. de Joya, ". . . What after Amnesty," Lansdale Papers, Box 18, #424.

56. Quoted in Kerkvliet, *The Huk Rebellion*, 147.

57. Ronald E. Dolan, ed., *Philippines: A Country Study* (Washington, D.C.: Library of Congress, 1993), 46.

58. *The Pentagon Papers*, 1:51.

59. Edward Lansdale, "Military Psychological Operations: Part Two," 7, 29 March 1960, Lansdale Papers, Box 12, #294.

60. Edward Lansdale, *In the Midst of Wars*, 74–75. During the height of the Vietnam War, Mary McCarthy would return to this phrase as well: "The Air Force seems inescapable, like the eye of God, and soon, you imagine . . . all will be razed, charred, defoliated by that terrible searching gaze." Quoted in Paul Boyer, *Promises to Keep: The United States since World War II* (Boston: Houghton Mifflin, 1999), 296.

61. William Whitson, "Informal Discussion with Col. Lansdale," 25 February 1957, 5, Lansdale Papers, Box 12, #292.

62. Edward Lansdale, U.S. Air Force Academy Oral History Interview by Kenneth Alwick 25 April 1971, 4, Maxwell Air Force Base, Ala.

63. Denis Warner, *Certain Victory: How Hanoi Won the War* (Kansas City, Mo.: Sheed Andrews & McMeel, 1978), 103–4.

64. Quoted in T. J. Jackson Lears, "From Salvation to Self-Realization: Advertising and the Therapeutic Roots of the Consumer Culture, 1880–1930," in *The Culture of Consumption: Critical Essays in American History, 1880–1890*, ed. Richard Wightman Fox and T. J. Jackson Lears (New York: Pantheon, 1983), 18.

65. A. H. Peterson, G. C. Reinhardt, and E. E. Conger, eds, *Symposium on the Role of Airpower in Counterinsurgency and Unconventional Warfare: The Philippine Huk Campaign* (Santa Monica, Calif.: Rand Corporation, July 1963), 50–52.

66. Quoted in Currey, *Edward Lansdale*, 367–68.

67. Lansdale Papers, Box 8, #260, 256–57.

68. Edward G. Lansdale, "Art of the Guerrilla War," pt. 1, *Christian Science Monitor*, 18 January 1964.

69. Currey, *Edward Lansdale*, 94–95; Lansdale, *In the Midst of Wars*, 51–52.

70. Larry Cable, *Conflict of Myths: The Development of American Counterinsurgency Doctrine and the Vietnam War* (New York: New York University Press, 1986), 55–56; Kerkvliet, *The Huk Rebellion*, 239.

71. Edward Lansdale, "Art of the Guerrilla War," pt. 2, *Christian Science Monitor*, 20 January 1964.

72. Lansdale to Major General E. L. Rowny, USA, Chief, United States Army Concept Team in Vietnam, 14 February 1963, Lansdale Papers (1990 declassified folder).

73. Lansdale Papers, Box 8, #259, 64; Box 9, #265, 64–65.

74. Francis Madlangbayan to Lansdale, 26 June 1962, Lansdale Papers (1992 declassified folder). The handwritten notation, "EGL feels he cannot interfere. . . . To be destroyed later," suggests Lansdale's response to this threat.

75. Lansdale to Carmen Nakpil, 5 December 1961, Lansdale Papers, Box 38, #938; Myron Cowen, "Memorandum by the Ambassador in the Philippines," 9 July 1951, *Foreign Relations of the United States, 1951: Asia and the Pacific* (Washington, D.C.: GPO, 1977), 6: 1550: "The Department feels, as I have long felt, that the use of napalm bombs by the Philippine armed forces is a hazardous venture to the extent that if any innocent Philippine citizens were inadvertently burned by the careless use of napalm we would be held at least morally responsible in as much as we had provided the Philippine armed forces with the napalm. . . . I discussed the matter briefly with Ed Lansdale a few days ago. Lansdale is of the opinion that a somewhat more liberal use of napalm should be given to the Philippine armed forces."

76. Fletcher Prouty to author, September 1992. The most effective rebuttal to this helicopter story was provided by the Vietnam specialist Douglas Pike, who told me in 1993 that every GI in Vietnam knew someone who knew someone who in turn knew someone who threw a VC guerrilla out of a helicopter. No one has yet actually seen or confessed to this deed in a way that can be corroborated.

77. Lansdale's most detailed discussion on U.S. policy in Central America during the 1980s is in his "Some Thoughts about Central America," 10 May 1983, Currey Collection. This same document sums up his assessment of why the United States lost in Vietnam: "We simply went home too soon." Also see Bonner, *Waltzing with a Dictator*, 34; Raymond Bonner, "The Salvador Strategy," *New Republic*, 7 October

1985, 19; Drinnon, *Facing West*, xv–xvii; Peter H. Stone, "The Special Forces in 'Covert Action': A Pentagon-C.I.A. Production," *Nation*, 7–14 July 1984, 8–12.

78. Edward Bernays, *Propaganda* (New York: Liveright, 1928), 9. Further on, Bernays modified his rhetoric, but only a bit: "Is this government by propaganda? Call it, if you prefer, government by education. But education, in the academic sense of the word, is not sufficient. It must be enlightened expert propaganda through the creation of circumstances, through the high-spotting of significant events, and the dramatization of important issues" (114).

79. Lansdale, address to National Strategy Seminar, National War College, "The U.S. Military in Non-Military Warfare," 23 July 1959, Lansdale Papers, Box 7, #239 (original emphasis).

80. Bruce Barton, *The Man Nobody Knows: A Discovery of the Real Jesus* (Indianapolis: Bobbs-Merrill, 1925), 100.

81. Edward Lansdale, U.S. Air Force Academy Oral History Interview, 25 April 1971, 7.

82. Lansdale, *In the Midst of Wars*, 376.

83. Quoted in Mark Crispin Miller, *Boxed In: The Culture of TV* (Evanston, Ill.: Northwestern University Press, 1988), 11.

84. Lansdale speech, "Soldiers and the People," 30 August 1962, Lansdale Papers, Box 7, #239, 6.

85. See, for instance, Stuart C. Miller, *Benevolent Assimilation: The American Conquest of the Philippines, 1893–1902* (New Haven: Yale University Press, 1982).

86. Norman O. Brown, *Life against Death: The Psychoanalytical Meaning of History* (New York: Vintage 1959), 220.

2. Selling America, Selling Vietnam

1. John Berger, *Ways of Seeing* (London: British Broadcasting Service, 1972), 130–31.

2. Journal No. 4, 26 December 1946, Lansdale Papers, Box 7, #237.

3. Lansdale to Frederick Praeger, 6 July 1962, Lansdale Papers, Box 5, #181.

4. "Memorandum of Conversation with the President," 7 June 1955, John Foster Dulles Papers, Seeley Mudd Library, Princeton, N.J., Box 12.

5. Joseph B. Smith, *Portrait of a Cold Warrior* (New York: Putnam, 1976), 101.

6. Edward Lansdale, interview by Cecil Currey, 16 May 1984, Currey Collection.

7. Lansdale Papers, Box 9, #261, 367–68. Even if Lansdale actually did read the book, it would not have been terribly helpful, since it dealt with China and its revolution. In a 1982 letter to the Congressional Research Service, Lansdale added that he began to read other French works in preparation for his trip to Vietnam: "The most useful of these was by Major A. M. Savani, *Visage et Images du Sud-Vietnam*, about French pacification efforts along the Mekong. It gave me insights into the Hoa Hao, particularly their leaders. I note as I look at my copy now, it is very thumb-worn from my study. I had many dealings later with the people in its pages." Quoted in Gibbons, *The U.S. Government and the Vietnam War*, 264 n.122.

8. Lansdale, *In the Midst of Wars* 110.

9. Edward G. Lansdale, interview by William Gibbons and Patricia McAdams, 19 November 1982, Lansdale Papers, Box 79.

10. Ibid., 3; U.S. Department of State, *Foreign Relations of the United States: Indochina, 1952–1954* (Washington, D.C.: GPO, 1982), memorandum of discussion at the 180th NSC meeting, 14 January 1954, 13: 961–64.

11. Quoted in George Kahin, *Intervention: How America Became Involved in Vietnam* (New York: Anchor, 1986), 81.

12. Edward Lansdale, interview by Ted Gittinger, 5 June 1981, Lyndon Baines Johnson Library, Austin, Tex.

13. Lansdale to Robert Shaplen, 30 May 1965, Lansdale Papers, Box 40, #1111. The popular French publication *Paris Match* had a 1965 article about the Vietnam War that was not only profoundly anti-American but included a brief, nasty description of Lansdale, whom it blamed for the Vietnamese hatred of the French. Alfred W. McCoy, *The Politics of Heroin: CIA Complicity in the Global Drug Trade* (Chicago: Lawrence Hill Books, 2003), 140. See Raymond Cartier, "S.O.S.: Amitié Américaine en Péril," *Paris Match*, 4 June 1965.

14. Lansdale Papers, Box 9, #261, 369.

15. Currey, *Edward Lansdale*, 176.

16. Lansdale to Diem, 12 September 1960, Lansdale Papers, Box 39, #1052.

17. Lansdale to Walter Stoneman, AID, Department of State, 14 May 1963, Lansdale Papers, Box 49, #1373. The Strategic Hamlet Program involved a series of fortified enclosures created by Diem with the help of American forces in an effort to withstand Vietcong incursions. This program failed for a host of reasons, including the isolation of these hamlets from the peasants' fields. See Kahin, *Intervention*, 140–44.

18. "The Village That Refuses to Die," Lansdale Papers, Box 49, #1375.

19. An American Officer [Lansdale], "The Report the President Wanted Published," *Saturday Evening Post*, 20 May 1961, 3, 8.

20. *The Village That Refuses to Die*, 1962 television program, KCRA, Sacramento, Calif., film in author's possession.

21. Lansdale and Harry Boardman correspondence, 25 February 1964, Records of Meetings, vol. 49, Council of Foreign Relations Archive, New York, N.Y.

22. Lansdale Papers, Box 16, #391; Rockefeller Archives Center, Sleepy Hollow, N.Y.

23. Lansdale Papers, Box 9, #264, 27.

24. John Mecklin, *Mission in Torment: An Intimate Account of the U.S. Role in Vietnam* (New York: Doubleday, 1965), 84–85.

25. Quoted in Gibbons, *The U.S. Government and the Vietnam War*, 263.

26. Lansdale, *In the Midst of Wars*, 159.

27. In a typical example, a message from Rufus Phillips (acting as the American intermediary) to Lansdale specified that Diem "is not too disposed to listen to anyone else except you I'm afraid" (Lansdale Papers, 4 May 1963, Box 40, #1080). For other examples, see Chapter 3.

28. Central Intelligence Agency, Country Report: South Vietnam, "Situation Appraisal as of 5 October 1963," 8 October 1963.

29. Seymour Hersh, *The Dark Side of Camelot* (Boston: Little, Brown, 1997), 427. Lansdale related this event to Daniel Ellsberg, who worked for Lansdale in the mid-1960s, and Ellsberg later told it to Hersh; however, Robert McNamara told Hersh that he could not recall whether or not it happened.

30. "The Beleaguered Man," *Time*, 4 April 1955, 22–23.

31. Demaree Bess, "Bright Spot in Asia," *Saturday Evening Post*, 15 September 1956, 127.

32. Copy in Lansdale Papers, Box 65, c. 1956.

33. Lansdale to Dr. Frith, Foreign Service Institute, 8 February 1963, Lansdale Papers, Box 49, #1373.

34. Lansdale interview by Currey, 19 December 1984. Currey Collection.

35. "The Beleaguered Man," 23.

36. Johnson, during his May 1961 visit to Vietnam, quoted in Ellen Hammer, *A Death in November: America in Vietnam, 1963* (New York: Dutton, 1987), 35.

37. Thé had split off from the Cao Dai in 1951 to head his own Lien Minh militia. Lansdale viewed these Lien Minh troops as a valuable asset, in essence a private army that could be hired to protect Diem. See Lansdale, *In the Midst of Wars*, 153, for his description of this history. *The Pentagon Papers*, quoted in Gibbons, *The U.S. Government and the Vietnam War*, 293 n. 41.

38. "Lansdale's Team Report on Covert Saigon Mission in 1954 and 1955," reprinted in *The Pentagon Papers*, 1:578.

39. Bernard Fall, *The Two Viet-Nams: A Political and Military Analysis*, 2d rev. ed. (New York: Praeger, 1967), 246. This single passage epitomized a long-standing dispute between Lansdale and Fall. In an 1964 edition of this book, Fall added: "In all likelihood, the total amount of American dollars spent on bribes during March and April 1955 by Diem may well have gone beyond $12 million." This was deleted in later editions, and in its place Fall added this curious footnote: "In a communication to this writer in 1964, General Edward Lansdale, then an adviser to Diem, stated that no bribes were given, but merely 'back pay' due the sect troops and paid in cash to their leaders." Fall remained incredulous, even as Lansdale's lieutenants defended the actions and Lansdale's overall innocence on these matters. See also Currey, *Edward Lansdale*, 380 n. 81. Of interest here is that one of Lansdale's closest aides at the time, Rufus Phillips, later characterized the SMM's actions in the following way: "It is known that money was provided by the CIA Station at Ed's request to President Diem to pay Thé's troops." (Phillips to Currey, 5 July 1988, Currey Collection). Phillips considered those payments as legitimate expenses, not bribery, and believed that Fall was biased against American efforts.

Lansdale's and Fall's relationship was often marked by differing visions of American power. During a 1966 lecture at the Far East Training Center in Hawaii, Fall said—and in front of Lansdale—"The Americans have an emotional hangup on the word 'colonialism.' That's why this place here [Hawaii] wasn't called a colony but a territory, right? Of course, it's six of one, half dozen of the other" (Lansdale Papers, Box 16, #390, 3). Lansdale, in turn, in a letter to a friend, pointedly noted: "On Indo-China, I feel strongly that any listening we do to the French (and Bernard Fall in particular) be done with a highly critical ear. The French went from glorious defeat to glorious defeat (Indo-China to Algeria), while being highly articulate on how to win a war. It's a bad habit, a contagious one, and all too easy for Americans to catch" (Lansdale Papers, 4 February 1963, Box 37, #887).

40. "Operation Exodus" was the term used by the United States Operations Mission for overseeing foreign aid programs; "Operation Passage to Freedom" was the term used by the U.S. Navy, which provided the ships to transport the refugees.

41. Gertrude Samuels, "Passage to Freedom in Viet Nam," *National Geographic* 107 (June 1955): 866.

42. Leo Cherne to Admiral Richard E. Byrd, n.d., Box 31, "IRC Business," Leo Cherne Papers, Boston University Special Collections, Boston, Mass.

43. Seth Jacobs, "'Our System Demands the Supreme Being': The U.S. Religious Revival and the 'Diem Experiment,' 1954–55," *Diplomatic History* 25, (fall 2001): 618.

44. Robert Schulzinger, *A Time For War: The United States and Vietnam, 1941–1975* (New York: Oxford University Press, 1997), 81.

45. Fisher, *Dr. America*, 58.

46. Lansdale, *In the Midst of Wars*, 226–27; Sheehan Papers, Box 71.

47. Edward G. Lansdale, U.S. Air Force Oral History Interview, Office of Air Force History, 9–10 September 1969, 51–52.

48. Lansdale, *In the Midst of Wars*, 168–69.

49. Lansdale memorandum to Taylor, "Resources for Unconventional Warfare," in *The Pentagon Papers*, 2:648.

50. History of Operation Brotherhood, Lansdale Papers, Box 35, #804.

51. Gloria Emerson, *Winners and Losers: Battles, Retreats, Gains, Losses, and Ruins from the Vietnam War* (New York: Harvest/HBJ, 1976), 294.

52. Fisher, *Dr. America*, 40.

53. Quoted in Agnes W. Dooley, *Promises to Keep: The Life of Dr. Thomas A. Dooley* (New York: Farrar, Straus, 1962), 62.

54. A photo of the ceremony can be found in Dooley, *Promises to Keep*, and the award is discussed in detail in Fisher, *Dr. America*, 34, 60. Unknown to Dooley, the CIA was also keeping extensive records on his activities at home and abroad. In 1978 and again in 1986 the agency released its records on the man, not only mundane newspaper clippings and congressional testimony that lauded Dooley's efforts but also more sensitive telegrams and memorandums on his actions—some of which continue to show deletions for "national security" reasons—and private letters that Dooley sent to friends, telling of his exploits. Clearly, the CIA considered the doctor an asset to their activities but someone who must be watched for fear that he was something of a loose cannon.

55. Thomas A. Dooley, *Deliver Us from Evil: The Story of Viet Nam's Flight to Freedom* (New York: Farrar, Straus, 1956), 71.

56. This point is explored in Jacobs, "Our System Demands the Supreme Being," 589–624. Jacobs makes a convincing argument that the U.S. supported Diem over other potential leaders because "Diem's trump . . . was his religion" (599).

57. Lansdale Papers, Box 22, #522.

58. *United States–Vietnam Relations: 1945–1967*, a study prepared by the Department of Defense (Washington, D.C.: GPO, 1971), 10:937.

59. Anderson, *Trapped by Success*, 111–19, details how Lansdale convinced Diem to initiate the battle between the government and the sects. Also see Daniel Greene, "Tug of War: The Eisenhower Administration and Vietnam, 1953–1955" (Ph.D. diss, University of Texas, 1990), 399–405. The key documents that outline Lansdale's maneuvers both within Washington and in Saigon are in U.S. Department of State, *Foreign Relations of the United States: Vietnam, 1955–1957*, vol. 1 (Washington, D.C.: GPO, 1985). An editorial note in this volume details Lansdale's actions, including his series of telegrams back to Washington urging U.S. support of Diem during the sect crisis. In one telegram he argued that "United States prestige in Vietnam would seriously decrease and the United States could not be a major factor in supporting such a government, which, lacking popular support, would be forced to depend heavily upon the French" (303).

60. Lansdale, "Memorandum for Review Panel," Center of Military History, U.S. Army, 6 June 1979, Currey Collection.

61. Howard R. Simpson, *Tiger in the Barbed Wire: An American in Vietnam, 1952–1991* (New York: Kodansha, 1992), 172.

62. J. Lawton Collins, interview by David L. Anderson, in Anderson, *Trapped by Success*, 112. For Lansdale's partial history of these events, see his *In the Midst of Wars*, 282–311.

63. Lansdale, U.S. Air Force Oral History Interview, 52.

64. Lansdale, *In the Midst of Wars*, 333–34.

65. Quoted in Karnow, *Vietnam*, 223.

66. Lansdale, *In the Midst of Wars*, 333–34; *The Pentagon Papers*, New York Times (New York: Bantam, 1971), 21.

67. Lansdale, *In the Midst of Wars*, 347.

68. Kahin, *Intervention*, 101. The internal quote is from a CIA memorandum of 19 September 1964, 3.

69. Lansdale, *In the Midst of Wars*, 307–8.

70. Tran Van Don, *Our Endless War: Inside Vietnam* (San Raphael, Calif.: Presidio Press, 1978), 60.

71. Memo from Lansdale to Sec. of Defense and Deputy Sec., 17 January 1961, Lansdale Papers, Box 49, #1376, 9.

72. Robert Buzzanco, *Masters of War: Military Dissent and Politics in the Vietnam Era* (New York: Cambridge University Press, 1996), 97. Buzzanco cites a May 1961 memorandum from Lansdale to Deputy Secretary of Defense Gilpatric on the nature of U.S. combat forces in Vietnam. The memo does not dispute that more U.S. forces may be required, but its tone suggests that delay would be prudent, "since the deployment of U.S. combat forces in Vietnam is predicted on the request for them by the

Government of Vietnam, [and] since this request hasn't been made yet. . . . With concrete information, you will then have a firm position for further decisions." The memorandum can be found in *United States–Vietnam Relations: 1945–1967*, 11: 157–58. Later, Lansdale seemed a bit more open to the introduction of American forces. In his December 1961 "Memorandum for the Chairman, JCS" he argued: "It would seem that the increased U.S. military stake in Vietnam should afford some means for stabilizing the political relationship with the Vietnamese Armed Forces long enough for all concerned to get on with the war. Armed with facts about such a political stability, Nolting [Frederick Nolting, U.S. ambassador to South Vietnam] and McGarr [General Lionel McGarr, commander of Military Assistance Command Vietnam] should have little trouble in getting Diem to play ball" (*United States–Vietnam Relations: 1945–1967*, 11: 427).

73. A. J. Langguth, *Our Vietnam: The War, 1954–1975* (New York: Simon & Schuster, 2000), 148.

74. William J. Rust, *Kennedy in Vietnam* (New York: Scribners, 1985), 45; Marilyn Young, *The Vietnam War: 1945–1990* (New York: HarperCollins, 1992), 99. Lansdale also related this story in Harold Morse, "Marcos' Militant Stance Criticized," *Honolulu Star-Bulletin*, 7 January 1984, A-3.

75. Mark Scott Zicree, *The Twilight Zone Companion* (New York: Bantam, 1982), 363–65.

76. Lansdale Papers, 17 April 1963, Box 48, #1359. The history of *Reader's Digest* is of note, as it has not always been so conservative: during World War II it serialized Joseph Davies's memoirs, *Mission to Moscow*, with its popular-front message and depiction of Joseph Stalin as "Uncle Joe." See Stephen Whitfield, *The Culture of the Cold War* (Baltimore: Johns Hopkins University Press, 1991), 144; see also John Heidenry, *Theirs Was the Kingdom: Lila and DeWitt Wallace and the Story of the Reader's Digest* (New York: Norton, 1993), 468–94, for an extended treatment on the magazine and the CIA.

77. Lansdale Papers, 14 October 1957, Box 49, #1366.

78. "Lansdale's Team Report on Covert Saigon Mission in 1954 and 1955," reprinted in *The Pentagon Papers*, 1:581.

79. Memorandum from the Secretary of Defense's Assistant for Special Operations (Lansdale) to the Secretary of Defense (McNamara), 26 February 1962, *Foreign Relations of the United States, 1961–1963: Vietnam, 1962* 2:177.

80. Diary of Robert Coate, Lansdale Papers, Box 60, #1574, 63.

81. Bruce Jackson, "The Perfect Informant," *Journal of American Folklore* 103 (October–December 1990): 416.

82. C. Wright Mills, *The Power Elite* (New York: Oxford University Press, 1956), 197. Mills goes on to write about an individual like Lansdale and his public relations persona with insight: "In and out of uniform, generals and admirals have attempted to sway the opinions of the underlying population, lending the weight of their authority, openly as well as behind closed doors, to controversial policies," (198).

83. On the very same day (17 January 1961) that Lansdale was extolling an increased presence in Vietnam, President Eisenhower gave his farewell address to the

nation, his most famous speech. In it, he echoed C. Wright Mills in explicitly warning against the kind of alliances Lansdale was so adept at fashioning and spoke of a growing threat to American democracy by a confluence of forces: "In the councils of government, we must guard against the acquisition of unwarranted influence, whether sought or unsought, by the military-industrial complex. The potential for the disastrous rise of misplaced power exists and will persist. We must never let the weight of this combination endanger our liberties or democratic process. We should take nothing for granted." Quoted in Blanche Wiesen Cook, *The Declassified Eisenhower* (New York: Penguin, 1984), ix.

84. Roswell L. Gilpatric, interview, 5 May 1970, Oral History Collection of the John F. Kennedy Library, Boston, Mass., 99–100.

85. *The Pentagon Papers*, 2: 7; Memo from Lansdale to Sec. of Defense and Deputy Sec., 17 January 1961, in Lansdale Papers, Box 49, #1376, 3, 9.

86. Dean Rusk, interview by Dennis O'Brien, 2 December 1969, 43, John F. Kennedy Library, Boston, Mass.

87. John M. Newman, *JFK and Vietnam: Deception, Intrigue, and the Struggle for Power* (New York: Warner, 1992), 3–7.

88. *Foreign Relations of the United States, 1961–1963: Cuba, 1961–1962*, 10: 666; Roswell Gilpatric, Oral History Interview I, by Ted Gittinger, 2 November 1982, 2, Lyndon B. Johnson Library, Austin, Tex.

89. Mai Pobone to Lansdale, 2 May 1977, Lansdale Papers, Box 2, #25.

90. Edward Lansdale to Peter Richards, 28 March 1983, Currey Collection.

91. Bernard Yoh to Lansdale, 28 February 1966, Lansdale Papers (1991 recently declassified folder).

92. Karl Marx, *Capital: Volume 1* (1867), in *The Marx-Engels Reader*, ed. Robert Tucker (New York: Norton, 1978), 319.

93. For a succinct discussion of how Melville and Marx viewed the role of commodities, see Jean-Christophe Agnew, *Worlds Apart: The Market and the Theater in Anglo-American Thought, 1550–1750* (New York: Cambridge University Press, 1986), 202–3; Lansdale is quoted in Bart Barnes, "Edward Lansdale, Prototype for 'Ugly American,' Dies," *Washington Post*, 24 February 1987, B4.

94. Richard Fried, *Nightmare in Red: The McCarthy Era in Perspective* (New York: Oxford University Press, 1990), 5.

95. Barton, *The Man Nobody Knows*, 155.

96. Quoted in David Corn and Gus Russo, "The Old Man and the CIA: A Kennedy Plot to Kill Castro?" *Nation*, 26 March 2001.

97. *Foreign Relations of the United States, 1961–1963: Cuba, 1961–1962*, 10:807–9.

98. Church Committee, *Alleged Assassination Plots*, 144.

99. Lansdale, "The Cuba Project," 20 February 1962, Kennedy Library, National Security Files: Meetings and Memoranda, Special Group (Augmented), 1/62–6/62, Box 319.

100. David W. Belin, "History according to Hollywood," *Wall Street Journal*, 13 February 1996. Belin originally interviewed Lansdale on 16 May 1975 when he worked as counsel for the President's Commission on CIA Activities. In this "top secret" interview, he showed Lansdale the 13 August 1962 memorandum. Lansdale's response

was that he didn't recall writing it or advocating the assassination of Castro. Later, he argued that it was simply an idea that had been dismissed by others in the Special Group (Augmented). See "Deposition of Edward G. Lansdale," U.S. President's Commission on CIA Activities within the United States, 16 May 1975, Assassination Materials, 11–17, Box 5, Gerald R. Ford Library, Ann Arbor, Mich. The document can be found, with notation of text not declassified, in *Foreign Relations of the United States, 1961–1963:Cuba, 1961–1962,* 10:924–25.

101. *Foreign Relations, 1961–1963: Cuba, 1961–1962,* 10:830; Mark J. White, ed., *The Kennedys and Cuba: The Declassified Documentary History* (Chicago: Dee, 2001), 120; James Hershberg, "Before the 'Missiles of October: Did Kennedy Plan a Military Strike against Cuba?" *Diplomatic History* 14 (spring 1990): 178–79.

102. Corn and Russo, "The Old Man and the CIA"; Lansdale, "Memorandum for the Record: Meeting with President, 16 March 1962." This document was declassified in 1997 by the Assassination Records Review Board and provided to me by Professor Larry Hapapanen.

103. Church Committee, *Alleged Assassination Plots,* 142 n. 2. For detailed histories of this period, see Hershberg, "Before the 'Missiles of October," 163–98; Thomas G. Paterson, "Fixation with Cuba: The Bay of Pigs, Missile Crisis, and Covert War against Castro," in *Kennedy's Quest for Victory: American Foreign Policy, 1961–1963,* ed. Thomas G. Paterson (New York: Oxford University Press, 1989), 123–55.

104. Lansdale Papers, Box 71.

105. Lansdale, "Illumination by Submarine," Kennedy Library, National Security Files: Meetings and Memorandums: Special Group (Augmented), 10/62–12/62, Box 319.

106. Bissell to Lansdale, "Cuba," 5 January 1961 (declassified by the CIA in 1993).

107. James Bamford, *Body of Secrets: Anatomy of the Ultra-Secret National Security Agency* (New York: Doubleday, 2001), 82.

108. George Lardner Jr., "Military Had Plan to Blame Cuba If Glenn's Space Mission Failed," *Washington Post,* 19 November 1997, A02; Tim Weiner, "Declassified Papers Show Anti-Castro Ideas Proposed to Kennedy," *New York Times,* 19 November 1997, A25. The memorandum can be found in White, *The Kennedy and Cuba,* 100–105.

109. Bamford, *Body of Secrets,* 84.

110. At an international conference in 1989 on the origins of the Cuban missile crisis, it was reported that "Senior Cuban officials reportedly have told American participants in the conference that they knew about Operation Mongoose from an early stage, thanks to a well-placed informant. It is unclear, however, whether they were aware that October 1962 had been mentioned as a target date for Castro's overthrow." What this reporter does not mention is that the document was written by Lansdale. Michael Dobbs, "Document Details 62 Plans on Cuba," *Washington Post,* 26 January 1989.

111. David C. Martin, *Wilderness of Mirrors* (New York: Harper & Row, 1980), 146. Oddly enough, Lansdale had received two actual pet mongooses as a gift from General Thé during his time in Vietnam; he housed them in his villa there to keep rats and snakes at bay. Lansdale to family, 2 May 1955, Lansdale Papers, Box 4.

112. Special Agent E. B. Stone, "Report from Department of Justice. . . . Alleged Villista Activities," 13 September 1916, Record Group 165, National Archives, Washington, D.C. This plan is discussed in greater detail in David S. Foglesong, *America's Secret War against Bolshevism: U.S. Intervention in the Russian Civil War, 1917–1920* (Chapel Hill: University of North Carolina Press, 1995), 21.

3. The Power of Secrets

1. Pat Lansdale, interview by author.

2. It must be emphasized that as of 2002 there was only one relevant document in Lansdale's personal papers at the Hoover Institution detailing his relationship with the CIA. On 9 January 1951, Walter B. Smith the CIA director, wrote to Major General Leland S. Hobbs, chief adviser to the Joint U.S. Military Advisory Group: "We are pleased to be of service to you in extending the orders of Lieutenant Colonel Edward G. Lansdale . . . We have checked with Colonel Lansdale and find him willing and eager to be of service." Handwritten at the bottom of the letter is this additional notation: "I agree with you—he is almost as indispensable where he is. W.B.S." (Lansdale Papers, Box 34, #747).

3. Lansdale to Currey, 15 December 1985, Lansdale Papers, Box 70.

4. From a 1981 interview with Samuel Williams, LBJ Library, Austin, Tex. On 29 March 1972, Williams had written to friends about Lansdale: "He remained for about a year or so with me. At that time he was a Colonel, USAF, but with CIA. Although with MAAG [U.S. Military Assistance Advisory Group Vietnam] he was getting his orders elsewhere and I stayed out of his business." In Samuel Williams Papers, Box 17, #8, Hoover Institution, Stanford, Calif.

5. Quoted in Daniel Ellsberg, *Secrets: A Memoir of Vietnam and the Pentagon Papers* (New York: Viking, 2002), 99.

6. "Review of Lansdale Document Listings," 21 July 1981; "Plans for the Review of the Edward Lansdale Documents," 3 August 1981; "Status of Lansdale Document Review," 12 August 1981; "Lansdale Papers," 24 September and 23 October 1981. All these documents were sent to this author by the CIA's Security Analysis Group.

7. Lansdale, *In the Midst of Wars*, 126–27.

8. "Meeting of the President's Special Committee on Indochina," 30 January 1954, in *The Pentagon Papers*, 1:446. (Note: Allen Dulles is referred to throughout this document as "Allan.")

9. Brig. Gen. Millard C. Young, Air Force, from the Office of the Joint Chiefs of Staff, in Lansdale Tape Collection, Tape #121.

10. Lansdale Papers, Box 49, #1376.

11. "Lansdale's Team Report on Covert Saigon Mission in 1954 and 1955," reprinted in *The Pentagon Papers*, 1:573, 574, 583.

12. Ibid., 1:574.

13. Ibid., 1:578.

14. Lansdale, *In the Midst of Wars*, 270. Minh's loyalty would eventually falter; he helped engineer the successful coup against Diem in 1963.

15. "Lansdale's Team Report," 1:579.

16. William E. Colby, Oral History Interview I by Ted Gittinger, 2 June 1981, 33–34, Lyndon B. Johnson Library, Austin, Tex.

17. "Lansdale's Team Report," 1:580.

18. Ibid., 1:581.

19. Simpson, *Tiger in the Barbed Wire*, 144.

20. Lansdale to Bunker, June 1968, "Vietnamese Soothsaying," Lansdale Papers, Box 62, #1619.

21. Rudyard Kipling, *Kim* (1901; reprint, New York: Penguin, 1987), 62. The "little friend" phrase is repeated throughout the novel.

22. Obviously, there were individuals in addition to Lansdale who were known to be working for the CIA but this list was extremely small.

23. Quoted in Kai Bird, *The Color of Truth: McGeorge Bundy and William Bundy, Brothers in Arms* (New York: Simon & Schuster, 1998), 177.

24. Roger Hilsman Jr., interview 14 August 1970, 22, Oral History Collection of the John F. Kennedy Library, Boston, Mass.

25. Cited in Rust, *Kennedy in Vietnam*, 45. Lansdale, though, could give back in like manner. He said of Taylor: "A patrician, cold, thinking, short-sighted person. He doesn't understand human beings, I'm afraid" (quoted in Currey, *Edward Lansdale*, 237).

26. Brig. Gen. Lansdale to General Taylor, "Unconventional Warfare," 23 October 1961, National Security Files: Vietnam; Taylor Report, 3 November 1961, Rostow Working Copy, Tab III–IV, John F. Kennedy Library, Boston, Mass. (declassified May 1999).

27. Draft of memoir, Lansdale Papers, Box 9, #264, 20–21.

28. Lansdale to McNamara, 7 July 1962, Lansdale Papers, Box 49, #1374 (declassified 12 April 1989), 2.

29. Robert S. McNamara, with Brian VanDeMark, *In Retrospect: The Tragedy and Lessons of Vietnam* (New York: Times, 1995), 32.

30. Walt W. Rostow, Oral History Interview I by Paige E. Mulhollan, 21 March 1969, 37, Lyndon B. Johnson Library, Austin, Tex.

31. Memorandum from Walt Rostow to McGeorge Bundy, 30 January 1961, Papers of President Kennedy, Box 193, National Security Files: Vietnam, January 1961–March 1961.

32. Lansdale to President Kennedy, 24 May 1963, Lansdale Papers (recently declassified folder).

33. "Talk with General Lansdale," 3 December 1962, Richard Helms, Box 5 Assassination Files, Gerald R. Ford Library, Ann Arbor, Mich.

34. Michael Denning, *Cover Stories: Narrative and Ideology in the British Spy Thriller* (New York: Routledge, 1987), 3.

35. U.S. Senate, *Executive Session of the Senate Foreign Relations Committee, The Situation in Vietnam*, 1965, 17:35.

36. Ibid., 69.

37. Similarities exist between Lansdale's performance before Congress and that of Teamster witnesses appearing at Senator Estes Kefauver's hearings during the 1950s

on the nature of organized crime in America (though the latter wore bags over their heads to disguise themselves, presumably to prevent their being killed by fellow labor racketeers). The senators had listened intently to these crime stories perpetrated by unknown yet knowing individuals much as they listened to Lansdale's tales of intrigue and Cold War stories.

38. U.S. Congress, Congressional Hearings on Counterinsurgency, 16 August 1962, in Lansdale Papers (recently declassified box for 1990), 7–8, 23–24.

39. Lansdale to Sam Williams, Williams Papers, Box 29, #15.

40. "Night of the Generals," *Women's Wear Daily*, 19 January 1976, 4.

41. Lori Eggert, interview by author, 15 August 1991, Hoover Institution, Stanford, Calif.

42. Lansdale Papers, Box 36, #815.

43. Lansdale, *In the Midst of Wars*, 218.

44. This information was presented in Fletcher Prouty's commentary at the Society of Americans of Foreign Relations Conference, Poughkeepsie, N.Y., 21 June 1992. He went on to note: "In November 1960 shortly after John F. Kennedy had been elected President, Ed came to me in my office across the hall from his and said that he was going to Saigon to meet with Diem. He asked me to do a favor for him. He wanted me to go into Washington and purchase the biggest, gaudiest, and grandest desk ornament ever made. . . . I went into the city and found what he wanted. As I recall it cost about $800.00 which I paid. Ed was delighted with the gift and promised to repay me as soon as he returned."

45. Garry Wills, *The Kennedy Imprisonment: A Meditation on Power* (Boston: Little, Brown, 1982), 35.

46. Quoted in Donald White, *The American Century: The Rise and Decline of the United States as a World Power* (New Haven: Yale University Press, 1996), 296.

47. "The Insurgent Battlefield," 25 May 1962, Lansdale Papers, Box 44, #1266. Many of these themes were incorporated into other Lansdale lectures: e.g., "Our Battleground in Asia," and "The Free Citizen in Uniform."

48. Quoted in John Stockwell, *In Search of Enemies: A CIA Story* (New York: Norton, 1978), 235.

49. Neil Sheehan, "Conversation with Rufus Phillips," 27 January 1976, Neil Sheehan Papers, Box 71, Library of Congress Manuscript Division, Washington, D.C.

50. To be sure, anticommunism as an ideology existed well before World War II. For a perceptive discussion, see George Sirgiovanni, *An Undercurrent of Suspicion: Anti-Communism in America during World War II* (New Brunswick, N.J.: Transaction, 1990). Sirgiovanni's statement "Anticommunism has been one of the most significant and enduring issues in American political history" (1) is central to my understanding of this phenomenon.

51. Quoted in Alan Nadel, *Containment Culture: American Narratives, Postmodernism, and the Atomic Age* (Durham: Duke University Press, 1995), 163.

52. Evan Thomas, *The Very Best Men, Four Who Dared: The Early Years of the CIA* (New York: Simon & Schuster, 1995), 84–85.

53. Martin Lee and Bruce Shlain, *Acid Dreams: The CIA, LSD, and the Sixties Rebellion* (New York: Grove, 1985).

54. "Judge Dismisses Demand for C.I.A. Budget Data," *New York Times*, 23 November 1999.

55. NSC-4/A, "Psychological Operations," December 17, 1947, in *CIA Cold War Records: The CIA under Harry Truman*, ed. Michael Warner, (Washington, D.C.: CIA, 1994), 173.

56. Dean Acheson, *Present at the Creation: My Years in the State Department* (New York: Norton, 1969), 374.

57. Eisenhower to Dulles et al., 2 June 1954, in *Foreign Relations of the United States: East Asia and the Pacific, 1952–1954*, 12:531. To be sure, Eisenhower was not the first American to utter such imperial sentiments. The National Association of Manufacturers announced in 1897 that with the Philippines as "pickets of the Pacific standing guard at the entrances to trade with the millions of China . . . it would be possible for American energy to . . . ultimately convert the Pacific Ocean into an American Lake." Quoted in Richard Van Alstyne, "The Open Door Policy," in *Encyclopedia of American Foreign Relations*, ed. Alexander DeConde (New York: Scribner, 1978), 714.

58. Quoted in Lloyd Gardner *Approaching Vietnam: From World War II through Dienbienphu* (New York: Norton, 1988), 351. Although Eisenhower's memoir, *Waging Peace: The White House Years, 1956–1961* (New York: Doubleday, 1965), gives a very generous reading of American policy during his time, the book's inner cover may be more illuminating: an arresting map titled "The Ring of U.S. Alliances" shows the United States and its various allies surrounding the Soviet Union. The map leads one to ask, who was threatening whom?

59. Niall Ferguson, *Colossus: The Price of America's Empire* (New York: Penguin, 2004), 6–7. Ferguson is indebted to others for this phrase, including Walter Lippmann's 1926 remark that "our imperialism is more or less unconscious."

60. Secretary of State John Foster Dulles, *Department of State Bulletin*, 18 June 1956, 999–1000.

61. Dean Acheson, *Present at the Creation: My Years in the State Department* (New York: Norton, 1969), 214.

62. James Edgington related this information to me in a 27 May 1993 phone conversation. Since then, a number of documents have been declassified but nothing on this scale.

63. Quoted in Thomas Paterson, "The Clandestine Response: The CIA, Covert Actions, and Congressional Oversight," in his *Meeting the Communist Threat: Truman to Reagan* (New York: Oxford University Press, 1988), 239.

64. Richard and Gladys Harkness, "The Mysterious Doings of CIA," *Saturday Evening Post*, 30 October, 6 November and 13 November 1954; "Allen Dulles: America's Master Spy," *Cavalier*, April 1954.

65. Thomas, *The Very Best Men*, 165.

66. Martin, *Wilderness of Mirrors*, 128.

67. Harkness and Harkness, "The Mysterious Doings of CIA," 165.

68. Heidenry, *Theirs Was the Kingdom*.

69. Tom Braden, "I'm Glad the CIA Is Immoral," *Saturday Evening Post*, 20 May 1967, 11–12.

70. Philip Agee, *Inside the Company: CIA Diary* (New York: Stonehill, 1975); William Colby, *Honorable Men* (New York: Simon & Schuster, 1978).

71. Stanley Kutler, *Abuse of Power: The New Nixon Tapes* (New York: Touchstone, 1997), 85.

72. Victor Marchetti and John Marks, *The CIA and the Cult of Intelligence* (New York: Dell, 1974); Howard Frazier, ed., *Uncloaking the CIA* (New York: Free Press, 1978).

73. Marchetti and Marks, *The CIA and the Cult of Intelligence*, 3.

74. These nefarious acts are detailed in U.S. Senate, Committee on Foreign Relations, *Hearing on CIA Foreign and Domestic Activities* (Washington, D.C.: GPO, 1975); and Church Committee, *Alleged Assassination Plots*.

75. Don DeLillo, "American Blood: A Journey through the Labyrinth of Dallas and JFK," *Rolling Stone*, 8 December 1983, 27.

76. Johnson quoted from an interview with ABC newscaster Howard K. Smith; see Lloyd Gardner, *Pay Any Price: Lyndon Johnson and the Wars of Vietnam* (Chicago: Ivan Dee, 1995), 328–29; and Leo Janos, "The Last Days of the President: LBJ in Retirement," *Atlantic Monthly* 232 (July 1973): 35–43.

77. Lansdale, "The Cuba Project," 20 February 1962, Kennedy Library, National Security Files: Meetings and Memoranda, Special Group (Augmented), 1/62–6/62, Box 319.

78. Church Committee, *Alleged Assassination Plots*, 168.

79. Quoted in Kahin, *Intervention*, 96.

80. Currey, *Edward Lansdale*, xii.

81. Thomas Powers, "The Truth about the CIA," *New York Review of Books*, 13 May 1993, 49, 55.

4. The Perils of a Usable Past

1. Frances Fitzgerald, *Fire in the Lake: The Vietnamese and the Americans in Vietnam* (New York: Vintage, 1972), 104–5.

2. Lansdale, *In the Midst of Wars*, 126–27.

3. Gelb and Betts, *The Irony of Vietnam*, 253.

4. See Walter L. Hixson, *Parting the Curtain: Propaganda, Culture, and the Cold War, 1945–1961* (New York: St. Martin's, 1997); and Frances Stoner Saunders, *The Cultural Cold War: The C.I.A. and the World of Arts and Letters* (New York: New Press, 2000), for the heretofore secret history of American psychological warfare efforts to win the Cold War.

5. See Van Wycks Brooks, "On Creating a Usable Past," *The Dial*, 11 April 1918, reprinted in *Critics of Culture: Literature and Society in the Early Twentieth Century*, ed. Alan Trachtenberg (New York: Wiley, 1976), 166–69.

6. For a penetrating discussion of the "usable past" in American history, see Warren Susman, "History and the American Intellectual: The Uses of a Useable Past" in his *Culture as History*, 7–26.

7. Pat Lansdale, interview by author.

8. Lansdale's ancestor, Philip Van Horne Lansdale, was killed in Samoa in 1898, where he had been sent by the United States on an expedition to prevent German control of the burgeoning Asia market. Later, the U.S. Navy named three ships in his honor. The signer of the Constitution was also the only Catholic, James Carrellton, from Maryland. "Lansdale Family," November 1971, in Lansdale Papers, Box 1, #5.

9. Although the earlier drafts cannot be equated with a private diary, they are far more forthright than the published version about the series of interventions that Lansdale took part in. In fact, sections from the drafts were closed to public access by the CIA; declassified in 1993, they are in Lansdale Papers, Box 9, #262, 542–44.

10. Lansdale Papers, Box 8, #259, 6–7.

11. Lansdale Papers, Box 13, #329.

12. Arthur Link, ed., *The Papers of Woodrow Wilson* (Princeton: Princeton University Press, 1969), 6:181. Wilson's thought on this subject also demonstrated the influence of social Darwinism: "But since then we have been steadily receiving into our midst and to full participation in our national life the very people whom their home politics have familiarized with revolution: our own equable blood we have suffered to receive into it the most feverish bloods of the restless old world. We are facing an ever-increasing difficulty of self-possession with ever deteriorating materials: for your only reliable stuff in this strain of politics in Character." Although Lansdale was no social Darwinist, a more intriguing difference was that Wilson, unlike Lansdale, saw the American Revolution as comprising both a universalism that could be replicated in other historical moments *and* an exceptionalism that only Anglo-Saxons could appreciate. This contradiction, never truly resolved in Wilson's mind, never concerned Lansdale.

13. Lansdale Papers, Box 7, #239.

14. Speech notes prepared for "Guerrilla Warfare: Lessons Learned and Their Implications," 13 April 1964, in Edward Lansdale File, Council of Foreign Relations Archive.

15. Lansdale, *In the Midst of Wars*, xxxi–xxxii.

16. Lansdale Tape Collection, Tape #30–31, Appendix B, "In the Midst of War," 1965–67.

17. Lansdale to Alvin Turner, 21 March 1971, Lansdale Papers, Box 6, #215.

18. Lansdale to President Kennedy, 24 May 1963, Lansdale Papers (recently declassified documents section).

19. Whitfield, *The Culture of the Cold War* 89. Eisenhower's relationship to organized religion was tenuous at times. His famous declaration "Our government makes no sense unless it is founded on a deeply felt religious faith, and I don't care what it is" was typical of his public utterances on religion. Quoted in Jacobs, "Our System Demands the Supreme Being," 593.

20. Lansdale Papers, Box 12, #298 (capitals in original).

21. Lansdale to Diem, 2 April 1959, Lansdale Papers, Box 42, #1219.

22. *Washington Post*, 5 September 1965.

23. Classic consensus histories include Richard Hofstadter's *American Political Tra-*

dition (1948), Daniel Boorstin's *The Genius of American Politics* (1953), Louis Hartz's *The Liberal Tradition in American History* (1955), and David Potter's *People of Plenty* (1958). To be sure, there were fundamental differences among these historians. Hofstadter and Potter had far bleaker visions of American history than Boorstin, who can properly be seen as something of an intellectual cheerleader for the American experience.

24. Letter from L. Fletcher Prouty to author, July 1992.

25. Lansdale Papers, Box 8, #259, 7.

26. Although the Japanese had initiated land reform programs during their occupation of the Philippines during World War II, these policies were discredited after 1945 because of their association with the Japanese. See on this question Kerkvliet, *The Huk Rebellion*.

27. Lansdale Papers, Box 7, #239 (original emphasis).

28. Lansdale, "Vietnam and Beyond—Our American Role in the Pacific," 1968, Lansdale Papers, Box 12, #324.

29. Lansdale Papers, Box 8, #259, 10.

30. Lansdale to Bunker, 2 March 1968, Lansdale Papers, Box 7, #240.

31. Memorandum from the Ambassador's Special Assistant (Lansdale) to the Ambassador to Vietnam (Bunker), "Subject: Evaluation of Tet Offensive," 27 February 1968, *Foreign Relations, 1964–1968, Vietnam: January–August 1968* (Washington: Government Printing Office, 2002), 6:257–59.

32. Lansdale to John D. Rockefeller, "Some Thoughts on a Magsaysay Foundation," 12 April 1957, "Magsaysay Award," Box 114, Rockefeller Archive Center.

33. Ronald Steel, "The Imperial Residency," *New Republic*, 11 September 1989, 32.

34. Pat Lansdale, interview by author.

35. Quoted in a speech by Colonel Valeriano to American military officers, Fort Bragg, n.d., Lansdale Papers, Box 18, #426.

36. "The Reminiscences of Felix Stump," 25 June 1964, 340, in the Oral History Collection of Columbia University, New York, N.Y.

37. Lansdale, *In the Midst of Wars*, 37.

38. "The People's Choice," *Time*, 23 November 1953, 37. On counterinsurgency in the Philippines, see D. Michael Shafer, *Deadly Paradigms: The Failure of U.S. Counterinsurgency Policy* (Princeton, N.J.: Princeton University Press, 1988), 205–39; Cable, *Conflict of Myths*: 55–56.

39. Journal No. 2, 10 November 1946, Lansdale Papers, Box 7, #237.

40. Lansdale cited Jesus Magsaysay in the notes he prepared for a lecture during an "All-American Conference," n.d., Lansdale Papers, Box 8, #241. He was not alone in wanting to share American ideals with foreigners. In a press conference, John Foster Dulles expressed the same sentiments: "I have often quoted what Abraham Lincoln said about the Declaration of Independence. He said it meant hope not alone to the people of this country but hope for the world for all future time." In *U.S. State Department Bulletin*, no. 28 (18 February 1953): 330. And before he became radicalized Daniel Ellsberg (*Secrets*, 101) took copies of Lincoln's second inaugural address with him when he went to Vietnam to work on Lansdale's political team in 1965; he, too, believed that Lincoln best expressed what Americans were hoping to accomplish there.

41. Walter LaFeber, *The American Age: United States Foreign Policy at Home and Abroad since 1750* (New York: Norton, 1989), 284.

42. Lansdale Papers, Box 12, #303. Much of this same language was used eleven years later when Lansdale helped write South Vietnamese Prime Minister Ky's speech celebrating his first one hundred days in office. He ended this speech by having Ky say, "But the most important aspect of communism is that communism is anti-God." U.S. Ambassador Henry Cabot Lodge to Department of State, 27 September 1965, Declassified Documents Reference System.

43. Lansdale Papers, Box 22, #509. Lansdale's long-standing interest in constitutions led him to write out the preamble to the U.S. Constitution and give it to a Vietnamese friend, Phuoc, so that he might have a better idea as to what a constitution should say. After reading it, Phuoc said it was missing the concept of brotherly love. Lansdale replied that it was written in Philadelphia, which in Greek meant "city of brotherly love" and later added, "Thus the American drafters were surrounded by an expression of this ethic at the time and undoubtedly were most conscious of it when they started their first meeting with a pause for silent prayer. Phuoc thanked me for the explanation" (Lansdale Papers, Box 8, #259, 24–26).

44. One of Lansdale's associates during this period, Lucien Conein, confirmed that Lansdale brought Jonny Orenidan to Vietnam for this specific purpose. Lucien Conein, interview by author, McLean, Va., October 12, 1992.

45. Lansdale Papers, Box 8, #264, 1169.

46. Ibid., 1185–86.

47. The French Catholic philosopher Emmanuel Mounier developed the theory of personalism in the 1930s. Nhu learned of it while studying in Paris and shared it with Diem. Personalism was a particularly opaque philosophy, one that not only rejected fascism and communism as inherently evil political systems but virulently rejected the tenets of liberal capitalism with its emphasis on materialism and individualism. This history is detailed in Edward Miller, "The Professor and the President: Wesley Fishel, Ngo Dinh Diem, and the Struggle to Build a Nation in South Vietnam, 1950–1963" (paper presented at the Society for Historians of American Foreign Relations conference, June 2001, in possession of author).

48. Alexander Woodside, *Community and Revolution in Modern Vietnam* (Boston: Houghton Mifflin, 1976), 5.

49. John McAlister and Paul Mus, *The Vietnamese and Their Revolution* (New York: Harper & Row, 1970), 4.

50. Quoted in Young, *The Vietnam Wars* 6–7.

51. Stanley Karnow, "Giap Remembers," *New York Times Sunday Magazine*, 24 June 1990, 39.

52. *Vietnam: A Television History*, Episode 1: "The Roots of War," WGBH Boston, 1985.

53. This discussion of early Vietnamese nationalists is based upon William Duiker, *The Rise of Nationalism in Vietnam, 1900–1941* (Ithaca: Cornell University Press, 1976); Milton Osborne, *The French Presence in Cochinchina and Cambodia* (Ithaca: Cornell University Press, 1969); Samuel Popkin, "Colonialism and the Ideological Origins of

the Vietnamese Revolution—A Review Article," *Journal of Asian Studies*, February 1985, 349–57; and especially Woodside, *Community and Revolution in Modern Vietnam*.

54. See David Steinberg, ed., *In Search of Southeast Asia: A Modern History* (Honolulu: University of Hawaii Press, 1987), 314.

55. Quoted in Woodside, *Community and Revolution in Modern Vietnam*, 39. The irony becomes all the greater when it is noted that the earlier generation of Vietnamese nationalists were influenced by the Japanese novelist Shiba Shiro, who studied at the University of Pennsylvania. His travels abroad may account for the heavily idealized "histories" of colonial America which he and his students adopted.

56. Ibid., 38–39.

57. Quoted in Gibbons, *The U.S. Government and the Vietnam War*, 3.

58. Quoted in Alan Riding, "The Vietnam War, as Seen in Art from the Other Side," *New York Times*, 22 October 2002.

59. Edward G. Lansdale, "The Opposite Number," *Air University Review* 23 (July–August 1972), 25.

60. Draft of introduction for Allan Millet, Lansdale Papers, Box 8, #241. The final version of this essay appeared in Millett's *A Short History of the Vietnam War* (Bloomington: Indiana University Press, 1978), vii–xiv.

61. John W. O'Daniel, "When I Think of Ngo Dinh Diem," unpublished article, 5 November 1963, Lansdale Papers, Box 20, #472.

62. Informal seminar by Lansdale, "Our Battleground in Asia," 19 June 1957, Lansdale Papers, Box 12, #296.

63. Lansdale Papers, 30 January 1961, Box 39, #1052.

64. Young, *The Vietnam Wars*, 10.

65. "The Beleaguered Man," 22.

66. Sheehan, *A Bright Shining Lie*, 144. Diem's family also believed in their historical lineage. In 1972 his sister-in-law, Madame Ngo Dinh Nhu, wrote to Lawrence Spivak, producer of *Meet the Press*, referring to Diem "as the legitimate heir of Emperor Gia-Long (1762–1820)." In Lansdale Papers, Box 5, #158.

67. Joseph Alsop, column of 31 December 1954, reprinted in Fisher, *Dr. America*, 51.

68. "Vietnam," 23 November 1964, Lansdale Papers, Box 7, #239.

69. Rufus Phillips, Assistant Director for Rural Affaires/USOM to the chargé d'affaires, Mr. William Trueheart, 5 July 1963, "Recommendation for Immediate U.S. Action" (Lansdale Papers, Box 49, #1373).

70. Harvey Neese and John O'Donnell, ed., *Prelude to Tragedy: Vietnam, 1960–1965* (Annapolis, Md.: Naval Institute Press, 2001), 2.

71. Tranh Van Dinh to Lansdale, 18 December 1963, Lansdale Papers, Box 41, #1154.

72. Lansdale, interview by Currey, 16 May 1984, Currey Collection.

73. I. F. Stone to Lansdale, 17 May 1964, Lansdale Papers, Box 41, #1129; Theodore White to Lansdale, 24 November 1962, Lansdale Papers, Box 41, #1175. Another act of press "objectivity" involved Lansdale's good friend Robert Shaplen, the longtime Asian correspondent of the *New Yorker*, who wrote to Lansdale on 30 January 1969:

"Give Henry [Kissinger] my best, and remind him that if I can help him at all, I shall certainly try." (Lansdale Papers, Box 72).

74. Author unknown, *Research Institute Report*, 27 August 1965, in Lansdale Papers, Box 26, #601.

75. C. Wright Mills, "The Cultural Apparatus," in *Power, Politics, and People: The Collected Essays of C. Wright Mills* (New York: Ballantine, 1963) 406 (original emphasis).

76. Lansdale Papers, Box 9, #265.

5. Gazing at the Third World

1. "The Lady from Philadelphia," CBS Television, 30 December 1957, Museum of Television & Radio Archives, New York, N.Y. Marian Anderson's fame resided in her world-renowned voice and her political efforts to challenge and break down racial barriers in the United States. She had sung in front of the Lincoln Memorial in 1939 after being denied permission by the Daughters of the American Revolution to perform at Constitution Hall. Eleanor Roosevelt intervened and helped her perform at the Memorial, ensuring that this site that would become central to the civil rights movement.

2. Milton Osborne, "Fear and Fascination in the Tropics: A Reader's Guide to French Fiction on Indo-China," in *Asia in Western Fiction*, eds. Robin W. Winks and James R. Rush (Manchester; Eng.: Manchester University Press, 1990), 160.

3. Robert J. McMahon, *The Limits of Empire. The United States and Southeast Asia since World War II* (New York: Columbia University Press, 1999), 104.

4. Lansdale memo, 27 February 1957, Lansdale Papers, Box 12, #292.

5. Lansdale Papers, Box 8, #260, 168.

6. "Counterinsurgency: A Symposium," April 16–20, 1962, S. T. Hosmer, report prepared for the Advance Research Projects Agency, RAND Corporation (January 1963), 68.

7. Clifford Geertz, *Available Light: Anthropological Reflections on Philosophical Topics* (Princeton: Princeton University Press, 2000), 64.

8. Memorandum for Sec. McNamara, 7 August 1963, Lansdale Papers, Box 49, #1372.

9. Lansdale Memorandum, "Meanings of Colors for Vietnamese People," Lansdale Papers, Box 62, #1619.

10. Ellsworth Bunker, Oral History Interview I, by Michael L. Gilllette, 9 December 1980, 20, Lyndon B. Johnson Library, Austin, Tex.

11. Quoted in Currey, *Edward Lansdale*, 24.

12. Edward Lansdale, U.S. Air Force Academy Oral History interview, 25 April 1971, 3–4.

13. Ibid., 3.

14. Ibid., 5.

15. Lansdale to Adjutant General, Lowry A.F.B., Colorado, 15 December 1948, Lansdale Papers, Box 1, #2; Lansdale Papers, Box 32, #717.

16. Lansdale Papers, Box 32, #717.

17. Journal No. 19, 4 January 1948, Lansdale Papers, Box 7, #237.

18. Currey, *Edward Lansdale*, 28–30.

19. Photography section, May 1946, Lansdale Papers, Box FDI.

20. Ibid.,

21. Susan Sontag, *On Photography* (New York: Farrar, Straus & Giroux, 1977), 75.

22. Lansdale Papers, Box 32, #717.

23. Lansdale Papers, Box 34, #759.

24. Journal No. 13, 11 April 1947, Lansdale Papers, Box 7, #237.

25. Pat Lansdale and Lucien Conein, interviews by author.

26. Lansdale Papers, Box 36, #817.

27. Journal No. 13, 11 April 1947, Lansdale Papers, Box 7, #237. Note that early practitioners of anthropology (e.g., Bronislaw Malinowski) employed this *reportage* method as well.

28. Journal No. 1, 30 October 1946, Lansdale Papers, Box 7, #247.

29. Lansdale Papers, Box 9, #265, 5, 281.

30. Lansdale Papers, Box 9, #265.

31. Lansdale, U.S. Air Force Academy interview, 25 April 1971, 8.

32. Pat Lansdale, interview by author.

33. Currey, draft manuscript of *Edward Lansdale*, 67, Currey Collection.

34. Journal No. 16, 10 August 1947; Journal No. 21, 5 July 1948, Lansdale Papers, Box 7, #237.

35. "A Case History of Insurgency—The Philippines," 25 March 1964, Lansdale Papers, Box 8, #244.

36. Lansdale Papers, Box 9, #265. There is no date on this document, but it is included in the drafts of his memoirs, indicating that it was written between 1968 and 1971.

37. James Clifford, *The Predicament of Culture: Twentieth-Century Ethnography, Literature, and Art* (Cambridge: Harvard University Press, 1988), 13–14.

38. Finley Peter Dunne, "On the Philippines," in *Mr. Dooley in Peace and in War* (Boston: Small, Maynard, 1898), 43.

39. Lansdale to Samuel Williams, 27 April 1967, Williams Papers, Box 20, #15.

40. Quoted in T. Christopher Jespersen, *American Images of China, 1931–1949* (Stanford, Calif.: Stanford University Press, 1996), 164.

41. Lansdale, interview, U.S. Air Force Academy, 25 April 1971, 2.

42. Catherine A. Lutz and Jane L. Collins, *Reading National Geographic* (Chicago: University of Chicago Press, 1993), 38.

43. Quoted in Michael Hunt, *Ideology and American Foreign Policy*, (New Haven: Yale University Press, 1987), 163.

44. See Donna Harraway, "Remodeling the Human Way of Life: Sherwood Washburn and the New Physical Anthropology, 1950–1980," in her *Primate Visions: Gender, Race, and Nature in the World of Modern Science* (New York: Routledge, 1989), 186–232, esp. 197–203.

45. Christopher Shannon, "A World Made Safe for Differences: Ruth Benedict's *The Chrysanthemum and the Sword*," *American Quarterly* 47 (December 1995): 659.

46. Lansdale, U.S. Air Force Academy interview, 25 April 1971, 6.

47. Edward Steichen, *The Family of Man: An Exhibition of Creative Photography Dedicated to the Dignity of Man, with Examples from 68 Countries* (New York: Museum of Modern Art, 1955).

48. *A Franz Boas Reader: The Shaping of American Anthropology, 1883–1911*, ed. George W. Stocking Jr. (Chicago: University of Chicago Press, 1974), 22.

49. Nick Cullather "Development? It's History," *Diplomatic History* 24 (fall 2000): 647, has nicely summarized this process by arguing that anthropologists of this period "defined and enforced the binary classification of colonialism—tradition vs modernity, primitive vs. civilized, underdeveloped vs developed."

50. Franz Boas, "Scientists as Spies," in *Universities and Empire: Money and Politics in the Social Sciences during the Cold War*, ed. Christopher Simpson (New York: New Press, 1998), 1–2.

51. See David Price, "Anthropologists as Spies," *Nation*, 20 November 2000.

52. Quoted in Han F. Vermeulen, "Anthropology in Colonial Contexts," in *Anthropology and Colonialism in Asia and Oceania*, ed. Jan van Bremen and Akitoshi Shimizu (Richmond, Surrey, U.K.: Curzon Press, 1999), 14–15.

53. Jeffrey Race, *War Comes to Long An: Revolutionary Conflict in a Vietnamese Province* (Berkeley: University of California Press, 1972), xii.

54. While James Scott and Samuel Popkin depict Vietnamese society in vastly different ways, they agree that French colonialism so disrupted the lives of ordinary peasants that it became the major impetus for the series of protests, then rebellions, and eventually wars against French rule. In this respect, French colonialism bonded the Vietnamese together as no other force had until that time. See James Scott, *The Moral Economy of the Peasant* (New Haven: Yale University Press, 1976); and Samuel Popkin, *The Rational Peasant* (Berkeley: University of California Press, 1979).

55. Stanley Karnow, "Edward Lansdale," *Washington Post*, 25 February 1966, 1.

56. Lansdale Papers, Box 18, #462; Lansdale Papers, 4 April 1952 (1990 declassified box). There is a problem with the date of the latter document, as Lansdale had not yet gone to Vietnam in 1952, though most likely it is simply a typing error.

57. George Herring, *America's Longest War: The United States and Vietnam, 1950–1975*, 4th ed. (New York: McGraw-Hill, 2002), 63.

58. Lansdale Papers, Box 9, #261, 280–81.

59. CIA Report of April 1960, "Intelligence Survey: South Vietnam," *CIA Research Reports: Vietnam and Southeast Asia, 1946–1976*, cited in Edward Miller, "American Universalism and Vietnamese Difference: Race, Culture, and Nation Building in Vietnam, 1955–1965" (unpublished paper, in possession of author), 10.

60. Lansdale Papers, Box 9, #261, 370–71.

61. Lansdale to Bunker, 4 June 1968, Lansdale Papers, Box 62, #1619 (declassified in 1991); Lansdale to the Ambassador, "Wedding," 27 July 1967, Lansdale Papers, Box 59, #1535.

62. Lansdale to McNamara, 25 July 1963, Lansdale Papers, Box 49, #1372.

63. Edward G. Lansdale, *In the Midst of War: Folk Music, Viet Nam, 1965–1967*, Library of Congress Folklife Collection, Washington, D.C., 14.

64. Nixon to Lansdale, 4 May 1967, Lansdale Papers, Box 54, #1455.

65. The full list of songs can be found in the register compiled at the Hoover Institution, where Lansdale's other papers and artifacts are stored.

66. Quoted in James Scott, *Domination and the Arts of Resistance: Hidden Transcripts* (New Haven: Yale University Press, 1990), 80.

67. Quoted in Gene Roberts, "Lansdale Retires from Saigon Post," *New York Times*, 16 June 1968, 10.

68. Lansdale Papers, Box 9, #265.

6. Fictions of Quiet and Ugly Americans

1. Norman Sherry, *The Life of Graham Greene, vol. 2, 1939–1955* (New York: Viking, 1994), 412–20.

2. Michael Sheldon, *Graham Greene: The Enemy Within* (New York: Random House, 1994), 322.

3. David Halberstam, "The Americanization of Vietnam," *Playboy*, January 1970. (in Lansdale Papers, Box 26, #600).

4. In Richard West, "Graham Greene and 'The Quiet American,'" *New York Review of Books*, 16 May 1991, 49.

5. Graham Greene, *The Quiet American* (Middlesex, U.K.: Penguin, 1955), 25. This passage is in essence recreated in Greene's memoir, *Ways of Escape* (New York: Simon & Schuster, 1980), 161.

6. Greene, *Ways of Escape*, 146; Grahame Smith, *The Achievement of Graham Greene* (New York: Barnes & Noble, 1986), 130.

7. Graham Greene, "Indo-China: France's Crown of Thorns," *Paris Match*, 12 July 1952, reprinted in Graham Greene, *Reflections* (New York: Reinhart Books/Viking, 1990), 129.

8. Greene, "Indo-China," 145–46 (original emphasis).

9. The question of whether Greene is practicing orientalism is discussed in Zakia Pathak, Saswati Sengupta, and Sharmila Purkayastha, "The Prisonhouse of Orientalism," *Textual Practice* 5 (summer 1991): 195–218; and Eric Solomon, "Notes toward a Definition of the Colonial Novel," *North Dakota Quarterly* 57 (summer 1989): 16–23. West, "Graham Greene and 'The Quiet American,'" 49–50, discusses the last point raised in this paragraph.

10. Quoted in Gardner, *Approaching Vietnam: From World War II through Dienbienphu*, 21.

11. Greene often returned to this theme in his novels. In *Our Man in Havana* (New York: Viking, 1958), 143–44, for instance, he wrote of the insidious and pervasive impact of Americana upon the people of Cuba: "The skyscrapers of the new town stood up ahead of them like icicles in the moonlight. A great H. H. was stamped on the sky, like the monogram on Hawthorne's pocket, but it wasn't royal either—it only advertised Mr. Hilton."

12. Greene, *The Quiet American*, 11, 181.

13. Curiously, Greene seemed to be in agreement with the American political theorist Louis Hartz's *The Liberal Tradition in American History* on this question. Indeed, the consensus tradition that Hartz was so influential in establishing after

World War II argued that America was "born modern" and was thus unable to come to terms with the varieties of economic and political changes occurring in the rest of the world. For a succinct description of Greene along these lines, see Christopher Hitchens, *Blood, Class, and Nostalgia: Anglo-American Ironies* (New York: Farrar, Straus & Giroux, 1990), 369.

14. The Pyle quote is in *The Quiet American*, 36; W. J. West, *The Quest for Graham Greene* (New York: St. Martin's Press, 1998), 158–59; Greene, "Last Act in Indo-China," *New Republic*, 9 May 1955, 11.

15. Quoted in David Stafford, *The Silent Game: The Real World of Imaginary Spies* (Athens: University of Georgia Press, 1991), 190–91.

16. Graham Greene, interview by Martin Amis, *Observer*, 23 September 1984, reprinted in Graham Greene, *Yours Etc.: Letters to the Press* (New York: Viking, 1989), xiv.

17. Greene, *The Quiet American*, 184.

18. This argument is put forth with a great deal of passion by both conservative and Marxist critics. See Peter Glenville, "The End of the Chase," *National Review*, 27 May 1991, 57–58; Terry Eagleton, "From Swiss Cottage to the Sandinistas,"*Times Literary Supplement*, 16–22 September 1988, 1013. Noting that Greene favored the poor over the weak, I realize, contradicts much of the earlier discussion about Greene and empires. "Greeneland"—the term employed by literary critics—is filled with contradictions; for a concerted attempt to sort them out, see Maria Couto, *Graham Greene, On the Frontier: Politics and Religion in the Novels* (New York: St. Martin's, 1988).

19. Terry Eagleton, *Exiles and Emigrés: Studies in Modern Literature* (New York: Schocken, 1970), 127; Smith, *The Achievement of Graham Greene*, 131–32; West, "Graham Greene and the Quiet American," 49–52.

20. A. J. Liebling, "A Talkative Something-or-Other," *New Yorker*, 7 April 1956, 148.

21. Greene, *The Quiet American*, 17, 18. A particularly good reading of Pyle is by William Chace: "He [Pyle] is not so much a 'child' as a 'liberal,' which to Greene is a person with a willed ignorance of the world. Pyle's innocence is dangerous." William Chace, "Spies and God's Spies: Greene's Espionage Fiction," in *Graham Greene: A Revaluation, New Essays*, ed. Jeffrey Meyers (New York: St. Martin's, 1990), 167.

22. Lansdale Papers, 4 April 1952 1990 declassified box. Later, Lansdale wrote a memo to Ambassador Ellsworth Bunker, 13 July 1967, on the merits of a "third force," relating a conversation with a long-standing Vietnamese political friend, Nguyen Ngoc Tho: "Tho switched subjects abruptly by asking me about a 'a third party or force.' I asked him in turn what he was talking about. He grinned and said the local press was publishing hints that I was engineering the forming of a 'third party or third force,' but was quite mysterious about the names of Vietnamese involved. I told Tho that this was the first I'd ever heard of it and couldn't help but wonder what the first two forces might be." Lansdale Papers, 1991 declassified box.

23. Lansdale to Pratt, 6 February 1985, Lansdale Papers, Box 76; Keyes Beech, interview by Ted Gittinger, 22 March 1983, Lyndon B. Johnson Library, Austin, Tex., 4.

24. Greene, *The Quiet American*, 167–68.

25. Robert Payne, *Red Storm over Asia* (New York: Macmillan, 1951), 3, 202.

26. Greene, *The Quiet American*, 157. The question of Greene himself as Fowler is necessarily open. At the time of the publication of the novel, Greene told a journalist, "Everybody thinks I am Fowler—well, I share some of his views about the Americans. But I'm not as bitter about them as he is. I didn't have my girl stolen by an American" (*British Evening Standard*, 24 August 1956, cited in *Yours Etc.*, 57). Other clues to connections between the two include the use of opium. Charlotte Loris, an American attached to the American Embassy in Saigon during the mid-1950s, knew Greene at this time: "So we got together a number of times and one evening we were discussing the ethnic background of Chinese and Asians and I said, I've always wanted to go to an opium den. . . . So we get in the cycle and the guy pedals us out to this opium den. Graham Greene was an habitue of opium dens and he knew Asia. . . . It was just like I expected it to be. Absolutely fascinating. I wouldn't have missed it for anything. I did want Graham Greene to buy me the silver opium pipe but he didn't. So he smoked nine pipes and I smoked three. But I didn't inhale because I was scared shitless. But it was fun. "An Interview with Charlotte Loris," 8 June 1989, Foreign Affairs Oral History Program, Georgetown University, Washington, D.C.

27. Greene, *The Quiet American*, 94–95.

28. Lansdale to Secretary of Defense and Deputy Secretary of Defense, 17 January 1961, Lansdale Papers, Box 49, #1374.

29. Greene, *Yours Etc.*, 126.

30. Ibid., 127.

31. Quoted in Christopher Robbins, letter to the *New York Times*, 18 June 1989.

32. Lansdale, interview by Currey.

33. Greene, *Ways of Escape*, 169–70.

34. Judith Adamson, *Graham Greene and Cinema* (Norman, Okla.: Pilgrim Books, 1984), 79.

35. Herbert Mitgang, "The Quiet American," *San Francisco Chronicle*, 21 August 1966, 25.

36. Lansdale, "The 'True American,'" 3 June 1960, 3, 6, Currey Collection.

37. Lansdale to Peter McInerney, 4 September 1980, Lansdale Papers, Box 79.

38. "To Get Rave Reviews, Write an Anti-U.S.A. Novel," *Saturday Evening Post*, (6 October 1956, 10. Tom Lambert, "The Savvy American," *New York Herald Tribune*, 20 August 1962. Language, again, plays an important part in this discussion. Placing an adjective in front of the word "American" was quite popular at the time, and began to take on aspects of parody with both supporters and critics of Lansdale and American actions abroad trying to attach ever more mindless words to describe him and his mission. Words such as "compelling," "splendid," and "smart" were used by numerous writers to familiarize Lansdale to their audience.

39. "Graham Greene," *Times* (London), 19 July 1988, in *Yours Etc.*, 249.

40. Herbert Mitgang, "The Prophetic American," *New York Times Book Review*, 8 June 1975, 35.

41. U.S. House of Representatives, Select Committee on Intelligence, "U.S. Intel-

ligence Agencies and Activities: Risks and Control of Foreign Intelligence," 94th Congress, 1st sess., (Washington, D.C.: GPO, 1975), part 5, 1706–7.

42. Quoted in David Thomson, "Greene in the Dark," *Film Comment*, July–August 1991, 19.

43. In Greene's memoir, *A Sort of Life* (New York: Simon & Schuster, 1971), 134, he relates how he joined the Communist Party with the hope that he might be sent to the Soviet Union, "which six years after the Revolution still had a romantic appeal."

44. Saunders, *The Cultural Cold War*, 293–301.

45. Monica Pritchett (quoting Greene) to Robert Lantz, 29 May 1956. Museum of Modern Art folder, "The Quiet American."

46. Lansdale to Mankiewicz, 17 March 1956, Lansdale Papers, Box 35, #785. A small curiosity is attached to this letter: the "p.s." is not currently available with the original document in Lansdale's papers; I obtained it from a fellow researcher who had copied it years earlier from another archive.

47. Gilbert Jonas, the public relations executive who worked on behalf of the Diem regime, simply observed that Lansdale "actually helped in the rewriting of 'The Quiet American' script." Quoted in Morgan, *The Vietnam Lobby*, 52.

48. John Gates to Alfred Katz, n.d., "Quiet American" folder, Museum of Modern Art Film Archives, New York, N.Y.; William Russo, *A Thinker's Damn: Audie Murphy, Vietnam, and The Making of The Quiet American* (Xlibris, 2001), 41.

49. Vo Van Hai, Special Secretary of the Presidency, "Letter of Introduction," 21 January 1957, In "Quiet American" folder, Museum of Modern Art Film Archives.

50. Joseph Mankiewicz to President Diem, cable, 3 November 1957, "Quiet American" folder, Museum of Modern Art Film Archives.

51. Greene, *Ways of Escape*, 171. The novel describes this scene in much the same way: "The legless torso at the edge of the garden still twitched, like a chicken which had lost its head. From the man's shirt, he had probably been a trishaw driver" (*The Quiet American*, 162).

52. For the very convoluted history involving the Eastern Construction Company and these other front groups organized by Lansdale, see Douglas Valentine, *The Phoenix Program* (New York: Morrow, 1990), 27. Lansdale's unvarnished history of Eastern Construction appears in a 1961 top-secret memorandum to Gen. Maxwell D. Taylor and other national security managers in the Kennedy administration: "Eastern Construction was started in 1954 as Freedom Company of the Philippines . . . with President Magsaysay as its honorary president . . . 'to serve the cause of freedom.' It actually was a mechanism to permit the deployment of Filipino personnel in other Asian countries, for unconventional operations, under cover of a public service organization having a contract with the host government. Philippine Armed Forces and government personnel were 'sheep-dipped' and served abroad. Its personnel helped write the Constitution of the Republic of Vietnam, trained Vietnam's Presidential Guard Battalion. . . ."

In the same document, Lansdale wrote concerning Operation Brotherhood that it "was started in 1954 by the International Jaycees, under the inspiration and guidance of Oscar Arellano. . . . The concept was to provide medical service to refugees and provincial farmers in South Vietnam. . . . Their work was closely coordinated with Vietnamese Army operations which cleaned up Vietminh stay-behinds." Lansdale then discussed Civil Air Transport and its involvement in "air lifts of refugees from North Vietnam." *Pentagon Papers*, 2:647–49.

53. Lansdale to O'Daniel, 28 October 1957, Lansdale Papers, Box 39.

54. Morgan, *The Vietnam Lobby*, 34.

55. Marie McNair, "Dragon Visits 'Quiet American,' " *Washington Post*, 23 January 1958, C1.

56. Tran Van Chuong to Lansdale, 8 November 1960, Lansdale Papers, 1991 declassified documents folder.

57. Quoted in Morgan, *The Vietnam Lobby*, 52–53.

58. Sheehan, *A Bright Shining Lie*, 177; Kenneth Geist, *Pictures Will Talk: The Life and Films of Joseph L. Mankiewicz* (New York: Scribner, 1978), 274.

59. These scenes are recounted in some detail in Gene Phillips, S. J., *Graham Greene: The Films of His Fiction* (New York: Teachers College Press, 1974), 141–45.

60. Greene, *The Quiet American*, 189.

61. Quoted in Arthur Knight, "One Man's Movie," *Saturday Review*, 25 January 1958, 27.

62. Quoted in Don Graham, *No Name on the Bullet: A Biography of Audie Murphy* (New York: Viking, 1989), 268–69.

63. Michael Redgrave, *In My Mind's I: An Actor's Autobiography* (New York: Viking, 1983), 216.

64. Rose Mary Mankiewicz, interview by author, 4 January 1997, Katonah, N.Y.

65. "Quiet American" folder, Museum of Modern Art Film Archives. (Tess Trueheart was Dick Tracy's girlfriend in the comic strip.)

66. Quoted in Thomas Pryor, "Producer Finds 'Quiet American,' " *New York Times*, 14 December 1956; Kenneth Geist, *Pictures Will Talk*, 268.

67. Ibid., 275.

68. Alfred Katz to Harold Oram, 13 February 1956, American Friends of Vietnam Papers, Box 12, Center for the Study of the Vietnam Conflict, Texas Technology University, Lubbock.

69. Geist, *Pictures Will Talk*, 275–76.

70. Rose Mary Mankiewicz, interview by author.

71. Pauline Kael, *Kiss Kiss Bang Bang* (New York: Bantam, 1969), 422; Bosley Crowther, *New York Times*, 6 February 1958, 24.

72. Jean-Luc Godard, *Godard on Godard* (New York: Viking, 1972), 104. In Godard's curious review, there is no discussion of how Mankiewicz altered the ending of the film, though he chastises Mankiewicz for being too literary a filmmaker even as he "improves a hundred percent on Graham Greene's novel" (84). One reason Godard may have championed the movie was that it shared qualities with his own film *Breathless* (1959); in both, the camera follows characters around a city in which they seem dominated by their surroundings, while the audience is not sure with whom to place their allegiance.

73. Lansdale to Diem, 28 October 1957, Lansdale Papers, Box 39, #1052.

74. Quoted in Geist, *Pictures Will Talk*, 268. Mankiewicz later denied telling Lantz this and said his intent was simply to show how "emotions can very often dictate political beliefs."

75. Kenneth Geist, *Pictures Will Talk*, 267, 270.

76. Greene, *Yours Etc.*, 57–58.

77. "The Reminiscences of Joseph Mankiewicz" November 1958, 17, Oral History Collection of Columbia University, New York, N.Y.

78. Peter Flint, "Joseph L. Mankiewicz, Literate Skeptic of the Cinema, Dies at 83," *New York Times*, 6 February 1993, 10.

79. Seth Mydans, "'The Quiet American': Backward to When the Road to Vietnam Was Paved," *New York Times*, 9 September 2001.

80. Anne Thompson, "Films with War Themes Are Victims of Bad Timing," *New York Times*, 17 October 2002.

81. Rick Lyman, "British Star Speaks Up For 'Quiet American,'" *New York Times*, 18 November 2002.

82. U.S. International Cooperation Administration, "Reply to Criticism in the Ugly American" (Washington, D.C., 1959), 1–23. The *Saturday Evening Post* initially refused to publish excerpts of *The Ugly American* for fear that it would be confused with Greene's earlier novel. See Joan Iversen, "*The Ugly American*: A Bestseller Re-Examined," in John F. Kennedy, The Promise Revisited, ed. Paul Harper and Joann P. Krie, (New York: Greenwood, 1988), 153–54, 168, for indications of the popularity of the novel. Also see Yvonne Daley, "The Persistence of The Ugly American," *Boston Globe Magazine*, 2 December 2001, for the remarkable longevity of the novel and how it led President Eisenhower to commission studies of U.S. military aid programs, including the work of the Draper Commission, which Lansdale was involved in.

83. John Hellmann, *American Myth and the Legacy of Vietnam* (New York: Columbia University Press, 1986), 4.

84. Lansdale to The Director, no title, 21 March 1954, Lansdale Collection.

85. William Lederer and Eugene Burdick, *The Ugly American* (Greenwich, Conn.: Fawcett, 1958), 93.

86. Ibid., 95.

87. Robert Hewitt, "Major General Edward G. Lansdale," 22 October 1965, Lansdale Papers, Box 1, #7, 8–9.

88. Lansdale Papers, Box 8, #260, 145; Box 9, #261, 497–98.

89. Lederer and Burdick, *The Ugly American*, 152, 157.

90. Mitgang, "The Quiet American," 25.

91. Sheehan Papers, Box 71.

92. Lansdale, interview by Buell, 9.

93. Arthur Schlesinger Jr., *Robert Kennedy and His Times* (Boston: Houghton Mifflin, 1978), 476.

94. J. Graham Parsons, John F. Kennedy Oral History interview, 22 August 1969, 23, John F. Kennedy Library.

95. Edward Lansdale, interview by Kenneth Alnwick 25 April 1971, Oral History Collection of Columbia University; Lansdale, interview by Buell.

96. To Lansdale from "Tommy" (no last name), 23 January 1959, Lansdale Papers, Box 2, #25 (original emphasis).

97. Lansdale, interview by Buell; Lansdale, interview by Alnwick.

98. Stern wrote the screenplays for a number of other major Hollywood productions, including *Rebel without a Cause.* Englund had previously directed only theater, but his friendship with Brando paved the way for his work on this movie. See Kent Brown, *The Screenwriter as Collaborator: The Career of Stewart Stern* (New York: Arno, 1980), 146.

99. Richard Schickel, *Brando: A Life in Our Times* (New York: Atheneum, 1991), 145–46; the film *The Ugly American.*

100. "Fulbright Hits Producers of 'The Ugly American,'" n.d., newspaper clipping file, Museum of Modern Art Film Archives.

101. William Lederer and Eugene Burdick, "The Ugly American Revisited," *Saturday Evening Post*, 4 May 1963, 78, 80.

102. Quoted in Brown, *The Screenwriter as Collaborator*, 147–48.

103. Ibid., 151–52.

104. Marlon Brando with Robert Lindsey, *Brando: Songs My Mother Taught Me* (New York: Random House, 1994), 288.

105. Cited in Schickel, *Brando*, 147.

106. "Juggle the Hot Potato," *New York Herald Tribune*, 15 April 1962.

107. Richard Schickel (*Brando*, 146–47) describes Brando's MacWhite as an "Ivy League twit" whose only oddity is a "pencil-thin mustache, more suitable to a shoe clerk than to a member of the Foreign Policy Association. . . . [I]t is a very sly mustache, not a boldly flaunted one."

108. Brown, *The Screenwriter as Collaborator*, 146.

109. Cullather, "Development? It's History," 641.

110. Modernization theory stems from nineteenth-century German sociology and details the revolutionizing effect of capitalism on traditional societies. It has long been a model favored by American historians in understanding the development of the United States from an economic outpost to a world power. See Dwight Hoover, "The Long Ordeal of Modernization Theory," *Prospects* 11 (1986): 407–51. Classic works on the theory include Daniel Leaner, *The Passing of Traditional Society: Modernizing the Middle East* (New York: Free Press, 1958); Walt Rostow, *The Stages of Economic Growth: A Non-Communist Manifesto* (Cambridge: Cambridge University Press, 1960); Cyril Black, *The Dynamics of Modernization: A Study in Comparative History* (New York: Harper & Row, 1966); S. N. Eisenstadt, *Modernization:Protest and Change* (Englewood Cliffs, N.J.: Prentice-Hall, 1966). Rostow was influenced by historical sociology works such as David Reisman's 1950 *The Lonely Crowd*. Reisman's arguement that societies evolved from "inner directed" to "outer directed" was cited approvingly by numerous academics in the 1950s and 1960s. His case studies of countries that shared this cycle of development ranged from India to the Soviet Union to the United States.

111. Rostow, *The Stages of Economic Growth*, 90. Rostow's book has gone through a series of editions, attesting to its popularity. Its fame (or notoriety) is such that the man and his argument were parodied throughout the Vietnam War, for instance, in a 1968

publication by the Students for a Democratic Society, John H. Coatsworth, *Walt W. Rostow: The Stages of Economic Stagnation*. David Halberstam's critique of Rostow and his unwavering enthusiasm for modernization theory, *The Best and the Brightest*, 156–62, remain insightful.

112. Roger Hilsman, for one, had a deep distrust of Rostow and later related that Kennedy referred to Rostow as the "air marshal" whenever problems developed in Vietnam, since bombing was his immediate answer to all problems there (JFK Library, Oral History Collection, Hilsman Jr., interview, 23).

113. Wesley Fishel, "Vietnam's Democratic One-Man Rule," *New Leader*, 2 November 1959, 10–13. Fishel was well aware of the contradictions inherent in Diem's rule—thus his choice of the title of his essay. He argued that American-style democracy was simply not possible in a South Vietnam that remained an overwhelmingly peasant society. Diem knew of this problem, argued Fishel, and was preparing the groundwork by making the country more modern.

114. Warren Hinckle, "The University on the Make," *Ramparts* 4 (April 1966), 20. In a statement on his own part in helping to create South Vietnam, Stanley K. Sheinbaum, one of the members of Michigan State team wrote: "Looking back I am appalled how supposed intellectuals . . . could have been so uncritical about what they were doing. There was little discussion and no protest over the cancellation of the 1956 elections. Nor were any of us significantly troubled by the fact that our Project had become a CIA front. . . . This is the tragedy of the Michigan State professors: we were all automatic cold warriors" (Hinckle, 13).

115. Braun, *The Screenwriter as Collaborator*, 153.

116. Lansdale Papers, 1990 recently declassified document section (original emphasis). On a more farcical note, when Vice President Lyndon Johnson toured South Vietnam in 1961 he was taken to Bien Hoa on a newly built, American-funded highway. Keyes Beech recalled: "and Johnson jumped out of that car and he went striding over to this Vietnamese old lady alongside the road and said, "You know who built this?" And she said, "No, I didn't do it! I didn't do it!" Keyes Beech, interview, 43.

117. National Security Files, Meetings and Memorandum. Countries: Vietnam, Box 193: 4/1/61–4/24/61, State to White House, 4/14/61, #6. John F. Kennedy Library.

118. Ibid., 6/3/61–6/18/61, Diem to Kennedy, 9 June 1961, 6.

119. William Trimble oral history, 12 August 1969, 8, John F. Kennedy Library Oral History Program.

120. For further elaboration, see Michael Adas, *Machines as the Measure of Men: Science, Technology, and Ideologies of Western Dominance* (Ithaca: Cornell University Press, 1989), 402–18.

121. *Foreign Relations of the United States, 1961–1963: Cuba, 1961–1962*, 10:666.

7. The Half-life of Celebrity

1. Norman Mailer, *Harlot's Ghost* (New York: Random House, 1991), 1023. This very long novel (1,282 pages) has wonderful depictions of individuals such as Lansdale. After its publication, Mailer said, "I've always been fascinated with spies and actors and

people who take on roles that are not their own and then take on that role more than they might like to. I wouldn't say actors equal spooks, but they each have experience of entering a role that could become more real than their life" (quoted in Scott Spencer, "The Old Man and the Novel," *New York Times Magazine*, 22 September 1991, 42, 47).

2. Leo Braudy, *The Frenzy of Renown: Fame and its History* (New York: Oxford University Press, 1986), 589.

3. Joe Banzon to Lansdale, 5 April 1961, Lansdale Papers, Box 36, #832.

4. Lansdale Papers, 1991 recently declassified box.

5. Lansdale Papers, Box 9, #265. Conein was no stranger to fictional representations either. His CIA roots and especially his involvement with the coup against Diem in 1963 led to increasingly imaginative stories about his own life. Stanley Karnow ("Spook," *New York Times Sunday Magazine*, 3 January 1999, 34), who knew Conein well, wanted to write a biography of the man but gave up because of Conein's penchant for tall tales. A series of speakers at the conspiracy conference "From Dallas to Watergate: Eyewitness Report," San Francisco, 6–7 September 1992, argued that Conein, along with Lansdale, was a key link between the CIA and the various plots to kill President Kennedy.

6. Dulles quoted in Currey, *Edward Lansdale*, 355 n. 9; Lansdale Papers, Box 1, #2; "The Reminiscences of Edward Lansdale," 1973, 8, in the Oral History Collection of Columbia University.

7. Bonner, *Waltzing with a Dictator*, 34; "The Road from Laos to Nicaragua," *Economist*, 7 March 1987, 35; Dan Morgan, "North Marched into a Vacuum; Unfettered NSC Aide Became a Man of Covert Action," *Washington Post*, 1 March 1987, A21.

8. Quoted in Rust, *Kennedy in Vietnam*, 28. State Department objections to Lansdale's methods are well documented. For example, officials discussed the need to censor one of his talks even as they noted, "The truth of what he says cannot be challenged, but we would question the propriety" (State Department memorandum to Lansdale, 11 June 1957, Lansdale Papers, Box 43, #1260).

9. Lansdale, interview by David Mabon and Ron Landa, 6 September 1984, 9, U.S. Department of State, Office of the Historian.

10. Halberstam, *The Best and the Brightest*, 128.

11. "A Political Warfare Lesson," April 1954, Lansdale Papers, Box 12, #299, 9. By subscribing to a "top-down" approach to the dissemination of culture, I realize that I am engaging in a historiographical debate among cultural historians that dates at least from Van Wycks Brooks's formulation in his " 'Highbrow' and 'Lowbrow' " essay from 1915, "America's Coming of Age." In the early stages of the Cold War, for example, Senator Arthur Vandenburg advised President Truman that achieving passage of Truman Doctrine in 1947 required the president to "scare hell out of the country" (quoted in Gardner, *Architects of Illusion*, 218). One must ask why he thought it necessary for Truman to take this approach if the evidence was so overwhelming. Yet I am struck by how elites (government leaders, publishers, religious leaders, and so on) during the Cold War era did not just manipulate or coerce other social classes into combatting

communism. Instead, a process of legitimation was always at work, one that elites tapped into and at times found themselves trying to contain. Indeed, the non-elite classes so enthusiastically took part in "witch hunts" and calls to wage war against all foes that elites were often afraid that they might not be able to contain the "democratic" urges they had helped set in motion. Clearly, anticommunism had breached the high/low distinction, and I believe it was continually doing so throughout Cold War era.

12. A. J. Langguth, "Our Policy-Making Men in Saigon," *New York Times Magazine*, 28 April 1968, 102.

13. "Gen. Lansdale: Mystery Man of S. Viet Nam," 13 February 1966, *New York Journal-American* (Lansdale Papers, Box 1, #6).

14. Nguyen Cao Ky, *Twenty Years and Twenty Days* (New York: Stein & Day, 1976), 74.

15. Richard Critchfield, "Lansdale Works Invisibly," *Washington Star*, 18 October 1965, A-1, A-6.

16. Jerry Greene's "Capital Circus," *New York Daily News*, 23 March 1961.

17. Phil Jeckyl, "Lansdale: Top Secret Agent of the World," in unidentified pornography magazine, circa 1965 (Lansdale Papers, Box 1, #6).

18. Jack Lasco, "Our Mysterious Edward G. Lansdale: America's Deadliest Secret Agent," *Saga: The Magazine for Men*, March 1967, 92 (Lansdale Papers, Box 1, #6).

19. Evans and Novak, "Viet Nam's Quiet War," 1965 (Lansdale Papers, Box 1, #6).

20. Jim Lucas, "Bad News for Red Warlords—Lansdale Heads for Viet Nam," *Washington News*, 14 October 1961.

21. David Martin, "The CIA's 'Loaded Gun,' " *Washington Post*, 10 October 1976. The material was incorporated into Martin's 1980 *Wilderness of Mirrors*.

22. Raymond K. Price Jr., "Bringing the Dream to the Ghettos." There is no date or publication information with this clipping in Lansdale Papers, Box 66.

23. Braudy, *The Frenzy of Renown*, 576.

24. Zalin Grant, *Facing the Phoenix*, 86.

25. Godfrey Hodgson, *America in Our Time* (New York: Vintage, 1976), chap. 1, is particularly good on the political as well as the psychic transformations that manifested themselves in post–World War II America. Also see Thomas Paterson, "Red Fascism: The American Image of Aggressive Totalitarianism," in his *Meeting the Communist Threat* (New York: Oxford University Press, 1988), 3–17, for a perceptive analysis of how Americans transformed the "other" immediately after World War II. Finally, Andrew Ross, "Containing Culture in the Cold War," in his *No Respect: Intellectuals and Popular Culture* (New York: Routledge, 1989), 42–64, makes the provocative argument that policymakers presented communism as a contagion to explain its danger to American society. Lansdale, lecturing on the evil nature of communism, often used such terms as "virus" and emphasized its contagious qualities.

26. By stating that the Cold War was lacking in "villains," I am describing a phenomenon in which the term "communism" was used quite generically, and phrases such as "the faceless enemy," "one billion reds," and "they even eat their young" were

routinely employed by media and government to describe America's enemy. Of course, individuals such as Joseph Stalin, Mao Zedong, and Ho Chi Minh were well-known enemies of America, yet I am struck by the paucity of foes named by J. Edgar Hoover or Richard Nixon when making their case about the mortal threat facing the United States. In many ways, a communist was at once a durable yet inchoate figure.

27. "The General from the CIA," *Pravda*, February 1966, translated by the *Foreign Broadcast Information Service*, (Lansdale Papers, Box 27, #625).

28. Lansdale Papers, Wesley Fishel to Lansdale, 6 August 1957. Interestingly, *Depeche*, 28 October 1961, contrasted the "evil" Lansdale with President Kennedy's "friendly gesture" toward the people of Cambodia (Lansdale Papers, Box 47, #1326).

29. "Asia's 007?" *Wall Street Journal*, 15 November 1968. Sihanouk was so consumed by visions of Lansdale that he insisted the American wanted to kill him. In a draft of his memoirs Lansdale reflected on his effect on the Cambodian leader: "I learned that Prince Sihanouk had convinced himself that I was visiting his country as an assassin and thus my 'protection' [by Phnom Penh's chief of police] was to make sure that I would get nowhere near the Prince!" (Lansdale Papers, Box 9, #264, 15). Sihanouk may have had some reason for his intense feelings toward Lansdale. *My War with the CIA: The Memoirs of Prince Norodom Sihanouk* (Middlesex, U.K.: Penguin, 1974) and the travel logs carefully reconstructed by Currey in *Edward Lansdale*, 200–204, indicate that Lansdale's movements in Cambodia in 1959 were indeed unusual. When he visited Cambodia's most famous tourist site, Angkor Wat, an abortive coup took place in Cambodia. The extent to which Lansdale, or any American, was involved in such plots is unknown, though America's relationship with Sihanouk was always unstable and culminated in the American-sanctioned coup against him by Lon Nol in 1970. See William Shawcross, *Sideshow: Kissinger, Nixon, and the Destruction of Cambodia* (New York: Simon & Schuster, 1981), 51–62.

30. Lansdale related this story in the drafts of his memoirs, Lansdale Papers, Box 9, #261, 283.

31. Richard Critchfield, "Lansdale Still a Saigon Force," *Washington Star*, 2 April 1966, A-3.

32. Phan Can Thanh, "The Man Sentenced to Death by Ho," *Thoi Nay*, 1 September 1967 (Lansdale Papers, Box 59, #1535).

33. Richard Critchfield, "Was He Col. Hillandale or the Quiet American," *Washington Star*, 26 March 1972, E-2.

34. *Time*, 1 April 1966, 24; President Nixon asked Lansdale in 1984 to examine the dangers posed by the growth of communism in El Salvador and Nicaragua and what threat this posed to U.S. national security (Currey Collection).

35. W. C. Bullock to Lansdale, 8 November 1960, Lansdale Papers, Box 37, #856.

36. Jean Lartéguy, *Yellow Fever* (New York: Dutton, 1962, 1965), 196, 200.

37. The other classic French *reportage* of the time was Gontran de Poncins, *From a Chinese City* (New York: Doubleday, 1957), reissued with an introduction by Edward Robinson (not the movie star), which briefly mentions how Lansdale helped bring "color" to South Vietnam at the time Poncins was an observer there. And three decades later, Marguerite Duras's fictionalized memoir *The Lover* (New York: Harper & Row,

1985) also uses many of the details favored by French writers when observing their colonial subjects.

38. Lartéguy, *Yellow Fever*, 199.

39. Joan Didion, *Democracy* (New York: Simon & Schuster, 1984), 90, 36.

40. Ibid., 40.

41. Michael Herr, *Dispatches* (New York: Avon, 1978), 50–51.

42. Ward Just, *A Dangerous Friend* (Boston: Houghton Mifflin, 1999), 2.

43. Michael L. Kurtz, "Oliver Stone, *JFK*, and History," in *Oliver Stone's USA: Film, History, and Controversy*, ed. Robert Brent Toplin (Lawrence: University Press of Kansas, 2000), 174.

44. The quoted phrase is from Thomas Powers in "The Black Arts," *New York Review of Books*, 4 February 1999, 20. An additional point: one does not have to subscribe to Hersh's breathless and corrosive take on Kennedy in *The Dark Side of Camelot* to recognize that JFK's private life led to complications in his public dealings with, for instance, J. Edgar Hoover; the remarkable aspect is how JFK compartmentalized his public and private life.

45. Reeves reviewed the film in *Journal of American History* 97 (December 1992): 1263; Heffner's "Last Gasp of the Gutenbergs" appeared in *Los Angeles Times*, 19 February 1992, B7. The quantity of literature generated by *JFK* is immense. For a representative samples, both pro and con, see Stone and Sklar, *JFK: The Book of the Film*, 187–529; and the forum in *American Historical Review* 97 (April 1992): 487–511. Marcus Raskin's essay in the *AHR* forum, "*JFK* and the Culture of Violence," 487–99, is typical of the muddle this discussion has become in that it both implicates and exculpates Lansdale: "It does not seem likely that as hawkish as Lansdale or the first-level advisers were, they would have been involved in a plot to kill President Kennedy in order to press a war and prove their ideological doctrines. However, it should be noted that most of Kennedy's advisers were far more hawkish than he" (497).

46. Norman Mailer, "Footfalls in the Crypt," *Vanity Fair*, February 1992, 126.

47. Gary Crowdus, "Clarifying the Conspiracy: An Interview with Oliver Stone," *Cineaste* 19 (1992): 25 (original emphasis).

48. Stone and Sklar, *JFK: The Book of the Film*, 182–83. To certain Kennedy conspirators, three "hobos" (or tramps as they are commonly called) photographed on the scene of the assassination in Dealey Plaza are considered prime suspects. Adding to the mystery, the tallest of the three tramps was later identified as Charles Harrelson, father of actor Woody Harrelson, who was convicted for the contract killing of a federal judge in a subsequent case. See Bob Callahan, *Who Shot JFK?: A Guide to the Major Conspiracy Theories* (New York: Simon & Schuster, 1993), 73. Prouty was equally forthcoming with one of the deans of the JFK conspiracy, Mark Lane, who wrote in *Plausible Denial: Was the CIA Involved in the Assassination of JFK?* (New York: Thunder's Mouth Press, 1991), 103: "When Prouty and I had lunch on Capitol Hill during June 1991, he showed me a photograph that had been taken in Dallas that day [22 November 1963]. It displayed a man striding away from the camera at an angle and therefore provided only a right side–back view. "There is no doubt in my mind," Prouty told me, 'that's Ed Lansdale'." After learning of this "evidence," I contacted Fletcher

Prouty and asked him for additional proof that Lansdale was in Dallas and that he was associated with the conspiracy. His response was curious: on the one hand he categorically denied that he had ever said Lansdale was a part of the assassination, even as he told me that he had further evidence (from unnamed sources) that linked Lansdale with the assassination (Fletcher Prouty to author, September 1992).

49. This "fact" is raised in Christopher Sharrett, "Debunking the Official History: The Conspiracy Theory in *JFK*," *Cineaste* 19 (1992): 11; the individual who served as the go-between for Lansdale and Oswald is said to be the CIA agent David Atlee Phillips. For a "history" of Phillips's role in the Kennedy conspiracy, see Lane, *Plausible Denial*, 189–200.

50. Another point raised repeatedly during the conference "From Dallas to Watergate: Eyewitness Report," was that there were no other well-known CIA agents who fit the bill.

51. Thomas Pynchon, *Slow Learner* (Boston: Little, Brown, 1984), 18.

52. Allen Dulles, ed., *Great True Spy Stories* (New York: Harper & Row, 1968).

53. A very brief sample of films involving CIA malevolence include Warren Beatty as an investigative journalist who becomes both victim and victimizer by unseen forces in *The Parallax View* (1974); Robert Redford as a CIA agent who finds himself the patsy to higher-ups in *Three Days of the Condor* (1975); Jack Lemmon and Sissy Spacek stumbling upon governmental misdeeds in *Missing* (1982); the never revealed reasons why American POWs were left behind in Vietnam in *Rambo* (1985). The CIA keeps even the president of the United States in the dark about the existence of aliens in the witless *Independence Day* (1996).

54. Tim Weiner, "Standing Tall at the Intersection of Clout and Pomp," *New York Times*, 25 July 1993, 22.

55. Quoted in Tom Wolfe, "Stalking the Billion-Footed Beast," *Harper's Magazine*, November 1989, 48.

56. In Spencer, "The Old Man and the Novel," 42, 47. This unreality continues; Tim Weiner has uncovered CIA payments to Haitian military leaders throughout the 1980s and into the 1990s: see his "Key Haiti Leaders Said to Have Been in the C.I.A.'s Pay," *New York Times*, 1 November 1993; and "Anti-Drug Unit of C.I.A. Sent Ton of Cocaine to U.S. in 1990," *New York Times*, 20 November 1993.

57. Quoted in Julian Loose, "Conspirators," *New Statesman & Society*, 8 November 1991, 40.

58. Critchfield, "Lansdale Works Invisibly," A-1; Erwin Canham, "U.S. Press Playbacks," *Christian Science Monitor*, 1 September 1965.

59. "The Lansdale File," *Economist*, 2 October 1965.

60. Maximo V. Soliven, *Manila Times*, 14 August 1968. (Lansdale Papers, Box 63).

61. This point was related to me by an attendee at the conference "From Dallas to Watergate: Eyewitness Report."

62. "Lansdale's Team Report on Covert Saigon Mission in 1954 and 1955," in *The Pentagon Papers*, 1: 573.

63. Garry Wills, "CIA's Schoolboy Bent," *Washington Star*, 30 December 1975, A-9.

Epilogue

1. Quoted in Drew Pearson, "Inside the White House," *Washington Post*, 11 July 1966.

2. Quoted in Langguth, *Our Vietnam*, 429.

3. Ward Just, *To What End: Report from Vietnam* (1968; reprint, New York: PublicAffairs, 2000), xxi.

4. Memo from Rufus Phillips to William Jordan, "The Vietnamese Elections—Ed Lansdale's Key Role," 22 September 1966 (Lansdale Papers, 1991 declassified folder).

5. Quoted in Bonner, *Waltzing with a Dictator*, 35.

6. Memorandum from the Ambassador's Special Assistant (Lansdale) to the Ambassador to Vietnam (Bunker), "Talk with Thieu," 2 September 1967, *Foreign Relations, 1964–1968: Vietnam, 1967,* 5:746.

7. Memorandum John Roche, Special Consultant to the President, 13 November 1967, Folder November 1967 [2 of 4], Box 26, Handwriting File, Lyndon B. Johnson, Library, Austin, Tex.

8. Co Van Hai to Lansdale, Lansdale Papers, Box 36, #814 (this Christmas card was declassified only in 1990).

9. From Liberation Radio (Clandestine) in Vietnamese to South Vietnam, 17 March 1966 (Lansdale Papers, Box 62, #1602).

10. Edward Lansdale, "Two Steps to Get Us out of Vietnam," *Look*, 4 March 1969, 67.

11. Lansdale to David Martin, 6 February 1972, Lansdale Papers, Box 5, #143, 3.

12. Sheehan Papers, Box 71.

13. Lansdale had correspondence until November 1986 with the United States Committee for a Free Indochina. Likewise, until 1986 he was in contact with the U.S. Army War College about how the United States could manage low-intensity conflicts around the world (Lansdale Papers, Box 74).

14. Lansdale to Harriman, 26 February 1977, Lansdale Papers, Box 3, #87.

15. David Brion Davis, *Revolutions: Reflections on American Equality and Foreign Liberations* (Cambridge: Harvard University Press, 1990), 3.

16. Karnow, *In Our Image*, 9.

17. See *CIA World Factbook* at www.cia.gov/cia/publications/factbook/geos/rp.html.

18. Marcus Brauchli, "Movie Tough Guy Fights Crime for Real in the Philippines," 8 September 1993, *Wall Street Journal*, 1; Bruce Lambert, "On Scavengers' Mountain, a Few Scraps of Hope," 16 June 1993, *New York Times*, A4.

19. Arjun Appadurai, "Disjuncture and Difference in the Global Cultural Economy," *Public Culture* 2 (spring 1990): 3.

20. Memorandum from the U.S. Joint Chiefs of Staff, 20 September 1945, quoted in Stephen R. Shalom, "Bases by Another Name: U.S. Military Access in the Philippines," *Bulletin of Concerned Asian Scholars* 29 (October–December 1997): 78.

21. *New York Times*, 4 August 1990, 2; Alan Berlow, "Way off Base," *New Republic*, 31 December 1990, 20.

22. Raymond Bonner, "'Yankee Don't Go' Is Message in Philippines Antiterror Rally," *New York Times*, 25 February 2002.

23. Emilio Aguinaldo, *A Second Look at America* (New York: Robert Speller, 1957), 236.

24. Hedman, "Late Imperial Romance," 184.

25. "Chronicle," *New York Times*, 12 February 1991, B18. The article added, "She also took reporters to her bedroom to prove that she could not hide under the bed because there was not enough space."

26. Seth Mydans, "Ousted Philippines President Officially Charged with Plunder," *New York Times*, 11 July 2001.

27. "Philippines: Marchers Oppose President," *New York Times*, 2 May 2002.

28. Seth Mydans, "National Pride over a Virus in Philippines," *New York Times*, 12 May 2000, C1.

29. *CIA World Factbook* at www.ciagov/cia/publications/factbook.

30. Karnow, *Vietnam*, 27–28.

31. "Tran Do, Vietnam's Leading Dissident," *New York Times*, 10 August 2002, A24.

32. Craig R. Whitney, "Ex-Follower of Ho Chi Minh Scolds Vietnam in Broadcasts," *New York Times*, 29 December 1990, 1. Bui Tin (a colonel in the Vietnamese army and deputy editory of the Communist daily, *Nahn Dan*) was using the services of the BBC in Paris to tell the Vietnamese that they needed to abandon their current political and economic policies. For another example see Philip Shenon, "In This Author's Book, Villains Are Vietnamese," *New York Times*, 12 April 1994, A4.

33. Quoted in Walter A. McDougall, *Promised Land, Crusader State: The American Encounter with the World since 1776* (New York: Houghton Mifflin, 1997), 190.

34. The article said that Peterson drives by the hotel two or three times a day, "and it doesn't bother me which is good. It means I have healed." David Shipler, "Robert McNamara and the Ghosts of Vietnam," *New York Times Magazine*, 10 August 1997, 34.

35. Seth Mydans, "Vietnam Hangs onto a Relic: The Propaganda Poster," *New York Times*, 14 November 2000.

36. "Vietnam Publishes Plan for Economy," *New York Times*, 4 December 1990, A7; Murray Hiebert, "The Tilling Fields: Vietnam Regains Role as Major Rice Exporter," *Far East Economic Review*, 10 May 1990; Craig R. Whitney, "Hanoi Now, Meet Saigon Then," *New York Times*, 28 December 1997, 4–6; Seth Mydans, "Visit the Vietcong's World: Americans Welcome," *New York Times*, 7 July 1999.

37. Walter LaFeber, *Michael Jordan and the New Global Capitalism* (New York: Norton, 1999), 148.

38. Wills, *The Kennedy Imprisonment*, 285.

39. Jerome Doolittle, "And This Was the Thanks I Got," *Washington Post*, 25 June, 2000.

40. The status of the bill can be found at www.house.gov/hefley/legis.htm (Summer 2004).

41. According to Electronic Arts, a computer software company, "research indi-

cates that the Hollywood Vietnam is the only representation of the war that much of its target audience knows." Stephen Totilo, "A Belated Invasion: Vietnam, the Game," *New York Times*, 1 April 2004, E1, E6.

42. George H. W. Bush, "Inaugural Address," 20 January 1989, *Public Papers of the Presidents of the United States: George Bush, 1989* (Washington, D.C.: GPO, 1990), 3.

43. Henry Kamm, *Dragon Ascending: Vietnam and the Vietnamese* (New York: Arcade, 1996), 11.

44. Apropos of Clinton's visit, in a poll taken by a Vietnamese newspaper (whose translated name is "Youth"), Clinton was voted twice as popular as the Vietnamese prime minister. Pico Iyer, "Welcome to Sunny Vietnam," *Time*, 3 June 2002, 79.

45. Quoted in Philip Shenon, "Vietnam Welcomes U.S. Decision on Embargo," *New York Times*, 5 February 1994, 1.

46. "Russia Returns Naval Base to Vietnam," *New York Times*, 3 May 2002.

Index

Accuracy in Media, 224n. 36
Acheson, Dean, 5, 39, 95, 96–97
Adamson, Judith, 160
Adventures in Chaos (Macdonald), 227n. 22
advertising: in Cuba, 71–75; empathy in, 47;
    in foreign policy, 27–28; future in, 49;
    Lansdale and, 22, 26–31, 46–48, 54, 68–72,
    226n. 11; in modern world, 46–47; nature
    of, 29–30, 46–48; in Philippines, 31–45; po-
    litical uses of, 49–50; power of, 28–29, 41;
    in Vietnam, 53–68
Aguinaldo, Emilio: *A Second Look at America*,
    213–14
aid: foreign, 34–35, 44, 59–60, 82, 185, 229n.
    37; humanitarian, 154
*Alleged Assassination Plots involving Foreign
    Leaders*, 14, 73–74, 102, 188–89. *See also*
    assassinations
Alsop, Joseph, 123
American Friends of Vietnam (AFV), 54, 57–
    58, 167, 170–71
America, United States of: Americanization of
    other countries, 7, 49–52, 110–18, 140–41,
    216; American Revolution, 107–10, 179;
    anti-Americanism, 42, 152–55, 172, 233n.
    13; arts, 172–73; cartoons and American
    values, 50; Cold War impact on, 217; devel-
    oping world, understanding of, 162, 175;
    empire, 153–54; foreign aid to Philippines,
    35, 44, 229n. 37; foreign aid to Vietnam, 59–
    60, 82, 185; foreign policy: *see* foreign pol-
    icy, American; ideals of, 246n. 40; interest
    in Asia, 5–6; legacy of Vietnam War, 218–
    19; in Philippines, 51, 113–15, 160–61, 212–
    15, 213, 227n. 22; popular culture of, 17–
    19, 67, 187–88, 197–207, 212–13; power of,
    48, 96; press: *see* press, American; propa-
    ganda, 44, 46–47, 232n. 78; role in world,
    96; State Department, 79, 174, 180–81,

191, 260n. 8; transformation after World
    War II, 261n. 25; United States Committee
    for a Free Indochina, 224n. 36, 265n. 13; in
    Vietnam, 51–67, 212, 215–20, 236n. 72. *See
    also* colonialism; imperialism, American
Anderson, Marian, 127, 249n. 1
Angelton, James Jesus, 91
Another Vietnam (exhibit), 219
anthropology, 142–44, 251n. 49. *See also* mod-
    ernization theory
anti-Americanism, 42, 152–55, 172, 233n. 13
anticommunism: American art influenced by,
    172–73; generally, 6–10, 242n. 50; John F.
    Kennedy and, 175; Lansdale's embrace of, 8–
    10, 81; legitimation of, 260n. 11; rhetoric
    of, 69; tourism and, 141. *See also*
    communism
antiracialism, 142–43
Appadurai, Arjun, 212–13
Aquino, Corazon, 214
Arroyo, Gloria Macapagal, 214–15
arts, 172–73
Asia: American interest in, 5–6; Americaniza-
    tion of, 7, 110–18, 140–41; Lansdale's eth-
    nography of, 130–37, 140–48; Lansdale's
    love for, 137; view of Lansdale, 21. *See also*
    Philippines; Vietnam
assassinations: Church Committee Report, 14,
    73–74, 102, 188–89; Fidel Castro, 2–3, 71–
    75, 101–2, 204, 239n. 100; John F. Ken-
    nedy, 17–20, 201–3, 263n. 45
astrology, 177
Atkinson, Stan, 55

"Ballad of Ed Lansdale, The"
    (www.blackopradio.com), 18
Bamford, James, 74
Bao Dai, 3, 64
Barton, Bruce, 72; *The Man Nobody Knows*, 47

Beech, Keyes, 157

Belin, David W., 73

Benedict, Ruth, *The Chrysanthemum and the Sword*, 142

Berger, John, 49

Bernays, Edward, 46, 232n. 78

Best and the Brightest, The (Halberstam), 259n. 111

Betts, Richard, 7

Bigart, Homer, 221n. 7

Binh Hung (Vietnam), 54–56

Binh Xuyen, 223n. 33

biography, nature of, 11

Bissell, Richard, 74

blackmail, and Lansdale, 45

Boas, Franz, 143

Bond, James, 193–94

Bonner, Raymond, 213; *Waltzing with a Dictator*, 214, 227n. 22

Braden, Tom, 98–99

Brando, Marlon, 181–82, 258n. 107

Braudy, Leo, 188, 194

Bright Shining Lie, A (Sheehan), 11–12, 223n. 31

Brown, Norman O., 48

Bundy, William, 85

Bunker, Ellsworth, 112, 131

Burdick, Eugene, 2, 139, 149, 173, 180. See also *Ugly American, The*

Buz Sawyer (comic strip), 56

Caine, Michael, 173

Cambodia, 262n. 29

Cao Dai sect, 122, 144–45, 156, 223n. 33, 234n. 37. *See also* sects; Vietnam

capitalism, 48, 50–52, 141–42, 216–17. *See also* consumerism

cartoons and American values, 50

Castro, Fidel, 2–3, 71–75, 101–2, 204, 225n. 51, 239n. 100. *See also* Cuba; Operation Mongoose

Cavalier, 97

Central Intelligence Agency (CIA): anthropologists used by, 143; Cold War and, 94–103; Commission on CIA Activities, 73; covert actions of, 10, 14–15, 93–94, 100–102; credibility of, 102–3; establishment of, 96–97; exposés of, 100; front groups for, 255n. 52; Hollywood and, 163–64, 201–5, 264n. 53; image of, 97–100; investigations of, 73, 94–95; John F. Kennedy and, 94; myths of, 99–101, 201–5; political alienation and, 102–3;

power of, 97–98; press, American, and, 97–100; public understanding of, 204; *The Quiet American* (film) and, 163–64, 166; spies and, 88–89, 91, 143. *See also* Central Intelligence Agency (CIA) and Landsdale; Cuba; Philippines; Vietnam

Central Intelligence Agency (CIA) and Lansdale: documents, 240n. 2; in fictional portrayals, 187–89; generally, 2–3, 22, 240n. 4; image of, 197; impact of celebrity on, 191; press, American, on, 221n. 7; relationship concealed, 30, 77–80, 89–91, 221n. 2

Chace, William, 253n. 21

Chandler, David, 3

Cherne, Leo, 60

China Gate (film), 219

China Lobby, 223n. 34

Christian Science Monitor, 43–44

Chrysanthemum and the Sword, The (Benedict), 142

Church Committee Report, 14, 73–74, 102, 188–89

CIA. *See* Central Intelligence Agency (CIA)

Civil Air Transport, 256n. 52

Clifford, James, 139

Coca-Cola Company, 35

Colby, William, 16, 78, 83, 162

Cold War: CIA and, 94–103; commemoration of, 217–18; consensus on, 9, 110–11, 245n. 23, 252n. 13; cultural knowledge in, 131; historiography of, 110–11; Hollywood and, 163–64; humanitarian aid, 154; impact on American world view, 217; Lansdale selling, to public, 67–72; legitimation of, 260n. 11; origins of, 7–8. *See also* history, use of in Cold War

Collins, Jane, *Reading National Geographic*, 141

Collins, J. Lawton, 63–64

colonialism: American vs. European, 69; anthropologists on, 251n. 49; culture and, 50; Greene on, 152–54, 157–58, 252n. 11; impact on Philippines, 137; Lansdale on, 9; in Vietnam, 251n. 54. *See also* empire, American; imperialism

Commission on CIA Activities, 73

commodities, power of, 72

communism: Christianity used to counter, 109–10; dangers of, as motivational tool, 123; domino theory, 7–8, 152, 158–59; fear of, 95–96; Lansdale on, 109; nature of,

261n. 25, 261n. 26; psychological warfare, 39–42, 74–75, 82–83, 109. *See also* anticommunism

"Comparative Counter-Insurgency Strategies in the Philippines" (Dillon), 227n. 22

Conein, Lucien, 6–7, 189, 260n. 5

confidence man, 25–26, 48

Confidence-Man, The (Melville), 25–26

consensus school, 110–11. *See also* Cold War

conspiracy theories, 17–20, 203, 263n. 48, 264n. 49. *See also* assassinations

consumerism: American empire and, 153–54; conflation with heroes, 27; future-orientation of, 226n. 17; in "Kitchen Debate," 141–42; modernization and, 29; power of, 49–51; in Vietnam, 216–17. *See also* capitalism

consumption. *See* consumerism

containment, 7–8. *See also* domino theory; Kennan, George

Continental Hotel explosion, 165–67

Cooper, Chester, 52–53, 85

corporations, American, in Philippines, 212

counterinsurgency, 1–2, 90–91. *See also* Central Intelligence Agency (CIA)

covert actions, 10, 93–94, 100–102, 114–15

Craft of Intelligence, The (A. Dulles), 99

Critchfield, Richard, 192; *The Long Charade*, 224n. 47

Crowther, Bosley, 171

Cuba, 71–75, 101–2, 225n. 51. *See also* Castro, Fidel

Cuban Missile Crisis, 75

"Cuba Project," 225n. 51

Cullather, Nick, 183; *Illusions of Influence*, 227n. 22

culture: Americanization of other countries, 7, 49–52, 110–18, 140–41, 216; American popular, 17–19, 67, 187–88, 197–207, 212–13; colonialism and, 50; consumer: *see* consumerism; dissemination of, 260n. 11; encounters of differing, 127–28; folk music, 13, 138, 146–47, 225n. 52; folk traditions, 147–48; knowledge of, used in Cold War, 131; Lansdale as cultural bridge, 140–41; Lansdale's insensitivity to foreign cultures, 116–18, 129, 136; Lansdale's knowledge of foreign cultures, 39–41, 43, 129–31, 143–44, 209; Lansdale's naiveté about other cultures, 30; tolerance, 142–43. *See also* films; Lansdale, Edward G., fictional portrayals

Currey, Cecil, 15; *Edward Lansdale*, 3–4, 206

Dangerous Friend, A (Just), 200

Davis, David Brion, 211

Dean, Robert, *Imperial Brotherhood*, 16

DeLillo, Don, 101; *Libra*, 205

Deliver Us from Evil (Dooley), 62–63

Democracy (Didion), 199–200

Dennings, Michael, 88

dependence theory, 212. *See also* colonialism

Desilu Productions, 55

developing societies, 143–44, 162, 175

Didion, Joan, *Democracy*, 199–200

Diem, Ngo Dinh. *See* Ngo Dinh Diem

Dillon, Dana R.: "Comparative Counter-Insurgency Strategies in the Philippines," 227n. 22

Dispatches (Herr), 200

domino theory, 7–8, 152, 158–59

Donovan, Bill, 29

Dooley, Tom, 235n. 54; *Deliver Us from Evil*, 62–63

Dragon Ascending (Kamm), 218–19

Drinnon, Richard, 15

Dulles, Allen: *The Craft of Intelligence*, 99; *Great True Spy Stories*, 99, 203; on Lansdale, 36, 189–90; on *The Quiet American* (film), 166; request to send Lansdale to Vietnam, 78, 221n. 2; on Vietnam, 52. *See also* Central Intelligence Agency (CIA)

Dulles, John Foster: on American ideals, 246n. 40; on America's role in the world, 96; on Lansdale, 51, 190; Lansdale and, 78, 221n. 2

Dunne, Finley Peter, 140

Duong van "Big" Minh, 82

Duras, Marguerite, *The Lover*, 262n. 37

Eagleton, Terry, 155

Eastern Construction Company, 255n. 52

Economic Development Corporation (EDCOR), 44

Economist, 205–6

Edward Lansdale (Currey), 3–4, 206

Eisenhower, Dwight, 51, 52, 95–96, 110, 175, 237n. 83, 245n. 19

elections, foreign, 32–37, 45, 64–65

Elimination by Submarine (plan), 74. *See also* Castro, Fidel

Ellsberg, Daniel, 11, 16, 80

Emerson, Gloria, 62

empire, American, 153–54. *See also* colonialism; imperialism

Encounter, 99

Englund, George, 178, 258n. 98
Estrada, Joseph, 214
ethnography of Asian cultures, 130–37,
    140–48
Evans, Rowland, 193
"eye of God" technique, 40, 42, 230n. 60. See
    also advertising

Facing the Phoenix (Grant), 194, 224n. 47
Fall, Bernard, 59–60, 234n. 39
Family of Man, The (exhibit), 142–43
Ferguson, Niall, 96
films: China Gate, 219; Fire and Shadow, 58;
    JFK, 19–20, 201–3, 225n. 54; In the Line of
    Fire, 203–4; power of, 168; The Village That
    Refuses to Die, 55–56; We Were Soldiers Once,
    219. See also Quiet American, The (1958
    film); Quiet American, The (2001 film); Ugly
    American, The (film)
Fire and Shadow (film), 58
First Indochina War, 52–54, 152–53. See also
    Vietnam
Fishel, Wesley, 183–84, 259n. 113. See also
    Michigan State University
Fisher, James, 62
Fitzgerald, Francis, 104
folk music, 13, 138, 146–47, 225n. 52
foreign aid, American: to Philippines, 35, 44,
    229n. 37; power of, 145; to Vietnam, 59–60,
    82, 185
foreign policy, American: advertising in, 27–
    28; Greene's critique of, 150–51; Lansdale
    functioning within structure of, 94–96, 102;
    Lansdale's role in, 225n. 51; nature of, 29–
    30; Open Door policy, 8; Vietnamization
    policy, 125
Fowler, Thomas: anti-Americanism of, 155,
    172; on colonialism, 157–58; Greene as,
    254n. 26; Michael Caine as, 173
France: on American role in Vietnam, 198;
    Lansdale on, 53, 145–46; in Vietnam, 52–
    53, 92, 120–21, 251n. 54
Fraser, Brendan, 173
Frederick, J. George, 47–48
From a Chinese City (Poncins), 262n. 37
Fulbright, J. William, 9, 89, 180
Fursenko, Aleksandr, 15

Garrison, Jim, On the Trail of Assassins, 18–19
Geertz, Clifford, 130
Gelb, Leslie, 7
Giap, Vo Nguyen. See Vo Nguyen Giap

Gibbons, William Conrad, 56–57
Gilpatric, Roswell L., 70
Girling, J. L. S., 3
Godard, Jean-Luc, 171, 256n. 72
Grant, Zalin, Facing the Phoenix, 194, 224n. 47
Great True Spy Stories (A. Dulles), 99, 203
Greene, Graham: on Alden Pyle, 159–60; on
    American foreign policy, 150–51; anti-
    Americanism of, 152–55; on colonialism,
    152–53, 158, 252n. 11; Communist Party
    and, 255n. 43; generally, 2; as journalist in
    Vietnam, 150–52; Lansdale and, 150, 159–
    61; Lansdale depicted by, 19, 149–50;
    Mankiewicz and, 163; opium use of, 254n.
    26; orientalism of, 252n. 9; on The Quiet
    American (film), 166–67, 168, 172; on "third
    force," 156–58; writing style, 160, 163. See
    also Quiet American, The (Greene)
Greene, Jerry, 192
Gunfighter Nation (Slotkin), 227n. 22

Halberstam, David, 15, 17, 151; The Best and
    the Brightest, 259n. 111
Hao Hao sect, 223n. 33
Harlot's Ghost (Mailer), 101, 187–88, 199, 204–
    5, 259n. 1
Hartz, Louis, 252n. 13
Harvey, William King, 193
Hedman, Eva-Lotta E., 228n. 22
Heidenry, John, 98
Hellmann, John, 174
Helms, Richard, 88, 225n. 51
Henares, Hilarion M., Jr., 42
"Hero of the Week" (advertising campaign),
    27–28. See also advertising
Herr, Michael, Dispatches, 200
Hershberg, James, 73
Hillandale, Edwin, 175–78
Hilsman, Roger, 85–86, 259n. 112
Hinckle, Warren, 184
historiography, 110–11, 245n. 23, 252n. 13,
    260n. 11
history, use of in Cold War: Lansdale and,
    104–13, 125–26, 166; in Philippines, 111–
    15; in The Ugly American (film), 179–80; in
    Vietnam, 115–24. See also "usable past"
Hoa, Father, 54–56
Ho Chi Minh, 7, 118–22
Hofstadter, Richard, The Paranoid Style in
    American Politics, 18
Hollywood: CIA depicted by, 163–64, 201–5,
    264n. 53; government and, 180; Mankiewicz

on, 172; "secret government," 203–5; Vietnam War depicted by, 218–19, 266n. 41
Hughes, Richard, 36
Huk Rebellion, The (Kerkvliet), 229n. 50
Huks, 38–44, 229n. 50. *See also* Philippines
Huks, The (Lachica), 230n. 50
humanitarian aid, 154
Humphrey, Hubert, 9

identity, political, 213
Illusions of Influence (Cullather), 227n. 22
Imperial Brotherhood (Dean), 16
imperialism, American, 5–7, 113, 212–20, 243n. 57, 243n. 58. *See also* colonialism; empire, American
indifference, political, 179–80
Indochina. *See* First Indochina War
indoctrination, 55
In Search of Enemies (Stockwell), 100
internationalism, liberal, 9, 115
International Refugee Committee, 60. *See also* resettlement programs
In the Line of Fire (film), 203–4
In the Midst of Wars (E. Lansdale), 2–3
Iran-contra scandal, 190. *See also* North, Oliver

Jackson, Bruce, 69–70
Jacobs, Seth, 60
Japan, 114–15, 134
Jeckyl, Phil, 192
JFK (film), 19–20, 201–3, 225n. 54. *See also* assassinations; conspiracy theories; Kennedy, John F.
Johnson, Lyndon: on Americanization of other countries, 216; on Diem, 59; on Lansdale, 208, 210; and Nguyen Can Ky, 140; transportation projects and, 259n. 116; and Vietnam War, 223n. 30
Joint Chiefs of Staff, 74–75
journalism. *See* press, American
Just, Ward, 209; *A Dangerous Friend*, 200

Kael, Pauline, 171, 181
Kahin, George, 65
Kamm, Henry, *Dragon Ascending*, 218–19
Karnow, Stanley, 144, 217, 228n. 29, 260n. 5; *Vietnam*, 15
Kennan, George, 7–8, 141
Kennedy administration, 66–67, 71, 87–88, 93
Kennedy, John F.: anticommunism and, 175; assassination of, 17–20, 201–3, 263n. 45; on

CIA, 94; conspiracy theories, 17–20, 203, 263n. 48, 264n. 49; on covert actions, 14–15, 93; Diem and, 57, 66; *JFK* (film), 19–20, 201–3, 225n. 54; Lansdale and, 57, 71, 191; private life, 263n. 44
Kennedy, Robert, 71–72, 74, 102
Kerkvliet, Benedict: *The Huk Rebellion*, 229n. 50
Kim (Kipling), 84
Kipling, Rudyard, 5–6; *Kim*, 84
Kissinger, Henry, 93
"Kitchen Debate" (Nixon and Khrushchev), 141–42. *See also* consumerism; Nixon, Richard
knowledge, cultural, use of in Cold War, 131
Kornbluh, Peter, 74
Ky, Nguyen Can. *See* Nguyen Can Ky

Lachica, Eduardo, *The Huks*, 230n. 50
Lacy, William, 51
LaFeber, Walter, 115, 217
land reform, 38–39, 230n. 51, 246n. 26
Langguth, A. J., 191
Lansdale, David, 21
Lansdale, Edward G.: as adventurer; affinity for people, 47, 92, 111, 133, 137–38; belief in his own benevolence, 159; "friendly American" persona, 92–93; harmonica playing, 138–39; as hero, 123–24; idealism of, 4–5, 68; image, 1–2, 14–21, 149–50, 188–97, 189–97; influence on people, 54, 139; interest in U.S. Constitution, 247n. 43; legacy of, 212–20; as liberal anticommunist, 45–46; limits of power, 12–13; *In the Midst of Wars*, 2–3; normalizes the foreign, 111, 129, 133, 139–40
Lansdale, Edward G., career of: ambassador position sought, 70–71, 191; basis of methods, 47–48; CIA association: *see* Central Intelligence Agency (CIA) and Lansdale; as Cold War theorist, 104–5; as explorer, 22; government agencies and, 191; impact of fame on career, 205–7; justifications for interventions, 115; as keeper of secrets, 88–89; later career, 75–76; methods, 9–10; as military man, 28–29, 70, 132–33; policy formulation role, 225n. 51; preference for persuasion over military tactics, 46–47; retirement, 210–11; role of economic support in successes, 82; as secular missionary, 93–94, 140–41; self-promotion as means to political power, 69–71, 81–82, 146; Senate

Lansdale, Edward G. (*continued*)
testimony, 89–91, 241n. 37; tactics adopted
for use elsewhere, 42; use of knowledge as
power, 144; use of language, 69; use of
secrets, 80–94. *See also* advertising; Magsaysay, Ramon; Ngo Dinh Diem; Philippines;
Vietnam
Lansdale, Edward G., fictional portrayals, 19–
22, 149–50, 155–62, 175–78, 186–89, 192–
205. *See also specific authors and titles*
Lansdale, Edward G., life of: early life, 26–27;
family history, 106–7, 245n. 8; marriages,
137; obituary, 1–2
Lansdale, Edward G., policymakers on: critiques, 85–87, 125, 189; John F. Kennedy
and, 57, 71, 191; John Foster Dulles and,
51, 78, 221n. 2; John Roche on, 210;
Kennedy administration and, 87–88, 93;
Lyndon Johnson and, 208, 210; Robert
Kennedy and, 71–72; Rufus Phillips on, 123–
24
Lansdale, Edward G., writings, 130–31; "Art
of the Guerrilla War," 43–44; "A Case History of Insurgency—The Philippines," 139;
on France, 145–46; "Fundamentals for
Americans," 111; "A High-Level Look at
the Cold War," 87–88, 109–10; "How to
select people for cold-war missions," 139; "
The Insurgent Battlefield," 93; memoir
drafts, 107; "Memorandum for the Chairman, JCS," 237n. 72; *In the Midst of Wars*, 2–
3; "Notes on How to Be a Prime Minister
of Vietnam," 56–57; on Philippines, 137; "
The Philippines Election, 1953," 32–33;
political intrigue in, 82; on Ryuku Islands,
133–36; "Some Thoughts about Central
America," 231n. 77; "Team Report" in *The
Pentagon Papers*, 80–85; "The 'True American,'" 160; "Two Steps to Get Us Out of
Vietnam," 210; "The Village That Refuses
to Die," 54–55; writing style of, 2, 64, 88,
105, 206–7
Lansdale, Pat, 91, 211
Lantz, Robert, 166
Lartéguy, Jean, *Yellow Fever*, 197–99
Lasch, Christopher, 28
Lasco, Jack, 193
Leach, William, 226n. 17
Lear, Jackson, 26
le Carré, John, 21
Lederer, William: on Edwin Hillandale char-
acter, 139, 177; generally, 2, 149, 173;

Lansdale and, 174–75, 180. See also *Ugly
American, The*
Lehman, William, 162
Lewis, Fulton, Jr., 20
liberal internationalism. *See* internationalism,
liberal
Liberation Radio, 210
Libra (DeLillo), 205
Liebling, A. J., 155
Lien Minh militia, 234n. 37
Lindsay, Vachel, 41
Lonely Crowd, The (Reisman), 258n. 110
Long An (Vietnam), 131
Long Charade, The (Critchfield), 224n. 47
Look, 210
Loris, Charlotte, 254n. 26
Lover, The (Duras), 262n. 37
Lovett, Jack, 199
Lucas, Jim, 193
Luce, Henry, 9
Lutz, Catherine, *Reading National Geographic*,
141

Macdonald, Douglas J., *Adventures in Chaos*,
227n. 22
Macmillan, Harold, 153
MacWhite, Harrison Carter, 178–79,
258n. 107
Mafia, 73
Magsaysay, Jesus, 115, 246n. 40
"Magsaysay March, The," 33–34
Magsaysay, Ramon: characteristics of, 33; for-
eign aid, 34–35, 44; Lansdale and, 1, 3, 31–
34, 114, 227n. 22, 228n. 26; press depictions
of, 36–38, 114. *See also* press, American; in
The Ugly American, 176; as viewed by poli-
cymakers, 51, 112–14; willingness to be in-
fluenced by U.S., 32. *See also* Philippines
Mailer, Norman: *Harlot's Ghost*, 101, 187–88,
199, 204–5, 259n. 1
Malraux, Andre: *Man's Fate*, 232n. 7
Mankiewicz, Joseph, 169–70; American
Friends of Vietnam (AFV) and, 170–71;
Greene and, 163; on Hollywood, 172;
Lansdale and, 164–65; personal life, 171–72;
on *The Quiet American*, 170, 172. See also
Quiet American, The (1958 film)
Man Nobody Knows, The (Barton), 47
Man's Fate (Malraux), 232n. 7
Mansfield, Mike, 64
Marchand, Roland, 29
Marcos, Ferdinand, 214

Martin, David, 193
Marxism, 38, 72, 119
McClure's Magazine, 222n. 14
McCone, John, 224n. 38
McMahon, Robert J., 129
McNamara, Robert, 57, 73, 86–87, 234 n.29
media. *See* press, American
Melby, John F., 38, 230n. 52
Melville, Herman, *The Confidence-Man*, 25–26
Michigan State University, 53–54, 259n. 114.
    See also Fishel, Wesley
military bases, American, in Philippines, 213
military-industrial complex, 238n. 83
Miller, Edward, 117
Mills, C. Wright, 70, 125
Mirsky, Jonathan, 3
Mitgang, Herbert, 161
modernization theory, 10, 29, 182–86, 258n.
    110. *See also* anthropology; developing
    societies
Moffat, Abbot Low, 7–8
Murphy, Audie, 169–70
Mus, Paul, 118

Naftali, Timothy, 15
napalm, use of, 231n. 75
National Geographic, 141
nation building, 53, 69, 121, 158–59
New York Herald Tribune, 161
New York Times, 37, 84–85, 174, 189
Ngo Dinh Diem: bribes, 60, 234n. 39; Ca-
    tholicism of, 63, 65, 236n. 56; Catholic po-
    litical base of, 61, 83; characteristics of, 58–
    59; coup and death of (1963), 66, 79, 124;
    coup attempt (1955), 63; and democracy,
    123, 185; election of (1955), 64–65; as fa-
    ther of South Vietnam, 117; foreign aid, 59–
    60, 82, 185; John F. Kennedy on, 57, 66;
    Lansdale and, 1, 3, 12, 53–59, 56–57, 63–
    67, 116, 123–24, 233n. 27; legitimacy of, 65,
    122; Lyndon Johnson on, 59; and Nguyen
    dynasty, 123, 248n. 66; origins of regime,
    51; policymakers' opinions of, 59, 85; politi-
    cal philosophy of, 117–18; press depictions
    of, 58–59; relationship with Americans, 121–
    22; "Report on the First 100 Days," 116;
    Tom Dooley and, 62; view of American
    troops, 66. *See also* Vietnam
Ngo Dinh Nhu, 65–67
Nguyen Can Ky, 140, 209, 247n. 42
Nguyên Thanh Phuong, 60
Nguyen Van Hinh, 83

Nguyen Van Thieu, 209
Nhu, Madame, 65, 248n. 66
Nhu, Ngo Dinh. *See* Ngo Dinh Nhu
Nitze, Paul, 8
Nixon, Richard, 33, 99, 141–42, 147
North, Oliver, 17, 190, 225n. 49
North Vietnam. *See* Vietnam
Novak, Robert, 193
NSC-4/A (document), 95
NSC-68 (document), 8, 95

O'Daniel, John W. "Iron Mike," 52, 121, 167
Office of Strategic Services (OSS), 189
On the Trail of Assassins (Garrison), 18–19
Open Door policy, 8
Operation Brotherhood, 61–62, 255n. 52
Operation Dirty Trick, 75
Operation Exodus, 60, 235n. 40
Operation Good Times, 75
Operation Mongoose, 2, 3, 71–75, 239n. 110
Operation Northwoods, 74–75
Operation Passage to Freedom, 60, 235n. 40
opium, 254n. 26
orientalism, 252n. 9

Parade Personality, 37
Paranoid Style in American Politics, The
    (Hofstadter), 18
Paris Match, 233n. 13
Parsons, J. Graham, 79, 177
Payne, Robert, 157
"Peace Fund," 44
peasant societies, 143–44, 162, 175
Pentagon Papers, The, 14, 59, 78, 80–85
People's Anti-Japanese Army. *See* Huks
People's Liberation Army. *See* Huks
personalism, ideology of, 117–18, 247n. 47
persuasion, art of, 41
Pham Van Dong, 215
Phan Boi Chau, 119–20
Phan Chu Trinh, 119–20
Philippine Armed Forces Journal, 136
Philippines: advertising in, 31–45; America
    and, 51, 113–15, 160–61, 212–15, 227n. 22;
    American corporations in, 212; "Compara-
    tive Counter-Insurgency Strategies in the
    Philippines" (Dillon), 227n. 22; corruption
    in, 214–15; culture, American, in, 49–52;
    education system of, 113; elections, 32–37,
    45; foreign aid, 34–35, 44, 229n. 37; frag-
    mentation of society, 214; history in, 111–

Philippines (*continued*)
15; Huks, 38–44, 229n. 50; impact of colonialism, 137; Lansdale and, 32–37, 42–43, 45, 115, 136–39; legacy of American intervention, 51, 212–15; military bases in, 213; resettlement programs, 44–45. *See also* Magsaysay, Ramon

Philippine Saturday Mirror, 36

Phillips, Rufus, 93–94, 123–24, 234n. 39

Pike, Douglas, 231n. 76

political identity. *See* identity, political

political indifference. *See* indifference, political

Poncins, Gontran de: *From a Chinese City*, 262n. 37

popular culture, American, 17–19, 67, 187–88, 197–207, 212–13. *See also* Lansdale, Edward G., fictional portrayals

pornography, 192–93

power, American, 48, 96, 186

Powers, Thomas, 103

Pratt, John, 157

Pravda, 195

press, American: on CIA, 97–100; on Diem, 58–59; ethnography and, 141; government and, 98–99; on Lansdale, 20–21, 36–37, 136, 188–89, 191–97, 206, 221n. 7; Lansdale and, 43–44, 54–55, 67–68, 124, 210, 248n. 73; on Magsaysay, 36–38, 114; *The Pentagon Papers* and, 84–85; on *The Quiet American* (film), 171; on *The Quiet American* (Greene), 155, 161–62; on *The Ugly American* (film), 181–82; on *The Ugly American* (Lederer and Burdick), 174–75, 257n. 82. *See also specific publications and journalists*

press, foreign, 36, 99, 195, 205–6, 233n. 13

Price, Raymond K., Jr., 194

progress. *See* modernization theory

propaganda, 44, 46–47, 232n. 78. *See also* advertising

Prouty, L. Fletcher, 225n. 54, 242n. 44, 263n. 48

psychological warfare, 39–42, 74–75, 82–83, 109. *See also* counterinsurgency

Pyle, Alden, 253n. 21; Audie Murphy as, 169–70; book vs. film versions, 169; Brendan Fraser as, 173; Greene on, 159–60; Lansdale and, 149–50, 155–59, 155–62

Pynchon, Thomas, 203

Quach Phong, 121

Quiet American, The (1958 film), 163–73; Allen

Dulles on, 166; CIA involvement with, 163–64, 166; critiques of, 168–71, 256n. 72; filming of, 169–70; Greene on, 166–67, 168, 172; Lansdale and, 164–67, 170–71, 173, 255n. 47; Mankiewicz on, 170, 172; South Vietnam government's cooperation with, 166

Quiet American, The (2001 film), 173

Quiet American, The (Greene), 149–62; American liberalism in, 151; critiques of, 155, 161–62; *A Dangerous Friend* and, 200; generally, 2, 205; impact of, 151, 161–62; model for Alden Pyle, 19, 149–50, 155–56, 159–60; portrayal of colonialism, 152–54, 158; "third force," 156–58; Vietnamese in, 151–52

Quirino, Elpidio, 36

Race, Jeffrey, 143

racism, 142–43

Ramos, Fidel, 214

Reader's Digest, 67–68, 98, 237n. 76

Reading National Geographic (Lutz and Collins), 141

Redgrave, Sir Michael, 169–70

refugees. *See* resettlement programs

Reisman, David, *The Lonely Crowd*, 258n. 110

reportage, 151, 197, 262n. 37

resettlement programs, 44–45, 60–61, 83, 233n. 17

Richards, Peter, 37

road development, 184–86, 259n. 116

Roche, John, 210

Rockefeller Commission, 73

Rosenberg, Emily, *Spreading the American Dream*, 29

Rostow, Walt: critiques of, 259n. 112; on Lansdale, 13; on Ngo Dinh Nhu, 67; *The Stages of Economic Growth*, 183, 258n. 111; on Vietnam, 87

Roth, Philip, 204

Rusk, Dean, 71, 191, 224n. 38

Ryuku Islands, 133–36

Saga, 193

Saigon Military Mission (SMM), 59, 80–81, 234n. 39

Sarris, Andrew, 181

Saturday Evening Post: on CIA, 97, 98; on Diem, 58; on Greene, 161; Lansdale memo in, 54–55; *The Ugly American* in, 174–75, 257n. 82

Schlesinger, James, 94–95

Schreiner, S. A., Jr., 37

Schudson, Michael, 29

Scott, James, 147

Second Look at America, A (Aguinaldo), 213–14

"secret government," 203–5. *See also* Central Intelligence Agency (CIA)

sects: Cao Dai sect, 122, 144–45, 156, 223n. 33, 234n. 37; Hao Hao sect, 223n. 33; Sect Crisis of 1955, 223n. 33, 236n. 59

See It Now (TV show), 127

Senate Foreign Relations Committee, 89

Shaplen, Robert, 248n. 73

Sheehan, Neil, 123, 177, 211; *A Bright Shining Lie*, 11–12, 223n. 31

Sheinbaum, Stanley K., 259n. 114

Sherry, Norman, 150

Shiro, Shiba, 248n. 55

Sihanouk, Prince Norodom, 21, 195, 262n. 29

Simpson, Howard, 64, 84

Slotkin, Richard, *Gunfighter Nation*, 227n. 22

Smith, Grahame, 155

Smith, Joseph B., 51

Smith, Robert, 68

Smith, Walter B., 240n. 2

South Vietnam. *See* Vietnam

space race, 75

Special Magazine Commemorating Two Years of President Diem's Government, The, 58

spies, 88–89, 91, 93, 143. *See also* Central Intelligence Agency (CIA)

Spreading the American Dream (Rosenberg), 29

Stages of Economic Growth, The (Rostow), 183, 258n. 111

State Department, 79, 174, 180–81, 191, 260n. 8

Stern, Stewart, 178, 180–82, 184, 258n. 98

Stevenson, William, 36

Stockwell, John, *In Search of Enemies*, 100

Stone, I. F., 124

Stone, Oliver, 19–20, 201–3, 225n. 54

Strategic Hamlet Program, 233n. 17. *See also* resettlement programs; Vietnam

Stump, Felix, 113–14

Taruk, Luis, 38–39, 43–44. *See also* Huks

Taylor, Maxwell, 66, 86

terrorism, 165–67

Terryman, Colonel, 197–98

Tet offensive, 112. *See also* Vietnam

Thé. *See* Trinh Minh Thé

Thieu, Nguyen Van. *See* Nguyen Van Thieu

"third force," 156–58, 253n. 22

Thoi Nay, 195

Thomas, Evan, *The Very Best Men*, 98

Time, 33, 58–59, 114

tourism, 128–31, 141

Tran Do, 215–16

Tranh Van Dinh, 124

transportation projects, 184–86, 259n. 116

Tran Van Chuong, 167–68

Tran Van Don, 65

Tran Van Soai, 60

Trimble, William, 185

Trinh Minh Thé, 60, 156–57, 165–66, 234n. 37, 239n. 111

Twilight Zone, The (TV show), 67

Ugly American, The (film), 178–86; American Revolution in, 179; critiques of, 181–82; Freedom Road theme in, 184; government response to, 180–81; history in, 179–80; Marlon Brando in, 181–82, 258n. 107; on modernization theory, 182–86; State Department influence on, 180–81

Ugly American, The (Lederer and Burdick), 173–78; on American attitudes toward developing world, 175; Edwin Hillandale in, 175–78; generally, 2, 149, 205; impact of, 174; Lansdale portrayal in, 139; Lansdale's involvement with, 174–75; Magsaysay in, 176; popularity of, 257n. 82; press and, 174–75, 257n. 82

United States. *See* America, United States of

United States Committee for a Free Indochina, 224n. 36, 265n. 13

"usable past," 105–6, 111–14, 119–21, 125, 244n. 6. *See also* history, use of in Cold War

Vann, John Paul, 223n. 31

Very Best Men, The (Thomas), 98

Vietcong, 55, 195, 210

Vietminh, 52

Vietnam: advertising in, 53–68; Allen Dulles on, 52; America and, 51–67, 66, 212, 215–20, 236n. 72; American Friends of Vietnam (AFV), 54, 57–58, 167, 170–71; Bao Dai, 3, 64; Binh Hung, 54–56; Binh Xuyen, 223n. 33; Catholics in, 60–61, 83; constitution of, 116; consumer culture in, 216–17; creation of South Vietnam, 12; culture, American, in, 51–52; early stages of American involvement with, 52–54; economic sabotage in North Vietnam, 82–83; elections (1955), 64–65; First Indochina War, 52–54, 152–53; folk traditions in, 147–48; foreign aid, 59–

Vietnam (*continued*)
60, 82, 185; French involvement in, 52–53, 92, 120–21, 251n. 54; history used in, 115–24; Hollywood depictions of, 218–19, 266n. 41; impact of colonialism, 251n. 54; legacy of war in America, 218–19; Lien Minh militia, 234n. 37; Long An, 131; Lyndon Johnson and, 223n. 30; medical assistance from Philippines, 61–62; nationalism in, 119–20, 248n. 55; nation building and, 53, 69, 121, 158–59; people's aspirations in, 158; promotion of in America, 68–69; resettlement programs, 60–61, 83; resistance to outside influences, 143–44; role of the individual in war, 223n. 30; Saigon Military Mission (SMM), 59, 80–81, 234n. 39; Sect Crisis of 1955, 223n. 33, 236n. 59; sects and. *See* sects; Strategic Hamlet Program, 233n. 17; Tet offensive, 112; tourism in, 216–17; uses of history in, 115–24; Vietcong, 55, 195, 210; Vietminh, 52; Vietnamese Communist Party, 215–16; war tactics, 209. *See also* Ngo Dinh Diem; Vietnam and Lansdale

Vietnam and Lansdale: ethnography, 144–48; failures in, 115–16; Lansdale's arrival in, 52–54; Lansdale's feelings on, 16, 110; Lansdale's return to, 205–6, 208; loss of war, 211; request to send Lansdale to Vietnam, 78, 221n. 2

Vietnamese Communist Party, 215–16

Vietnamization policy, 125

Vietnam: *Journeys of Body, Mind & Spirit* (exhibit), 219

Vietnam (Karnow), 15

Vietnam Lobby, 12, 223n. 34

Vietnam Syndrome, 218

Village That Refuses to Die, The (Atkinson), 55–56

"Villiers" (code name), 228n. 29

Visionary Vietnam Veterans, 194

Vo Nguyen Giap, 119

Waltzing with a Dictator (Bonner), 214, 227n. 22

war: political nature of, 224n. 47; psychological, 39–42, 74–75, 82–83; World War II, 30, 122, 132–33, 261n. 25. *See also* Philippines; Vietnam

Washington Post, 167, 189

Weiner, Tim, 204

Westmoreland, Kitsie, 91

West, Richard, 151, 155

West, W. J., 154

We Were Soldiers Once (film), 219

Wherry, Kenneth, 140

"White Man's Burden, The" (Kipling), 5–6

White, Theodore, 124

Williams, Raymond, 226n. 11

Williams, Samuel, 78

Wills, Garry, 93, 207, 217

Wilson, Woodrow, 108, 115, 245n. 12

Woodside, Alexander, 118, 120

World War II, 30, 122, 132–33, 261n. 25

Yellow Fever (Lartéguy), 197–99

Y, General, 201–2

Yoh, Bernie, 71